S0-AKR-593

COLUMBIA BIBLE COLLEGE
444 00003 9958

CONFESSIONS OF A THEOLOGIAN

Founding Editor, *Christianity Today,* 1956-'68

CARL F. H. HENRY

CONFESSIONS OF A THEOLOGIAN

AN AUTOBIOGRAPHY

WORD BOOKS
PUBLISHER
WACO, TEXAS

A DIVISION OF
WORD, INCORPORATED

CONFESSIONS OF A THEOLOGIAN

Library of Congress Cataloging in Publication Data

Henry, Carl Ferdinand Howard, 1913–
Confessions of a theologian.

Includes index.
1. Henry, Carl Ferdinand Howard, 1913–
2. Theologians—United States—Biography. 3. Evangelicalism—United States—History—20th century.
I. Title.
BX4827.H38A33 1986 230'.044'0924 [B] 86-5480
ISBN 0-8499-0455-2

Printed in the United States of America

67898 MP 987654321

Deo Gratias

OTHER BOOKS BY DR. CARL F. H. HENRY

God, Revelation and Authority (in six volumes)
Aspects of Christian Social Ethics
The Christian Mindset in a Secular Society
Christian Personal Ethics
Basic Christian Doctrines (Editor)
The Biblical Expositor (Editor)
Horizons of Science: Christian Scholars Speak Out (Editor)
Revelation and the Bible (Editor)

Contents

Teaching: Northern, Fuller, Eastern, Trinity

Foreword

Who am I? A mammal of the species *homo sapiens* weighing 190 to 200 pounds (depending upon whether it is July or December) and standing 6′ 1″ (especially when being measured for insurance). My brown hair conceals a few strands of gray; my blue-brown eyes prefer bifocals for reading (trifocals for lecturing). My head, arms, legs and feet are all in place—although that is no small marvel.

My beret was bought in Spain, my horn-rimmed glasses in Singapore, my shirt and suit in Seoul; the rest is "made in America." My over-the-calf socks may be dark blue when they ought to be black; I seem unable to tell the difference (or so my wife says).

My mind whirlwinds with memories of almost two million miles of air travel and ministry on all continents and in perhaps two-thirds of the 150 or more modern nations. My daily pocket calendar carries names, addresses and some telephone numbers of persons on several continents. A medic-card notes that I take a 200 mg. quinidine sulphate pill morning and evening for heart arrhythmia. My eel-skin Korean wallet often carries some spare foreign currency (enough for first-day arrival expenses). Notations include the license numbers of my 1973 Olds Cutlass (62,000 miles) and my 1981 Buick Century wagon (69,000 miles), which often patiently await my return from some distant journey. My luggage sports cosmetic scars inflicted in Bombay, Lagos, Taipei and Washington.

Another reference occurs on the identification page of my appointment book: "In case of accident notify. . . ." It then carries the name Helga B. Henry, spouse, and also the names of Congressman Paul B. Henry, son, and Dr. Carol Henry Bates, daughter, with appropriate addresses and phone numbers. The inside date book is crowded to the hilt with notations about board, committee, speaking and lecture commitments, and a quarterly reminder to see my physician, Dr. Nikos Kakaviatos, for a routine checkup.

My attitude toward humanity is on the whole—at least I think so—positive. Admittedly, I despise a few things: salesmen who phone me in the middle of a television program, people who send unsolicited manuscripts for review and don't even include postage, government bureaucrats who forget that they are civil servants, noisy hotel rooms and sinks with nonworking drain stoppers, ball point pens that don't write and paper clips that won't hold and Scotch tape that tears, winter retrieval of the *Washington Post* from the driveway when I pay for front-door delivery, vichyssoise and okra, a B or E plane seat between two overhanging passengers, local shops that advertise specials that they don't really stock and any surgeon who turns his operating duties over to an intern without saying so.

I also have some special likes; given enough time, I could prepare a list that outweighs my perturbances. Sauerbraten and potato dumplings, or prime rib medium well, for starters, or pecan or butter almond ice cream; or an A or F seat in an exit row on domestic flights, or the Chicago/O'Hare Hyatt Regency at special weekend rates. Or raising some choice azaleas from cuttings, or happening on a bargain in a remote antique shop. Better yet, finding a book treasure that unexpectedly illumines Scripture truth with encircling radiance.

The rumor that there can be only one Carl Henry in the world—and that in any event the cosmos could not tolerate more than one—is questionable. For many years somebody in the Brooklyn or New York area did a thriving mail order business merchandising Carl Henry Cigars; I have no idea how unworthy of the name they were. A few years ago I got a gracious letter from Colonel Carl Henry, resident of New York City's Fifth Avenue, commending an address of mine carried by *Vital Speeches.* At Moody Bible Institute I ran into the son of a Haitian minister whose father had given him the names Carl Henry. To these, one and all, I offer condolences as the real thing is about to be unveiled.

It is, in truth, with a sense of gratitude to God that I narrate my story. My hope is that it mirrors a buoyant witness while it preserves also the best traditions of candid reporting. Special thanks go to Irma Peterson who during secretarial duties kept my *Christianity Today* files in orderly condition; to Floyd Thatcher of Word Books who thought the story was worth the telling; to Helga, who spent long hours taming abrasive adjectives and making sure that all was seasoned with grace; to a select few friends who did me the service of a critical reading of certain chapters, even if their comments were too sparse;

and above all to the God of the ages who has enabled me to complete an autobiography that I was in many ways and for many reasons reluctant to venture.

CARL F. H. HENRY

January 22, 1986
My 73rd Birthday

Completing *God, Revelation and Authority,* 1976-'83

Confessions of a Theologian

Dr. Carl F. H. Henry, Chairman, and Dr. Billy Graham, Honorary Chairman, World Congress on Evangelism (Berlin, 1966)

1

A Difficult Delivery in New York

Hawkers of *The New York Times* and *New York Tribune* heralded no notable headlines on Wednesday, January 22, 1913. Manhattan weather was unusually pleasant and toward night it turned even warmer. In a small apartment at 92 East End Avenue a family physician, Dr. L. W. Harnisch, arrived hurriedly from his Lexington Avenue office to assist an immigrant mother's painful first delivery of a chubby baby.

My mother was Johanna Vaethroeder (Väthröder), born in Germany on October 8, 1891. Ferdinand Vaethroeder, her father, was a musician who taught violin and trumpet. Her mother was the daughter of Elizabeth Wohlfarth, whose brother was Bürgermeister in Lengfurt. Resident in Karbach, a county of Markenheidenfeld, the Vaethroeder family owned a farm; in summer they also offered for hire a horse and carriage and in winter a horse and sled. Mother was one of seven children; two, Josef and Emil, looked after the farm; one sister died soon after marriage, and another lived in Koblenz. Three came to America: my mother, her brother Gustave, who ran a small candy store on New York's East Side; and another brother Eddie, who for many years played in Goldman's Band.

My father was Karl F. Heinrich, son of a German pastry chef married to Hulde Mauersberger. Born on March 16, 1886, father was brought up in Triptis, a small city in the Thuringian state of Weimar, much of which was forest. After graduation from school in 1900 he became a specialty baker and about 1910 sailed to the United States, where he had a stint as pastry chef of the then famous Willard Hotel in Washington. He met Johanna Vaethroeder in New York where they married late in 1911 or early in 1912. They lived on E. 81st St. near where Father worked as a master baker. My father's sister, Paula, also came to the States and lived in New York.

I was the oldest of eight children, all of whom were given two middle names. Mine had an uncomfortably Prussian ring: Carl Ferdinand Howard Henry. In succession came Emil Gustave Cort Henry, born May 11, 1914; Frederick William Walter Henry, born August 16, 1915; Paula Johanna Elizabeth Henry, born June 13, 1917; Warren George Louis Henry, September 10, 1919; Eleanor Margaret Dolly Henry, April 21, 1922; Isabella Viola Vera Henry, November 20, 1925; and Johanna Katherine Marion Henry, November 27, 1927. Five of us were born in New York City before the family moved to Long Island.

About early school days I remember little. The family doctor came late in June, 1918, to give measles or smallpox vaccinations that fortified me for kindergarten in the Fall. The first day, after Mother walked me to Public School No. 77 and consigned me to the teacher, I promptly wet my pants. I became an eager student, always readied my homework and, in fact, managed to skip three grades. In those fantasy years, when relatives occasionally asked about future vocational interests, I mentioned chemistry as an option. That was mainly, I think, because of a Christmas present of harmless bottled liquids that could be combined in intriguing ways.

My New York family memories are slim. When World War I erupted in 1914 I was a mere babe and unaware of the fury that Kaiser Wilhelm had unleashed upon Europe. The German immigrant community was deeply troubled, however, for when the United States entered the war on April 6, 1917, feelings of hostility quickly mounted toward German immigrants. In New York German immigrants anglicized their names; our family name changed from Heinrich to Henry. We also stopped speaking German, even in private.

I recall how after a long and laborious day's work in a bakery, my father often arrived home too breathless and fearful to eat. German immigrants had entered America not to extend the Kaiser's frontiers but, like many others, to find a better life in a land of liberty and promise. But before the middle of 1918 American troops were arriving in Europe at a rate of 300,000 a month. Immigrants who held jobs while Americans fought abroad were harassed and intimidated; on one occasion my father, denounced as a "scab," was chased, caught and hurled over a fence; he reached home several hours late, his clothing in tatters.

On November 11, 1918, the war so hopefully fought to preserve the world for democracy came to an end. I was a kindergartner and then a first-grader when in January, 1920, the Versailles treaty was signed. When General Pershing's returning American troops made their New York victory march our apartment echoed with the sound of marching bands. I was just tall enough to peer over the windowsill to see and hear swelling throngs hailing the forces that had prevailed at St. Mihiel and then at Meuse-Argonne.

Another early childhood memory is the summer weekend with my mother's brother, Uncle Gus, and his wife, Katherine, who lived above their corner candy store and "take-out" delicatessen and where the neighborhood policeman on his beat stopped periodically to sample the German sausages. That Saturday afternoon Aunt Katherine took me to a vaudeville show that featured a trampoline troupe. Alas I soon learned that such feats couldn't be duplicated on an ordinary bed, at least not by me. An even greater lesson, however, related to Uncle Gus's invitation to help myself to whatever I wanted from his array of chocolates. An enormous ingestion of chocolate-covered peanuts proved my Waterloo. Never again did I pose a threat to the profitability of Uncle Gus's or any other candy store.

Manhattan memories of Christmas and Easter also persist. Easter mornings we youngsters could hardly wait to see whether the Easter Bunny had left our individual baskets of colored eggs, chocolates and jellybeans on the fireplace mantle. Christmas always meant a decorated tree. On Christmas Eve we customarily hung the biggest stockings we could find for Santa's anticipated benevolences that included an orange, a peppermint stick and German specialties like lebkuchen, pfeffernüsse and anise cookies; stollen and other goodies came later. Christmas dinner was always a sumptuous feast of soup, roast chicken or goose, dumplings, sweet-and-sour red cabbage, mince pie and other delights. Christmas gifts were usually necessary items of clothing, and these—to the dismay of younger family members—came mostly to me as the oldest while others would later inherit them as hand-me-downs. From uncles and aunts we received modest luxuries like games and simple toys.

Santa himself put in an annual appearance. Carrying a broom, whose handle he thumped insistently on the floor, he inquired (in an authoritarian German-edged voice that all too soon blew his cover) whether we had behaved during the past year and whether we promised to do better in the next.

In respect to church participation we were Christmas and Easter Christians. My father was Lutheran by family heritage and my mother Roman Catholic. But we had no family prayers, no grace at table, no Bible in our home. Only once do I remember Mother praying with me, when some stubborn illness confined me to bed and kept me home from school.

Both parents worked unsparingly hard. Mother cleaned the apartment, sewed clothes and washed and ironed, bore a youngster every few years, nursed the ailing ones, cooked endless soups and stews and baked bread and puddings, and urged us to stay abreast of our schoolwork. Father put in six full days a week, and sometimes overtime also, by the fiery ovens of a midcity bakery. For all the struggles of those years we never lacked food.

Our pleasures consisted of playing hopscotch with other youngsters on sidewalks outside our apartment, shooting marbles on the dirt shoulders of the walks or tossing pennies without gambling (none of us could afford to lose even one cent). Most of all, however, we looked forward to the annual family picnic.

On one such outing our family went by ferry to Red Bank, New Jersey, to join a gathering of the Mozartverein comprised of German musicians among whom Father played the zither. The musicians impressed me less than did the long tables of food and the display of prizes for participants whose admission ticket might carry a winning number. But most fascinating of all were the colorful soaring butterflies. Now and then they lighted nearby on small flowers, defying me, so it seemed, to catch them. Yet always they eluded my pursuit. While some picnickers captured them with nets, I simply gave chase up and over many green terraces. All at once I realized I was alone, without either butterflies or a sense of direction. No amount of scampering over the rolling hills produced any signs of life. It was several hours before a search party found an exhausted, weeping butterfly-chaser who now had forever lost all interest in that diversion. I had failed in catching butterflies but I had touched a world "out there" far larger than any I had heretofore known or even imagined.

One recollection of the early years I should like to forget, but can't. Father had returned home late, as he sometimes did when working overtime to decorate wedding or anniversary cakes, and we had already eaten. A sudden rumpus in the kitchen brought me running. What I saw shocked and terrified me. My distraught mother was pummeling my father with a broomstick because he had come home "drunk again." This introduction at the age of six to an unsuspected domestic problem left lingering scars.

As the family grew my parents dreamed of perhaps moving to a country setting on Long Island. The dream materialized in 1920 when we moved some fifty miles east of New York City to Central Islip, in the middle of Long Island.

Carl and Helga Henry, 1940 Wedding Picture

2

A One-Acre Long Island Farm

It was probably in the Sunday real estate ads that my father learned of a commodious two-story home situated on an acre of scrubland that might become serviceable as a farm. I have often wondered about the sales pitch that encouraged him to ride the Long Island Railroad to Central Islip—more than an hour's trip—presumably not only to see the property but also to weigh whatever problems he might encounter in commuting to his work in New York City.

Once the purchase was consummated the entire family migrated in one weekend. Most of the family came by train, but my father and I rode in the moving van, which on one side bore in large letters the legend: "Absolutely Fireproof Storage Warehouse."

The spacious white house with an open porch, and a large red barn some distance removed, stood on Wilson Boulevard, a long dirt road that served four or five other houses also. The nearest significant landmark was the tall wire fence, about a fifth of a mile distant, that surrounded Central Islip State Hospital, an institution for the mentally insane. Able-bodied patients occasionally scaled that barrier and escaped through the woods to freedom. That circumstance, plus the fact that the new Henry abode was more than a mile from the village and an additional quarter of a mile removed from the public school, accounted for the affordable price. The house had neither electricity nor running water.

After commuting daily by train before sunrise, and returning after sunset from work that kept him on his feet for long hours, Father nonetheless spent many weekends turning the wilderness into a garden. He removed small pines and scrub oak, coaxed an old horse named Franky to plow the fields, planted vegetables and flowers, installed a Delco power system to supplement the kerosene lamps, sank a twenty-one-foot basement well that enabled us to pump water and dug a cistern at the end of the grape arbor that sheltered the path to the outhouse.

Even so, contrasted with the comparative comfort of an economical New York flat, this setting was hardly a rose garden. A wood-burning stove in the kitchen served both for cooking and for heating water that we carried to the second floor bathroom for family baths. There were now more "mouths" to feed—Leghorn and Rhode Island Red chickens, a few guinea hens, three milk-producing goats, Franky the increasingly decrepit nag and a few pigs. Mother and the older children lent a helping hand not only on weekends but also on weekdays after a trek from school that involved a mile's walk along the highway and beyond that a narrow footpath etched for another half mile into the long pine and scrub covered hill.

Father sported a mustache and wore a fedora hat outdoors and, if the weather was cool, a vest without a coat. Somewhat regal in bearing, Mother was quite tall and had shoulder-length brown hair. In this new environment I was soon beneficently shorn of my long curls. But knee-length britches, knee-length stockings and a cap remained my usual dress until high school.

Saturday was a full workday, but Sunday mornings we children attended Sunday school at the Church of the Messiah, an Episcopal mission church, choice of which avoided a conflict over Catholic or Lutheran alternatives. The Reverend John Tilley, although very devout, was an ineffective minister; to hold the interest of the men of the church he played pinochle with them in the parish house. Robert E. O'Donohue, the realtor who had negotiated our move, was the Sunday school superintendent. He was also a lay reader as well as treasurer of the church; he personally assumed payment of many of its bills. A polio victim at the age of five, it was evident whenever he led the service that he had great difficulty in kneeling.

Whatever the weather, the Henry children trooped the long mile to Sunday school each week unless illness or deep snow interfered. Almost always we were awarded the annual silver bar for perfect attendance. We walked to Sunday school on the side of the street opposite St. John of God Roman Catholic Church, whose parish priests during the week required all schoolboys of whatever faith, as they passed, to tip their caps to the host on the altar. Little did they then dream that a half century later their successors would invite the Gideons to distribute 1800 copies of the New Testament to their parochial school.

The Episcopal church had an old foot-powered organ, but with its help we learned to sing the great hymns of the church and Christmas carols. My Sunday school teacher was Louise Bridger, a pretty junior high school teacher who wore a peekaboo blouse and year after year taught us the Gospel miracles or parables. For being the "most courteous" lad in class she took me to the first movie I had ever seen, a special featuring Jackie Coogan, the child film star. She later moved to New York and became a high school principal in Queens.

Sunday afternoon was fun-time. Mother bought a used bicycle and learned to ride it around the yard. The back wheel lacked a tire, but it functioned minimally with the help of a thick binding of grain sack strips. From sturdy tree branches hung two swings on which the girls, wearing brightly colored bloomers, would put on their dazzling neighborhood "free show." We fellows played ball in the street. Father usually caught a Sunday afternoon nap. The large rocker that he brought from New York in the van was seldom in use; his main relaxation was smoking his pipe while busy with other things.

In the Spring, wild blue lupine and pink lady's-slippers appeared in great profusion, although I was not much aware of them. In our yard, as we cleared the scrub oak, we first planted potatoes, corn, tomatoes, kohlrabi, cabbage, cauliflower and carrots. Then we added long rows of flowers—canna, dahlias and gladioli (always my favorite among the irises). Beyond the overarching grape arbor and tall lilacs that gave generous protection from rain and snow along the fifty-foot pathway to the outhouse Father planted a row of small blue spruces that struggled for survival.

On Saturdays during harvest the three oldest children—Emil, Fred and I—would load the wagon formerly tugged by the now deceased Franky and push and pull it three miles to Islip Manor, a thickly settled housing development. There we peddled fresh vegetables and flowers house to house at bargain prices. An hour before dusk we would head for home again so that our unlighted transport would not compete after dark with auto traffic. I usually walked in front of the wagon, carrying and steering the bars, while my brothers pushed from behind. Whatever produce was unsold was predictably a main part of our next week's table fare.

I soon became accustomed to the sight of my father chopping off the head of a noisy rooster the afternoon before Sunday dinner. Once drained of blood, the decapitated fowl was singed in a pot of boiling water and its feathers quickly plucked.

It was more gruesome, however, when on one occasion Father decided the time had arrived to butcher one of the pigs (with a sledge-hammer blow to the skull). It was then readied for curing in the smokehouse that Father had recently built over the coal stove in the cellar of our progressively modernized home. The ample basement stored all necessary equipment for stuffing the different kinds of home-made sausage that hung in the smokehouse to cure.

That pig episode was my father's one and only butchering effort and the family was fortunate indeed to escape with its life. In occasional wild dreams I still see an enormous red glow enveloping the interior of our country home. About three o'clock in the morning Mother roused us with the frantic call of "Fire! Fire!" and hurried us out of the smoke-filled house. She, my father and Uncle Eddie—mother's brother, who fortunately happened to be spending the night with us—had for a full hour fought the growing cellar fire but seemed unable to contain it. Drippings from hams and sausages suspended in the smokehouse had ignited atop the coal stove from where flames crept quickly along the basement ceiling. When smoke and crackling fire awakened my father, he quickly roused my mother and uncle. Then he furiously pumped pail after pail of water which the others carried as a bucket brigade in an effort to extinguish the flames. It was when they thought the cause was lost that mother awakened us children. We youngsters then took over pumping the water and together with the effort of the three-adult bucket brigade brought the fire under control and saved the house.

At the other end of the cellar from the coal-and-wood burning stove and smokehouse was a special room that housed fruits and vegetables preserved for the coming winter—quart jars of beans, corn, tomatoes, apples, peaches, pears and huckleberries. There were large grape-leaf-lined crocks of pickles and several dozen large bottles of cork-sealed home-made root beer. Periodically during the day or night one of the bottles would blow its cork, spurting its contents over the ceiling, and frightening us as if a basement intruder had fired a gun.

We had little success growing fruit. At the height of the apple season Father would rise early on a Sunday morning, an hour before dawn, and drive to nearby Brentwood where a large apple orchard bordered the main highway. Parking the car well off the highway near the orchard, he would fill several burlap bags with apples. He took me along to beep the horn if I noticed anyone approaching, an unwelcome sentry duty that terrified me. I have no memory that he ever stole anything but apples. He worked hard and paid for whatever he got.

But mention of a car has taken me ahead of my story. Father had acquired a used car so Mother could drive him to and from the train station. In bad winter weather the sheet-ice road was treacherous. Yet the arrangement worked well except for one morning when the jalopy slid off the highway and flipped on its side. Mother sustained a gash on her forehead. But the two of them righted the car, dressed the wound with handkerchiefs and carried on.

That first car was clearly too small to accommodate a family well on its way to eight children. So father "traded up" to a used van that had side panel folding-bench seats. This presumably would enable the entire family to survey Long Island scenery on summer Sunday afternoons. The difficulty was that only Father and Mother, who sat up front with the youngest, could see directly out of a window. Whenever the car unexpectedly turned a corner or swerved, all the side bench passengers were in danger of being hurled into space. The youngsters complained that they saw more of each other than of the world outside.

Father had a violent temper (some of which showered on me). When another car passed his lumbering bus on a hill, he would shout, "G-- d--- kike, so I'm not going fast enough for him!" And I remember how one time when I had neglected some chores, he cursed me and threatened to beat me into permanent awareness of my duties. Infuriated, I heaved a rock through a kitchen window, suddenly realizing that now I would get a double dose. I ran away from home and stayed that night in the village until a traveling medicine show closed for the day. I had planned to sleep in the woods. But out of the exciting crowd stepped my mother, who had been searching for me; in tears she took my hand and walked me home. The episode was never mentioned again.

All the bedrooms in our home, I recall, were upstairs and in winter were bitterly cold. There were window shades but no draperies. As we huddled under the covers we heard the periodic calls of small wild animals and the antiphonal echo of dogs howling to each other. Each room had a bare electric bulb that dangled from the center of the ceiling. I ran a string from the pull chain to the top of my bed, so I could turn off the light without emerging from my blanket-cocoon.

Father and Mother did a good job of keeping disagreements to themselves. But late one night, after everyone had retired, I heard my father shouting for my mother, apparently determined to shoot her, and presumably carrying a loaded gun. He demanded that she come out of hiding. I knew that now and then, although he was not a persistent drunkard, Father drank too much and altercations ensued. But never had I heard anything like this. I froze in my bed as the commotion continued. Finally I tiptoed to the window, quietly opened it and stepped back from the bitter cold. I do not know to this day how as a young lad I then had the temerity to do what I did. I swung open my bedroom door to the central hallway and stepped hurriedly to one side, called out in the darkness to my father and asked if he needed help. Next I walked out boldly, wrested the gun from his hand, ran back into my room and hurled the weapon into the snow-covered night. I trembled sleeplessly until dawn, but at least that terrifying fracas had come to an end.

During the prohibition era our home became, in fact, a sort of alcoholic spa when my father perceived it as an opportunity for earning extra dollars to help pay off the mortgage. National prohibition was adopted in January, 1920, not long after our family moved to Long Island, and was in force for almost fourteen years. Many railroad commuters voiced discontent over the federal definition of intoxicating liquor as one-half of 1 percent by volume, and covert speakeasies soon emerged. I do not know where or how my father got the still to start his boozing business, but he set it up in one corner of the kitchen where each day it regularly distilled a quart or more of alcohol from potato mash. Before long our dining room became a retreat where, during afternoon hours before the youngsters returned from school, and on Saturdays also, hospital attendants from the nearby mental institution whiled away an hour's leave by playing pinochle or poker and bought a "shot" of whiskey or a bottle or two of home-made beer. Prohibition enforcement was lax; it was aimed primarily at major offenders rather than petty violators and was often carried out by incompetent agents. There was little public enthusiasm for prohibition. If investigators conducted a surprise "train search" they seldom bothered a commuter who had "his own" bottle. Father carried a quart of distilled spirits in his satchel and built up a rather regular demand for undiluted whiskey that earned him the name of "100% Henry."

In the mid-twenties Cadman H. Frederick, a real estate developer, built a new community of houses several miles from our home. His extensive advertising drew large Sunday crowds to the site where salesmen doled out sandwiches and soda pop to prospective buyers. We got the food concession, so late Saturday nights Mother and I routinely made and wrapped (at 10 cents each from the realtors) 500 cheese sandwiches. The realty development encouraged my father to open, as an additional investment, a nearby hot-dog stand and small convenience store at a convergence of several streets called the "Five Corners." He operated it weekends, dreaming of the day when business would so improve that he could give up the daily commute to New York. At the same time he began risking occasional bets on horses, and now and then his bank checks bounced. It was then, as a young teenager, that I decided to use my middle and differentiating initials, and became Carl F. H. Henry.

I entered high school in September, 1925, with a solid academic record; Central Islip Union School had awarded me a gold pin for excellence. But now my main challenge became physical more than mental. I gained weight uncontrollably and developed what a physician diagnosed as rheumatism because of severe pains in my legs and ankles. Despite the prescribed jiggers of lemon juice twice a day, my condition worsened until I could hardly walk. I shuffled awkwardly among my classmates from classroom to classroom and it took me forever to get up and down stairs. I wondered whether I would live to be thirty-five.

One Saturday heavy-set Uncle Gus came to check my condition. Speaking from his own experience, he said: "You don't have rheumatism; you have fallen arches. Next Saturday we'll drive to Brooklyn and I'll buy you a pair of arch-support shoes." Meanwhile he tautly bandaged my arches and lower limbs. Uncle Gus's ministrations brought quick improvement. Once again I could share energetically in activities with Joe D'Amico, Sidney Benstock, Grace Cordingly, Rita Thornton, Margaret Ashby and other classmates.

Customarily Episcopal Sunday school students were confirmed when they turned twelve years of age. When my confirmation neared the parish priest was shocked to learn that I had never been baptized. He therefore quickly arranged a private Sunday afternoon baptism with close relatives as godparents. As we gathered around the font the priest dipped his fingers into the water, made a sign of the cross on my forehead and declared: "Dearly beloved, . . . this child is now regenerate, and an inheritor of the promises of the Kingdom of God." My father had slain and plucked a prize chicken that morning and presented it to Father Tilley as an honorarium. On Tuesday, November 9, 1926, the Bishop of Long Island, Dr. Ernest M. Stires, confirmed our class of candidates, including Carl Ferdinand Howard Henry, and thereafter we had the privilege of attending monthly communion services. I was, in fact, no more regenerate than the Long Island telephone directory.

I shared in the Lord's Supper a number of times. But then, like many teenage friends, I dropped out under the impression that I had inherited all that institutional religion could offer. I was born at the juncture of the Protestant Reformation—Mother a Catholic and Father a Lutheran; I had faithfully attended Sunday school, and as a most courteous participant at that; within two weeks I had been baptized and confirmed in the faith.

Whatever gifts I have, if any, I always suspected were not in music. I took 27 lessons on the piano (at 25 cents an hour), at which point my teacher quit. In all honesty, I should add that she moved out of town, and no other instructor was locally available. But it was just as well. I had difficulty correlating left hand bass and right hand treble notes. Under Maestro Webber, a gifted teacher and concert master who conducted the symphony orchestra at the nearby State Hospital, I also studied trombone. We met for the 50-cent-an-hour weekly lessons in a small office in the village, where he directed my one-man efforts with wide baton sweeps as if he were leading his orchestra. Once he had taught me the rudiments of trombone, he launched me on "America" as my first "piece."

At home I soon drove younger members of the family who were trying to study to near madness as I interspersed repeat performances of "My Country 'Tis of Thee" with simulations of a fire department siren achieved by bold manipulations of the trombone slide. Emil, my next oldest brother, finally ran out of patience. Wresting the trombone from me, he beat me over the head with it. The instrument acquired a bump in the number two slide position; thereafter the mouthpiece jarred my teeth whenever the slide moved beyond that point. Herr Webber had misgivings, too. Having mastered "America," I told him I wanted next to play "Bye Bye Blackbird," one of the current hits. He would have none of it; he would teach good music or nothing, he insisted. My devotion to the trombone thus ended as swiftly as my devotion to the piano. I am, I suppose, what is called a monotone; I have never been able to carry a song on more than one or two notes. In respect to musical nontalent, I was and still am an oddity in our family.

The move to senior high school required traveling from Central Islip to Islip eight miles away. That meant traversing the familiar oak and pine growth footpath and concrete highway to a bus stop for transport headed through Islip to Bay Shore, Babylon, West Babylon and Amityville.

Early mornings and late afternoons the bus was preempted by students carrying books and lunches. I remember especially Joe D'Amico and Sidney Benstock. D'Amico was the Italian barber's son, a personable lad with a full shock of wavy black hair. Benstock was short and slight of build, wore thick glasses and was the son of Jewish owners of a general store. Like most students, they boarded the bus downtown in the heart of the three-block business district; those of us who got on elsewhere had to cope unsheltered with the cold winds, rain and snow.

We who lived on the outskirts of the village were regarded somewhat as country boobs, although D'Amico always made me feel at home. Benstock's heavy lenses may have been an impediment to his studies. At any rate, at the end of our junior year, I won the annual award for "most improvement." On the homeward bus, Benstock forever alienated me by loudly proclaiming that I had deliberately done less than my best early in the year in order to win at the end. From then on I patronized the Benstock general store only when it was a matter of life or death, which it never was.

It was now the Fall of 1927. At the beginning of the junior year it was customary to choose between pursuing the precollegiate or the business secretarial course. No one in our family had ever gone to college. Since I had no plans to do so, and in any case would lack funds, I opted for typing, shorthand and commercial law rather than for ancient or foreign languages and creative writing. Besides the business subjects, I studied ancient history with Miss Maud Susan Sherwood (with whom until her recent death I exchanged annual Christmas greetings), and English with Miss Mary Goodrich; both were no-nonsense teachers. My general science teacher was Paul Hayward, who never hinted that he was a Wheaton alumnus. The commercial teacher, Miss Dorothy F. Henry, was a stickler for proficiency.

The events to which all high school juniors and seniors looked forward, apart from final graduation, were the Easter junior trip to Philadelphia and the Easter senior trip to Washington. To gather funds students did odd jobs like peddling greeting cards door to door and selling candy. On the 1928 Easter tour to Philadelphia our junior class stayed in the Bellevue-Stratford, then the city's most prestigious hotel. It was my first experience in a hotel room. The morning wakeup buzzer drove me wild, since I had no idea how to stop it. I bought stamps and postcards at the hotel drug counter and, naive as any fifteen-year-old could be, fell head-over-heels in love with the smiling, stunning redhead behind the counter. Once home, after visiting all the historical sites and museums in the City of Brotherly Love, I promptly sent an ecstatic postcard to the "Girl in Charge of Drug Counter, Bellevue-Stratford Hotel, Philadelphia, Pennsylvania." I am still waiting to hear from her.

Money was not easy to come by. In the Spring of my sophomore year our high school class planned a bus trip to the Museum of Natural History in New York; each of us was to bring $10 by a certain deadline day. I saw no prospect whatever of meeting that requirement, and it appeared that I would be the only member of the class unable to go. The night before the deadline I was alone in the living room, stretched out on a sofa and crying my heart out. I accidentally flailed my arm against a large painting, a rather amateurish effort by one of my uncles that we had mounted above the sofa. As the frame bounced and shifted, something fluttered down onto my face. It was an old 1917 ten-dollar bill, with crossbars printed on one side. No one knew anything about it, and no one claimed it. I kept it as an answer to unarticulated prayer, and the next day signed up for the New York trip.

During my early teenage years I caddied now and then at the Brentwood Golf Club on Saturdays and Sundays. To reach Brentwood one either hiked or hitchhiked several miles before carrying clubs for morning and afternoon rounds of 18 holes. On an exceedingly good day one might earn $5. I was on the course on Saturday, May 21, 1927, when the electrifying news came that Charles Lindbergh had crossed the Atlantic and landed the *Spirit of St. Louis* safely in Paris.

For a regular job during the summer of 1927 I felled tall pine trees on a tract of land that a local realtor was readying to sell. The pay was 25 cents an hour—$10 for a five-day work week. My right hand blistered so badly after the first few days that I cut trees left-handed as best I could while the other hand healed over the weekend.

But the next summer I worked at the nearby State Hospital. Although the minimum age was sixteen, because I was large for my fifteen years I was promptly hired. For two months I was an assistant attendant, first in a tuberculosis ward and then in a physical and social therapy section. I saw patients of every conceivable kind—the dying, the violent, those controlled by straitjackets or injections. Part of my job was to maintain constant watch against attempted escapes. It was a harrowing experience for a fifteen-year-old. Many of the regular guards or attendants were middle-aged and heavy-set. When some robust patient tried to run away, they simply blew their whistles to alert other guards. Among the well-known escapees was Pinky, a Yale alumnus whose dementia was alcohol-induced. Whenever he sped off, and he did so frequently, no one bothered to catch him. He inevitably showed up at the home of a relative who in due course simply recommitted him.

Among those in the therapy ward was a Persian who, when his mind was clear, designed beautiful large table covers for embroidery. Other patients worked hand looms. Still others simply pushed floor polishers hour after hour, day after day, trying to regain order for their disarranged lives. For a bit of extra money the Persian fashioned a specially lovely tablecloth for me to give to my mother who did magnificent needlework. Along with Mother's other handwork the tablecloth was stored in a closet for some special future celebration. When fire destroyed our home several years later, everything went up in flames.

Such were the economic pressures in our family that I dared not ask for even an occasional 25 cents to attend high school sports events like baseball and basketball. But by my junior year I was typing better than 85 words a minute and in the Fall of 1928 approached the local weekly newspaper about doing sports reporting of high school events. *The Islip Press* hired me at 5 cents a column inch. That gave me full and free entry to sports activities.

Like many country towns, Islip had competing weekly papers—the *Press* which was part of the Republican chain owned by W. Kingsland Macy, and the *Islip Messenger,* a Democratic opposition paper. So I inquired of the *Messenger* also whether they needed a sports reporter. In reply, Lawrence F. Deutzmann of the *Islip Messenger* as well as of the *Smithtown Messenger* invited me to submit, at 7½ cents a column inch, not only sports coverage for Islip, East Islip and Central Islip, but also local news of general interest. Since the rival editors were not on speaking terms and seldom used bylines, neither one knew that I was also reporting for the other.

From my slim savings I bought an overused Model T Ford which we stored behind our house. Since I was still too young for a driver's permit I could not legally operate it on public roadways, even on the seldom used dirt road that linked us to the outside world. I nonetheless ventured a few exploratory drives around the neighborhood; on one of the first a sputtering carburetor set the floorboards afire and I was fortunate indeed to salvage my investment. But the worst liability lay ahead.

The graduating class of 1929 was invited for its commencement party to the home of its president, George Kube, son of the local justice of the peace. The night was foggy with intermittent heavy rains. I set out on the six-mile trip to Islip at dusk in my rattling Model T, its dim headlights barely outlining the rain-swept roads. Time after time I tried to hand-wipe the clouded windshield. Despite the drenching downpour I had reached the halfway point of my journey when suddenly the headlights of an approaching vehicle pierced the fog and sent me veering sharply to the right on the barely visible two-lane highway. Directly in front of my swerving car I saw two women's umbrellas hoisted against the rain. I applied the brake as quickly as I could, but nonetheless sent both pedestrians off the shoulder of the road.

I pulled off the highway. The driver of another much newer car stopped to help the women lying on the water-soaked ground and moaning. The assisting driver suggested we help them into his car for a hurried trip to the hospital. I tried to follow in my car but could not keep up. Since I was but a few miles from the Kube home,

I drove there first, indicating that I had had an accident. A phone call to the nearest hospital elicited no information.

I stayed for the senior party with an uneasy sense of coming doomsday. The following morning a New York state trooper came to my home and summoned me to court on four charges: driving without a license, reckless driving, leaving the scene of an accident and failure to report an accident. Much of my life I have suffered from migraine headaches; that morning, I think, I experienced the first of them. I trembled like a leaf in the wind. I prayed desperately to God as if he were an ambulance or fire department poised to give emergency rescue. I spent more time on my knees and shed more tears than I had ever done in my life. I tried to strike a deal with God, but I had nothing to offer. My only plea was, "I'm sorry. . . . Please, God, help me."

The summons left two days before I was to appear in court. The first morning, after unprecedentedly fervent prayer, I felt constrained to go to the State Police headquarters in Bay Shore, an eight-mile walk shortened by hitchhiking. I arrived just before ten, and meekly reported that I wanted to speak with an officer about a summons. I stated my name, then sat and waited alone in a small office for two seemingly endless hours. Finally, just before noon, I was led into the main office of the lieutenant in charge. A towering and awesome picture of police authority, handsome in his khaki uniform and standing twenty feet tall, he announced laconically, "You're due in court tomorrow."

"I am sorry as I can be about all this," I said, choking on the words. "I would appreciate it if I could ask you something about the summons." He nodded. I left the scene of the accident, I explained, to accompany the car carrying the victims to the hospital, although in the rainstorm I lost the trail. I then mentioned the accident to a justice of the peace, I added, but there was no hospital information about any emergency admission.

Making notes on my comments, the lieutenant told me to return the next day. By that time he had verified my story. Justice Kube had apparently indicated that I had no previous brush with the law. Strange though it seems, the two women were indeed taken to the hospital, but their injuries were not serious enough to even list them as emergency admissions; one was released with slight bruises, the other, after examination, insisted upon being hospitalized for a possible broken hip or other injury.

Accompanied by my Uncle Gus, standing six-feet tall in his brass-button attendant's uniform, I then called on the confined woman to apologize and console her. "He will pay your hospital costs," my uncle explained, "and in fact will give you a cash amount if you sign a release." Though she first wanted more, the lady eventually settled for $200. My uncle counted off ten $20 bills—a large share of his monthly salary. Once she signed the release, the patient quickly recovered and left the hospital.

State troopers settled the case out of court: charges were suspended and I was told never again to drive a car until I was sixteen years of age and had a license. From then on, except for an occasional startup to postpone its demise, the Model T rusted away undisturbed in its ruts on our farm. On one of those therapeutic startups I became careless in cranking the ailing engine; like an angry mule it backfired and left me with a fractured wrist.

Our 1929 senior class Easter trip to Washington put us into the Willard, "the hotel of presidents," just two blocks from the White House. That scintillating first visit to the nation's Capitol left indelible impressions, especially the Lincoln Memorial. But there were lighter hours as well. I dated Margaret Ashby, an Irish lass whose father worked as a State Hospital attendant. After stalking museums and galleries we went to an evening movie. I was so excited that at the box office I forgot to wait for change from my lone $20 bill. When I remembered midway through the film, I promptly excused myself and went to the box office, where a personnel shift had already taken place. Fortunately an honest cashier had left my change in an envelope with a note indicating that I would doubtless return for it. We were required by chaperones to be in the hotel by eleven o'clock. The fellows then gathered for a card game in one of the bedrooms. Here one of the chaps suspended from the chandelier a whole stalk of bananas that he had bought from a street vendor. The game for bananas continued through the night, and probably no company of tourists ever coped with sightseeing the next day with so bloated an inheritance.

My senior year of high school carried one great disappointment. Annually the Daughters of the American Revolution awarded a watch for the best student essay submitted on Lincoln. This year, too, a watch was expressly announced as the first prize award. My essay, which began "Abraham Lincoln was a common man," was deemed best in the competition. When the award was publicly made, I received not a watch but a bronze medal decorated with the symbol of an owl and inscribed with my name as first prize winner. I accepted it with appreciation and grace. But I often wondered whether the preannounced award would have been bestowed instead had I come from the other side of the tracks, rather than from Lincoln's side.

3

Ardor, Ambition and Adventure: The Late Teens

The ominous Great Depression was nearing when our senior class graduated from Islip High School on June 24, 1929. The fourteen-year economic decline set in motion that year became America's most severe and widespread recession to date; much of the Western world, in fact, was caught in its vortex. In November, 1928, Herbert Hoover had won a sweeping Republican presidential victory over Alfred E. Smith, whereas Franklin D. Roosevelt became governor of New York by only a slim margin. Signs of a collapsing stock market were already evident by the end of October, 1929. On November 8, 1930, a Democratic landslide re-elected Roosevelt governor; two years later he became president, and less than four months later he closed the banks and put an embargo on gold.

Work was hard to find already in 1929; for many graduates thoughts about choosing a career deferred to more urgent concerns about assured survival. As for me, there seemed no more natural or convenient place to seek full-time work than at *The Islip Press.* Presumptuous though it was, I actually probed a job as general news reporter.

At one of several desks sat a white-haired, middle-aged lady, Mrs. Mildred Christy, to whom during the past year I had routinely handed my weekly sports copy. I sat down and waited while she telephoned the president and general manager of Suffolk Consolidated Press Company and set up an appointment for me. I was to see him at the Bay Shore headquarters of the Macy-owned chain of six weeklies that published the *Press.* Then she handed me a nail file folded into a one dollar bill. Before you see Paul Bailey, she exhorted, get yourself a new shirt "and remember I'll be praying for you." In those years Saturday was washday for my two shirts, one set aside for weekdays and one for Sundays, and both frayed. Following her advice I hitchhiked to Bay Shore, bought a new shirt (yes, for $1 in those days), put it on in the store and carried away the old one in a paper sack. Before my appointment I carefully activated the nail file.

I emerged from Mr. Bailey's office as something rather less than a full-fledged reporter. For every $2 annual subscription I sold, I was to get a dollar commission, and for whatever general news or sports items the editors accepted a nickel a column inch.

For much of a week I knocked on doors in Islip Manor but nobody, it seemed, could afford a subscription. After this disconcerting start I tried another angle. Instead of peddling subscriptions, I presented myself as a *Press* reporter looking for local news. The next week I returned to ask sources of news items if they had seen their names in the paper, and left a sample copy. Once people saw their names in print, it seemed, they could no longer afford to be without a subscription.

As soon as my weekly sales topped a dozen subscriptions I was placed on a steady $12-a-week salary as reimbursement for both news copy and subscriptions. As I produced more and more usable news, my salary was raised to $15, and soon thereafter I also received an added publication day gas allowance for bulk delivery of papers to stores and street vendors.

From the very first summer when at fourteen I had cut down trees, I gave mother $10 a week to help buy family groceries and meet other expenses. As my wages crept slowly upward, I could now also bring home a surprise Saturday special like three soup chickens for a dollar. Besides doing odd jobs and caddying, my next oldest brothers helped maintain the one-acre farm.

There were the months and years also of welcome pleasures that might punctuate the necessary work routines. Most appreciated of my schoolmates was Richard Timm, who lived some three miles distant at the opposite end of Central Islip. The Timm home was regularly open Sunday afternoons and evenings to classmates and friends of Dick and his attractive teenage sisters, Jessie, Evelyn and Edna. Sunday afternoons the fellows played basketball outdoors on a long tree-mounted backboard. Evenings, after sandwiches and soft drinks, fellows and girls played cards or other indoor games and learned to dance to the music of the Twenties. After Jessie married Charles Murphy, we sometimes spent Sunday afternoon on Great South Bay as guests aboard their 35-foot cabin cruiser.

One of our group was Willy Warburg who later became a Seventh Day Adventist and went off to a Washington seminary. During vacation he once plied me with prophecies of impending eschatological doom and tried unsuccessfully to convert me to Ellen G. White's expectations of a fiery encroaching endtime.

In those years also, in my larger circle of acquaintances, I met and was enamored of—let me call her Yvonne, my teenage infatuation. She had blue eyes and honey-blonde hair that cascaded to her shoulders. She was somewhat shorter than I would have preferred and a bit more curvaceous than necessary. No girl I knew kissed as fervently and untiringly. A relaxed partner, Yvonne was attuned to soft dance music and to a full moon over Great South Bay. She looked specially nice and provocatively so in a black low-cut gown.

Yvonne lived with an aunt and uncle in a modest white corner house in Islip Manor. Her parents lived in Brooklyn; she never talked about them and I never met them. One weekend four carloads of us teenagers in rickety automobiles held together by divine providence drove to the Brooklyn apartment for a Saturday night slumber party. By the time we negotiated the weekend inner-city traffic we all arrived so tired that most of us fell asleep on the rugs before we could remove our shoes.

Sometimes Yvonne seemed so eager that she frightened me. I was not ready for commitments that I felt were increasingly implicit in our relationship. One night, when we were out driving, she fainted and, young newspaperman though I was, I was dismayed and unnerved. She admitted later that it was all a hoax. That was the last time I dated the one girl of my teens most difficult to forget.

In the Bay Shore headquarters offices I met and worked under the editorial staff. The most experienced among them was J. Edward Haley, editor of *The Bay Shore Sentinel* and *The Smithtown Star,* who for health reasons had left the dank newsroom of *The Brooklyn Daily Eagle* to work in clean country air. He was a skillful reporter, writer and copy-editor. An atheist, he routinely deleted from all copy any reference to God. I also soon observed and personally experienced his antipathy for shoddy copy. In the center of the editorial office stood a big, tall wastebasket; circling it around three walls were the staff's desks and typewriters including mine. When untidy copy reached Ed Haley's desk he simply crunched it into a tight ball and arched it with never a miss into the waiting basket. I then faced the embarrassment of silently retrieving the rejected effort and redoing it. I learned more from Haley about news writing than I ever learned from books. He demanded accuracy in journalism and brought to his work an even temperament that only poor copy could ruffle.

At another of the desks was Arthur P. Thompson, a rather earthy chap given to smutty jokes, who covered police and general news. He was also a suburban stringer for *The New York Times.* Married to an attractive wife, he boasted about their Saturday night swingers group who after dinner tossed and picked up house keys for a night's extramarital escapade.

Al Ruhfel, editor of *The Babylon Eagle* and *The Amityville Sun,* always spent press day in the Bay Shore headquarters office. A gifted reporter and editor, he covered also for *The Brooklyn Daily Eagle.* Like Haley, he was a family man and a gentleman.

Also in the newsroom from time to time was Julian Tuthill, women's page editor, a somewhat effeminate chap in his late twenties who handled food and fashion features. Once on a trip to New York City with him he persuaded me to visit a club to which he belonged, one that admitted only members whose names were secretly coded, and their guests. Never before or since have I seen such and so many weirdos at one time and in one place.

On press day during final stages before printing, I often joined Mrs. Christy in proofreading and correcting galleys. One day I made a blunder of sorts and expostulated, "Jesus Christ!" Removing her tortoise-shell glasses, she looked at me penetratingly and remarked in a soft voice: "Carl, I'd rather you slap my face than take the name of my best Friend in vain." I knew she was a widow. What I did not know then was that her teenage son, whom I apparently resembled, had recently died in California in a motorcycle accident. Nor did I know that she prayed God to give her a son in the ministry, or at least, in the Lord. What's more, she had alerted two friends in Ohio—with whom as a teenager she had often sung gospel songs in churches and rescue missions—to put me, of all people, on their prayer list. To be on the prayer list of that triumvirate, and of local believers like Martha Gorton, too, was like being at the mercy of an air assault.

As a journalist I often received complimentary tickets for boxing and wrestling events, auto races, county fairs, summer theatre, flower shows and even restaurant openings. There were tickets to the legitimate stage in New York, where I saw Katherine Cornell perform; to opera at the Hippodrome; to the rodeo at Madison Square Garden; to the Ringling Brothers and Barnum and Bailey circus. Less interested in stage than screen, I was encouraged to add to my reporting the movie editorship of our chain of six papers. That meant preparing the signed weekly column "Through the Moviescope." Complimentary tickets to Radio City Music Hall and other metropolitan theatres were readily available, although travel time discouraged frequent attendance there. Local theatres supplied reserved seats for me and a guest at any program I wanted; if the weekly column required it, I attended double features at two cinemas on one night.

My heart and mind were geared to the secular world and knew little of religious things. I joined the Bay Shore Lions Club. Many churches had liberal pastors whose sermons were book reviews or travelogues and attendance was slim. Faced by the deepening economic depression, churches and voluntary agencies lacked resources to cope with public hunger and unemployment. To help the cause I played the role of bride in a "Womanless Wedding" presented to a capacity crowd in Bay Shore at the First Methodist Episcopal Church, but we raised a paltry $75 for the local unemployment fund. As time went on, government was increasingly implored to meet mounting emergency needs. With Franklin Roosevelt's election to the presidency in November, 1932, federal agencies became the central and continuing social service resource.

During those years I also met Vasata the Great. He was head barber and usually the only barber in his rather large shop in East Islip where I went for haircuts. An immigrant from Eastern Europe, he was by birth a Czech, or, as we said then, a Bohemian. Slight of stature, with reddish hair, he spoke good English and was grateful to be living and working in America. His shop had two or three swivel chairs that faced floor-to-ceiling mirrors that reflected into similar mirrors on the opposite wall. I never surmised their full purpose until one day, on a routine every-other-week stop for a hair trim, I found Vasata performing complex card tricks before the mirrors.

Vasata, I discovered, was a magician—and somewhat more than an amateur at that. Having completed introductory and advanced Harlan Tarbell courses in magic he routinely performed at various clubs and gatherings. By the time I got to know him he had developed an impressive repertoire. Besides doing card tricks he also invoked spirits, did vanishing acts, sawed in half coffin-encased bodies, turned water into wine (and, moreover, wine back into water again).

As a young reporter I had a certain flair for humorous and human interest situations as well as a healthy curiosity. I consequently became much more interested in Vasata the magician than in Vasata the barber. I made it a point to schedule my shop visits at the end of his day's work, did occasional news items about him (in which he became Vasata the Great) and, most importantly, picked up the art of magic so well that within six months I became his assistant. I learned to put a deck of cards in my well-worn hat and summon a preferred card to leap accommodatingly from the mix, to turn water into what looked like wine and then back again into what looked like clear water, to produce a rabbit from apparently empty tubes, to invoke anonymous spirits to write messages on slates, to command a light bulb to turn itself on and float across the room, to banish a numbered dollar bill and then recover it inside a piece of fruit. On Saturday nights when no journalistic priorities prevailed I presided over Vasata's climactic act in which he was firmly secured in a coffin-like box and sawed in half.

Card tricks became my specialty. In my early teens I had learned to play pinochle. But when I met Vasata I learned to shuffle, cut and offer a deck to anyone who, despite every effort to avoid it, unwittingly took whatever card I preferred. I could toss a shuffled deck on the floor and request a particular card to leap out, or command that card to rise slowly out of a goblet or out of a hat into which I had placed the deck.

From Vasata, I must admit, I learned also about the *Daily Racing Form* and how to play the horses. I placed weekly bets, usually on Saturday races, wagering on any horse that in his previous race was nosed out in the final quarter turn after leading the field. Bets were placed in a small Islip drug store by handing a memo with a $5 or $10 bill to a certain employee. In my first year I succeeded in losing about $100—not a fortune, yet enough of a misfortune in a depression time. One day a fellow magician made one of his periodic visits to Vasata's shop. He mentioned that a friend, a trainer at a Southern track, knew when a certain mediocre horse was going to "run to win," and that he would share the word. Several months later we got the promised tip: John T. D., a critter that had not won for a long time, was marked to "go for the money." The official odds were 20 to 1. I bet $5 to win, $5 to place and $5 to show—my largest bet ever. John T. D. actually won, and I recovered all of my accumulated gambling losses. That was the end; I never placed another bet—unless one classifies Wall Street with Belmont and Pimlico.

News reporting and writing was, of course, my week-long commitment, and it often preempted my evenings. I covered political rallies and civic meetings, and on Sunday afternoons worked as confidential stenographer for W. Kingsland Macy, New York State Republican leader, who would have become ambassador to England had Herbert Hoover been reelected. This inside glimpse of politics lent a certain tempting fascination to see it as a possible future career option.

By late 1931, I was serving not only as a relief editor but had also become a suburban stringer in Suffolk County for Standard News Association, inheriting Art Thomas's work as suburban reporter for the *New York Herald Tribune* and periodically covering events for the *New York Evening Post.* Those were the *Herald Tribune*'s days of greatness, the Stanley Walker era, and that of Charles McLendon as day city editor. The *Tribune*'s rewrite men were word craftsmen who routinely contributed leading feature articles to *Collier's* and *Saturday Evening Post.* In human and humorous interest stories they saw as much drama and comedy—and even more—than did the alert suburban correspondents to whose reports they added literary flair.

I readily adopted some marks of the newsmongering profession as Hollywood and popular columnists like Walter Winchell depicted it, especially the slouch hat. Other distinctions I escaped, including the dangling cigar or cigarette. Back on the farm my brother and I had once experimentally smoked corn tassle "cigarettes." I became so desperately ill that puffing any kind of weed forever lost its appeal. Alcohol I had sworn off when I saw what three or four "shots" of homemade gin could do to customers of our country still. My besetting problem was weight, 200 pounds of it; weekend caddying had not walked it off, and news coverage of luncheons and dinners now kept it on.

I maintained almost weekly contact with "Mother Christy," not only for emergency proofreading help on press day, but by frequently driving her home at the end of the work-day. She lived with her attractive daughter, Helen McDonald, who had preferred raising her family to accepting a film offer. Her entrepreneur husband, George H. McDonald (or "Mac"), was active in county politics and in various enterprises, some of them secret. The family often invited me for dinner, especially on holidays when relatives interested in writing were also present. One day when I arrived, the McDonalds's fetching French maid was dusting the living room. Knave that I was, I picked up a beachball near the entry and tossed it playfully at her lace-edged derriere. Like many unscientific maneuvers the act had unforeseen and unfortunate consequences. The ball bounced up and against one of a matched pair of valuable porcelain vases on the piano, shattering it to smithereens. Helen McDonald entered at that unpropitious moment. With the grace and generosity that characterized her, she moved the surviving vase to the center of the piano and said, "You know, I have long thought that just one would look better, right there the way it now is."

On our occasional junkets together from office to home, Mother Christy tried to establish a beachhead for spiritual things. I listened respectfully as she spoke about biblical prophecy and things to come. One evening she told me of the absolute need to be "born again." "Except a man be born again," she quoted from the venerable King James Bible, "he cannot see the kingdom of God." For emphasis, she added, "Jesus said that, you know, and he knew more about the conditions for getting into heaven than anybody else." I felt the finger of destiny pointing at me but changed the subject to less personal matters.

Mother Christy was an inactive Methodist who lamented the forfeiture of the gospel by many local churches. She and other believers met periodically for prayer, often at the McDonald home. The Oxford Group, with Frank Buchman at its helm, was then making inroads on Long Island, and especially among nominal Episcopalians. At the Group's houseparties, as they were called, I heard leaders speak about moral and spiritual crisis and personal decision. During those days I also met the Welsh evangelist Peter Rees Joshua, minister at First Presbyterian Church of Islip before he moved to a long ministry in Huntington.

Another new contact made through Mother Christy was her friend Dozier N. Fields, now a local banker who as a former journalist had been press aide to then Secretary of Commerce Herbert Hoover. A disciplined writer and true intellectual, Fields was a stimulating host at dinner evenings at his home in which I participated. Some of my insights were honed by his penetrating mind and caustic wit.

All such activities were incidental, however, to my journalistic goals and concerns. At home I equipped a small downstairs room as my study, with a desk, telephone, some files and of course, a typewriter. The one-acre farm at 103 Wilson Boulevard, once derided as "Chickentown" by a number of former schoolmates, now became a communications center linked to several of the world's greatest news desks. Besides added duties with Standard News Association and the *New York Herald Tribune,* I now covered occasional crime and divorce stories for the *New York Daily News.* Since the *Daily News* featured photo journalism, I bought a top quality Zeiss Ikon to try my hand, but abandoned photography when the camera was stolen from my car. Those days when rum running was rampant off the Long Island coast, I wrote stories about it in our chain of weekly papers under the pseudonym C. Lincoln Howard to ward off possible gangster recrimination. But perhaps no experience in those years was more unexpected than that on Tuesday night, March 1, 1932, when I called the *Herald Tribune*'s city desk to report a gruesome automobile accident with several fatalities. "Sorry, Henry," was the hurried response, "the Lindbergh baby's just been kidnapped and we're holding all the space we have for that." As time passed I relayed hundreds of stories to the *Herald Tribune,* handled Suffolk county election returns and periodically filed human interest stories that disinterested my colleagues until, when prominently featured by the *Tribune,* their competing papers insisted on belated coverage. Writing had now become, as it were, not only my bread and butter, but my very being.

In 1932 together with Lloyd Record, another young Suffolk journalist, I enrolled for a course in short story writing that met periodically in New York City. It was taught by Thomas H. Uzzell in his Madison Avenue office. Record and I would drive fifty miles to Manhattan at dusk, sharing ideas along the way, and return home just before midnight. Uzzell had been fiction editor of *Collier's* and was now a successful literary agent and author of a book on *Narrative Technique.* He put us on notice the very first night: "Write a million words of your best," he said, "and toss them into a wastebasket. Then you'll be really ready to break into the fiction market." Having cleared story ideas and plots, we would return to New York a week or two later with a first draft, and after class criticism faced a weekend of manuscript revision. At that time I met or corresponded with a number of prominent writers who summered as a colony on Fire Island, among them Fanny Brice and Gene Fowler.

When Ed Haley died suddenly of a heart attack on September 16, 1932, at the age of 47, I was asked to take the editorship of *The Smithtown Star.* It was a remarkable entrustment. In three years I had climbed the ladder from cub reporter to reporter to relief editor, and now became, at 19, the youngest editor of a weekly newspaper in New York's second largest county, and probably in the entire state. What's more, the *Star* was in the heart of Suffolk county's society belt.

4

A Renegade Editor's Rebirth

Smithtown was a twelve-mile drive from home, mainly through woodlands whose villages bore old Indian names like Hauppauge, Ronkonkoma or Nesconset. The *Smithtown Star* office was located in a storefront building that housed an editorial and news room, storage facilities, the business-advertising unit directed by George Morsing and a double-duty secretary.

The opposition *Smithtown Messenger* welcomed me in September, 1932, by front-paging my picture with the derisive caption "Little Carlie, God's Gift to Journalism."

On the edge of my new appointment I preserved certain past activities, interrupted some, dropped some and added others. In addition to editorship of the *Star* I inherited from Ed Haley also the associate editorship of *Suffolk Every Week,* and continued as suburban stringer for both Standard News Association and the *Herald Tribune.* Interest in magic largely fell by the way; short story writing was reserved for the odd evening or free Saturday; social life was largely eclipsed; entertainment centered mainly around films reviewed in my work as movie editor of the Western Suffolk Group of six weeklies.

Occasionally I still attended an Oxford Group "houseparty" and heard speakers elaborate the theme that changed lives are the raw material for a new world order. At a Waldorf-Astoria international gathering leaders included academic, political and business notables like John A. Mackay and Samuel M. Shoemaker. At subsequent smaller meetings I met Vic Kitchen, author of *I Was a Pagan,* and heard men and women from all areas of life share how they had found spiritual vitality and ethical renewal. The Group's strategy was to reach professional leaders and through them still other leaders who exemplified and called for changed lives. Early in May, 1933, I briefly met a dynamic University of Pennsylvania alumnus, Gene Bedford, and several others who gave me a copy of A. J. Russell's *For Sinners Only* to help me understand a movement for which they encouraged publicity.

Local business and professional men promptly invited me into the Midday Club that met weekly at the Elk's Club for a fifteen-minute address and a dollar luncheon. Comprised mainly of physicians, lawyers, clergy, a few merchants and the two local editors, the Club brought me face-to-face with Editor Deutzmann of the competing *Messenger* who, even if he wielded a vitriolic pen, was a civilized Methodist deacon. Although no confidences were broken, this weekly gathering just before press day yielded a good bit of local news without extensive leg work.

After one such meeting, the Reverend John Runkle, rector of St. James Episcopal Church, indicated that a University of Pennsylvania alumnus was visiting him for a few days; the two of us, he thought, would enjoy getting acquainted. I promised to stop by on Saturday. But when Saturday came, I balked. After all, I mused, any chap who stays with a preacher for most of a week must be overly religious. At the next Midday Club meeting I expressed my regrets to the rector; something unforeseen, I said, had prevented my coming. Runkle was understanding, but noted that since his guest was staying a second weekend, I would be no less welcome Saturday next. I said I'd try. But when Saturday came, my reluctance multiplied: anyone who spent two weeks visiting a preacher, I decided, was incurably religious, and I had best beware. Once again I explained to Runkle at Midday Club that something had intervened, adding apologetically that such is the vulnerability of journalistic work. To my astonishment, he replied that because the weather was so exceptionally nice his guest was staying a third week; while he wouldn't pressure me, Runkle added, he hoped I'd make it this time. Did I, perchance, have Saturday morning or afternoon free? I had no commitment that I could think of right off, I said; no doubt I could come. My apprehension multiplied even more, however; here was a chap menacingly religious, and I was not going. For three Saturdays in a row, therefore, I broke that implicit commitment.

Even though I had shed the church in my mid-teens, certain remnants of a devout exposure remained. My one and only Bible, which I had pilfered from the pew racks of the Episcopal Sunday School, stayed near my bed. Sometimes before retiring I read and reread parts of it, especially the fascinating accounts of Jesus' resurrection. Mother

Christy kept reminding me that God requires and provides the new birth. Oxford Group meetings confronted me with college graduates and others who recounted how their lives were supernaturally changed. While I recalled certain phrases of the Episcopal prayer book, I had no prayer life. To all intents and purposes I was a pagan.

As the summer of 1933 approached a combination of circumstances propelled me toward definitive vocational decision. I was doing too many things, and enjoying them all, with the mounting danger that I would excel at none. There was the weekly newspaper editorship—should that be my future? What of alternative possibilities with the New York dailies? What of fiction writing? On my desk for two weeks, awaiting my signature, was a contract projected by one of the most successful writers of detective stories, Frederick C. Davis, who proposed that I flesh out his skeletal plots and we would split the take 50/50. In the mails was an invitation also from Uzzell that I sign a six-month preliminary contract to produce action fiction. And there were remote possibilities of political tie-ins through Kingsland Macy.

One early June night I stayed late at the Bay Shore headquarters where our six weekly papers were set in type and printed. I was giving "Lover's Merry-Go-Round," a 3000-word short story, its twentieth and, I hoped, final revision.

Not long into the effort the phone rang. It was Mother Christy, whom I had told to call me if ever she lacked transportation. Could I perchance drive her to a special gathering at St. Mark's Episcopal Church in nearby Islip, she asked, and better yet, attend as well? Yes, I'd take her, and pick her up later; no, I couldn't go, because I hadn't shaved and was redoing a short story. Warding off her counterproposals, I simply took her to St. Mark's and returned for her two hours later. "You must meet tonight's speaker," she greeted me; "he's not much older than you, and wonderfully dynamic." "Some other time," I replied hurriedly, eager to return to "Lover's Merry-Go-Round." The disappointment that swept her face annoyed me. Well, I thought, if a perfunctory journalistic "hello" and "good-bye" would crown her evening's pleasure, I could at least agree to that.

Some sixty people were gathered inside, among them, crowding the speaker, my former high school principal Earl B. Robinson and other community leaders. Mother Christy introduced me as "Carl Henry." A bit unsure, and taken aback, he replied: "You're in newspaperwork, aren't you?" When I nodded, he replied, "I'm Gene Bedford." For good or ill I had unexpectedly been thrust together with the chap with whom, in a village twenty-five miles away and weeks earlier, I had three Saturdays in a row broken an informal appointment.

"Is newspaperwork what you plan to do all your life?" Bedford asked. That ten-word question brought into focus the multiple and rival possibilities that pelleted my uncertainty about the future.

"I wish I knew," I responded candidly.

"Why don't you ask God about it?" Gene countered.

"W-h-a-t?" I replied, as if faced by a preposterous suggestion.

"You believe in God, don't you?" Gene asked.

"Y-e-s," I answered slowly.

"You believe he has a plan for your life?"

Again, more slowly still, I replied: "Y—e—s."

"Then why don't you ask him?"

I was embarrassed now by the presence of people who gathered to overhear the dialogue, and felt threatened by a sense of public exposure and nakedness. Sometimes, I thought to myself, not even the saints are smart enough to regroup when a conversation gets intimately private.

"I'd like sometime to get together and to talk to you about it," I countered.

"When shall we do it?" he asked.

"How about next Saturday?"

With that proposal we both exploded in uncontainable laughter, since my track record for three previous Saturday commitments was nil. But we agreed to meet at the Bay Shore offices in midmorning on Saturday, June 10.

What I did not know was that Bedford during summer months earned his living selling real estate in northern New Jersey and that Saturday, moreover, was his best day for sales. Yet he drove up as promised, and I was there, expected or not. After a brief greeting we dialogued for an hour about Christian commitment and then drove to the shores of Great South Bay to converse some more. I raised all the usual objections that one hears from those trying to rationalize their unbelief. Himself once a nonbeliever, Bedford told how he now found a daily walk with God so rewarding that he felt impelled to share the good life and good news with others. God would not coerce me, he said; the responsible choice was mine, and mine alone.

I did not tell Gene that a few nights earlier I had driven to the quiet shorefront at Blue Point and there had meditated and prayed and wrestled with God. I still felt, as when reading the accounts of Jesus' resurrection, like a moth circling a flame, daring neither to believe nor to disbelieve. I even fancied walking the high road of commitment, although the great biblical truths of Christ's atonement for sins and justification by faith were on but the rim of my monologue. But then a sudden squall followed by a furious storm sent me driving homeward through earth-piercing lightning and thunder. As I parked momentarily for the raging rain to subside before opening the large barn door for car entry, a fiery bolt of lightning, like a giant flaming arrow, seemed to pin me to the driver's seat, and a mighty roll of thunder unnerved me. When the fire fell, I knew instinctively that the Great Archer had nailed me to my own footsteps. Looking back, it was as if the transcendent Tetragrammaton wished me to know that I could not save myself and that heaven's intervention was my only hope.

At the end of three hours of dialogue with Gene Bedford that momentous Saturday in June I volunteered, "I'm ready"—and I somewhat understated my readiness by a fallback to Pascal's wager. "If I go ahead, and there's nothing to it, I have nothing to lose," I said; "if I don't go ahead, and there is something to it, I have everything to lose."

"Let's pray," he said.

We knelt down in the front of the car, Gene crowding down at the steering wheel and I beside him. There was a long silence during which I was unsure how to begin. A newspaper reporter and editor, and exposed in my youth to the Episcopal prayer book, I nonetheless lacked words appropriate to the moment.

"If I pray first," Gene volunteered, "will you repeat after me?"

I agreed.

Sentence by sentence Gene prayed the Lord's Prayer, and I followed. Then I acknowledged my sinful condition and prayed God to cleanse my life of the accumulated evil of the years, to empty me of self and to make resident within me the Holy Spirit to guide and rule my life.

By the end of that prayer the wonder was wrought. I had inner assurance hitherto unknown of sins forgiven, that Jesus was my Savior, that I was on speaking terms with God as my Friend. A floodtide of peace and joy swept over me. My life's future, I was confident, was now anchored in and charted by another world, the truly real world.

Gene suggested that we now remain quiet before God. "He has given us one tongue and two ears," he remarked. "We ought to listen twice as long as we speak, and let him tell us what we ought to do."

I waited and wept before God as the minutes passed, silently asking for guidance and direction and committing to him the whole panorama of future vocational possibilities. I now knew God to be King of my life. Had he dispatched me, I would have gone that very day to China or anywhere else in his cause.

Gene spoke again. "If you have good news to share, Carl, don't hoard it from others. Ask God to show you with whom to share it." Then he added, "Keep your morning quiet time with God. Read the Bible, perhaps John's Gospel at first, and pray and wait for guidance. Do what he says and God will nourish your spiritual life and reward you with joy."

I filled up Gene's gas tank and with gratitude bade him safe journey, unaware that he now faced a long drive to New York and thereafter through the Lincoln Tunnel to northern New Jersey for a few scant hours with realty prospects. He had ignored the high odds against my keeping a Saturday engagement and had won another seeker for the supreme Sovereign.

I shared the news almost immediately with two persons. The first was Mother Christy, who was overjoyed that I had found enduring treasure. She had me recount the entire morning's events and wanted especially to know what Gene Bedford had said about the Cross. It had escaped me that The Lord's Prayer says nothing about Christ's substitutionary death in the sinner's stead as the ground of salvation. Nor could I recall any explicit discussion or dialogue about it with Gene. Yet I assured her of my trust in Christ as the sinner's Substitute, and there came to memory now, from long-past Episcopal services, such reinforcing phrases as "We look to the shed blood of Christ and are thankful." In the incomparable providence of God I had found redemption through a plurality of contributory factors that included a pilfered Bible, fragmentary memories of the Episcopal prayer book, a Methodist friend's insistence on the new birth, an Oxford Grouper's daring call for changed lives, all coalescing around my need for vocational direction and crowned by the Holy Spirit's work of grace and inner assurance. I prayed with Mother Christy and we arranged to travel the next morning to hear Peter Joshua preach.

The second person to whom I spoke was my mother by birth. Our family was not a communicative family; we did not freely display affection, and seldom shared anything personal. Mother was alone in the kitchen preparing supper when I arrived. I greeted her with the rather disarming words: "Mom, I gave my life to Jesus today." Perplexed and somewhat astonished, she asked, "*What?*" "I gave my life to Jesus today," I reiterated. "That's good," she answered. That ended my first testimony. I walked quickly to my private study and sank to my knees. "O God," I said, "that wasn't much of a testimony, but thank you for helping me give it." Three months later Mother made a personal commitment with Sophie Smith, an Episcopal Sunday school teacher who in the interim had also found Christ.

On June 12, two days after my "great awakening," Gene Bedford wrote assuring me of his prayers and anticipating further fellowship later in the summer. "God has started a real work in you, and the future is full," he wrote. "There is grand adventure in this fellowship with God, and each of us must launch out into the full rich stream of his guidance and fit in with his plan. Don't ever limit his power in you, and so live that you *expect* real miracles to happen."

We had talked the previous Saturday about the need of witnessing in Bay Shore and to Long Island's entire South Shore. I drew up a list of sixty persons—friends, relatives, fellow-workers and former classmates—who might be invited to a group meeting in Bay Shore, where with other members of a team I would willingly testify to my experience of Christ. I also shared the word with my younger brothers and sisters, and involved them in home Bible study and prayer. A small group effort was underway in Sayville under George Bond, rector of St. Ann's Episcopal Church. Mrs. Christy and I drove over for a Friday night meeting in the rectory where I gave my testimony. Present was a garage mechanic, Al Graunke, who was touched by my witness; after talking together alone in another room we knelt in prayer and Al surrendered to Christ. A quarter century later he was active still in International Christian Leadership.

I kept an outreach prayer list and asked the Lord to burden me specially for some particular person. If a month passed without my helping lead someone to Christ I began to wonder about the depth of my commitment. Sometimes after inviting a friend to join me for some event in New York City, I used the homeward trip to talk about spiritual things.

Several weeks after my conversion I came to a time of enigmatic emptiness, however. As I waited before God for resolution of this problem I was rebuked for not having done what the Spirit had earlier prodded me to do, namely, to return to Islip High School a stack of books I had signed out as a student but had never returned. Since I was considered an outstanding graduate and local leader, I now walked without secretarial clearance directly into the principal's office. Thus it happened that one day I appeared in Mr. Robinson's office holding a load of books tucked precariously under my chin. "What's this?" exclaimed the principal. Without flinching, and to his amazement if not consternation I said, "I've committed my life to Jesus Christ, and he told me to bring these books back where they belong." Robinson thanked me without further inquiry, then changed the subject, perhaps thinking thereby to spare both of us embarrassment.

A few months later, at my Wilson Boulevard home, a knock came at the front door. It was Earl B. Robinson, Jr., the principal's son, an atheist home for a few days from Amherst. "Carl," he began, "my mother died recently, and I hear you have had an experience with God." Then he added: "I'd like to visit with you." The following week we called on Peter Joshua, with whom Earl made his commitment. He later attended Westminster Theological Seminary, taught at The Stony Brook School and at Gordon College, before serving in later years as a Baptist pastor in New England.

But there were disappointments too. I tried, for example, to win the *Star*'s business manager George Morsing. Member of a then very liberal Presbyterian church he firmly believed he was an authentic Christian because of his baptism as a child in Denmark. My own father likewise claimed to be a Christian because of his baptism as an infant in Germany.

Controversy erupted among both promoters and critics of the Oxford Group over whether the movement had an adequate doctrine of the atonement. Among the critics were Arno C. Gaebelein, Sam Shoemaker and Peter Joshua. After my decision for Christ, I wrote Gene Bedford asking what role the Oxford Group assigned to the Cross. His reply was that "without shedding of blood there is no remission. A price must be paid—and I start to comprehend somewhat the Cross in continued crucifixion of self and that which constitutes self. . . . The message of the Oxford Group is the message of the Cross. Christ—his life and death—are the mainsprings of the whole thing. . . . An articulate message will emerge from maximal living." This was the sort of ambiguity that encouraged doubts about doctrinal adequacy, or at least clarity. Under a cloud of evangelical criticism, enthusiasm for the Group faded and within a few years more traditional efforts took over evangelistic outreach.

My 1933 summer vacation plans had been made early. Supplied with press tickets for a late June trip to the Chicago World's Fair, I intended to take along Mother Christy. We would first stop in Ohio to meet other members of the "prayer triumvirate," Mrs. Alice Cooper in Toledo and Mrs. Blanche Garn with whom we stayed in Fremont, before continuing to the Windy City. Named "A Century of Progress International Exposition," the Fair proved to be a glittering success without governmental subsidy, even in the depths of the Depression.

Although it focused on engineering and on scientific and technological developments, the Fair's most publicized feature was Sally Rand, a 28-year-old "fan dancer" who stripped to the buff, or nearly so, while maneuvering yard-long feathers. My colleague, Art Thomas, delighted in circulating the hope that I would provide the office chaps full and detailed verbal coverage of the exhibition. Crowds on the Midway waiting to see Sally Rand's performance extended a city block long three or four abreast and, as I discovered, inched along at a snail's pace. As a half hour passed I coped first with a feeling of discomfort and then of inappropriateness and guilt about the whole prospect of lining up with pop-eyed oglers thirsting for eroticism. What I did next would perhaps have been considered insane by most folk in that waiting mob. I tore my two passes to the Rand show into bits and went to another exhibit. That decision put distance between myself and shoddy sexuality; moreover, it promoted decency and conserved valuable time and money. Sally was a sad case, a Quaker farm girl from Missouri and reportedly a graduate of a religious college. Her claim to fame rested on being arrested four times in a single day for indecent exposure. Across the years, despite dwindling appreciation, she was still on her ego strip in cheap hotels and small nightclubs at the age of 73.

To many Americans the high point of 1933 was Roosevelt's inauguration, Babe Ruth's home-run record or the inauguration of King Kong movies. For some it was the year when, in May and June, thirty-four humanists—including twelve prominent ministers—signed the Humanist Manifesto that declared "the time has passed for theism, deism, modernism"; rejection of the supernatural, it announced, would advance the goal of "a free and universal society in which people voluntarily and intelligently cooperate for the common good." For many Europeans 1933 marked the beginning of Hitler's concentration camps. As for me personally, that year began a relationship with God through Christ, Savior and Lord, that can survive the crush of planets and the end of this world.

On return from Chicago I became acting editor—and eight months later, editor—of the *Port Jefferson Times-Echo;* its circulation was the largest among our chain's six weekly newspapers and covered a large segment of north shore Long Island.

Editor Deutzmann of the *Messenger,* who had disdainfully heralded my arrival in Smithtown in 1932 to guide the *Star,* now compounded his abuse by a front-page tribute when I moved in November, 1933, to lead the more prestigious *Times-Echo:*

"Smithtown has been blessed (?) by the presence of 'Little Carlie' as God's gift to journalism. The fat school graduate once wrote a prize-winning essay in the Islip High School and immediately got the idea he was the world's best writer. So he went to work for the *Islip Press.* This week he has gone to Port Jefferson to edit the *Port Jefferson Times-Echo,* another bad odor of the Macy Western Suffolk Group of News-Manglers. In Little Carlie's place in Smithtown has appeared . . . Frank Catska . . . carrying explicit instructions to continue where Carlie left off. . . . Carlie's clothes will hardly fit you. . . . Carl Henry, as promotion for his wonderful journalistic endeavors, the Pickwickian Joe of the Macy Slingerbund—is transferred to the wilds of Port Jefferson as Editor of the *Times-Echo*. . . . Catska and Henry, the pink pills of Yellow Journalism, with instructions to make things hot. . . . Macy's little fat boys, Carl Henry and Paul Bailey, are rated, in their own organization, by Mr. Macy, not by their associates, even in Macy's organization, as coming big shots in politics. They love to make office holders squirm with headlines. Suppose we printed a headline: CARL HENRY, SMITHTOWN STAR EDITOR, KILLS SEVEN and then in small type added, Fleas in an Islip Restaurant, with a Stein of Beer. . . ."

At about the same time *The New York Times* asked me to cover 600 square miles comprising Long Island's northeast quarter. The two-year Port Jefferson stint was a time of vigorous journalism when spiritual experience and moral sensitivity added new dimensions to my understanding of life and human events. Whatever its category—tragedy or comedy, straight news or human interest—readable copy flourished and flowed: the Christmas eve discovery of the nude body of a beautiful teenager, an abortion casualty; police raids on a still that for many months had covertly consumed truckloads of sugar transported weekly to a woodland retreat; a numerologist who predicted the end of the world and was put to the test by a doubter's cash offer for his automobile; an evangelist who inveighed against everything from rouged cheeks to chewing tobacco ("You can go to heaven if you chew, but you'll have to go to hell if you want to spit"); the departure of a pet crow that survived only on a banana diet and became the object of an island-wide manhunt; the fire department so charmed by a silver-tongued salesman that it had to sell a fire engine to pay for its expensive new siren.

Long Island's north shore boasted exceptional scenic beauty and charm. On the hillock overlooking Belle Terre I often enjoyed my sack lunch and had a time of private meditation. Looking across Long Island Sound toward Bridgeport, Connecticut, one glimpsed fishing vessels, sailboats, scows and the Bridgeport-Port Jefferson ferry plying its course. Stately mansions obscured by summer foliage in winter came to view among the snow-covered hills. I sometimes imagined a day when I might settle down in a home of my own, one built to order on a hill above the harbor. But that bit of fancy was quickly shattered by a summons to a more mobile future.

The conviction that I must enter college or university to prepare for full-time Christian service overtook me gradually. Peter Joshua and I were walking the shoreline near Setauket one day when he twitted me about covering Long Island for the news media while he covered it for the Lord, a contrast that I considered not quite legitimate, although I indicated my openness to technical Christian work. In the Spring of 1934 I mentioned that possibility to Dr. Frank E. Gaebelein, headmaster of The Stony Brook School, whom I interviewed occasionally for news copy. Gaebelein asked if I knew of Wheaton College. Since I did not, he gave me a catalogue. I examined it that night and chuckled at its no-movie, no-dancing, no-card-playing code. But its emphasis on Christian world-life view attracted me and I was ready—if that was the price of admission—to subscribe to the negations. I wrote for application forms, knowing so little about biblical factualities that I addressed the postal card to Miss Enoch Dyrness, registrar, thinking Enoch to be a woman's name.

Yet the urge to attend college also disquieted me. For one thing, no one in our family had ever attended college or university. And my funds were very limited in this continuing depression time. In view of the national economic crisis the Roosevelt regime was projecting social security for the nation's thirty million elderly, sponsored unemployment compensation and housing loans, established a National Youth Administration to provide 3,000 jobs; almost half the population got part if not all of its income from the government. Adequate homes could be bought for $3,000 but many persons could not afford even a sandwich or cup of soup, let alone see a movie or the newsreels for 15 cents or dream about going to college. I knew I would have to work my way.

I wrestled with the idea of waiting until the Fall of 1936 to enter college, but God brooked no delay. If God directed, I finally decided, he would doubtless provide. But how? One night I fought out the matter in prayer. College cost money, and if we were going to cross this Red Sea, I wanted to know the divine mechanics. The answer came before I retired, in part perhaps because of my importunity, or in part or whole because of God's demonstrated adequacy of his promises in the present, and his surety for the future.

As if to bind God to a written contract, I penciled on a three-by-five card the funding assurances that overtook me in prayer: 1. Teaching typing; 2. Newspaper work.

I have always been open to some so-called mystical aspects of the Christian life, if in fact mysticism is really a term appropriate to the New Testament. Too many theologians have hastily dismissed the apostle Paul's teaching on "union with Christ." To be sure, the New Testament doctrine is remarkably different from what in philosophical circles is generally meant by mysticism. The Christian's relationship to Christ involves no absorption or disappearance of the self into the Infinite; distinctions of personality are not cancelled, but rather are intensified in man's relationship to the Deity. Equally important is the fact that the Bible anchors the most intimate divine-human relations in redemption, even if that experience rests upon Christ's prior mediation in creation and revelation. Scripture knows nothing of a sinful humanity with immediate access to the holy God in man's own right or on man's own terms; communion with God presupposes the God who speaks and saves. God has revealed his nature normatively to the inspired prophets and apostles as set forth in Scripture. That does not mean, however, that he enters into no significant relations today. New truth about God there is not; a novel God about whom we must affirm only revisable predications is a modernist invention. But when God becomes *my* God, when divine revelation penetrates not only the mind but rather the whole self, when the Spirit personally illumines the believer, dynamic fellowship with God opens possibilities of spiritual guidance in which the Holy Spirit personalizes and applies the biblical revelation individually to and in a redeemed and renewed life.

The Oxford Group emphasis on personal guidance stirred a hornet's nest. At a Stony Brook Bible Conference Arno Gaebelein caricatured houseparties at which Groupers carried paper and pencil awaiting divine guidance while they left their Bibles behind. When I produced a Bible and noted that many of his Bible conference hearers did not carry one, he argued that there must be several brands of Groupers. Yet there was indeed need for criticism, since some Groupers told of being divinely led in the most trivial matters that called simply for common sense. The Group's emphasis seemed to blur the frontier between guidance and revelation.

Yet any statement of evangelical experience that does not include the possibility both of communion with God and the communication of the particularized divine will to the surrendered life seems to me artificially restrictive. Some persons no doubt open the Bible magically for a verse of counsel. While God can speak even through Balaam's ass, it is well to remember that Satan who spoke through the Serpent may at times come as an angel of light. Yet the Spirit-led life is not reducible to a game of chance, any more than it is devoid of spiritual interaction and decision. Nor ought it discourage the development of a sanctified common sense, with growing maturity and insight into the providential purposes of God.

Tests for genuine guidance in the life of the believer have long been charted by evangelical writers: conformity with what is revealed in Scripture about God's nature and dealings with men, consistency with the previous leading of God for the same individual, joy in the prospect of undertaking the venture as a divine constraint, congruity of the proposed action with the emerging pattern of relevant circumstances and with the counsel of trustworthy spiritual advisors.

Few circumstances in my life have been as striking as that small white card on which, on that night of fervent prayer in my study, I jotted down in stipulated sequence the provisions by which God promised to see me through college. It would not have required a prophet to anticipate the possibility of a newspaperman in a new location reengaging in the word business in quest of funds. After all, that had become my life. Yet God's answer to my prayer for assurance strikingly inverted the order by stipulating first of all "teaching typing," whatever that implied. In some ways, in fact, it seemed incredible. I enjoyed typing, and the constant pressure of deadlines had encouraged me to rattle along at about 86 words a minute whenever my thoughts moved in high gear. But I had no reason to think that I could teach anyone to type, nor that I would want to.

There were, indeed, two exceptions. One of the printer's devils at our plant had aspirations for self-improvement, and asked me as a personal favor to teach him the touch system with its obvious advantages over the frustrating hunt and peck used even by many reporters. So, one night a week, in the large barn behind his home, I thumped a small board against the side of a barrel to supply the rhythmic beat to which Johnny Mills learned the a-s-d-f and ;-l-k-j routine on his decrepit typewriter. Apart from other ailments, the machine had a broken tension spring. We solved the problem by stretching a piece of elastic from one end of the carriage to a wall beam, so that the carriage could shuttle from right to left. In time, Mills developed a respectable speed, so perhaps heaven took cognizance of my ingenuity in teaching typing.

But a second effort was a notable failure. Mother Christy, suffering from arthritis, hoped mastery of the keyboard might eliminate the difficulty of hand-written letters. But the hope was dashed in less than a month.

Between Spring and Fall of 1935 when I entered college, came three surprise government offers of a job as junior typist—one in the U.S. Treasury Department in Washington, another in a medical hospital and a third in some obscure now forgotten place. Although I declined each opportunity, the offers came my way through a remarkable back-door entry.

When one of my friends, Evelyn Timm, applied to take the civil service examination for typists at the U.S. Veterans Hospital in Northport not far from my Port Jefferson office, I volunteered to transport her and her typewriter on exam day. On arrival I decided to wait while she took the examination, instead of making a return trip later. The exam room was a dither of uneasy, tense and excited applicants. I was unexpectedly told I could take the exam if I wished, and so jumped in as an adventure. No sooner had the test for speed and accuracy begun when the left rear leg of my typewriter, having worked itself loose, somehow dislodged and rolled across the floor. The machine dipped whenever the carriage moved beyond the left middle, and then righted itself and dipped again back and forth as I banged away. Come what may, I determined to finish the test. A few months later the Civil Service Commission sent word that I had scored 87.83 and that federal job offers would soon be forthcoming.

The Treasury Department invitation of September, 1934, prompted me to request catalogues from all universities in Washington, D.C., including Howard which, unbeknown to me, was then largely an institution for blacks. Howard cautioned me that I might have social problems if I attended. More than twenty years later when I went to Washington as an editor, I looked down from my office in the Washington Building on the Treasury Department across the street where in 1934 I had been offered a typist's job.

By early 1935, I had applied for admission to Wheaton in the Fall. During the summer I heard Wheaton's president, Dr. J. Oliver Buswell, Jr., speak at the Stony Brook conference grounds on faith, reason and the importance of Christ's resurrection. Much of what he said was theologically beyond my grasp, but what I made of it was that faith without reason is not worth much, and that reason is not an enemy but an ally of genuine faith, and moreover that the resurrection of Jesus is an historical event.

My relationships on Long Island and with New York City editors were so solid that I thought it only fair to give them substantial advance notice of my leaving. My resignation, I told them, stemmed from the conviction that God had led me to prepare academically for Christian service.

Letters of appreciation and profoundly gratifying commendations reached me. The editor of the *Herald Tribune,* Charles McLendon, sent along a letter "to whom it may concern": "Mr. Carl Henry, editor of the *Port Jefferson Times,* has served as Suffolk County correspondent for the *New York Herald Tribune* for the last three years. His excellent news judgment and spirit of initiative made him the best correspondent the *Herald Tribune* ever has had in this important center. I recommend him to the attention of any editor who could use a really live newspaperman." Similarly appreciative letters came from Standard News Association and *The New York Times.* About the same time came an invitation from Inter-Continental Communications to provide spot news from Suffolk county to its affiliated radio broadcasting stations; I declined with appreciation.

By summer of that year my father and mother, to my surprise

and distress, had come to a parting of the ways. I still lived at home—or at least spent my nights there. Despite dim and disconcerting rumors of parties involving women and drink, I was unaware that my father's weekend and then routine lodging at the convenience store had deeper implications than protecting the property against breakin.

My father proceeded to deed all interest in the Wilson Boulevard property to my mother. Not until she was served with legal papers did she have any intimation, however, that a foreclosure action had been initiated or that awaiting her was an unpaid and overdue mortgage charge plus interest, taxes and foreclosure costs totaling $679.50, a significant amount in those days and times.

With but five weeks to go before I was to leave for college, I saw the attorney and arranged for payment. That left me $300 and an old car with which to launch a college career.

I had resigned effective August 31, 1935, to allow a week to pack and prepare for Wheaton. The staff gave me a pleasant farewell party and I did my best to make a call to ministry seem at once ideally universal and yet a distinct personal privilege. I had the good will of all my colleagues, including Art Thomas, who delighted in introducing me to visitors as "that oddity among editors" who neither smokes, nor drinks, nor uses profanity, "but prays us all into heaven." News releases had gone out for month-end announcement that I was resigning to attend Wheaton College and then seminary to prepare for the ministry. "At the age of 22," commented one paper, Henry "had attained not only the editorship of one of Long Island's leading and most widely circulated weekly newspapers, but was a news representative in Suffolk county for several New York dailies. His resignation came at the end of six years of journalistic work, during which he became Suffolk's youngest editor."

Within a few short days the bottom seemed to fall all at once out of my plans. Crisis threatened my transition from journalism to college. It seemed to frustrate God's purpose for me, and to raise a serious question, among skeptical friends as well as in my own reflection, about the whole matter of specific divine guidance. So clear had the will of God for my life seemed that, six months before I was to begin studies, I had tendered my resignation. The *Tribune*'s city editor had sent me a personal memo, commenting that the world seemed in such desperate straits that only the Christian message has sufficient vitality to redeem it, and wished me well in my new endeavors. I had endured some considerable caricature of my intimacy with God, especially from a few colleagues who were sure only of their nonacquaintance with him. Even at the final farewell, at which they publicly conceded the remarkable change that becoming a Christian had effected in my life, several privately doubted the wisdom of my abandoning a promising newspaper career; some thought that what I claimed to be the will of God might be mere autosuggestion.

Events of the next few days encouraged these apprehensions. For the first time in my life I became desperately ill. I was stricken suddenly with such acute appendicitis that Dr. Goldschlager, my gifted Jewish physician, refused to take professional responsibility unless I submitted immediately to surgery or secured a second-opinion consent to delay it. My predicament was more than embarrassing; it was desperately perplexing. The clear will of God was to begin college studies that Fall, which meant being in the Midwest, a thousand miles away, within two weeks. Such an operation in those days and its consequent hospitalization would have meant a semester's postponement of academic pursuits; more than that, the spiritual witness given to newspaper coworkers and acquaintances was at risk. Surely God would not so reverse his purposes that I must return to the newspapers from which I had resigned now to apply for another position.

My convictions about divine healing were somewhat ambivalent. Some months earlier, I had received a review copy of a book, in which the author suggested that all bodily illness is due to personal sin and unbelief; Christ died, he contended, for the sicknesses and not only the sins of mankind. One night I drove the long distance to New York City to see first-hand a so-called Pentecostal "healing campaign" in which a dynamic and voluble preacher professed to cast out everything from arthritis to demons. The theatrical features, the disorder and confusion, and a strange inner chill combined to drive me away from the whole enterprise. Actually, I had made the trip after also reading another book, *Whipping Post Theology,* by the evangelist W. E. Biederwolf, who objected to any "healing is in the atonement" thesis, but on the other hand seemed insufficiently to acknowledge the healing power of God. The New York healing campaign had not won my enthusiasm, for it seemed remote, indeed, from anything in the Gospels. I did, however, believe that God *could* heal and, for my part, I was ready to put him to the test in circumstances that, if he did not intervene, would surely frustrate his clearly revealed plan for my life.

Doubled up in pain, I stood outside the Southside Hospital in Bay Shore, waiting for the moment when, unobserved, I could slowly ascend the long flight of steps to the entry. The excruciating pain was that of broken rotor blades running amuck in my abdomen. Once inside the hospital I asked for a surgeon and expressed preference for Dr.

Raymond Hildreth. Former missionary to India and an active Methodist temperance worker, he might, I thought, perhaps understand a highly unusual request.

"Doctor, I'm not a fanatic," I began. "I'd submit to an appendicitis operation in five minutes," I added, "if I weren't convinced that in two weeks God wants me in college. I believe in hospitals, doctors and medical missionaries. But I believe also that, for his own glory, God sometimes heals without them."

I hurriedly narrated the circumstances. "If you'll let me stay out of the hospital overnight," I concluded, "I'll promise that if God hasn't touched my body by tomorrow morning, I'll return promptly for an appendectomy."

Remarking on the evidently intense pain, Doctor Hildreth lectured me on the dangers of my condition. Reassured, however, that I would indeed return in the morning, he reluctantly gave way on the condition that I stay reasonably close to the hospital, should an emergency operation be necessary. I agreed.

The logical place to stay was nearby at Mother Christy's, where the "Friday Night Group," a band of soul-winners and prayer warriors, met each week. While I suffered into the night, that dispersed but alerted company of fellow believers interceded to God on my behalf. Sometime after midnight I fell asleep, exhausted.

On the following morning Dr. Goldschlager paid his scheduled call. He examined the abdomen. There was no pain even in the appendix area. He punched lightly, then harder. There was still no pain, even when he accelerated the punching. I pointed above my bed to a painting of Christ weeping over Jerusalem. "The Lord is good, doctor," I said. He resumed punching and even harder than before. Still no pain. "The Lord is good," I repeated. With a professional look, he simply said, "There is nothing I need to do. If you have any further trouble, give me a ring."

At the newspaper office some of my skeptical friends were already anticipating the possibility of my return for a job after an appendectomy. But their plans to accommodate me proved needless. The story of God's power to save and to heal now spread not only throughout newspaper ranks but also through the community at large. God had used faith and prayer in the midst of pain and suffering to advance his glory.

I knew there was a healing power of nature, for the cosmos owed its source and sustenance to a providential Creator. I respected the healing power of doctors and the marvels of medical science that had transformed modern hospitals. I knew there was a healing power also of mind over matter, and that a patient's will to recover is sometimes half the battle. But I knew something more, that the great God who is sometimes glorified by the courageous and victorious bearing of one's thorn in the flesh is, on other occasions, equally glorified in the direct healing of the body no less than of the soul. I left for college in good time, reassured that God would and could supply every need.

5

God and a Newspaperman at Wheaton

My reception at Wheaton was hardly spectacular. When I rang the front doorbell of my preassigned lodgings, The Green Lantern, the middle-aged housemother Mrs. Betty Roy came to the door, took one look at the six-foot-one visitor toting a briefcase and mistook me for an insurance salesman. Closing the door, she said: "No thanks, I'm not interested!"

My roommate at 320 East Seminary Avenue was C. Adrian Heaton, a bumptuous music major who, when coming in late, seemed unable to avoid ramming his long trombone case into my head or feet if I was already asleep on my cot. Son of a distinguished leader of the Fundamentalist Fellowship in the American Baptist Convention, he felt that Wheaton's selective admissions policy made it a mark of distinction to graduate even with a C average.

Other housemates came from near and far, including Dayton Roberts and Sam and Howard Moffett, missionary sons who had been graduated from high school in Pyengyang, Korea; Selden H. Ward from Oswegatchie, New York, a geographic spot that we housemates immortalized by frequent references; Orla Blair, Bill Claudon, Edver Erickson, Henry Northey, Walter Oliver and Bernard Peterman. During our sophomore year Ward became house cook to hold down our expenses until his repetitious servings of liver fomented a rebellion.

Beyond registration, my prime concerns were to prepare for classes and to find a job. Six months earlier, in April, I had sent an application with a fact sheet and recommendations to the editor of *The Wheaton*

Daily Journal. In reply, the business manager, Gay Reinig, commented on the "exceptionally fine recommendation" given to one "at such an early age." She noted, however, that editor George Smith found "student help . . . very unsatisfactory" and added: "Trust you know what you are doing." I learned later that what Smith really thought was that either my recommendations were forgeries or that I was insane to give up so promising a career to enter Wheaton.

I made myself known several times to the college employment secretary, Johanna Voget, so I'd not be forgotten when something turned up at the going rate of 25 cents an hour. My first such job was to supervise the Academy study hall for two hours daily during the noon break. My green "dink" with its orange insignia "Class of 1939" that Freshmen were required to wear invited an assortment of snowball pelting and light campus hazing in which Academy students now also joined.

Mother Christy's Chicago friend Mrs. Victor (Babe) Burnett, whose husband was an invalid, sent me a laundry case with prepaid return stamps and offered as a Christian service to do my laundry and mending every week or so. Years later I learned that she volunteered the same help to about eighteen students, particularly missionary candidates, who attended different evangelical schools. When Wheaton conferred an honorary doctorate in 1968 I invited her as a special guest.

One day the college bulletin board invited applications for the post of typing instructor; due to illness the present teacher could not continue beyond the first semester. Remembering my late night prayer vigil that had issued in the Lord's reassuring message "teaching typing," I went directly to the interviewing dean of the college and expressed my interest.

"What degrees do you have?" asked Dr. Emerson.

"Degrees?" I repeated. "That's why I came to Wheaton . . . to get one."

"I don't doubt you can do it," he replied magnanimously, "but an accredited college is responsible for maintaining certain requirements. The accrediting agencies won't be easily persuaded of your professional eligibility."

To mitigate my embarrassment I volunteered apologetically that "I type 86 words a minute with considerable accuracy, but I have only a Civil Service job rating."

"In typing?" he asked.

Then I told him about the three government job offers, including the Treasury Department invitation just before coming to campus.

The upshot was that at midyear I began teaching first and second year typing to academy and college students four hours a day, five days a week, a job that I kept until my junior year. I taught typists who eventually went around the globe to places like Iran, the Belgian Congo and Latin America, not to mention many parts of the United States.

One typing aspirant I shall never forget, and it is unlikely she will forget me. Registered for beginning typing this last semester of her Senior year was Helga Bender, daughter of Baptist pioneer missionaries to the African Cameroons. Her hazel eyes had a sparkling radiance, I wrote Mother Christy, "like the light of heaven." Miss Bender—no first name familiarities in those years—was startled that first day in typing class when I inquired, "*Sprechen sie Deutsch?*" Five years later she interrupted her work as a college dean of women and professor of German to marry me.

If my typing commitment brought surprise blessing it also hindered my full participation in the great campus spiritual revival of February, 1936. Dr. Robert C. McQuilkin, founder of Columbia Bible College, had come to campus as victorious life speaker but, taken suddenly ill, was confined to the infirmary. President Buswell accordingly used the chapel hour for hymn-singing and testimonies. When Don Hillis, a respected Senior who pastored the local Gospel Tabernacle attended by many students, rose to confess prayerlessness and other shortcomings, a tide of conviction and sense of shared guilt swept over the chapel. Students stood one by one, holding back or yielding to tears, acknowledging their spiritual need and asking for God's touch. At times spontaneous singing or praying interspersed the testimonies and confessions. Hour after hour class bells rang, but only a few people left. I felt obliged to tiptoe out to meet my 1:30 typing class but no one came. As it turned out, no one came to any classes. The revival carried on through the day, through the night and through the following day. For hundreds of students what transpired was the spiritual high point of their Wheaton years, and something never to be forgotten.

Since the *Wheaton Daily Journal* had offered only a closed door, I probed the *Chicago Tribune* about coverage in Wheaton where it had no correspondent. After checking my credentials, the *Tribune* hired me before yearend as DuPage County reporter at $5 a week plus supplemental stipend for special coverage. Wheaton city police were sometimes displeased over candid reporting of their activities; one offended sergeant phoned to report a police headquarters rumor that the coroner was on the lookout for me. That incident apart, my relationships with police were decent and friendly.

By yearend I was scooping the Wheaton *Journal* with stories that I funneled to the *Tribune,* and began coverage also for the suburban *Aurora Beacon* and *Elgin Courier-News.* At that point, the *Journal* invited me to join their crew. By early 1936 I was "doing newspaper-work" as anticipated in my three-by-five Lord's promise card. I was a suburban reporter for the *Chicago Tribune,* the Wheaton *Journal* and several other dailies; later that year Associated Press asked me to handle its presidential election coverage in DuPage County.

At that time the United Presbyterian Church was feuding over modernism which J. Gresham Machen and other evangelical leaders assailed. As part of the controversy a Presbyterian commission was trying Wheaton's president, J. Oliver Buswell, Jr., for disobeying a 1934 General Assembly order to resign from the Independent Board for Presbyterian Foreign Missions of which he was a founder. Presbytery wanted this Board disbanded because it was diverting denominational giving to preferred missionary causes.

Unaware that college authorities hoped to set Buswell's denominational controversy apart from his presidency of Wheaton and to minimize the trial in the community, I interviewed Dr. Buswell for a story that early in 1936 frontpaged in the Wheaton *Journal.* Buswell refused to comply with the 1934 order because he considered the General Assembly's mandate unconstitutional, and in 1936 he was prosecuted by Professor Andrew Zenos of McCormick Theological Seminary and unfrocked. Soon thereafter the General Assembly sustained the verdict. In June, 1936, the first General Assembly of the Presbyterian Church of America was organized with J. Gresham Machen as moderator. On November 12, 1936, Buswell was elected moderator of its second General Assembly, with Cornelius Van Til offering the nomination and Carl McIntire seconding it.

The college had hired a secular journalist, L. M. Aldridge, to conduct its news bureau and to publicize the school in the nonreligious media. He was furious when my articles on campus-related news appeared independently and when secular papers reimbursed me. He circulated a report that I was a pseudo-journalist with no professional experience. Unwittingly he repeated this charge to my roommate with whom he happened to be seated on a train ride from Chicago. My roommate went to the dean of the college, stating that since either Aldridge or Henry was a liar, something should be done. It was arranged, therefore, that all college-related stories would originate with the college news bureau, but that I could transmit them to the newspapers I represented. Since this meant that I was reimbursed for news bureau effort whenever such items were used, Aldridge remained unhappy.

Because of this dissension the college became more fully aware of my journalistic experience and asked me the following year to teach courses in journalism. In one of those courses, a class on feature story writing, I enlisted for part of the final examination the help of Richard Halverson, a classmate who decades later would become chaplain of the United States Senate. After distributing the final exam I led the class in prayer, as is customary at Wheaton. Suddenly a masked gunman burst into the room, leveled his pistol and, having told the class not to move, asked me to hand over my wallet. I did so, protesting that it contained a month's pay. After the gunman escaped I told the class to "write the story." Those who handled the incident as straight news fared worse on the exam than those who saw its feature story possibilities.

On occasion my commitment to "teaching typing" and "newspaper work" collided somewhat awkwardly. Typing classes met Monday through Friday in four successive periods from 1:30 to 5:30—twenty hours a week at 50 cents an hour. Since news reports for the earliest evening editions were due in late afternoon, I used the five-minute break between classes to phone the local police and sheriff's offices from a pay phone in the hall. If there was important news, I launched the next period's students on a ten-minute speed test and exited the room to relay information to the *Tribune.*

Such overlap was infrequent, however, and journalistic work was carried on mainly at The Green Lantern where I had a private phone. As my work expanded, the once-hostile *Journal* now carried banner headlines on both straight news and feature byline stories. Class preparation had its problems since, day or night, it might be unpredictably interrupted by a summons to hurry to the scene of some breaking story. Sometimes during that first year of college, after all night coverage of a gruesome accident, fire or murder—on one occasion a double murder and suicide—I barely made it, unshaven, to the eight o'clock Latin class taught by Miss Harriet Blaine. Such mornings I wished that Caesar's troops had marched less swiftly, and that all Gaul, instead of being quartered into three halves, had been splintered into much smaller parts. In her exposure to the classics, I mused, Miss Blaine had perhaps been infected by a bit of Stoicism. She would follow an unprepared student's flawed translation with the sorry announcement that "a zero on Tuesday counts just as little as a zero on any other day of the week" or would chant the principal parts of her specially crafted verb: "*Flunko, flunkere, faculty flunktus!*"

My respect for President Buswell was very high, and for most of my professors also; each made some specific contribution. When appointed to Wheaton's presidency in 1926 Buswell, at thirty-one, was the youngest college president in America. Aware of the growing inroads of modernism and humanism into denominational colleges, he also recognized clearly the antisupernaturalistic biases that underlay John Dewey's philosophy of education; the daily press quoted him as a critic of Dewey's theories. His emphasis on high academic standards brought swift accreditation to the college and attracted one record-breaking enrollment after another, until the student body tripled in size and within less than ten years Wheaton became the largest liberal arts college in Illinois. Besides holding the presidency, he was J. P. Williston Professor of Philosophy and Bible and regularly taught the required Senior courses in ethics and theism. His ultimate vision for Wheaton was a Christian university. He added Phi Beta Kappa evangelicals to the faculty, seeking equivalent status for Wheaton's Scholastic Honor Society. Christian students and graduates were already impacting on a society whose drift toward secularism World War II would soon accelerate. But Wheaton's contribution was then largely to the ranks of missionaries, pastors, medical doctors and teachers; it had yet to infiltrate seriously many other legitimate vocations.

Mainstream secular education had already lost a unifying referent. Philosophy departments that were expected to clarify the metaphysical disputed instead the reality and nature of God. The long prevalent idealism of the forepart of the century was crumbling, and biblical theism was shunned. Transitional modernism—which affirmed God but stripped away the miraculous and was open to experimental redefinitions—was unable to hold the line against an insistent humanism. To integrate campus learning, academics looked to shared ethical values, but these, too, were under fire from those who insisted on empirical verification of all intellectual matters.

Many denominational colleges sought to taper biblical theism to greater contemporary acceptability, unaware that Christian supernaturalism stands or falls as a whole, and cannot be effectively preserved by philosophical mayhem. Wheaton led the way among interdenominational colleges in insisting that the Christian world-life view is not only intellectually tenable, but that in fact it also explains reality and life more logically and comprehensively than do modern alternatives.

At Wheaton, not only Bible survey but also theism and ethics were required courses. Accrediting agencies may have smiled at reducing the number of curricular electives to accommodate such requisites, but they were satisfied that Wheaton met all standard requirements. Even if pedagogy was sometimes mediocre and content stuffy, serious exposure to the concerns of religion and morality was nonetheless preferable to the best pedagogy elsewhere that championed bad metaphysics. But evangelical colleges, too, had their own outstanding teachers. In any case, the unifying center of the whole circle of knowledge was at Wheaton acknowledged to be the transcendent self-revealing God known supremely in the Bible and in Jesus Christ. The college motto was "For Christ and His Kingdom."

Actual integration of campus learning in this context was, to be sure, something less than proclaimed. Here and there revelational truth was defended in the name of the Father, the Son, the Holy Ghost and Aristotle—or Aquinas. Now and then naturalism was countered by philosophical idealism or some other subevangelical alternative. One outstanding alumnus, moreover, later commented that only years after graduation did he learn of alternatives to the Bible department's marked orientation to Scofield dispensationalism.

Rhetoric and logic—Aristotelian and inductive, not symbolic—we absorbed less than adequately from Darien A. Straw. He concealed his defective hearing by seating the entire class around the four walls and on every issue required us to vote Roman arena style: thumbs up or down—or extended sideways for acknowledged ignorance. Quick-witted even on his seventieth birthday when I asked to what he attributed his longevity, he replied, "Solely to the fact that I was born so long ago."

Bible we learned from Merwin Stone, a devout teacher who often lost us in extended alliterative outlines, whether the M's of John's Gospel or the P's of Hebrews or whatever, but who nonetheless conveyed the essence. Psychology we studied with Wallace Emerson, whose true-false tests sometimes repeated from previous classes were nonetheless the bane of our existence, yet who on a meager salary occasionally took students out for dinner to prod and discuss dreams and ambitions. Theology, precariously balanced between Calvinism and Arminianism, came from Henry C. Thiessen, sensitive and conscientious head of the graduate school. He was essentially a New Testament scholar trained in the Dallas mold, meticulously demanding in his field but not at his best in the ancient philosophy course that had fallen his way. He knew the main critical interpretations and their implications, and was as interested in details as in comprehensive theories. But he was quite unaware of the massive upheavals in contemporary European theology where Karl Barth ten years earlier had declared the death of classic modernism. Apart from the fact that neoorthodoxy held critical views of the Bible, we hardly knew that there was a Barth.

Primitive religions I studied in the skeleton-laden office of anthropology-obsessed Alexander Grigolia, who set his alarm to go to bed at midnight, but who nonetheless found time to instruct me privately when my schedule ran into conflict.

Philosophy we learned from one of the most brilliant faculty members, Gordon Haddon Clark, whom Buswell had persuaded to come from the University of Pennsylvania. Clark and Grigolia made philosophy and anthropology the most popular majors during the Buswell era. Because of Clark's consistent Calvinism and scrupulous application of logic to the hesitations of less astute teachers, however, a number of faculty colleagues conspired to make his departure inevitable. When V. Raymond Edman, with a doctorate in history, came from the mission field to succeed Buswell in the presidency, he yielded to pressures from college donors who complained about Clark's emphasis on divine election; it was eroding, they charged, the missionary call of a number of students. Edman had a warm evangelistic heart, and he was popular among students; the 1939 Tower was dedicated to him. But his commitment to the importance of philosophy was less than that of Buswell. Contending, for example, that theism and ethics had never led anyone to salvation, he substituted a course in Scripture memorization and soul-winning for those erstwhile required courses.

A quiet, Stoic-mannered figure, Clark knew how to ask the right questions, how to make the worst answers show themselves for what they are and followed logic more devotedly than he followed Dale Carnegie. I specially recall his statement: "A satisfactory religion must satisfy. But satisfy *what* and *why?* The Greek mysteries satisfied the emotions; brute force can satisfy the will; but Christianity satisfies the *intellect* because it is *true,* and truth is the only everlasting satisfaction."

Among my other professors were Glenn Cole in criminology, Marian Downey in literature, John W. Leedy in botany, Herbert Moule in ancient history and Clarence Nystrom in homiletics. Moule taught the history text as if he were expounding a verbally inspired document. Miss Downey frequently commented on my newspaper byline stories, gleefully chiding me when she found a mixed metaphor.

Buswell celebrated his tenth anniversary as Wheaton's president in 1936. After his election as moderator of the Presbyterian Church of America in November of that year, divisions arose between him and Machen over the purity of the Church and over eschatology. By June, 1937, some dissidents were proposing a new group, and in September, 1938, the first General Synod of the Bible Presbyterian Church was formed with Buswell as moderator. Buswell's fracas with northern Presbyterianism was his undoing at Wheaton. Influential alumni felt that the college ought not be involved in a denominational controversy, and certain denominationally minded Presbyterians felt that Buswell's conflict with the General Assembly, like Machen's, was disruptive. A somewhat antidenominational spirit settled over the campus not only because of the theological decline of many established religious colleges, but also because of forces sympathetic to the newly founded Orthodox Presbyterian Church. Some fundamentalist trustees tended to brand conservative pastors apostate if they kept their churches in the mainline denominations. With mingled pathos and humor, one student group roamed the campus singing a parody of "Win Them One by One":

You split the one next to you,
And I'll split the one next to me;
In no time at all
We'll split them all
So split them, split them, one by one.

Those became drab and dark days for Wheaton. The wounds were not easily healed. Evangelicals inside and outside the large denominations were at odds with each other. Even faculty members suffered a period of unfortunate internal tension. Whatever early inclination I then had of possibly seeking Presbyterian ordination and ministry was discouraged by the condemnatory spirit and one-sided propaganda of the "come-out-ers" and the machine-loyalty of the "stay-in-ers." While many of the latter preached the gospel, they were suspected of currying favor for the sake of personal denominational advancement instead of contending boldly in ecclesiastical circles for evangelical truth.

The simmering controversy over Buswell's involvement came to a head in a meeting of Wheaton's Board of Trustees in January, 1940. The Board requested Buswell's resignation, but he refused. He was therefore summarily dismissed from the presidency and faculty. He moved immediately to Wilmington, Delaware, to teach at Faith Theological Seminary until 1941, when he became president of National Bible Institute in New York, later known as Shelton College. In 1955 he lost the Shelton presidency after differences with Carl McIntire.

Much of this continuing smoldering conflict escaped student notice; college learning and recreational life carried on more or less routinely. When I first arrived on campus in 1935, there came with me a magic wand, an assortment of colored silk handkerchiefs, mechanical contraptions for producing or obscuring pigeons and rabbits, magic slates and a generous supply of "woofle dust," a semantic inanity introduced to confuse viewers at the precise point of some misleading maneuver. Except at occasional student houseparties I performed little magic on campus until the annual Homecoming festivities sponsored in 1936 by the campus literary societies. The growing student enrollment was overcrowding the societies so that two new chapters—Knights and Ladies—were formed to ease the pressure for membership. Not being addicted to tradition, I became a Knight on December 6, 1935, as did my roommate. The "Lit" societies met Friday nights for an hour's program that involved original poetry or prose readings, musical numbers, extempore speeches, debates and drill in Robert's rules of order.

Annual homecomings brought alumni back to their societies that competed for the largest attendance. Knights proposed breaking campus tradition with a magic program jointly sponsored by all the societies. The burden of performance fell on me.

To tell the truth, I had lost enthusiasm for magic in the interval between June, 1933, when I became a Christian, and September, 1935, when I entered Wheaton. Even occasional performances at Sunday school parties and other small events left me with an uneasy feeling that the spiritual ambassador was being lost in the worldly entertainer. I have never been persuaded that the magical arts are an ideal or even proper context for the presentation of Christian truth. The former depend upon subtle deception, or at any rate, misdirection, whereas the latter is nothing if it is less than what it professes to be.

I remember well only a few things about that 1936 Homecoming night. It would perhaps be better if I could remember none. For one thing, there was a capacity audience. One of the stunts, moreover, required a live rabbit; failing to locate one, my roommate borrowed a chicken from the small flock in a nearby yard. Ultimately said chicken was to emerge from bright red tubes (painted stovepipes of varying sizes) passed through each other to "demonstrate" that they were empty. The restless chicken emerged, indeed, at the proper moment. But at three in the morning my roommate awakened me; had he, he wondered, returned the bird to the right yard? I do not know to this day whether some Wheaton resident was defrauded of a two-pound fowl.

The magic program closed with the crude sawing in half of a coffin-like box in which, while four volunteers watched, we secured both the victim's hands and feet. After a bit of reassurance Olive Drechsel, a short, thin student from New Jersey, volunteered for the act. Inside the specially made pine box we placed large plastic tubes of catsup which, when ruptured by my big-toothed lumber saw, spewed gruesome globs of red sawdust over platform-protecting sheets of newspaper and lent "empirical confirmation" of a body's dismemberment. Observers meanwhile held taut the ropes that presumably were tied to the victim's limbs.

Years later, in Madison, New Jersey, I spoke at an evening church service to a large congregation. I preached my heart out for decisions for Christ. After the benediction I walked briskly to the foyer of the sanctuary to greet departing worshipers. Hardly had I arrived at the door when a woman in her forties, with three teenagers in tow, rushed toward me. "Tell them," she entreated, as if her family was an aggregate of doubting Thomases, "tell them that once during college you sawed me in half!" I had been striving that night to help put fragmented souls together again, but the imaginary dismemberment of years long past had risen to haunt me.

What I remember most vividly about that Homecoming night, however, preceded the closing act and had much more disturbing repercussions. Ordinarily, slate-writing trickery was rather incidental. It depended (although this was but one of several techniques) on a false inside cardboard flap that flipped from one slate into the other as the two slates were combined into one and turned over. The invisible "spirits" would be asked to write the answer to some question on which the audience had agreed after a bit of humorous prodding. What complicated the Wheaton performance was the audience's insistent demand for prediction of the final score of the next day's Homecoming football game between Wheaton and its archrival. Seldom if ever had Wheaton won more than a consoling "moral victory" against North Central ("at least we played it clean"). In such circumstances it was clear why my assistant—a classmate hidden behind the platform's rear draperies—was unsure whether he, ready as he was to inscribe a dummy set of slates, should be a realist or a partisan. A pianist playing soft background music muffled conversation on stage. When the concealed assistant implored, "What score?" I nonchalantly circled the platform and at the curtainfold whispered back, "Wheaton 7, North Central 6." On my next circuit of the platform I managed an exchange of slates with my accomplice. Pandemonium broke loose when the audience realized that even the invisible spirits were on Wheaton's side.

What lay ahead was something quite unforeseen. For one thing, Wheaton did in fact defeat North Central by a seven to six score. That was hardly to strike pay dirt, however. Among the college faculty members was Florence Cobb, my speech teacher, a very proper graduate of the Curry School of Elocution in Boston. When she heard of my invocation of spirits, and the outcome of the football game, she was appalled and insisted that there was surely something demonic in all of this. That was the last time I did magic at Wheaton. Not eager to be leagued by the faculty with Beelzebub, I gave away much of my paraphernalia and, except for a weak moment now and then, said farewell to that aspect of my life.

Although college had its lighter side, my primary aim was to get a Christian education that opened a more comprehensive window on life and the world, and it was high time to concentrate all my energies in pursuit of the liberal arts degree with a philosophy major and an anthropology minor. Two years of Latin under Harriet Blaine prepared for two years of classical Greek under Robert Stone, and for two years of German under Fred Gerstung and Dora Soldner. Since the first year of languages was always most difficult for me, I would hire the leading student in class to drill me for two hours before the midterm and final exams.

The philosophy major was demanding. The ancient philosophy course under Thiessen, to be sure, was largely a memorization of factual data with little awareness of the schematic connection or disconnection between successive systems. That information I wrested from the classic works by Ueberweg and Windelband. Gordon Clark taught medieval, modern and contemporary philosophy and drilled us in the importance of words, ideas and sentences. When he taught Augustine, or Aquinas, or Spinoza, he was for a time the living incarnation of each thinker, defending a given philosopher's affirmations against all counterattack, and driving us to formulate our criticisms ever more lucidly and logically.

I first met Clark in my Freshman year when he stayed in his office late one night and was preoccupied with books. I got up courage enough to interrupt and ask what engaged him so late. He had just received F. R. Tennant's two-volume *Philosophical Theology,* he said, and had to prepare a book review. I asked how long it took him to read two volumes like that. "Not too long," he replied; "the more one reads, the easier it is to take in stride whatever comes down the pike."

Clark gave us periodic true-false or completion tests of 20 questions, and never scaled the grades on the basis of 100. It was a routine comment that not even the Pope could fare better than 20 points on Clark's exams, and he would be lucky to get that.

For my third and final year (by attending four summers I was graduated in August, 1938, rather than with the class of '39 the following June) I moved to the Kay residence at 600 College Avenue where Fred Baer, Bradley Gough, Harold Lindsell and Al Shepard roomed. Lindsell, member of a state championship debate team with Kenneth Taylor, was ever ready to take the other side of a discussion either in conversation or in forensics, but he was an earnest student. I had been elected to Alpha Delta, the national journalistic fraternity, and to Pi Gamma Mu, national social science honor society. But Lindsell's reminder that "what a student does with his last thirty minutes at night, when everybody wants to 'goof off,' is the difference between a B and an A," gave me added incentive to make Scholastic Honor Society, which I did.

During the '37–'38 academic year I served as editor of the 1939 *Tower,* with Howard Moffett as business manager and Pearl Hetrick and Betty Varnell as chief aides. Together we produced the largest yearbook to date in Wheaton's history, a prize-winning effort that was also a gratifying business success.

My change in graduating classes meant that I joined the 1938 Senior "sneak," a long weekend retreat at an unpublicized resort hotel. The following year in appreciation of labors on the *Tower* the '39ers invited me to their affair as a graduate chaperone. The '38 "sneak" was held at French Lick, Indiana; the '39 "sneak" at the Spink Wawasee also in Indiana. On arrival at the latter hotel one Senior as a lark invested a quarter in one of the few lobby slot machines and hit the jackpot. Word spread like wildfire—to everyone's dismay, since gambling fell outside Wheaton's code—about a Wheatonite's unexpectedly high return on his investment.

The Spring of my Senior year posed crucial decisions about the future. Moody Bible Institute approached me about becoming director of promotion and heading a large staff of writers, artists and secretarial aides. After wrestling whether journalism or theology would be my major pursuit, I felt constrained to decline the Moody opportunity. A year later Russell Hitt, whom Moody persuaded to leave the *Detroit Free Press* to fill the Chicago post, drove to Wheaton to personally thank me for declining, since the position was exactly what he had been wanting.

With theology as my choice, the next question was where to study. Seminary options were a high priority in campus discussions that involved not only Seniors but undergraduates like Billy Graham who was already weighing seminary possibilities. I applied to Northern Baptist Theological Seminary on Chicago's West Side, then the largest evangelical divinity school in the Northern Baptist Convention, and was accepted for the Fall of 1938 for the bachelor of divinity program.

By a strange turn of events Wheaton announced at about the same time that it was launching a two-year master's degree in theology that same Fall, and encouraged some of the Seniors to consider that option. Wheaton had for many years resisted graduate offerings in theology because denominationally oriented alumni did not want the college to compete with mainline seminaries. But two sisters in Philadelphia had bequeathed modest funds to Wheaton for just such studies provided the program was instituted before both had died. Since one of the sisters had recently died and the second was not well, Dr. Buswell promptly established the John Dickey Memorial Theological Seminary training course. Wheaton offered me a graduate fellowship and free tuition. After comparing and contrasting course requirements, I decided to pursue studies simultaneously at Wheaton and Northern, since each offered specific advantages; one granted a two-year master of theology degree and the other a three-year bachelor of divinity degree. I set up class schedules that allowed manageable driving between the two campuses from September to June and some additional summer courses at Wheaton.

In the late Spring of 1938 I became burdened for a larger witness to students on secular campuses. In my behalf Ted Benson, president of Wheaton's chapter of Scripture Distribution Society, wrote to Cyrus N. Nelson, editor of *Light,* a slick monthly launched by Gospel Light Press in 1937 to reinforce Christian education. Cy accordingly invited a monthly article beginning in September, 1938, under the general title of The Cross and the Campus. I also wrote articles for *The Sunday School Times* and *Good News* to stimulate interest among students, and Clyde Dennis of Good News Publishing Company invited me whenever convenient to discuss mutual concerns with him in Minneapolis. I corresponded with C. Stacey Woods, general secretary of Inter-Varsity Christian Fellowship of Canada, and with John Herrmann, general chairman of Christian Youth League of America, and proposed to Cy Nelson that *Light* publish a special single issue for distribution to university students. He responded enthusiastically, projecting its distribution prior to Easter of the following year. Discerning suggestions about content came from classmates Roger McShane and Dayton Roberts.

Because my remaining science requirement was completed at Wheaton's Black Hills summer science station in South Dakota, I was graduated in absentia on August 12, 1938, with the bachelor of arts cum laude. Although the class of 1939 had its own evangelical frontiersmen, I was now cast with soon-to-be-illustrious alumni like Norris Aldeen, John Ballbach, Harold Lindsell, Samuel Moffett, Dayton Roberts, Eleanor Soltau and Kenneth Taylor.

I returned to Wheaton in the Fall of 1938 as a graduate fellow in publicity while completing the first year's graduate work in theology. The $400 fellowship, supplemented by exemption from tuition fees, compensated for services in the News Bureau. For the 1939–40 academic year I was exempted from tuition fees and given a $500 stipend as compensation for teaching journalism five hours each semester.

Wheaton's graduate program in theology suffered evident birth-pangs. From graduate studies at University of Chicago Dr. Buswell remembered a conservative Methodist minister who had earned his doctorate, and prevailed on him to come out of retirement to teach Hebrew and Old Testament. Dr. Jacob Hoffmann spoke with a heavy German accent. He made more critical concessions than Buswell would have approved, but his intentions were constructive. He was devout, indeed at times superdevout. On occasion he would open a class with prayer, make a few announcements and assignments, then forgetfully lead the class in prayer a second time.

First-year classes were small—six or seven students. Exegeting a portion of Genesis, Hoffmann in his emphatic German accent read: "Und Chakup wowed a wow" ("and Jacob vowed a vow"). When the class chuckled he was momentarily flustered. Thinking he had misread the text, he repeated the performance even more vigorously: "Und Chakup wowed a wow!" This time we laughed outright. He hurriedly adjusted his spectacles, peered at the text and made yet a third effort, slowly stressing every word. When we exploded unrestrainedly, Hoffmann removed his glasses and, facing us intently, remarked: "Ah, chentelmen, I know vy you are laffink; you know vat sort of scountrel diss man Chakup vass, don't you?" To his credit, Hoffmann stayed near the text rather than circumventing it or undermining it, even if his accent required him to stay with it longer than necessary.

Class assignments were demanding, with Dr. Henry Thiessen handling much of his specialty, the New Testament courses. Fortunately my Wheaton and Northern courses meshed well without wasteful overlap.

In October I suggested to *Light* magazine the content for the specially projected student issue. We would depict Jesus Christ as the only leader worthy of complete trust, devotion and sacrifice. Brief articles by outstanding scholars would present straightforward doctrine alongside personal testimonies by leading professors and prominent students on mainline university campuses. The issue would be enlivened by pictures of campus action. I set aside the Christmas holidays for a drive to California to finalize plans. Student passengers shared the driving and my aging car made the trip in 60 hours, almost matching the 56-hour run by the Santa Fe. When I arrived I found that a letter must just have missed me at Wheaton in which Cy Nelson indicated that *Light* had ceased publication due to lack of funds.

I encouraged the Class of '39, since their cash balance was due in large part to the successful yearbook, to channel some funds to this cause. Howard Moffett, the business manager, supported the idea. In addition, we solicited tithes and invited evangelical student movements and campus groups to underwrite distribution costs. We then published a limited edition of an exceedingly attractive and evangelically potent issue called *Youth Looks at Life.* Quite widely distributed, the stock was soon gone.

Among requirements for the graduate degree in theology were a thesis and three days of final comprehensive written examinations. My thesis on The Parables of Matthew 13 was a modest first such effort. Preparation for comprehensives was rigorous. I had discovered during undergraduate days that student distractions and tensions run highest at exam times and concentration is difficult. So I armed myself with the five-volume *International Standard Bible Encyclopedia* edited by the Glasgow apologetics scholar James Orr and for 75 cents a night signed into the college infirmary for three days and nights. Having reviewed all my class notes, I considered that particular encyclopedia an excellent integrating resource; during Freshman days I had in fact sold some twenty sets to fellow students for $38 each, for which the Howard-Severance Company, publishers, paid me the Depression-era commission of one dollar a set. The pleasant school nurse Ada Rury cooperated eagerly. Since the infirmary had no patients at the time she assigned me a private room where I read as many major I.S.B.E. articles as possible for a comprehensive grasp of biblical and theological issues.

It was James Orr's great work, *The Christian View of God and the World,* used as a Senior text in theism, that did the most to give me a cogently comprehensive view of reality and life in a Christian context. I had brought to college life a dramatic conversion and decisive dedication; what I wish by way of hindsight is that I might have found in my collegiate experience a still deeper comprehension of the essential Christian virtues and their even more disciplined manifestation in christlikeness, and a fuller awareness of the frontier dilemmas of our society and of realistic possibilities of Christian confrontation. That I did not experience an all-engaging volitional crisis, and in some ways a deeper intellectual crisis, is probably due to several things. For one, I had no home or church educational supports on which to build an academic career. Moreover, I spent four or five hours daily earning my expenses, a schedule that involved great physical drain and also absence from many of the weekly student prayer meetings. Although newspaper work constantly linked me to the secular world, and precluded confinement within an evangelical ghetto, so to speak, the human social situation then attracted at Wheaton little academic analysis. Student conversations with deans or faculty usually concerned rule infractions or course requirements rather than character development and life perspectives. In a few important courses, moreover, my teachers, while generally competent, were not exceptional.

Obviously each person enters and leaves college at a different cognitive, volitional and emotional stage, and I have much more to applaud than to criticize about Wheaton. The life friendship of godly classmates, the focus on Christian truth during a cognitively confused era, the meeting of a devout life companion, daily chapel services that introduced me to globally respected evangelical leaders, the emphasis on faithful vocational service for Christ, are part of that inheritance. I only wish the inheritance were even greater. I personally do not think that the focus of a liberal arts college should be reoriented toward student activism and campus politicization, nor do I think that the emphasis on metaphysical system and logical consistency are Graeco-Roman liabilities rather than Judeo-Christian strengths. In fact, I see the current radical assault on traditional Christian learning to be more corruptive than corrective. What I do maintain is that all Christian learning must be for the sake of worship and service of God in the world, and that we are deceived if we think that our own schematic skills or speculative theories or politico-economic proposals make the Bible meaningful and credible to the contemporary world. The case for Christianity does not rest upon our ingenuity; it rests upon the incarnate and risen Lord. The Bible is meaningful and credible as it stands; it is we, not the Scriptures, that need to be salvaged. Unless evangelical education understands Christianity's salvific witness in terms of the whole self—intellect, volition, emotion, conscience, imagination—and of the world in its total need—justice, peace, stewardship and much else—it cannot adequately confront a planet that has sagged out of moral and spiritual orbit.

On June 16, 1941, I received two degrees—the Master of Arts in Theology from Wheaton College, and the Master of Arts from the Orlinda Childs Pierce Memorial School of Theology (as the Dickey school was renamed for supplementary funding). I was now ready to throw undivided energies into completing the bachelor of divinity course already well underway at Northern Baptist.

6

Helga

In my Freshman year Mrs. Katherine Shapleigh, the stately dean of women, took female students aside periodically for motherly counsel. Hand-holding, they were told, was acceptable but such intimacies as a waist-encircling arm and a good-night kiss were prerogatives of engaged couples. Such close encounters therefore went underground.

On a brisk autumn Saturday morning my feelings got the better of me. I borrowed the dress form that Mrs. Roy used at The Green Lantern as a sewing model. Marvin Veerman and I adorned the figure with a lady's coat, used a mop for a wig and in snug waist-encircling arms then escorted the monstrosity all over campus. Rightly or wrongly, word spread that we were willing to hold out arms to the fair sex but, understandably, none such damsels volunteered as mere manikins.

I dated little during my first semester except on Friday nights after literary society. There were invitations to numerous house parties. Never to be forgotten was one to East Gate near my later student lodgings at the Kays. I wore white flannels that had been closeted for several years. At some point during the party I bent over to pick up a paper clip and split the rear seam of my trousers from stem to stern, though nobody else was aware of it. I asked a friend to retrieve my raincoat, excused myself for a hasty retreat to my lodgings and returned shortly in more customary attire.

For Sophomore and Junior students the conventional wisdom was to "play the field" to learn the assets and virtues of each companion and then to court the most engaging and compatible. In the Senior year there were always a number of soon-to-be-interrupted friendships. But for me during college years there was really only one true love—Helga.*

In Wheaton's fateful typing room the machine-laden tables were arranged in three rows of six each, the middle row directly facing the instructor and the others ranged on left and right. Helga Bender had taken the last seat on the left. The very first day I reseated the entire class and located her directly in front of my desk. Since she was registered for the last hour of the four successive classes, she could stay overtime to work on the next day's lesson, and occasionally did. I sometimes made it a point to tarry also, especially if she was alone.

I learned a few things about many of my students, but not too much about Helga, since she was reserved. She was a Senior, she volunteered, and had opted for typing in her last semester, expecting to be taught by Miss Edna West rather than by a mysterious male replacement. Occasionally when returning her papers I added a postscript, one that could mean as little or as much as one preferred.

In those days the Washington's Birthday Banquet was the year's gala social event. Since Helga was a Senior and I was an instructor even though a Freshman, I decided to ask her to be my banquet guest. But she had already made a commitment. So I asked her to accompany me to the Tower concert a month later. She thanked me and declined again because of an earlier engagement. My pride was somewhat piqued; another negative response, I mused, would indicate clearly that she preferred no entanglement with me. I decided to make a final try: would she be my guest at the Naitermian literary banquet in June? This time she said yes; from then on our relationship took on an added aura.

In one afterclass conversation in early March we exchanged thoughts about future hopes and plans, including the sort of marriage, if any, each of us envisioned and the relative priority of spirituality, talent, attractiveness, character, wealth and whatever else we looked for in a life mate. By mid-March I asked her to accompany me to a Sunday night service at Moody Memorial Church. Since chaperones were required for out-of-town automobile junkets, this prerequisite was duly arranged.

My old car had developed an asthmatic condition from being parked

* At Helga's intervention, to spare them possible embarrassment, I have not named others of the fair sex whom I dated at Wheaton. But I wish nonetheless to indicate my appreciation to Wheaton lasses who added zest and luster to those campus days.

in the campus outdoor parking lot. It was still somewhat serviceable, but I faced it downhill so that if inclement weather strained the battery and I was called out for a late night news story the car could, if need be, propel itself into action. During the Moody date night the Chevy developed a flat tire, but I mounted the spare without vocalizing my feelings.

Since Helga's June graduation was approaching, I sent her a note asking if we could spend the evening of April 5 together. She was at that time—although I was unaware of it—dating three other fellows. One, with whom she was going out quite regularly, had groundlessly circulated the gossip, Helga replied, that I had "a crush" on her; she sensed pending problems, and thought she had best "go into hibernation." I should therefore "be prepared for her declination," she added, if I were minded to invite her again. She addressed the letter "Your Honor" and signed it "H. B." I was aware, of course, that except for those with more permanent ties Senior classmates would soon be saying "au revoir," and I was quite willing to commit the durability of romantic impulses to divine providence. So I offered use of my car to Helga's suitor, should he wish to take her out of town during the final weeks of classes. He declined.

Several days near the end of April Helga was absent from class without apparent reason. I stopped briefly at her lodgings at 200 West Franklin, inquired about her and left a personal note. She was at the music conservatory all week, I learned, helping her roommate, Pauline Eppley, prepare for a graduation speech recital that week. She sent her first typewritten letter, addressing me as Carl and signing it Helga. A handwritten postscript invited me to attend the recital at which she would be an usher, and alluded to the pedagogical value of low pupil-teacher ratios. I replied that I'd welcome a one-to-one ratio any time. The following Monday came her memo: "Carl: How about a private conference Wednesday around eight? H. B." After that Helga and I dated quite regularly.

In the final June weeks we met classday mornings at "The Stupe" (Student Union) for a 15-cent breakfast—coffee and a "long john." She always insisted on paying her way. Friday nights we met after Lit Society. We walked Wheaton sidewalks in rain or shine; one route took us from the college to the poorhouse at the city limits.

One Sunday after church I met her mother who because of family illness had returned early from the mission field. She invited me to dinner. For the first time I sensed how frugally Helga lived. I did not know that in her Freshman year, while her parents were still in Cameroun, Helga had arrived by train in Wheaton with a half-crate of eggs that a saintly and well-meaning soul had sent along from a

Wisconsin farm. During that first year Helga cooked her meals on a sterno can in the basement of Professor Alice Spaulding's (sister-in-law of President Buswell) home where she roomed. Sometimes she survived that year on fallen fruit gleaned from curbsides. She had fainted of hunger several times. At 30 cents an hour she worked her way through college in the German department.

She was certainly not born into intellectual poverty, however. Her father was a graduate of the college and divinity school of Rochester Baptist Seminary in New York whose German division had been established by American Baptists to assist increasing numbers of German-American ministerial students. Helga's mother, a missionary deaconess-nurse, had been trained in Germany. The six Bender children routinely won awards for academic excellence, the five older ones having received highly acclaimed *Gymnasium* education in Berlin before continuing studies in the United States. Reading, music, art and literary pursuits flourished in the Bender home.

After graduation with a major in German and a minor in French, Helga moved to Chicago to live with her now widowed mother and two of her four brothers, Armin and Carl; I remained in Wheaton for summer school. While I was coping with Vergil's *Aeneid* and readings from Cicero, Helga, like other Depression era graduates, probed for work opportunities.

In her first letter to me from Chicago she mentioned that she had begun writing me "the first evening, but then I decided to discipline myself so I waited" a full week. She had spent evenings in "the lonely big city" reading poetry by Edwin A. Robinson and Rupert Brooke and even Schopenhauer's "Studies in Pessimism." She missed me, she said, but if I asked her why, she added, she would respond with silence. In devotions she'd been reading Hebrews and memorizing Scripture. Although she felt at this transition stage like Abraham going into a strange country, she was "bubbling with joy in the Lord." She recalled our relationship of the past months as "inexpressibly beautiful." She had been reading Spurgeon and about his great ministry. She wanted in no way to be a hindrance to my calling, she said, but wanted me to know that her mother concurred in an invitation to visit should that ever be convenient.

But then she wrote again: "We're very different in many ways. I can't remember ever having a friend so unlike me in attitudes and general principles. You look at life much more wholesomely, vigorously. . . . All in all that is the best policy, but somehow I can't do it." Next she wrote that she wished she had never enrolled for typing class, and had determined that she would never accept another letter from me, nor see me again. Then she wrote on July 7 that she looked forward to "those familiar envelopes" and if I cared to write or visit, she would be glad.

In the background of these letters, among other things, were admonitions given by her older brothers, more worldly wise than she, against taking at face value all that a journalist might say. She wrote again that I must understand her caution: "I don't want to influence you one way or the other concerning me. I could play the game and do everything in my power to sway your decision but I don't intend to do so. . . . I think a lot of you (that's as much as I dare say); for that reason I want to do the right thing."

We were both at the stage of wanting to avoid overcommitment, striving to discern God's will and to avoid mistakes we might later regret.

Helga's periodic letters were good reading. Reflecting knowledge of the literary masters and creatively crafted, they ran the gamut from introspection to critical analysis but always voiced the need for spiritual integrity. For all that, while it became evident our relationship was not merely a treasured fellowship, Helga on her part hesitated to speak of love lest the word be immature or premature; I patiently suspended my own profession of affection on divine confirmation.

Since no proper teaching post had opened, Helga sought alternatives. When Wheaton announced plans to inaugurate graduate studies in education during the 1936–37 school year, Helga wondered whether some kind of college assistantship might subsidize such studies. In mid-July she tentatively outlined a schedule that in a year's time would lead to a master's degree in education. With "not a single cent" in reserve and the desired assistantship in German far from certain, she nonetheless declared herself ready for another walk of faith. On July 26 she formally registered for the Fall graduate program.

We met again at the end of July. A week later, just as she began probing Wheaton work possibilities in exchange for room and board, came an invitation from the dean of women for Helga to proctor and chaperone The Barracks, a converted army hut that housed twenty-six undergraduate women. We would now have to be all the more circumspect in our relationship, she wrote. By mid-August she indicated that her inclination not to write had "almost survived" but she needed to try out a new pen.

I wrote in jest that, now that she was an alumna and would soon be a graduate student and, moreover, a dorm proctor, she was apparently becoming "sophisticated again." I addressed her, provocatively, as "Dear Hel. . . ," which she promptly declared an act of extreme mental cruelty.

"It really hurts," she replied, "because I've tried really hard for so long to overcome my reserve. Was that appellation your early impression of me too? I certainly remember my first impressions of you. I took you to be in the late twenties, very matter-of-fact, efficient and self-confident. What nettled me was a seeming disdain for women . . . and from the first I determined to 'double dare' you. But then I recoiled from such pseudo-warfare. After the first date to Moody Church I couldn't come to any satisfactory conclusions about you. As time went on you came to be more understandable; in fact one thing that I liked particularly about you was the challenge that you presented (to me, at least) in comprehending your way of thinking and doing."

When Helga began her Fall, 1936, graduate studies and work at The Barracks, she learned that she would also serve as graduate assistant in German to Dr. Fred Gerstung. Less than a month earlier, confident that something would indeed materialize at Wheaton, she had declined an assistantship at the University of Iowa.

The temptation to claim her for my own was at times a living fury. Ours was an emotional tug of war. "It's madness to go on as we have been," Helga wrote in November. "Emotions and the heart can be charged to only a certain point; beyond that lies either happiness or regret. Good-bye—thanks for teaching me how to smile, thanks for being such a Prince to Cinderella, thanks for enriching my life in so many ways. I'll always pray for you." A week later she wrote again: "If it's the Lord's will one way or the other, must we both necessarily know at the same time? If his will is 'no,' does that mean that neither of us can or should harbor affection for the other? People can sincerely and deeply care for each other, yet never have the Lord's leave for them to marry, or even contemplate marriage." Next morning we prayed together and attended church, confident that divine providence sheltered us and our relationship.

During Spring break Helga wrote again from Chicago on April 11, 1937, knowing that I would be steeped in term papers. She, too, was "up at six, as usual, and late to bed" and was anticipating "the fatal day in June" that will "really be liberation. . . . Mom repeats her invitation to come whenever it is convenient." I drove to Chicago for a day's visit that prompted the observation in her next letter: "My mother has come to the conclusion that you like me considerably. . . . I enjoyed seeing you off—may I do it again? If we remain 'platonic friends' what would our meeting be like after a year's separation?"

Wheaton had a science station in the Black Hills of South Dakota offering summer courses in botany, forestry and geology. When I became a Christian something remarkable happened to the world of flora and fauna. Lupines, lady's-slippers, cornflowers, daisies, violets and other wildflowers and ferns that populated the woods near our Long Island home revealed in intricate and lucent beauty what I had missed until I recognized nature as the Creator's gift and handiwork. I projected the possibility of completing my science requirement in the Black Hills during two month-long summer school terms in 1937 and 1938, and registered for botany. Helga agreed that joining the camp kitchen crew might be a relaxing interlude between mid-summer completion of a master's degree and full-time teaching that hopefully would eventuate in September. Back with her family in Chicago, she finished her master's thesis and prepared for final exams before the Black Hills junket.

Anticipating August commencement exercises when she would receive her M.A. in education, Helga on June 14 wrote jubilantly of applying for an advertised post as dean of women and German teacher at a teachers' college in North Dakota—"beginning salary, $135 a month, which is the best financial offer to date." The $1500 salary for twelve months would include room and board. "I'd really be thrilled to have that kind of a job, because it offers excellent possibilities for getting into closer contact with students than merely a straight teaching position ever could. It's a splendid opportunity for Christian service, and oh, how I long to be used consistently! I know you'll pray, won't you, Carl—if the Lord wants me there, he'll open the door."

Following a college bus, we traveled from Wheaton to the Black Hills in a caravan of a half dozen cars, one of them my aging vehicle. But we all finally made it to Rapid City.

Those of us taking botany had to collect wildflowers and then identify them with the help of Gray's *Manual.* My favorite find was the beautiful white mariposa lily, always a delight to discover. Base camp was near Rapid Creek where, if we wished, we could on a good day fish for trout, even if without much success. We steeped ourselves in the lore of the historic Black Hills, entered both abandoned and active gold mines and attended the passion play in Spearfish Canyon. After study hours there were game times, although Helga's kitchen duties at the wood-burning stove conflicted somewhat with nonstudy hours. The rattlesnake-infested hills discouraged romantic walks even when the moon was bright and nights were clear and brisk. We took part in group activities and found some time for ourselves on weekends. Friday nights were reserved for campfire prayer meetings at which some students confessed Christ and others dedicated themselves to Christian careers. One student, I remember, acknowledged a missionary call to Africa but indicated that she wanted divine assurance that she could take along a refrigerator wherever she served. Someone told her she'd need to pack a long extension cord.

I greatly enjoyed botany and Professor John W. Leedy approved my proposal to return the following summer to complete science requirements by preparing a comprehensive manual that identified the wildflowers native to the Black Hills.

On return from the Black Hills to Chicago, Helga readied for her move to North Dakota. Meantime I returned to Long Island for a few weeks with my family, and made an important contact with the First Baptist Church of Babylon. Bible study had convinced me that New Testament baptism was by immersion, and is intended for believers only. I asked Pastor Burgess E. Brown to explain believer's baptism to me in detail, as if I were hearing about it for the very first time. He made clear its significance as an open personal identification with the death, burial and resurrection of Jesus Christ, and as one's witness to the world at large of new citizenship in the kingdom of God. I was immersed at the next midweek prayer meeting. My option for future theological studies now looked specifically toward Baptist ordination, a decision made easier by the current Presbyterian controversy over doctrinal fidelity.

I returned to the Midwest about the time that Mother Christy and Blanche Garn arrived in Chicago to visit Babe Burnett for a reunion of the prayer triumvirate. All three were delighted to meet Helga in the days just before she left for North Dakota. Helga and I reminded each other that neither of us could afford a mistake in the matter of life companion and co-worker, especially if Christian ministry were in view, and she emphasized that a sacred conception of love and its expression was also at stake. "Words of affection may be a vista into a realm of holy joy, or a snare into unforgettable despair. Better to wait perhaps even a long time for God's sure leading, than to spend a lifetime in regret. This period of separation I definitely believe is in his plan. . . ." We agreed to write once a week and, since we were not formally engaged, to date others as we wished, in full confidence that God would preserve whatever relationship he intended.

The first letter to reach me, posted September 7, indicated that Helga had arrived by train and was met by the college president himself who escorted his new dean into the life of the city and campus. She twitted me about my forthcoming ethics and theism courses, classes that involved several hundred alphabetically seated students, and where my H would place me halfway toward an exit! "Don't forget me," she added.

There was a variety of endeavors indeed. Besides Senior studies I was editor of the 1938 *Tower,* covered the *Chicago Tribune* and DuPage County dailies and was preaching at the Presbyterian Church in Oswego where the pulpit committee became interested through commendation by the *Chicago Daily News* religion editor of a series I was doing for the campus *Wheaton Record* on "Men Who Turned Back" and "Men Who Pressed On."

I assured Helga of how much I missed her. She wrote of her daily activities, and, as weeks passed, of a possibility of coming East for Christmas holidays with stops en route in Emery, South Dakota, where her brother Thorwald was then pastoring, then in Watertown, Wisconsin, to visit her mother and then on to Chicago and Wheaton. Several weeks later her brothers gave up their Chicago apartment, however, Armin to work for the president of the University of Rochester and Carl Ronald to live elsewhere in Chicago as he continued his architect's career. Helga therefore invited her mother to come to North Dakota. Now it became impractical for her to come to the Midwest at year's end, and financially unfeasible. When she wrote of being condemned to the Siberian snows of North Dakota for the yearend holidays I borrowed a Sears, Roebuck catalogue and prepaid a pair of heavy flannel pajamas to be dispatched as a Christmas gift to the dean of women.

Our next possibility for meeting would be in late May, 1938. Helga's academic year would end May 27, 1938. If she got East by May 30, she asked, would I like to blow out her twenty-third birthday candles? Again she wrote: "We know no more than before what the future holds; yet there is a richer, finer quality about our regard for one another." And again, "Absence isn't engendering doubt, but I often wonder if trying to preserve and cultivate a deep friendship and trying to make it elastic, so to speak, through the years, isn't destroying the beauty and intangible loveliness of it. Its own intensity burns it out. And that mustn't ever happen to us."

For all the wearying load at the college Helga was consistently happy in her work, with its opportunities for encouraging, guiding and shaping students' lives. Her $1500-a-year plus room and board Depression days salary embraced supervising the dormitory—the girls, their guests, their activities; chaperoning dances and other social affairs; counseling; directing physical maintenance of the premises; planning dining hall menus, hostessing the meals; directing kitchen personnel; requisitioning quantity food and housekeeping supplies; inspecting off-campus housing; assisting with student employment; helping the campus doctor; sponsoring the campus Y.W.C.A.; and teaching beginning and scientific German. Yet hardly a letter came from her that was not spiritually buoyant. She and a few Christian students had organized a vigorous Bible study class. She had become active in local churches and invited students to join her in attending services. She was praised by townspeople and faculty for her moral and spiritual earnestness and for "a most charming, ever-ready smile." Yet she was known, too, and respected for maintaining campus discipline and attention to serious study.

Her situation, as dean of women, was one in which dating locally was imprudent, even though as an attractive 22-year-old dean who walked in line after the president in academic processions she was an alluring prospect. My situation as *Tower* editor in my Senior year at college was very different; literary society banquets, house parties, the *Tower* artists' series and other social affairs offered opportunity to establish friendships with fellow classmates. In the Spring I now and then walked Wheaton streets with a petite and popular Southern belle who, rumor later had it, would ask the local florist to deliver roses to her dormitory room with a card attached bearing the name of any imaginary campus lover that suited her mood. Helga and I had put our relationship on Platonic hold. From correspondents at Wheaton she was getting reports that my Platonic hold was slipping into Neoplatonic activism.

In the summer of 1938 both of us returned to the Black Hills summer camp, where I finished my science requirement and in August was graduated cum laude, but in absentia. Helga was assistant director of the camp's kitchen crew. As time permitted we had great fellowship sharing the experiences of the past academic year and wondering what lay ahead. Our plans were still on the altar of providence. In September, 1938, she returned to North Dakota and I to commuting between Chicago and Wheaton for theological studies, a schedule that required me to discontinue newspaper work.

There was really no one for whom I carried a torch but Helga. But we were not certain that we should marry. In any case, this was not yet the right time for marriage; it would interrupt Helga's career and it could possibly hamper my post-graduate studies if such were in the offing. Helga had indicated that the single life could for her be no less a divine vocation than marriage; marriage was not to be seen as life's highest good. I assured myself that she had no overseas missionary call, since I would want to protect that, and asked whether, if the Lord led us together, she would gladly add her literary talent to whatever were my gifts in ministry, whatever its direction. At that time the pastorate seemed a prospect for me, but we were both open to other ministries.

In response to an inquiry from a professional bureau near the end of 1939 the administration rated Helga superior in knowledge of subject matter, class management, pupil motivation, cooperation with superiors, participation in community life, personal habits and character and health. Personality, poise and morals were listed as outstanding, and subject matter presentation, professional attitude and participation in school life, very good. "She is happy in her work," the report read, "and we hope she has no intention of leaving." In less than two and a half years of administration and teaching Helga was, at the age of twenty-four, no longer the free-wheeling companion of a few years past, but a surprisingly mature educator with a remarkable professional career in her grasp.

In the late Fall Harold Lindsell had indicated to me that he had an excellent New York contact for diamonds. Since during the summer I had playfully slipped off a ring that Helga was wearing and put it on my finger for size, I could now purchase a beautiful diamond of which Helga knew nothing.

Helga traveled to Chicago for the holidays, and stayed with her mother who had returned there. She planned to continue to Asbury College in Wilmore, Kentucky, to interview for an available position teaching German. I was a Christmas Day guest at the Benders, and late in the day, after small gifts had been exchanged, Helga and I went for a walk. It was then that I fumbled for one more gift that I admitted I was unsure she would really welcome. I slipped it on her finger. She was shocked but pleased. Before she could say a word, I gave her a stormy embrace. Never has a dean of women been constrained to surrender under such unpredictable circumstances.

Before Helga left for North Dakota—she cancelled her Asbury trip—we set Friday, August 17, 1940, as our wedding day. On the train she posted word from Aberdeen: "Each time I've written the news to friends I've been happier and more thrilled. You have made the vacation period one of the most beautiful experiences of my life. More important is the fact that this is only the beginning of this avenue in our lives. The Lord has graciously led; we must acknowledge him together in the days before us. Meanwhile our responsibility is prayer, and a holding up of one another in thought and deed. I only hope and strive, my dear, that God may make me a blessing and joy in your life, and that he'll permit my bringing you the glorious degree of happiness you've brought into mine."

Helga had wondered how best to break the news in North Dakota, but arrived to find the campus already reverberating with the news. *The New York Times* on Sunday, December 31, had carried prominent word of the engagement in its society pages, and from that notice it spread like wildfire through the campus. Chicago and Long Island papers, and the *Wheaton Daily Journal,* also told the news.

My letters to Helga were warm, spirited, even passionate. They were typed, hurried and direct; since they were for her only, I made no carbons. Helga either lost them or scrapped them, for my sake or hers, or they self-destructed under the weight of fervent ardor. They were in any case neither self-analytical nor deeply meditative, nor did they have the literary charm and power of Helga's correspondence. But I left no doubt that I counted her an incomparable treasure and rejoiced that she would soon be mine.

She warned in late February, 1940, however, that I should not value her as "an ideal wife" because she wanted "to be my ordinary self." She did not say so, but she may have wondered, and with good reason, whether marriage would mean an end to her professional usefulness. Or she may have been voicing a preference for simple weddings. Too, she had "been trained to think a woman should be preferably very reserved and not given to the display of undue emotion and affection. Such rudimentary things, when instilled for years, are almost as unchangeable as a Catholic heritage." For whatever reason, she wrote: "Marriage, for me, never has worn a halo. It's just one of two alternatives. . . . I sometimes think I'll be hanged before I give anyone the satisfaction of making me part of the game. . . . I dislike pompous church weddings. The spirit is lost beneath the brilliance of fancy dress, perfect hair-dos, beautiful bouquets, measured professionals. And I loathe the weeping. . . . You'll probably reconsider whether you still want to marry me."

A few days later came another letter, that crossed mine in the mails, "to make amends . . . for being cruel and cynical." She was fearful she had sacrificed "the most meaningful friendship I've ever had. . . . I know I have checked the spirit of a beautiful love, and have temporarily destroyed a keenly motivating force in both our lives. . . . If you can accept a firm resolve on my part to battle against those onslaughts, please take me once more into your good graces."

Helga was heartened by a letter from her youngest brother, Armin, approving our marriage: "I have always liked Carl Henry; I am very glad indeed that you are going to marry him. He has qualities that I admire: tact, courtesy, sincerity and the courage of his convictions. I like his sense of humor; the fact is that, although he is an idealist committed to life in an idealistic service, he has his feet on the ground. We need more men in the ministry who fit as easily into the men's club of a church as they do in the ladies' aid or missionary society." By early March Helga and I had arranged a simple wedding to be held in the chapel of Northern Baptist Theological Seminary. Anticipating the event now less than six months away, Helga wrote: "I'm only yours. . . . I'm glad for that. And I shall be yours more and more, as we learn new privileges and responsibilities. Some day, too, I'll hold in my arms the children we wait for, children we'll dedicate as God directs us to his supreme purpose."

7

Cloistered Years at Northern

A strange sense of monasticism gripped me when in September, 1938, I moved my scant possessions to Northern Baptist Theological Seminary located three miles west of the inner city at 3040 West Washington Boulevard. An iron fence protected the small, attractive campus long years before hoodlums and squatters invaded the area and finally left it a ghost town.

Now, leaving the secular city far behind, I would for some years focus on biblical languages, church history and theological concerns. In my solitary room I explored the New Testament in Greek, stretched my prayers around the world, and at times sank to my knees and wept, entreating God before an open Bible to forgive my sluggish spirit, redeem the failings of a religious life, and make me a worthy witness to his grace.

Wilkinson Hall's two upper floors constituted the men's dormitory. A long concrete corridor that echoed the clatter of inconsiderately slammed doors separated identical rooms on both sides. Each room included an army-type cot with well-worn mattress, a metal dresser, a bookcase, lamp, desk and chair and a closet that conferred invisibility on one's belongings. Toilets and showers were down the hall. Yet the lodgings were agreeably warm, easy to clean (which we did ourselves) and at least had a window on the outside world. Their simplicity spurred us to wander to lower floors—the basement bookstore run by Will Bisgaard and the nearby student-run barber shop; on the street floor was the quite spacious and serviceable library and classroom complex where we encountered the "faculty greats." Chapel met daily on the third floor of nearby Byrne Hall, an architecturally interesting old mansion that stood beyond a plaza of grass and a few welcome trees.

On its lower floors Byrne Hall housed administrative, business and faculty offices. There in that same Fall of 1938 President Charles W. Koller began his twenty-four-year span of seminary leadership. In the course of those years controversy engulfed the Northern Baptist Convention over the appointment of liberal candidates by the Foreign Mission Board. The denominational split that followed issued within a decade in the founding of Conservative Baptist Seminary in Denver and in 1947 of the rival Conservative Baptist Association of America. When I entered seminary in 1938 bureaucratic ecumenism was at high tide: 47 percent of American Protestants—especially Congregationalists, Presbyterians, Methodists and Northern Baptists—favored one large Protestant church. Koller was both denominationally loyal and evangelically orthodox. He felt that intensive production of evangelical ministers as at Northern would sooner or later overtake enough Baptist pulpits to shift the stance of liberal Convention machinery.

Northern's theological conservatism attracted the largest student body of any Convention seminary. In all, more than 300 ministerial candidates were enrolled, about half of them for the bachelor of divinity offered to those with a liberal arts degree, and the rest with lesser backgrounds for the bachelor of theology. The faculty, largely conservative, certainly reflected no insistent liberalism.

Across the hall from where Dr. Koller conducted frequent student interviews, Registrar William Mefford Fouts and sister Alice plodded through applications and unending paper work. Various nooks of the building provided shoebox office space that neither allowed much privacy nor encouraged research and writing.

My Northern mentors were Peder Stiansen, Julius R. Mantey, Ernest E. Smith, Faris D. Whitesell, William Emmett Powers, William Fouts and J. N. D. Rodeheaver. The last named was a brother of Homer Rodeheaver, song leader for Billy Sunday's evangelistic crusades. Since I had already taken homiletics in college, I was excused from Rodeheaver's preaching instruction, which was just as well; unfortunately, President Koller was not yet offering his expository preaching course which later became legendary in many evangelical circles and motivated the pulpit ministry of hundreds of Baptist pastors. Neither evangelical preaching nor liberal pulpiteering were plowing deep furrows. A noted churchman of the day suggested that a two-year moratorium on sermons and pulpit lectures could markedly enhance the influence of American churches, and Episcopalians, Congregationalists and Jews especially were prone to agree. I did take Rodeheaver's course in song-leading, however, since it was assumed that Baptist preachers often were obliged to lead congregational singing, or at least should know how it was done. I coped successfully with $\frac{3}{4}$ and $\frac{4}{4}$ hymns, and could beat out $\frac{6}{8}$ numbers, but ended up—probably by a touch of professorial generosity at that—with the lowest grade in my seminary studies, a flat C.

Peder Stiansen, the church historian, was then at his prime. His burly body lunged around the room as he recreated main events of the past as if they had occurred last week. His heavy Norwegian accent intensified the decline and fall of the Roman Empire and tales of how "the Goats, the Wisigoats and the Wandals swept down from the Nord." Who could ever forget Stiansen's dramatization of Luther's posting of the 95 "teesees" on the door of the Wittenberg Castle Church and his passing comment that "the Pope—he vas *roaring* mad!"? Stiansen brought down the house when he asked fellow class members to comment on a reporting student's "pro*noun*ciation." But he had high standards and demanded accuracy in quotation and spelling as threshold essentials in term papers. His jokes lightened the lessons—annually told, according to upperclassmen, at the same point in his lectures. A favorite was his story of a Swede who, during surgery, somehow got up and escaped while doctors in an adjoining room were examining his temporarily removed brain. When the brainless Swede was located three years later, "Ver do you tink dey found him?" Stiansen demanded, and then proclaimed, straightfaced but with eager delight, "In a Swedish seminary teaching church history." A vigorous lecturer with broad historical perspective, Stiansen mediated a sense of the shaping currents of history. We were prone to question his insights only when he extolled the virtues of the denomination's Foreign Mission Society, the growing storm center of Northern Baptist policy.

The other exhilarating mentor at Northern was Dr. Powers, who in addition pastored a Chicago church. A powerful preacher, he could when at his best wrench one's very soul, it seemed, from one's body and speak directly to individual conscience. His field was philosophy of religion more than systematic theology. He was a disciplined sampler of the best in modern trends rather than a logically coordinated critic of their weaknesses. He had taken graduate studies at Loyola and became a convinced Thomist until he came upon Edwin Lewis's *The Faith We Declare* and Emil Brunner's *The Mediator* and other neoorthodox works. Ever open to extended class discussion, his insistence that students "sharpen" their questions later encouraged dedication to him of my volume, *Giving a Reason for Our Hope.* In such classroom exchanges he was at his finest—reminding students of their presuppositions, cutting their ground from behind when the case was weak, firing acute criticisms at competing theological views and on the wing offering gifted insights. His plea for God's revelatory initiative and his emphasis on the singular uniqueness of Christian redemption stirred Northern Baptist Convention pastors and seminarians alike at a time when the denominational machinery was firmly in the grip of modernism, although most local congregations were conservative. While he did not systematically dissect opposing views, he punctured them rather at specially vulnerable places. Doubtless his nonsystematic approach reflected not so much a dislike for system per se as the failure to achieve a personal tidy cognitive edifice—hospitable as he was at times to Thomism, at other times to Augustinianism, and then again to neoorthodoxy. But he required at least some critical familiarity with contemporary religious tensions and brought us in direct touch with molders of the twentieth century mind like William James, C. Lloyd Morgan, John Dewey, Henry Nelson Wieman, Karl Barth, Emil Brunner and Edwin Lewis.

Powers did not publicly flaunt his dedication to personal evangelism but conducted it on a high level, often among professional men. One day he went to lunch after class with his family physician. "I phoned him first," Powers told us, and noted that "across the years you have talked to me about my body, and I'd like to get together and talk with you about your soul."

At least half the Convention seminaries—usually the larger ones—were still firmly evangelical. Powers's barbs at liberals and humanists were soon matched by digressions of discontent over Northern's administrative policy, and he finally resigned in favor of Eastern Baptist Theological Seminary, where he became increasingly disdainful of fundamentalist critics.

Julius R. Mantey was more effective as a research scholar than as a teacher, and already in those days a heart condition impaired his energies. The Dana and Mantey volume, *A Manual Grammar of the Greek New Testament* (1927), was in wide use and highly regarded. But in the classroom Mantey enforced little academic discipline. Students in the Greek Gospels course kept English translations alongside the Greek New Testament text and used them in moments of difficulty. A gentle and kind teacher, Mantey encouraged prospective preachers disinclined toward study of biblical languages and seldom questioned their excuses for unpreparedness. One year, upon Mantey's sudden illness at the beginning of the semester, I was privileged to teach his course in Greek Gospels. In previous studies I had fortunately taken two years of classical and one year of biblical Greek.

Seminary study of Hebrew was unrewarding. Fortunately the

teacher, Dr. Fouts, had almost wholly mastered a stuttering problem that had plagued him in earlier years. Fouts was an amazing collector of books on the Old Testament; not only his apartment and his office but all available hallspace as well almost everywhere on campus seemed to house extensions of his library. I diligently prepared lessons and got a top grade (even discovering a Hebrew error in the final exam). But I forgot what little Hebrew I learned almost as quickly as I acquired it.

Faris D. Whitesell, whose proficiency in practical theology was in the ascendancy, stood apart from his colleagues in Christian friendliness and in emphasis on the life of prayer. From him I learned the essentials of church ministry and how to extend an orderly evangelistic appeal. A personable and readily accessible teacher, he became a good friend during my later years on Northern's faculty. I suggested that he write the book *100 Ways to Extend an Evangelistic Invitation.*

Courses in Christian education disappointed me. Dr. Ernest E. Smith placed little emphasis on the implications of scriptural truth for the whole range of the humanities, arts and sciences. What principles we were taught were more compatible with philosophical idealism than with biblical theism.

I made good use of library resources, often signing out books that paralleled the assigned text, and thus familiarized myself with other perspectives. On chilly nights I often fell into bed with a book. First on my list of choice reading was J. Gresham Machen's *The Origin of Paul's Religion,* which I could not put down until I had completed all but the last chapter. I was drawn to conservative Anglican divines of the turn of the century more than to Continental luminaries who often walked a very narrow strip of recent theological controversy.

In seminary it was radio bulletins and the daily newspapers that jolted us into the world outside. The international tranquillity of my undergraduate years seemed suddenly to be exploding into a hemisphere in peril. Northern had no courses in social ethics; public matters intruded mainly through concerns in opening classroom prayers or expressed during mealtime conversations marginal to academic engagement. Now came the ominous news of the German Army's unrelenting drive beyond the Reich's borders. Prime Minister Neville Chamberlain took off by plane in mid-September to personally plead with Hitler to avert war. Weeks and even months of international suspense would soon collapse into ever worsening news. Despite Hitler's talks with Italian, French and British leaders, and a plea by Roosevelt, the German dictator proceeded in 1939 to scrap existing pacts with Poland and Britain. Before I began my second seminary year Germany and Russia had, on August 23, 1939, signed a ten-year nonaggression pact.

Britain and France then mobilized for war in case of Germany's invasion of Poland. On August 31 German troops attacked Poland and claimed the port city of Danzig for the Reich. On September 2, 1939, Britain and France issued a final unheeded ultimatum and then declared themselves at war with Germany. On the following day, September 4, Germans torpedoed a British liner. By mid-September Soviet troops marched into Poland and fierce fighting raged along the Western front.

During the 1938 and 1939 academic years classes divided my time between the Northern and Wheaton campuses some twenty-five miles apart, since I was simultaneously pursuing the bachelor of divinity at Northern and the master's degree in theology at Wheaton. I had already brought newspaper activities to an end, although I carried a Chicago Police Department reporter's pass. I planned to complete course requirements by summer school studies. On Wheaton days I also taught late afternoon courses in journalism.

The main faculty attraction in Wheaton's graduate school then was Henry Thiessen, a gifted New Testament exegete who had studied Greek under A. T. Robertson. Thiessen's examinations were exacting and thorough. At exam time we covertly referred to him as "the Pharaoh of the Oppression"; at other times students used the more affectionate term "Uncle Hank." Wheaton's strength was its perception of the unbridgeable gulf separating historic Christianity and Protestant modernism; its weakness was its lack of touch with contemporary European trends. Schleiermacher and Ritschl and their modernistic puppets we knew, but of the revolt against modernism and of existentialism we knew little.

Northern's lack of Sunday preaching and teaching assignments was disconcerting. Upperclassmen understandably preempted most of the opportunities. But I was asked in my first year to trial teach a large adult Sunday school class at First Baptist Church of Oak Park, then liberally oriented. That door then opened permanently, and at least one businessman was helped to an evangelical confession of Christ.

During the summer of 1939 I attended classes at Winona Lake School of Theology. Although still unaccredited, the school nonetheless always featured a few scholars from mainline campuses and in earlier years had enlisted men like G. Campbell Morgan, A. T. Robertson, J. Gresham Machen and Melvin Grove Kyle. There I took Old Testament Introduction from Princeton's Henry S. Gehman who in the conservative Winona Lake environment concealed his critical concessions. In the early 1940s, after I married, we spent brief summer vacations at Winona Lake, then a flourishing Bible conference ground. These visits were usually coordinated with speaking engagements or with a brief course offered by the summer school of theology, or later, with my own teaching on the Winona campus.

Ten months after I was immersed there, on October 5, 1939, the Babylon Baptist Church, on its own initiative, licensed me to preach. Subsequently, during the 1939 Christmas holidays, Helga and I announced our engagement. Her credentials, by then, included library skills. At the North Dakota campus a fine librarian, a Catholic colleague about Helga's age, traded extensive and intensive weekly tutoring in library science for Helga's similar help in German. When President Koller heard just before yearend of our engagement, and surmised that we might marry the following summer, he asked to see us. Since married students apartments in Taft Hall were in short supply I had already put my name on the waiting list for the Fall of 1940 to snap up a possible vacancy. In our conference, Dr. Koller indicated that Northern needed a trained librarian. Gratified to know that the post would not intimidate Helga, he invited her to begin work in September, hoping that divine providence and Northern's offer might facilitate our plans. We had set our wedding date tentatively for August, 1940. Although it runs ahead of the story to say so, the fact is that at the end of her first month's full-time work as librarian Helga was astonished by her first compensation. Her unstipulated salary, it developed, was $65 a month; in North Dakota her stipend as dean of women and German professor had been twice that plus room and board, little as that was. Fortunately, our wedding and honeymoon were blissfully spared any awareness of the financial details of her work as seminary librarian.

By early April, 1940, the Germans had occupied Denmark and bombed Oslo, provoking Norway to enter the war. By May 9, the Nazis had invaded Holland, Belgium and Luxembourg. A week later they had pierced French lines on a 62-mile front. Before seminary commencement exercises on May 22, 1940, they were but 60 miles from Paris; three weeks later the French government forsook the capital and Italy entered the war. By mid-June German troops occupied Paris. The implications for American military intervention were still unsure, and prolonged suspense hung over all human planning.

Saturday, August 17, 1940, was a humid Chicago day if ever there was one. Months in advance we cleared use of Byrne Hall chapel, otherwise in disuse through the summer, for an early afternoon wedding ceremony. I prearranged for necessary cleaning and seating arrangements with the building superintendent. Taft Hall Apartment 200, our future home, became available and Helga and her mother readied it for occupancy, and gradually we transferred our belongings. Helga's mother sewed a new lining in my suitcoat while I checked the readiness of my '37 Ford sedan for honeymoon driving.

Finally came the W-Day. Before guests were due I went to the chapel, only to discover that the florist had not yet delivered palms and flowers. The first guest was now in view before ushers were in place. Wearing a white satin dress, she seated herself in a front row. On second thought she opted for another location. The imprint on her dress was unmistakable: the building superintendent had forgotten to dust the chairs. I hurriedly dispatched arriving ushers to do double duty.

Mother Christy came from Long Island with the Joshuas and sat with Marjorie, the pastor's wife. Nearby were Mother Bender and Helga's theologian-brother, Thorwald, who gave Helga away. President and Mrs. Koller and other faculty and wives, students, members of churches where I had ministered and other friends came as well. Harold Lindsell was best man and Enid Platts, with whom Helga had shared Black Hills kitchen crew chores, was maid of honor.

As the wedding procession began I coped with a monumental migraine. Peter Joshua conducted the simple, devout ceremony. I recall at one point his urging me to say, "I do." I did. I know that I intended the vows sincerely, until death do us part. Helga was a picture of beauty, charm and dignity—as she was when first I greeted her less than five years earlier.

That evening we welcomed guests to a delectable dinner at The Spinning Wheel in suburban Hinsdale. We waited as long as we could for the Kollers, who had driven to the wrong place in the wrong city.

In early evening we said farewell and left on our honeymoon. It had begun to rain ever more heavily. Accommodations were not under great pressure that August so we planned to drive as far as we wished before stopping whenever and wherever we desired. The rains poured with ever greater intensity. Cars and even trucks had pulled off the roads to wait out a seemingly never-ending storm. About midnight we reached the small town of Harvey, Illinois, where I inquired about lodgings. The inclement weather had filled all vacancies, we were told; nothing was available for miles around. We could, however, have an unused upstairs room with twin beds and a sofa. We hesitated momentarily until fierce lightning and thunder encouraged quick acceptance. No honeymoon was ever intended for a migraine night anyway.

Our trip took us next to Cedar Lake, Indiana, where Torrey Johnson, preaching to a Bible conference on "The New Relationship" (2 Cor. 5:17), spotted us in the congregation and used us as a five-minute sermon illustration. As a consequence, some prankster doctored our car; on startup it popped like a hundred balloons. After a stop at Winona Lake we continued to Fremont, Ohio, and then to the Niagara Falls area. At Houghton College we stopped with the beloved Claude

Rees family before traveling through the Finger Lakes district and on to Long Island where Helga met my family and friends for the first time. Not much given to seafood, Helga, one night after we were served a delicious clam dinner, came home and from her purse poured—like so many quarters—an assortment of ingeniously concealed mollusks.

We went on to Carlisle, Pennsylvania, where friends of Mother Christy served us on beautiful ruby glasswear. On a lark we drove to New Martinsville, West Virginia, only to learn that the glass factory there had just been sold to Viking and all old patterns had been discarded. A Baptist deacon whom we met in church the next day, a factory foreman, salvaged for us virtually a full service of magnificent rubyware which we still treasure.

God graciously gave favor to my preaching, although early efforts were hardly remarkable. In my college Freshman days I joined a gospel team for Mother's Day and preached my only sermon, titled "Blood on Your Hands" based on Ezekiel 33. That morning I tried to find the Scripture reading in the huge pulpit Bible only to be confronted by books I had never seen before: Maccabees, Tobit and so on. Only the presence of an index rescued me from ignominy. During college years I spoke on Long Island one Sunday night in Central Presbyterian Church, Huntington, on "The Tyranny of Death," based on Romans 5:12–21, and plowed so deep that Peter Joshua rescued his service only by singing a solo after I concluded. My weakness was a long introduction, too much information and a lack of illustrations. I was still unaware that pauses can be as important as verbalizing if one knows what to do with them. My voice was quite monotone; in any case, I had not learned to use it well.

But from February through May, 1938, I preached regularly at Oswego Presbyterian Church in Illinois. After that, many small churches invited me. In the summer of 1940 I served at $15 a week as interim minister at First Baptist Church of Elmhurst. I was called as full-time pastor, but declined because fulfilling my degree requirements would deprive the church of the pastoral attention it merited.

Still another factor added to my reservations about opting for a preaching ministry, that of coping with the problem of death. Newspaper work promotes objectivity amid even the most terrible tragedy. A reporter routinely intrudes into others' grief in quest of photographs for the next day's front pages and sometimes breaks the first news of death to an unsuspecting family only to exploit the conversation for press purposes. A heavy burden accompanied preaching, but my attitude toward death was more impersonal than what seemed right for a Christian minister.

When I was called to a student pastorate in October, 1940, the congregation was comprised mainly of elderly people. The Humboldt Park Baptist Church adjoined the German Baptist Old People's Home, and for some occupants, if they could manage, the nearby church provided their only outside stroll. I had conducted both the Oswego ministry and the Elmhurst ministry without the death of a church member, but Humboldt Park would be different. I prayed with double unction that God would restore the sick and that the angel of death would not come near.

I was not without personal feelings about death—that is, my own death. I shared the fear of death common to the human race, yet knew that Christ by his resurrection had removed the sting of death and bequeathed to his followers a life fit for eternity. But the fact of Christ's victory over death, the power of resurrection truth at the final brink, the comfort of the gospel in time of personal grief, were not yet a deeply appropriated experience. Death seemed to me, and seems still, an evil, the last enemy that Christ will obliterate. I was uncomfortable about preaching funeral sermons on short call. The question also remained whether years of newspaper work had schooled me in a rather Stoic indifference to death and quite eroded the capacity for a pastor-heart which bears the grief of the bereaved in the shadow of the valley of death. A newspaper obituary preoccupation with the "who, what, when, where and why" does not leave one experientially at home amid the enduring concerns of spiritual death and spiritual life, future destiny and the resurrection of the body.

The light that Christianity casts upon the pallor of death astounded me unexpectedly. Just a few days before Thanksgiving, on November 23, 1940, a Western Union messenger came into the seminary library with a telegram: MOM PASSED AWAY AT 3 PM COME HOME IF POSSIBLE. The news stunned me, but within the hour I was aboard a crack Pennsylvania Railroad train from Chicago to New York City.

Ours was not a closely knit family, but a bond of affection existed between my mother and me, even if seldom expressed in so many words. She wept when I went to college, not because she would have changed God's will, but because home was such an empty place—empty of companionship and durable things—except for the nook that Christ was now able to occupy there. In her clothes closet I would find, unopened because she treasured it, the box of chocolate-covered cherries (into which I had inserted a bill) that some months previously I had sent on her forty-ninth birthday. None of us dreamed that a heart attack complicated by pleurisy and pneumonia would sweep her away at the onset of the cold Long Island winter.

When I walked into 103 Wilson Boulevard a stupefied look blanketed the children's faces. Never, I think, did bereaved brothers and bereaved sisters love each other so much as in that moment of emptiness when they jointly looked at me as if for some great reversing miracle of faith. Johanna, the youngest, was twelve; Isabella had just turned fifteen, and Eleanor was eighteen. Quietly and confidently I assured them that we could trust God who makes no mistakes.

My father, holding back threatening tears, asked me to go to the funeral home with him. We climbed into the old car, just the two of us. He told me that he had completed all arrangements. "I gave Mama the best we could from the insurance money," he said. "Don't try to change anything," he added, breaking down. "She didn't have very much in life," he explained; "let's give her the best we can in death."

I repressed my feelings, knowing that neither God nor Mother would want things thus—that she should have on earth so little of genuine love and understanding and of things that truly matter, and now, when decision time was past, that the children would have little if anything of what she had left, and the undertaker most of it. I said nothing. Funeral arrangements had been made and any protest would have seemed a lack of affection, just as some mortals gauge love by the extravagance of a gravestone.

Father had been overly generous to patrons of his convenience store. Customers ran up large bills that they failed to pay. After having for several years moved out of the family home, he had returned there late in 1939. He then rented the store early in 1940, giving the tenant option to buy within ten years, which he did. Unknown to me, Mother had meanwhile taken up doing housework in Brightwaters and Bay Shore to help meet the mortgage payments. After Mother's death in November, 1940, Father lived at the homestead until the end of 1942 when on December 30 he married Mae Wilcox, a Central Islip resident. He then rented the home and lived elsewhere in the village. A few years later, in 1945 or 1946, he converted the homestead into two apartments, one of which he rented, and lived with Mae in the other.

As we walked toward the viewing room Father whispered: "Mama is in here!" I rested my hand softly on her lifeless mere stick of a self, and after brief meditation and a prayer said softly, "No, Mama is not here; this is only the body. Her soul is already with Jesus." Father looked at me with big, curious eyes.

We returned home, where the children were weeping. I gathered them around the large circular dining room table and told them again that Mama was with Jesus. At the funeral service the body would be placed in the grave, I said, but it, too, would someday be raised.

They looked at me eagerly. Mama was with Jesus—that removed half the sting of death, nor was the funeral service the last word.

Then I opened the Bible to First Corinthians, the fifteenth chapter. Never was there a more intent and solemn congregation. There was no need to think about an effective introduction, about moving illustrations. The Word of God alone sufficed. I read the long passage about Christ's resurrection and ours, from the opening verses ("For I delivered unto you first of all that which also I received: that Christ died for our sins according to the scriptures; and that he was buried; and that he hath been raised on the third day according to the scriptures. . . .") through the words, "For as in Adam all die, so also in Christ shall all be made alive. But each in his own order."

For the next half hour we reverently discussed questions about death and immortality. Then we asked ourselves what Mother would now have us do. The youngsters knew that she had become a Christian, that there had been a transforming experience in her outlook, that she had encouraged them to pray and to trust in Christ. We had a circle of prayer, and seemed momentarily encamped just outside of heaven. The tears that flooded the youngsters' faces when I first arrived gave way to confidence and trust. They slipped off to bed quietly. Tomorrow we would all go to church knowing that Christ's resurrection and his living power had dealt death its ultimate defeat.

During the westbound return trip a surprising realization overtook me. To minister to the bereaved would no longer be the intimidating dreaded task it once seemed; it would be a wider opportunity to display the triumph of the gospel of grace, even as I had experienced it in my own and my family's time of need. It should then have surprised no one that when invited I shared eagerly in activities of the Soldier Field Easter Sunrise Service committee in Chicago, and later spearheaded the Pasadena Rose Bowl Easter Sunrise Service committee in California.

It was Harry Saulnier, then a member of the Christian Endeavor cabinet, who in 1932 first shared with Chicago friends his youthful vision of a citywide Easter sunrise service. Although such a service was considered impractical, he and his young people's committee in 1933 gathered 15,000 persons for the first program. Thereafter the annual Soldier Field Easter Sunrise Service attracted turnouts that often exceeded 50,000.

In 1935 trustees of Chicago's Pacific Garden Mission, the oldest rescue mission in the Northwest and second oldest in the nation, added Saulnier to their board. Soon he was spending three nights a month at 650 South State Street speaking at the mission to human derelicts that drifted in. An electrician with Commonwealth Edison, Saulnier soon became known throughout the city as a dedicated Christian layman. When the mission early in 1940 lacked a superintendent and no qualified person seemed available, board members drew up individual lists of preferences for the position. One member proposed Saulnier, who was flabbergasted. After a week of prayer with his wife, Saulnier resigned secular work and undertook the rescue mission superintendency.

Helga and I were not long settled into Taft Hall as young marrieds when I got to know Saulnier. Over six feet and weighing 220 pounds, every inch and ounce dedicated to evangelism, he would soon expand the mission's frontiers. Although founded in 1877, it had little promotional material except for occasional tracts about some dramatic conversion. Saulnier talked with me both about writing the story of Pacific Garden Mission and about volunteering to serve on the publicity committee for the Soldier Field Easter Sunrise Committee.

In 1942 Zondervan published *A Doorway to Heaven* with an introduction by Dr. Harry A. Ironside, then pastor of Moody Memorial Church. It went through twelve editions and for years served as a descriptive volume of the mission's life-transforming ministry.

The book was really a family production to which Helga and I surrendered not only our efforts but our apartment. First we gathered from skimpy and disorganized files anything from its 1877 beginnings onward that had ever been printed by or about the mission. This material was lugged in boxes to our one-bedroom Taft apartment, where for several months we yielded almost the entire living room to the mission project. Inside a closet were my office desk and typewriter. First we stacked material in piles separated by decade from the 1870s to 1940. Then we further separated accounts of spectacular developments or outstanding conversions. With some twenty chapters tentatively in view, we each went to work on different sections of the book, noting gaps that we would ask former workers and board members to fill in.

Before writing anything I felt I must anonymously spend a night at the mission, absorbing its atmosphere as an overnighter submitting to delousing and other standard procedures. When I learned that Saulnier would be in Kansas for much of a week of meetings, I decided to use an alias and to scout the mission unrecognized. I taught my Northern theology classes that Friday morning unshaven, and in late afternoon donned the oldest suit in a meager wardrobe, and boarded an elevated train to the inner city. I shuffled along State Street making brief notes on what I saw. Finally I reached the mission doors at dusk just after nightly prayer meeting had begun.

The routine mission menu was "prayer meeting then soup and sandwich," and finally a shower and bed. With wide, sweeping gestures the songleader that night beat out the hymns as if he were conducting some massive choir. Finally came testimony time. Here and there someone rose to speak a hesitant word for Jesus, until a crescendo of voices took up the witness. I, too, ventured a word of anonymous gratitude that Christ had changed my life since first he became my Savior and Lord. At that, the songleader unwittingly blew my cover. "Now you know," he said, "why I've been so nervous all evening. That man, who just gave his testimony, is one of my professors at Northern Baptist Seminary." It was the first—and last—prayer meeting out of which I walked as soon as heads were bowed. I returned to campus for the night.

Because of my journalistic experience I was invited to serve on the steering committee for the annual Soldier Field Easter Sunrise Service. The committee of twenty gifted laymen divided into twenty subcommittee heads, each of whom then enlisted four other appropriately talented evangelicals from churches of various denominations. In this way the central committee grew to one hundred active lay leaders. To promote the service, the steering committee met monthly from New Year's onward, then weekly the month before Easter and finally at Soldier Field all day Saturday before Easter. The night before Easter we spent as guests of the Congress Hotel in the Loop, where at 5 A.M. we met for prayer before moving to the site of the sunrise service where with soon arriving multitudes we fellowshiped in transdenominational praise to the Risen Lord.

The whole effort was an uncompensated volunteer event in every respect from usher to musicians to featured speaker. One Easter Saturday, Saulnier received a wire from an already publicly announced speaker that he must withdraw; the awesome burden of his responsibility had overwhelmed him. Saulnier promptly fired back: THIS IS GOD'S SERVICE. YOU ARE ONLY HIS SERVANT. WE ARE PRAYING FOR YOU AND EXPECT YOU IN THE MORNING. Come Easter dawn and the speaker was indeed present. On another Easter 65,000 people attended in weather so frigid that a committeeman kept maneuvering an electric light over the organ keyboard to warm the musician's hands.

If seminary seemed a cloistered life removed from the secular city, and I no longer moved in the world as I did during newspaper years, these dedicated evangelical lay people kept before me the vision of a lost city, of a nation in need of the gospel, of a world task that far transcended the bickering and rivalries at work in ecclesiastical circles.

My bachelor of divinity degree was conferred by Northern on May 26, 1941, and the master of arts in theology by Wheaton on June 16, 1941. I was committed to completing the doctorate in theology at Northern, although the national and international context in which I ventured my theological studies in undergraduate days had now altered greatly. In June, 1940, France had capitulated to the Reich. When divinity classes resumed in September, Britain reciprocated the German bombing of London by bombing Berlin. Two months later on November 5, a day after Franklin D. Roosevelt had on his own authority traded destroyers to Britain in exchange for seaports, he was elected for a fourth term. At the end of 1940, 59 percent of Americans expected the U.S. to enter the European War; 52 percent declared the German people—not simply the Nazi government—our enemy. Although the vast majority (over 80 percent) favored staying out of the war, 68 percent said that future American safety depended on British victory, and 60 percent said that the U.S. should therefore help Britain even if it meant getting into the war. About 66 percent thought that the U.S. should go to war against Germany and Italy if that alone would guarantee those nations' defeat. Such developments shaped student discussions late into many nights as we parried questions of vocational priority, patriotic loyalties, draft exemption for ministerial students and career possibilities of chaplaincy.

In June, 1941, Hitler went to war against Russia and in August the Germans invaded Czechoslovakia and Greece. By mid-August, 1941, 65 percent felt that U.S. entry would require dispatching our fighting forces to Europe.

Northern manifested very little pacifist sympathy in face of the horrendous destruction loosed upon the West by the Nazis. As seminary classes reconvened in September, 1941, 57 percent of Americans felt America should surely enter the war; 56 percent thought the U.S. should bomb German warships and submarines on sight. Among both students and faculty many were convinced that in case of war Northern should be ready to supply competent candidates for the chaplaincy.

I was not wholly sure what was at stake for me. I was not a pacifist, believing that too optimistic a theory of human nature undergirds that view, and moreover, that biblical realism requires an alternative. The evils perpetrated by Nazi aggression called for resistance. I had a call to technical Christian service, and also knew that I could not qualify physically for military service. Helga's brothers Armin and Carl Ronald served with U.S. naval intelligence with the Pacific Fleet. Northern Seminary had enlisted me in 1939 to teach English and American literature and religious journalism at the theological college level, and then in systematic theology also; it also held out the prospect, once I completed my doctorate in theology, of a full-time faculty post in theology and philosophy of religion.

On October 6, 1940, a month and a half after our marriage, I had begun serving as student pastor of the Humboldt Park Baptist Church in Chicago, a congregation of the German Baptist (later North American Baptist) Conference. The call to minister there came literally "out of the blue" without my candidating, not because of any supposed preaching gifts but for two quite different reasons. First, the church was in decline with a morning attendance of about thirty-five persons and twenty at night, mainly elderly. Second, I was the husband of Helga whose family had served the German Baptists in a distinguished missionary career in Africa. The first Sunday I preached on "Why a Church Calls a Pastor," a nonexpository message appended to Peter's words to Cornelius in Acts 10:21: "Therefore came I unto you without gainsaying, as soon as I was sent for; I ask, therefore, for what intent you have sent for me?" My stipend, for two Sunday services and leading midweek prayer meetings, was $60 a month, whether four or five Sundays, and remained so for well over a year. Within six months regular attendance had almost doubled, with the supportive help of Albert Gernenz, a Northern student who became Sunday school superintendent. Since a Baptist Old People's Home adjoined the church we installed a sound system that carried the services to those who could not come in person. We put a phono-chime system in the steeple to alert the neighborhood to new vitality in the church.

News from Europe was specially disconcerting to German-Americans trying to think their way through the worsening conflagration abroad. Sooner than anyone dreamed American entry into the massive conflict became inevitable. On Sunday, December 7, 1941, Japanese bombers struck Pearl Harbor and the U.S. declared war; five days later our country was at war also with Germany and Italy. Chicago radio first carried news of the Pearl Harbor attack about 12:30 P.M. Sunday. Having heard it before mid-afternoon, I knew instinctively that the message I had prepared for that night was inappropriate. Walking across the campus I happened into Dr. Stiansen and asked, "What does this mean for the future of the Church?" What would global war imply for the worldwide presence of the missionary cause? Stiansen replied in bold confidence: "I have lived in Norway," he said, in fond recollection of his youth in Trondheim, "and I have seen the tide go out and the tide come in, go out and come in, go out and come in. 'On this Rock will I build my church!' said Jesus, and I have no fears for the future of the Church." I opened and closed my Humboldt sermon that night with Stiansen's reassuring comment.

It was at Humboldt that I was ordained to the ministry in 1941, an experience stripped of some of its sacred aura by denominational politics. To avoid irregular ordination by local churches, the Chicago

Baptist Association named a prudential committee to examine credentials and interview candidates and then recommend or not recommend ordination. Because the University of Chicago Divinity School (Baptist by origin) and Northern Baptist Seminary were theologically divergent, it had become the practice to let local churches establish candidates' theological acceptability, and the prudential committee to certify character, academic fulfillment and general competence. When both a theologically liberal candidate and I, a theological conservative, appeared before the committee, nonevangelicals pressed me—contrary to established procedure—for a statement of faith. As a point of beginning and identification I recited the Apostles' Creed and was criticized for not being creative. A modernist committeeman asked why I believed that Jesus was "born of a virgin" when neither Mark nor John say so. I replied courteously, and expanded my beliefs. Both of us candidates were approved by voice vote. Later in time alone with God I was grateful, indeed, that what often now passes for ecclesiastical ordination is answerable ultimately to a higher court.

I carried the ministry at Humboldt Park into January, 1943. My teaching at Northern brought further invitations to minister in Baptist and other churches, like First Baptist of Rockford, Illinois, First Baptist of Hammond, Indiana, and First Baptist of Eugene, Oregon. By 1944 I was addressing Saturday night Youth for Christ meetings, as in Kiel Auditorium, St. Louis, with 1600 attending, in the Detroit Arts Arena with 1300 present, in Rockford with 1300, in Grand Rapids with 1600 and in Cleveland, Indianapolis and elsewhere. During the five summers spent in New England for doctoral studies I spoke in various East Coast pulpits, including Park Street Church, Boston, in 1945, and Tremont Temple, Boston, a year later. Meanwhile invitations came to address Inter-Varsity groups at the universities of Chicago, Illinois and Michigan; and in the summer of 1947 Campus in the Woods in Huntsville, Ontario, simultaneously scheduled Cornelius Van Til and me.

In 1942 when Harold John Ockenga and others decided that orthodox Protestants should launch the National Association of Evangelicals, I was still a graduate student but supported the cause from its beginning. Carl McIntire had hastily organized the American Council of Christian Churches in St. Louis in 1941 when rumors arose that an organizational challenge to the Federal Council (later National Council) of Churches was in prospect. Conservative Christians felt increasingly that without some such effort they could not effectively confront the Federal Council's liberal reorientation of theology and socio-political perspectives, its control of foreign missions boards and its monopolizing of Protestant chaplaincy appointments. In contrast to N.A.E.'s welcome to evangelicals in mainline denominations, McIntire rejected all clergy and laity in ecumenically linked churches as apostate.

Among Northern Baptists these issues were fueled by increasing debate over the doctrinal views of missionary appointees and the tendency of Convention spokesmen, despite their denomination's emphasis on local church autonomy, to act in concert with Federal Council leaders. Independent Baptists opted for the General Association of Regular Baptists as an alternative sphere of ministry. Many Northern seminarians felt, as I did, that the Convention had an official evangelical heritage through its historic commitment to the New Hampshire Confession of Faith. If the Convention ever officially adopted a contrary statement, then we would by conscience be compelled to withdraw, but unless such development transpired our mission and commitment remained to preserve the Convention's official standards, whatever any liberal leadership might think.

When N.A.E. was organized, and in subsequent years also, I handled convention publicity as an annual contribution. For many years I was literary (book) editor of *United Evangelical Action,* the movement's monthly publication, and also served on its board of administration for several terms. I applauded N.A.E.'s determination to rise above a protest mentality and to shape a positive program.

My final year of doctoral studies at Northern in the Fall of 1941 brought me into contact with a devout and dedicated teacher, T. Leonard Lewis, later my faculty colleague and treasured friend. When Dr. Powers moved to Eastern Baptist, Lewis came to teach seminars in both Old Testament and New Testament theology. He soon also taught the graduate level course in systematic theology while I as assistant professor taught the college level course for Th.B. students. Helga meanwhile taught theological college courses in English and American literature. When in 1945 she completed the M.R.E. degree under Dr. Harold C. Mason, she added Christian education courses to her teaching; in that same year her brother, Thorwald, received his doctorate in theology.

Faculty office space was at a premium. Leonard Lewis, another teacher and I shared a small corner office where we carried on theological discussions, took phone calls and interviewed students. In those days Lewis and I projected a comprehensive revision of A. H. Strong's three-volume *Systematic Theology,* the standard text for Northern Baptist Convention seminarians. We often parried those plans at Sunday dinner and in evening fellowship even after Lewis became pastor of the fast-growing First Baptist Church of Hammond, Indiana. When he became president of Gordon College on the Boston Fenway, I taught there for five summers while pursuing doctoral studies in philosophy at Boston University. My Boston dissertation was a critical examination of the impact on Strong's later theology of personal idealism—a philosophical stance perpetuated by Edgar S. Brightman. When Gordon Divinity School, now Gordon-Conwell Theological Seminary, moved to a new suburban campus, Lewis held open for me the seminary's academic deanship for several years, until in 1947 I went instead from Northern to the West Coast.

I received the Northern doctorate in theology on May 22, 1942. That was six months before U.S. forces landed in French Africa to open a second front, and a year or so before General MacArthur launched the Allied offensive in the Pacific. Once I had my doctorate, Northern added me to its full-time faculty. Helga and I moved in the Fall into the English basement quarters at Heinrichs Hall, the faculty apartment building. Rental was to be deducted from my $3600 annual salary as Professor of Systematic Theology and Philosophy of Religion. I persuaded President Koller to forego the rental charge.

In June, 1942, I ventured for the first time since prechristian newspaper years to buy a new car. My second-hand 1937 Ford sedan had been totalled by an uninsured oncoming driver. For $1037, discounted 10 percent and by another $100 for the wrecked Ford, Floyd Baughman, a dedicated Baptist layman who owned the Buick agency in Downers Grove, sold me a new Buick sedan. Ten gallons of gas added to the tank at delivery cost $1.75. In May, 1946, I traded the Buick for another new model, and was allowed $1128 toward the $1690 purchase price.

During the war years we coped as did others with ration coupons for foodstuffs, gasoline and other items. We waited in long lines at store counters. Baked Spam was a frequent Sunday dinner item. These inconveniences were trivial, of course, compared to the risks borne by our servicemen. We moved in the early summer of 1943 to the upper floor of Heinrichs Hall where the apartment space accommodated Helga's architect-brother, Carl Ronald, when he returned from the war, and also Helga's widowed mother, who in her retirement years insisted on working at an inner city establishment and thus entered Social Security (there was no missionary retirement fund in those days).

Faculty salaries at Northern were painfully low. When President Koller first announced a raise, he permitted teachers to retain from their preaching and other church engagements any honoraria exceeding the first $600. This practice not only disadvantaged faculty who had little preaching skill but also put most faculty in the undesirable position of concentrating on pulpit supply rather than on teaching, research and writing. My Northern salary rose in 1943 to $3,795 and in 1945 was $3,900 plus a $585 increment for living quarters.

One way of holding down expenses was to shop at Chicago's Farmers Market where on Saturday mornings truckers peddled bushels of fruits and vegetables. Faris Whitesell and I often arrived there just before noon, when most produce had been sold and farmers eager to return home were ready to dispose of remaining merchandise at bargain prices. Instead of buying items we preferred, we often ended up dividing closeout produce between us and then descended on our somewhat perplexed wives with a half bushel of tomatoes or peppers or grapes. One afternoon I bought a bushel of pomegranates, a fruit Helga had enjoyed in Africa. On Monday afternoon, reinforced by Sunday worship, my tolerant spouse by prayer and good works moved the mountain of pomegranates into the best jelly we have ever tasted.

Paul arrived on July 9, 1942, in Wesley Memorial Hospital, after a false alarm two weeks earlier. The maternity ward waiting room contained a scrapbook into which expectant fathers, each on a separate page, recorded their impatience. One exhausted husband counted and charted all the tiles on the maternity ward floor. Another wrote: "Three days ago I wanted a boy. Yesterday I would have been delighted with a girl. Today I'll take anything." Paul was a large, healthy child whose robust voice he exercised vociferously during night hours.

Heinrichs Hall lacked an elevator and daily Chicago soot blackened its back stairs. After Carol was born Helga not infrequently lugged both youngsters, one under each arm, up three flights of front or back stairs to our third floor apartment.

Carol's arrival was no routine matter. We had anticipated her coming possibly by mid-August, 1944. To be in Chicago in good time I wrote early exams at Indiana University where I was taking summer graduate courses. But the babe had its own ideas about a timely appearance. I had a long-scheduled two-day engagement to speak just before monthend to the day and night shifts at the LeTourneau plant in Peoria. The morning after my arrival came a telegram signed CAROL JENNIFER HENRY. That she was born in Wesley Memorial Hospital was a matter of "specialized" providence. Wartime restrictions limited taxi service as well as private car use. Well past midnight Helga called the police, indicated she was alone and faced the imminent birth of a baby. Police arrived at the Seminary in a long "Black Maria." Unfortunately their precinct regulations limited their service to Cook County Hospital. For the only time in her life Helga slipped a bill under the steering wheel, so to speak. Within moments the police wagon was underway to Wesley Memorial Hospital where within fifteen minutes Carol arrived on August 31.

During that summer of 1944 my graduate courses in philosophy at Indiana University were under W. Harry Jellema and Henry Veitch, the former a staunch Calvinist and the latter an equally staunch Thomist. Some years earlier I had studied Thomas Aquinas and Duns Scotus at Loyola University in Chicago for first-hand exposure to Catholic thought. But neither the Loyola nor now the Indiana experience convinced me of the validity of the fivefold Thomistic proof of God's existence. Jellema was a master teacher who taught history of philosophy from 1935 to 1947 and in 1939 had become head of the department. He lectured methodologically and magisterially, sweeping over the broad cognitive vistas of Western thought with special alertness to the dilemmas of modernity. His interest in ontology and epistemology was at the same time an interest in moral philosophy and spiritual reality. He knew how to communicate and how to challenge students, and pressed philosophy's abiding concerns on minds and consciences. He not only held Christian world-life intellectual convictions, but promoted Christian perspective as well, that is, the need to think and live christianly. Jellema made helpful suggestions on my volume *Remaking the Modern Mind* (1948) and when I became editor of *Christianity Today* in 1956, came aboard from the first as a contributing editor.

In the mid-'40s the chairman of a Presidential Search Committee asked me to address the Sioux Falls College student body and to meet with trustees. The leaders wanted, they said, to turn the college into a "Baptist Wheaton" since hundreds of Baptist students were attending interdenominational campuses. They asked about my accepting the presidency, if it were offered. On inquiring about the proposed transformation to Wheaton-likeness I learned of two ironclad stipulations that would hardly encourage that objective: first, faculty must not be required to sign a formal doctrinal statement, and second, that already entrenched social practices (such as campus community dances) remain in place. I replied that within their projected framework no Baptist Wheaton would or could emerge and I wished the search committee well.

Early in 1945 I was approached about considering the presidency of Western Conservative Baptist Seminary in Portland. The school had emerged from Baptist Bible Institute formed in the mid-'20s under Dr. W. B. Hinson. When in 1934 Dr. Albert G. Johnson assumed the pastorate of Hinson Memorial Baptist Church, he and the congregation forthrightly opposed the "inclusive policy" of the Northern Baptist Convention and designated all church giving to specific missionaries. Later when the Conservative Baptist Foreign Mission Society was formed Johnson served as president and became increasingly involved in the Seminary's leadership as well. I met with trustees and addressed the Seminary chapel. On February 25 I spoke on the same Sunday to Johnson's 1200 members at Hinson Memorial and to 900 persons at the White Temple (First Baptist) where more strongly Convention-aligned Dr. Ralph Walker pastored. The Seminary's five-acre campus, it seemed, was at the stage where I could possibly give leadership in maintaining doctrinal soundness, lifting academic standards and enlarging various ministries. I had the board's unanimous enthusiasm. I assured Johnson that "circumstantially my acceptance seems 99 percent assured"; I was returning home, I said, "to clear it with the Lord." To conserve time I prepared and sent—prematurely, it developed—a full-page ad at my expense to *Watchman-Examiner,* the denomination's conservative magazine, announcing "A New Star in the Sky" and ranging Western/Portland alongside Conservative Baptist/Denver, Northern Baptist/Chicago, Eastern Baptist/Philadelphia and Gordon/Boston. Helga was not reluctant to go, but pressed me over whether—as in my previous major decisions—I had "an unqualified 'yes' from the Lord." We prayed earnestly, until on the Ides of March—when I had promised final word—I mailed a declination. Once again I was divinely diverted from administrative work.

The fundamentalist-modernist conflict in the Northern Baptist Convention reached its zenith at the Grand Rapids convention in May, 1946, where conservatives, despite their superior numbers, were outmaneuvered and outvoted. Notwithstanding growing protest over the appointment of theologically compromised missionary candidates, the Convention committed itself to support of the Federal Council of Churches and to an inclusive policy. My nomination as recording secretary of the Convention by the Fundamentalist Fellowship together with their other nominations was defeated. But this turn of things nonetheless publicized my evangelical loyalties throughout the Convention.

Marked restlessness beset Northern in the mid-'40s. The neighborhood had deteriorated, street crime increased, prostitutes walked the area, whites were on the move as minorities enlarged their geographic sites. While President Koller was committed to buying up more and more property, others felt the campus should be relocated, and that the purpose of a seminary should not be confused with the role of a church in neighbor relations. Increased modernist-fundamentalist tensions in the denomination now climaxed in the formation of Denver Conservative Baptist Seminary. Certain Northern faculty complained that the school's expanding budgets accommodated property and building acquisitions more than faculty personnel and their office and secretarial needs. Although I shared conservative Baptist indignation over

Convention appointments of theologically compromised missionaries, I considered the opening of Denver seminary premature and costly, since Northern's competent faculty offered sound evangelical training.

Although doctoral studies and related written work preempted most of my creative time, I regularly churned out newspaper and magazine features from 1942 onward, increasingly for evangelical publications, to advance evangelical causes, to preserve writing contacts and to supplement income. In 1943 Zondervan published *Successful Church Publicity: A Guidebook for Christian Publicists,* my Northern doctoral dissertation for which William F. McDermott, onetime religion editor of *The Chicago Daily News,* wrote an introduction. In November, 1945, I spent a long evening at my desk on an essay, "The Relationship of Belief and Conduct," which won the Langhorne Orchard essay contest sponsored by Victoria Institute of Great Britain. Rain had turned to snow during the hours in Byrne Hall and on leaving I bounced down six concrete stairs and incurred a long-troublesome coccyx injury.

Inspired by correspondence with Gordon Clark, then at Butler University in Indianapolis, by Jellema's lectures at Indiana University, by a continuing reading of some of Van Til's syllabi and on the edge of Brightman's courses at Boston University, I began shaping for early future publication a work on *Remaking the Modern Mind.* Set up and printed by Eerdmans in September, 1946, it appeared before yearend with a dedication to "Three 'Men of Athens' G. H. C.—W. H. J.—C. V. T. who have sharpened my convictions by action and reaction, in delightful philosophical interchange." A second edition appeared in 1948; later it was reissued in a twentieth century Christian classics series. My doctoral dissertation at Boston was not due until 1949; Van Kampen Press published it in 1951 under the title *Personal Idealism and Strong's Theology.*

In 1946 Helga and I were invited into the Gnosis society, a half-century-old Chicago literary and social club devoted to preparation, presentation and discussion of scholarly papers. In the Spring of 1946 I handled publicity for the Life Begins Campaign held for thirty-six nights in the Chicago Arena from April 28–June 2 where Paul Rood, John R. Rice and Bob Jones, Sr., were the featured speakers.

That summer while I was teaching and studying in Boston came word that Mother Christy had died on August 5, 1946, and that the family wished me to conduct funeral services. I drove to Long Island to pay last respects to the saintly woman to whom I owed so great a debt, and committed the remains in Oakwood Cemetery, Bay Shore, in confident expectation of the future resurrection of the body. Her devout spirit, I knew, was already with Christ the Risen Lord.

During the 1945–46 and 1946–47 academic years I also drove to Wheaton to teach Senior classes in theism and ethics, filling the gap left by Dr. Henry Thiessen's move to Los Angeles. Helga accompanied me and in addition to her Northern work taught first and second year German to help meet the post-war GI enrollment boom. In 1947 I was elected president of Wheaton Alumni Association, but my forthcoming impending move to the West Coast made difficult any effective implementation of that office.

Denominational leaders began to question Northern's loyalty. In protest against equal distribution of funds for theological education to Baptist schools irrespective of their enrollment differences, President Koller rejected participation in the inclusive budget. He thereupon appealed directly and successfully to a supportive constituency disinterested in doctrinal pluralism. Although Northern later reentered the denominational funding channel, it maintained its theological integrity and in 1947 was the Convention's largest seminary with more than 600 students in its graduate school and theological college. But denominational patriotism increasingly encroached on campus perspectives. By two decades later, although entrenched on a splendid new suburban campus, Northern had engaged a liberal theologian and its student body had dwindled at one point to 27. Thereafter, although now openly accepting certain critical emphases that its founders had deplored and shunned, it strove energetically under new leadership to reaffirm its heritage and rebuild its enrollment.

When I left Northern in 1947 the graduate school faculty included President Koller, Dean Stiansen, Registrar Fouts and Professors Mantey, Whitesell, Groom, Mason and Shultz. In the theological college were J. S. Congdon, F. E. Eastburg, Adrian and Ada Beth Heaton, Dale Ihrie, William Kerr, Harold Lindsell, John Mostert, Martin Schlichting, Warren Young and Helga.

During the mid-'40s Eerdmans had begun publishing a monthly evangelical digest similar in format to *Reader's Digest.* I began in 1946 to shape a series of eight monthly articles constructively critical of contemporary fundamentalism. That summer I gave the series a trial run at Gordon College of Theology and Missions and then probed the magazine's interest. William B. Eerdmans, Sr., expressed a wide welcome for the material but warned that it would be a mistake to run it as a series of successive monthly essays. Since I proposed to "'perform surgery' on Fundamentalism," he explained, those who most needed to hear the message would turn it off prematurely and not follow it through. Eerdmans therefore proposed a small book with a dollar price tag. "If people spend a dollar," he said, "they'll read it whether they agree or not." So *The Uneasy Conscience of Modern*

Fundamentalism appeared in 1947. It was dedicated to T. Leonard Lewis, "Christian friend and former colleague," who was now entrenched as president of Gordon; its introduction was by Harold John Ockenga, pastor of Park Street Church.

Uneasy Conscience, really ventured as a tract for the times, made quite a stir. Not only did reformed scholars immediately welcome it, as reaffirming the Christian's dual citizenship, but so also did many traditional evangelicals who felt that fundamentalist withdrawal from society was just as ill-advised as its pessimism about evangelistic renewal. *United Evangelical Action* handled the book gingerly, not wishing to offend a diverse constituency. It offered a $10 reward for the best essays *pro* and *con* on the question, "Is Dr. Henry Right?" Bernard Ramm, then on the faculty of Bible Institute of Los Angeles, won the *con* award.

Ockenga was then in the process of convening a week-long summer conclave of influential evangelical scholars and authors to discuss evangelical literary needs and to identify projects already on the evangelical agenda. Funding for the conference was provided by John Bolten, a wealthy Park Street businessman. He was also meeting periodically and quietly with radio evangelist Charles E. Fuller about formation of a new West Coast Bible school or seminary for preachers.

Early in 1947 Dr. Wilbur M. Smith, noted editor of *Peloubet's Notes on the Sunday School Lesson* and professor of English Bible at Moody Bible Institute, spoke in Northern Seminary chapel. Later when he asked me: "Has Harold Ockenga been in touch with you about a new seminary on the West Coast?" I said, "No." "Well, he will," replied Smith, as he hurried back to Moody classes. Some months later Smith invited me to lunch. "I have just received pictures of the new campus," he said, "and it is a veritable Garden of Eden!" "If so," I remarked humorously, "there is a fall just around the corner."

8

Fuller and Its Fortunes

In May, 1947, radio evangelist Charles E. Fuller, Harold John Ockenga, Wilbur M. Smith, Everett F. Harrison, the New Testament professor at Dallas Theological Seminary, and I met at the Palmer House in Chicago to talk and pray about launching an evangelical seminary in California in September of 1947 or 1948. As we continued discussions, the earlier date, however close at hand, seemed our preferred option.

For one thing, Fuller's father had left a sizeable trust fund for Christian education. For another, Charles Fuller cited immediate availability of the choice 5½-acre Cravens Estate on Pasadena's prestigious South Orange Grove Avenue. As beginning publicity, the Old Fashioned Revival Hour network could announce the new seminary and its faculty to millions of Christian homes without undue delay. More than that, Harold Ockenga declared himself ready to come as president.

Smith, Harrison and I were entrenched in major theological posts with large student enrollments but were open to the will of God. There were several problems, however. Dr. Frank Gaebelein, who had been approached about coming as dean, gave late word of his unavailability; moreover, no registrar was yet in view. I mentioned that Harold Lindsell, who had recently joined the Northern faculty, had previously been registrar at Columbia Bible College. When queried, Lindsell agreed to fill that post, provided he could also teach a course in church history and missions.

We spent unhurried time in prayer. A common conviction gripped us of the need for what we envisioned: an evangelical seminary of uncompromising academic and spiritual priorities, and that granted professors built-in time for research and writing. Each of us knew that only the sovereign God could create such a seminary *ex nihilo* in less than four months. A spiritual imperative urged us on. A first announcement, we decided, would be made by Dr. Fuller on the Old Fashioned Revival Hour in June, mentioning names of faculty, Pasadena as the location, and inviting inquiries from graduates of accredited colleges and universities. Meantime those of us involved would resign our present posts.

Ockenga asked me to become dean. Indicating that among other things the proposed school attracted me because of its prospects for completing writing projects already under way, I declined the offer unless I could wait a year, and then come as dean in 1948. Ockenga insisted that as original faculty Smith, Harrison and I should come together in 1947; presumably he too would be with us.

After summer doctoral studies and teaching in New England, I returned to Chicago for final evacuation of our Northern apartment and the drive to California that would end at the Cravens estate, meanwhile purchased by the Fuller Foundation. Everett Harrison and his family reached campus from Texas at about the same time. We moved our belongings into the mansion's erstwhile servants' quarters before probing the matter of renting or buying homes. I had hardly arrived when a telegram from Ockenga named me (contrary to our understanding) acting dean for the first year. He himself, we had learned on arrival, would not be joining us in the initial year.

In any case, 27 of the entering class's 39 students were already on hand. Many represented Big Ten universities and mainline colleges. Some students came with memories of a call to Christian service during World War II in theatres of military combat. We announced that C. Gordon Brownville, former pastor of Boston's Tremont Temple and currently of the Eleventh Avenue Baptist Church in Los Angeles, would supplement faculty offerings with a course in evangelism, and that Lindsell was registrar and acting professor of missions. Many students were missionary-minded. Al Strong in time became a missionary leader in Ethiopia, John Winston a seminary president in France, Gary Demarest head of the Fellowship of Christian Athletes, Ralph Winter missionary in South America and implementer of the U.S. Center for World Mission, to mention but a few. Dan Fuller, the founder's son, also enrolled. All but one of the initial class ended up in technical Christian service.

On the second day of classes uniformed police arrived to serve papers for violation of zoning restrictions. This shock was the first intimation to any of us that city authorities had disallowed a zoning variance authorizing use of the Cravens estate for educational purposes. The assurances given by Dr. Fuller in May apparently evaporated when a city election brought into office new directors who feared that possible additional variances would in time downgrade the city's famous residential avenue. We were stunned.

Dr. J. Henry Hutchins, long-time and beloved pastor of the Lake Avenue Congregational Church, a godly man active in many evangelical and community enterprises, came promptly to the rescue: until the Seminary found alternative quarters we could use his congregation's facilities for week-long classroom purposes. Fortunately this arrangement also solved problems of parking and public transportation, since the church was centrally located and in fact within walking distance of many students' living quarters.

Faculty stayed tentatively at the Cravens estate while probing the area's comparatively expensive housing market. Many realty offers required more funds than some of us like Everett Harrison and I could muster. Wilbur Smith had bought housing sight unseen in order to move into a residence on arrival. In due time and with trust in divine providence, Harrison bought a place he did not really want, unpacked only essential items and expected a more suitable alternative to emerge before long (and it did!).

For Sunday dinner on September 14 we invited the Lindsells to join us at the Cravens estate. The previous evening while scouting for a house we came upon a two-bedroom bungalow with detached one-car garage and small garden plot a block from Lake Avenue Congregational Church. The owners were offering 400 North Hudson Avenue at $11,500 and were eager to move. Our total savings were but $4,000, and we had no experience whatever in real estate. We asked nonetheless to go through the property and after some discussion boldly offered $10,000 as our one and only bid. After an hour's friendly conversation the owners accepted. We needed, of course, to make a deposit to bind the agreement. Helga and I emptied purse and wallet and put on the table all the resources we had—$102, $20.46 of it in cash plus checks for $46.54 and $35. Four thousand dollars was to be paid in escrow eight days later, and the balance by monthend. Our Chicago belongings, inventoried at a value of $1,122, were scheduled to arrive at about the same time. The next day, since we were totally without funds to augment our larder, our first guests joined us for left-over meat loaf.

From the beginning the Seminary had an excellent support staff: Mary Ashley, assistant registrar; Irma Peterson, general faculty secretary; Doris Loeding, Dr. Smith's secretary; Ernest Buegler, outstanding chef; and Hilding Carlson, groundskeeper.

Late in September Ockenga arrived for conferences with Dr. Fuller and the faculty and to address the opening convention that on October 1 attracted 2500 people to Pasadena Civic Auditorium. Speaking on "The Challenge to the Christian Culture of the West" he was at his finest, addressing the mind and stimulating the will of his audience. Fuller Seminary was no mere provincial effort, he declared, but was here to stay, and with national significance for the mainline churches and for the country. Undergirding the school, he stressed, was the authority of the Bible and commitment to sound theology with an apologetic mission and responsible Christian awareness and involvement in social concerns. Announcement was made, to the disappointment of faculty and students, that Ockenga's presidency would be *in absentia* for the first three years.

At that time Ockenga coined and approved the term neo-evangelical which in short order Bob Jones, Sr., Carl McIntire and other fundamentalist critics targeted for abuse. The term, they argued, signified a compromise of biblical orthodoxy and so-called "old-time religion." I myself had previously written of a "new evangelicalism" that reaffirmed cognitive and apologetic concerns and social engagement, although I considered the term "evangelical" in and of itself adequate, preferable and noncontroversial. In the series of essays on "The Vigor of the New Evangelicalism" that appeared in *Christian Life and Times* between January and April, 1948, I noted: "The new evangelicalism voices its plea for a vital presentation of redemptive Christianity which does not obscure its philosophical implications, its social imperatives, its eschatological challenge, its ecumenical opportunity and its revelational base." Apart from such emphases, I added, fundamentalism's "forward march" will merely "mark time."

Actually extremist fundamentalist spokesmen decried the term "evangelical" no less than "neo-evangelical," and went to incredible lengths to deride and embarrass the new Seminary and its friends. As acting dean I invited Bob Jones to speak in Fuller chapel, where he deplored sustained academic pursuit as based on intellectual pride. *Christian Life and Times* carried a letter to the editor bent on discrediting my essays. Signed by Richard E. Day, c/o Jefferson Ranch, Sunnyvale, California, it warned readers: "In spite of all the big words . . . all of this has . . . a very sinister connotation." I wrote Day a personal letter that the post office returned with the message: UNKNOWN. Apprizing the magazine of this development, I then wrote a letter to the editor myself using the unknown Day's name and address. "I take back everything I said," it stated. "I am now convinced that Henry is right after all." That was the end of the matter. Ockenga's convocation address had unequivocally identified the new Seminary as interdenominational; it had just as unequivocally, however, repudiated any support of "come-out-ism." "We want our men to be so trained that when they come from a denomination," Ockenga had said, "they will go back into their denomination adequately prepared to preach the gospel and to defend the faith and to positively go forward in the work of God." Ecumenically oriented denominations nonetheless perceived Fuller as an impediment to pluralistic ecumenism and in rivalry with denominational institutions.

The United Presbyterian Church sought, in fact, to block Presbyterian faculty members from teaching at Fuller by requiring consent not only of the presbyteries from which the men came but also of the presbytery to which they moved. First Presbyterian Church of Pasadena, under the ministry of Dr. Ganse Little and then of Dr. Eugene Carson Blake, was hostile. Under these circumstances Dr. Wilbur Smith, Dr. Everett Harrison and later Dr. William S. LaSor and Dr. Gleason Archer, transferred to other denominations.

When I informed the Ministers and Missionary Benefit Board of the American Baptist Convention of my new work, I was cut from its retirement plan and my cumulative payments were summarily refunded. At the same time Dr. Henry Nelson Wieman, who retired from the University of Chicago Divinity School to teach at an ecumenically oriented college in Texas, retained his retirement status. Presbyterian Ministers Fund, to which I transferred, has never been hostage to such theological bias even within its own denomination.

Further petty prejudices by even mature leaders continued to harass us. Twice on Friday nights when I was scheduled to address Inter-Varsity meetings at the University of Southern California, rooms that had been prearranged in the School of Religion were locked and we had to meet in a nearby church instead. Fuller faculty were snubbed at regional meetings of the Society of Biblical Exegesis. Intimidated by the increasing number of participating Fuller scholars, it voted that while those teaching on unaccredited campuses could become dues-paying members, they were ineligible to hold office in the Society. Full acceptability rested not on personal competence but on one's institutional alignment.

No seminary faculty ever faced a student body more eager and dedicated than that group of pioneer seminarians. From the first we determined to press upon them both the intellectual demands of an effective evangelical ministry and the spiritual disciplines of an authentic witness. That the theoretical might outrun the practical or that discouragement could overtake certain students were recognized dangers. College graduates without even Sunday school input but who had met Christ in wartime foxholes now wanted to enter the ministry; young engineers and scientists totally devoid of theological exposure came as new converts. We made curriculum changes as needed. My course in The Problem of Religious Knowledge (Religious Epistemology), for example, that analyzed the diversity between D. C. Macintosh, Emil Brunner and B. B. Warfield, became a second rather than first year requisite. Difficulties, whether academic or denominational, only seemed to challenge and motivate these early students all the more. When denominations thwarted Fuller graduates from church posts, they opted gladly for service instead on distant mission fields or in small homeland parishes that soon prospered.

In addition to maintaining his weekly national broadcast, Dr. Fuller energetically probed alternative campus site possibilities; Henry Hutchins and I did so as well, but to no avail. To build a new campus required zoning approval and several years' wait from blueprint to completion. Meanwhile the Seminary faced an intensive job of public relations with community and churches. It seemed imperative to me that in the cultured context of Pasadena, evangelical Christianity be seen as an intellectually viable and vibrant faith and not as a suspect cult.

Early in 1948 I addressed the Pasadena Christian Business Men's Committee at a luncheon. Recounting the energetic efforts of Chicago's Soldier Field Easter Sunrise Committee and how, even in harsh weather, the Easter dawn service drew tens of thousands of participants, I asked why the Rose Bowl was known mainly for its New Year's Day football classic. To be sure, Chicago offered bus transport and an elevated system that eagerly cooperated, but Pasadena, I indicated, had its own special advantages.

Just before Easter, announcements appeared that Bob Pierce and Los Angeles Youth for Christ would sponsor such a service. Pierce was then a young evangelist and on rather short notice arranged such dramatic features as airplanes flying over the Rose Bowl in the form of a cross. Since no offering could be solicited on city property, the bills that accrued to Pierce for arrangements he had made independently were staggering. Years later, when we became personal friends, he told me how he had mortgaged his home for the needed funds.

C.B.M.C. subsequently asked me about the logistics for a sunrise service. The event must not be turned over to others, I stressed, but must be carried through by local lay leaders themselves. Before long we organized the Pasadena Rose Bowl Easter Sunrise Committee, on the Chicago pattern of a steering committee of 20 persons and a central committee of 100. Across the years of sunrise services that followed, speakers included, among others, evangelicals like Professor Norman C. Hunt of Edinburgh University, Dr. Elmer Engstrom of R.C.A., Lt. Gen. William K. Harrison, Dr. V. Raymond Edman,

Senator Mark Hatfield, Congressman John Anderson, Dr. Paul Rees, Dr. Charles Fuller, evangelist Merv Rosell, R. G. LeTourneau, Russell V. DeLong and Clarence Jones. Bob Pierce was invited in 1961 with special appreciation. I myself was speaker both in 1962 and 1963. Among frequent attendees in the services was Mrs. Hannah Nixon, the devout mother of Richard Nixon.

Throughout my Pasadena years I served as chairman of the committee—or as co-chairman with A. Lewis Shingler. In 1963 the City of Pasadena marked the twenty-fifth anniversary of the Rose Bowl service and expressed appreciation for community enrichment by "one of the founding professors of Fuller Seminary" who "conceived the idea of the world-famous Pasadena Rose Bowl as a setting to proclaim Christ's Resurrection from death, bringing eternal life to all mankind, thereby instituting the annual Rose Bowl Sunrise Service. . . . Dr. Henry's influence has been felt throughout the Southern California community and the world, which is better for his having been among us, as he has touched perceptively the lives of countless numbers of people, pointing always to a fuller, more meaningful and significant life."

June, 1948, took me back to the East Coast for the fourth successive summer of doctoral studies at Boston University and of teaching at Gordon College on the Boston Fenway. Initially I had hoped to study for a doctorate in philosophy at University of Chicago divinity school. But the influence there of Henry Nelson Wieman and others was then so great that candidates for a degree were expected to subscribe in advance to the scientific method as the *open sesame* to all knowledge. What largely clinched the decision to attend Boston University, instead, was a less restricting academic atmosphere. I knew that Edgar S. Brightman, prominent Methodist personalist, advanced his theory of a finite God on two fronts—on the one hand, against atheistic naturalism, and on the other, against biblical or miraculous theism, whether evangelical or neoorthodox. My studies could therefore interact with the contemporary clash of ideas, yet do so without surrendering a keen awareness of the history of philosophy.

The Boston locale renewed contacts with Edward John Carnell who, in September, 1948, would leave Gordon to teach apologetics at Fuller. It also shaped early associations with other Gordon Divinity School men like George Eldon Ladd and Roger Nicole.

Carnell and I were in some ways utterly different and in others remarkably alike. Six years younger than I and slim, he was reared in a parsonage by strict Baptist parents. My heritage was totally different. But we both were philosophy majors under Gordon Clark at Wheaton, where he was graduated in 1941 and I in 1938 and 1940.

Since we both worked our way through school we really did not know each other on campus. Although we eventually received our Boston doctorates at the same commencement exercises, we were in few classes together since I pursued doctoral work only during the summer months. But I came to respect Carnell from the very first as a gifted young scholar and in time as a cherished friend.

Carnell went from Wheaton to Westminster Theological Seminary where, under Van Til, he earned the Th.B. and Th.M. degrees in apologetics in 1944. Further work at Harvard yielded the S.T.M. in 1945. Ordained to the Baptist ministry in 1944 he pastored the Baptist Church of Marblehead, Massachusetts, from 1945–46, while also serving, until 1948, as professor of philosophy and religion at Gordon College and Gordon Divinity School. In 1948, after completing Harvard course requirements and his dissertation on "The Concept of Dialectic in the Theology of Reinhold Niebuhr" (published in 1950 as *The Theology of Reinhold Niebuhr*), he received the Th.D. His Ph.D. from Boston University after he completed a dissertation on "The Problem of Verification in Søren Kierkegaard" (published in 1965 as *The Burden of Søren Kierkegaard*) came in 1949. His extensive graduate program and exposure clearly afforded a more rigorous and sustained wrestling of contemporary theological concerns in epistemology than I had acquired in my own graduate studies.

Carnell was an indefatigable worker and a disciplined and inquiring student. Periodically we walked the Boston streets and talked philosophy. Except for odd moments of humor and banter, Carnell was almost always serious and intellectually engaged; he wrestled speculative problems as personal inner tensions and pressed for precision. We argued over the empirical proofs for God and the problem of common ground and rational probability and had many refreshing conversations about frontier issues and problems. A literate devotee of evangelical orthodoxy, he was unqualifiedly committed to scriptural authority, alert to the importance of propositional revelation, champion of a rationally consistent and coherent Christian world-life view and alive to the epistemic importance of presuppositions. For Carnell systematic theology was not a semantic game but a matter of life or death for evangelical theism. On several occasions, when expressing his distaste for Protestant liberalism as a logically deficient religious sentiment, he indicated that if he felt it necessary to depart from evangelical Protestantism he would find Catholicism more congenial than modernism, although Rome had its own vexing dilemmas.

Whereas my *The Uneasy Conscience of Modern Fundamentalism* (1947) then seemed but a tract for the times, Carnell already in 1948 produced his durable *An Introduction to Christian Apologetics* that won an Eerdmans book contest award. My *Remaking the Modern Mind* appeared about the same time as a work in philosophy of religion.

My four qualifying exams were in history of philosophy, metaphysics, history of ethics and philosophy of religion. I had successfully completed all but the one in ethics when I learned of a qualifying exam in ethics scheduled for the following week. Brightman assured me it would not jeopardize my candidacy for a degree were I to take the exam on short notice and fail; I would have three opportunities to pass, but no more. I took the plunge and made a 99, a higher grade than on my other qualifying exams, and as high a score as that of any of Brightman's former students.

Since Pasadena and Boston were on opposite ends of the nation, train travel was prohibitively time-consuming and driving too exhausting. So in the summer of 1948 I made my very first plane flight: a $99 special from Los Angeles to New York. I recall how when the lumbering old propeller plane readied for takeoff I bowed my head to the God of miracles and prayed that the regularities of nature which he also sustains would maintain their constancy. A second flight came the next summer when Carnell and I flew East together to defend our dissertations. Before continuing by train the next day to Boston we stayed in New York overnight, and at the Sloane House Y.M.C.A. to save money. But it was a terribly noisy night and neither of us got much sleep.

Among the examiners when I defended my dissertation was Dr. Albert C. Knudson, professor of Old Testament. Later when we went to lunch together, Knudson, recently widowed, observed that he was now thinking much about an afterlife. "There must be immortality," he said, "or all the values we cherish would simply come to an inexplicable end." "Dr. Knudson," I commented reassuringly, "There *is* immortality; Jesus said, 'If it were not so, *I would have told you.*' " Knudson paused for some moments and then remarked, "You know, I have never before thought of those words that way." He then invited me to his home to see his library. After introducing me to his sister, she asked, "Is Fuller Seminary connected with Dr. Charles Fuller of the Old Fashioned Revival Hour? Why, I listen to that all the time!"

On commencement day Brightman accompanied me to the ceremonies for a parting conversation. Remarking that a professor is always pleased when a student genuinely shares a teacher's convictions, but quickly perceives when students are merely parroting what they hear, he turned to me and said: "I know you don't fully hold my views, but you have done good work; I'm glad to have had you in my classes and wish you well." It was, I thought, the mark of a truly liberal spirit. Knudson, by contrast, was unwilling to view evangelical Christianity other than in terms of irrationalism, although he regarded it as perhaps preferable to neoorthodoxy.

In the 1940s when evangelical colleges and seminaries were more competitive than cooperative, many evangelical scholars were seeking a bridge to fellow scholars. Some Gordon Divinity School faculty, especially Burton Goddard, Edward Dalglish and George Ladd, accordingly promoted the idea of a convocation of evangelical scholars that would encourage conservative theological literature. A meeting was projected for December 27 and 28, 1949, in the downtown Cincinnati Y.M.C.A. after twenty-five scholars from as many campuses endorsed the proposal, among them Oswald T. Allis, Clarence Bouma, J. Oliver Buswell, Jr., Gordon H. Clark, Ralph Earle, R. Laird Harris, Harold Kuhn, Allan MacRae, Walter A. Maier, Merrill C. Tenney, Merrill F. Unger, Cornelius Van Til, Edward John Young and myself.

Wilbur Smith had accepted an invitation to give the keynote address at the dinner meeting. A month before the gathering he had to decline because of unmet writing commitments, however, and suggested the committee ask me. When the telegram of invitation arrived I surrendered Thanksgiving and much of the Christmas holidays to research a topic of my own suggestion, "Fifty Years of Protestant Theology," a critical overview of the immediate past half-century's theological drift. In Cincinnati I gave it extemporaneously to about sixty attending scholars; Dr. Cyrus H. Gordon was a special guest. Later the material was expanded in a small book; in a review of it in *Theological Studies* (September, 1951) the Jesuit apologist Gustave Weigel called it "an admirable presentation of the subject, which entailed the knowledge of an immense literature. . . . Fundamentalists were once dismissed impatiently as unscholarly and ignorant, but no one who reads this book will believe that such a charge can be legitimately hurled against all fundamentalists. Dr. Henry is certainly a shattering refutation of so easy an accusation."

As we discussed the group's future, I moved we take the name, The Evangelical Theological Society. For its doctrinal statement the Society approved: "The Bible alone, and the Bible in its entirety, is the Word of God written, and therefore inerrant in the autographs." Alexander Heidel, Burton Goddard, Julius Mantey and I were named to the editorial committee. Later in 1969–70 I became president.

On January 31, 1950, Fuller Seminary's faculty and board of trustees adopted a succinct ten-point statement of faith. Its second article affirmed that "The books which form the canon of the Old and New Testaments as originally given are plenarily inspired and free from all error in the whole and in the part. These books constitute the written Word of God, the only infallible rule of faith and practice." The ten-point statement carried the introductory reminder that "annual signing of the creed is a sacred act as well as a sacred commitment." Faculty and trustees formally affirmed the statement each year. Even a decade later records show official subscription to the creed by Harold Ockenga and Charles Fuller, trustees Edward L. Johnson, Gerritt P. Groen, H. R. Walker, Rudolph C. Logefeil, C. Weyerhauser, Dean E. Stephan, Paul Van Oss, Robert G. Taylor, Charles Pitts and Billy Graham, and faculty members Rebecca Price, Wilbur Smith, Edward Carnell, Robert Bowers, George Ladd, William LaSor, Everett Harrison, William Lantz, F. Carlton Booth, G. W. Bromiley, Clarence S. Roddy, Daniel P. Fuller, Gleason L. Archer, Jr., Harold Lindsell and Paul K. Jewett. I, too, signed the statement annually until 1956 when I left Fuller to become editor of *Christianity Today.*

In time, although annual signing continued, differences and tensions arose both in definition and interpretation of biblical and theological matters.

From the outset Fuller was projected as a faculty-centered institution. Largely because of his *in absentia* relationship, Ockenga did not customarily interfere with week to week operations. But when he came each semester for a week of lectures or theological sermons he helped negotiate policies and resolve major problems. In 1948 the Seminary enthusiastically added to its faculty Gleason Archer as professor of biblical languages and acting dean, Edward Carnell as associate professor of apologetics and Arnold Ehlert as librarian. Archer, who had served as Ockenga's assistant at Park Street Church, was a gifted linguist and, like Carnell, had Harvard credentials.

The following year Ockenga interviewed and encouraged William S. LaSor, who held a doctorate from Dropsie, and Bela Vasady, of the University of Debrecen, Hungary, to join Fuller in the Fall of 1949, LaSor as professor of Old Testament and Vasady as professor of biblical theology and ethics. Herbert S. Mekeel, on leave as pastor of First Presbyterian Church of Schenectady, came as Dean and acting professor of practical theology. LaSor stood to the left of other faculty members by his late dating of some Old Testament books, but subscribed to Fuller's doctrinal statement; two decades later Fuller colleagues would view him as too far on the right. Vasady, influenced by Barthian theology, tended to emphasize the Holy Spirit's internal confrontation and witness more than an objectively inspired and inerrant Bible. Mekeel's task as dean to operate a growing seminary with a library of 29,000 volumes in the confines of church facilities was more than frustrating. He called frequent faculty meetings to discuss moving the Seminary lock, stock and barrel to other quarters, other cities, other states. The number of trustees at that time to help wrestle such problems was small; there were Arnold Grunigen, Jr., Dr. Logefeil and H. J. Taylor. Richard Curley was business manager.

If the Rose Bowl Easter service as a community event gave thousands of people access to the gospel, no less so did the Mid-Century Rose Bowl Rally in 1950. The Pasadena-Los Angeles area was known for its civic and cultural activities, for Huntington Library in San Marino and for numerous universities and colleges, not least among them the California Institute of Technology. Late in 1949 Billy Graham launched his evangelistic crusade in Los Angeles. Church attendance at the time was low, cynicism about religion rampant and the term evangelical still shunned by ecumenical enthusiasts. Graham was then 31. The nightly tent meetings drew thousands of persons to the "canvas cathedral" where songleader Cliff Barrows, soloist George Beverly Shea, organist Lorin Whitney and associate Grady Wilson served as a support team. Cliff's wife Billie played the piano and Ruth Graham assisted in prayer and counseling sessions. Reports of the tent-meeting response so impressed news mogul William Randolph Hearst that he wired Hearst editors: "Puff Graham." No one sensed that this Los Angeles campaign was the start of a worldwide ministry. In time Graham crusades would gather cumulative live audiences of 94 million persons as well as unprecedented radio and television outreach.

Before Graham went from Los Angeles to the Pacific Northwest for a short crusade, he had agreed to a one-night appearance in the Rose Bowl sometime in June, 1950, to be organized by Fuller Seminary and known as the Mid-Century Rose Bowl Rally. As a college graduate Graham could bring to evangelism marks of dignity and respect, let alone credibility. Although a graduate school, Fuller Seminary was unapologetically committed to the importance and necessity of evangelism. The Rose Bowl seemed an excellent setting in which to combine academic and evangelistic forces.

Aided by Dick Curley, the Seminary's genial business manager, I expended almost all my time and energies for three months to preparation and promotion of the effort. When the meeting night finally came, 50,000 persons turned out to hear Graham and Ockenga, who flew in for the event. My first reaction was one of disappointment that not all 100,000 seats were filled. But the press rightly hailed the rally as the largest religious event in the history of the Pacific Southwest; the front-page news reports at one and the same time multiplied interest both in Graham and in the Seminary. Unfortunately, Ockenga who had pledged to assume a resident presidency that Fall of 1950 once again delayed his coming.

As interest widened in evangelicalism, so did interest in my writings.

Friday nights I met regularly at First Baptist Church of Hollywood with students from a dozen or more colleges and universities, lecturing and answering questions about Christianity and the Christian world-life view. Tapes of these question-answer exchanges later appeared as *Giving a Reason for Our Hope* (1949). Extensive materials for a college-age Sunday school class at Immanuel Baptist Church in Pasadena appeared as *Notes on the Doctrine of God* (1949). A followup volume to *Remaking the Modern Mind,* entitled *The Protestant Dilemma,* also appeared in 1949. At yearend 1950 Graham urged me to come the following Spring for the first series of W. B. Riley Memorial Lectures at Northwestern Schools of which Graham was president. Titled *The Drift of Western Thought,* they appeared in print in 1951, the same year my Boston doctoral dissertation was published.

I now determined to concentrate on research and technical writing that would help give formative intellectual direction to the evangelical cause. By arrangement from the beginning the founding faculty taught eight hours each semester followed by a three-month summer break, of which two months were intended for teaching and writing and the third for vacation and travel. In addition, faculty were assured a full complement of secretarial help for correspondence and for typing of manuscripts. During my first two summers at Fuller I studied in Boston and completed my doctoral dissertation. Now, once beyond the Mid-Century Rose Bowl Rally, I projected major works on Christian personal ethics, religious epistemology and Christian social ethics. Afternoons and evenings, and Saturdays as well, found me routinely at work in these subject areas.

On July 31, 1950, we bought directly from the owner a charming Dutch Colonial home on the edge of the estate section. Substantially built by a contractor during World War I, it was without doubt the most enjoyable home we have ever had. Located at 942 South Oakland Avenue, a mile from the Seminary and from the Tournament of Roses parade route, it cost us $21,000. We had long outgrown our Hudson Avenue lodgings; Carol shared her bedroom with Helga's widowed mother, Paul and I shared a bedroom, and Helga slept on a daybed in the dining room. We determined to make a move as soon as our savings permitted.

Our $4,000 down payment on July 31 included my Fuller check for the month. The unpublicized fact was that we now faced a month without funds for even staples except those that we moved from our small bungalow. Helga was at that time teaching a college-age Sunday school class at Pasadena Mission Covenant Church whose members surprised her one evening with a housewarming gift, a huge assortment of canned food. There was only one problem, however: in good humor, to which we responded with many a laugh, they had removed all the labels! To be sure, sometimes we had beans when we would have preferred corned beef or soup, but beans fit in much better with what little we then had than nothing at all.

The Oakland Avenue property had an inviting entry, large living and dining rooms, kitchen and walk-through pantry, glass-enclosed breakfast nook, downstairs bedroom and bath, three upstairs bedrooms and two baths, an upstairs study with sundeck, a yard with covered outdoor patio and enclosed garage and almost perpetually blooming roses. It offered all the incentives one could want for pleasant family living and entertaining as well as privacy for study. Helga staked claim to the basement for her private study; we named it Purgatory since whenever she entered she seemed self-condemned to remain there forever. When in 1951 she began teaching at Pasadena College, Purgatory increasingly became her hideaway. During the illness of Dr. Rebecca Price in 1952–53 she also taught Christian education at Fuller.

The Seminary's entire atmosphere encouraged and reinforced academic application. As he dictated replies to correspondence, Wilbur Smith paced his office, peered from time to time out of the windows or stared intently at the ceiling. Other times he was buried in books from his vast library. Once a week the two of us had lunch at The Clock, where we discussed things of mutual interest. "Your ideas sometimes aren't worth much," he once joshed, "but they're always big!" Carnell in his office, Archer and LaSor and Harrison in theirs, seemed to be perpetually at their typewriters or deep in drafts of manuscripts. Although each was at work on some major project, the faculty, in the absence of a resident president, was more a series of individual stars than an interrelated constellation of scholars. By the 1950–51 academic year Harold Lindsell had been named dean and professor of missions, with Charles J. Woodbridge teaching the courses in church history. Fuller graduates were already located on distant mission fields in Africa and Asia, others were in graduate schools pursuing doctorates and still others in pastorates. Some became educators; J. Robertson McQuilkin began teaching theology and Greek at Columbia Bible College where he succeeded his father as president.

The American Association of Theological Schools had indicated that it would not consider an application for accreditation by Fuller until after its first class was graduated. With this requirement now met, Lindsell's task was to coordinate the necessary data. Daniel Day Williams of Union Theological Seminary in New York came as A.A.T.S. representative for a preliminary meeting. Williams promptly asked how an academic institution that requires signing of a doctrinal statement can maintain academic freedom. Carnell asked in turn whether Union Seminary would welcome an atheist on its faculty. When Williams said that he doubted it, Carnell pointed out that both institutions drew a line, but simply drew it in different places.

I deliberately maintained links to the National Association of Evangelicals although it probed few ties to Fuller. Among my concerns was to engage evangelicals in a discussion of social and cultural problems and to help define authentic involvement. The March 1, 1951, issue of *United Evangelical Action* carried my essay on "Evangelicals and Social Action." For the ninth annual N.A.E. convention in April of the same year I arranged a special forum in Chicago on Evangelicals and labor relations, race relations, temperance activity and other issues. N.A.E. subsequently established a Commission on Social Ethics, and in 1952 I became its co-chairman. Dialogue on social concerns then became a regular feature of the annual conclaves. Unfortunately the Commission became defunct when evangelist H. H. Savage became N.A.E. president; he felt that too much interest in social ethics might erode the priority of evangelism and misdirect evangelical agencies toward the imbalances and objectionable commitments of ecumenical groups.

By the late Spring of 1951 the Seminary acquired choice land at Oakland Avenue and Ford Place near downtown Pasadena. Chapel announcement was made of groundbreaking in October for a $300,000 three-story edifice to be named the Charles E. Fuller Memorial Building. This first unit would provide space for administrative, teaching and study requirements. As funds became available additional buildings would follow for chapel, library and dormitory purposes. Already in hand, we were told, was $50,000 in gifts, but a quarter of a million dollars remained to be raised.

Much would have been gained, I suggested to Dick Curley for relay to Dr. Fuller, had Fuller made the announcement at commencement to a capacity audience in Pasadena Civic Auditorium instead of a small in-group, and coordinated it with effective releases to the secular and religious press. Thereupon Fuller asked me to give some thought and time to suggestions for a sound promotional campaign. I volunteered to make periodic suggestions about mail solicitations and public announcements if a promotional office were staffed and equipped, but wanted no part in solicitation of funds or responsibility for the success or failure of a funding effort; moreover, any time lost from research should be compensated by an adjustment of my teaching load. Alas, when Fuller made a second chapel announcement, he referred again to the new building, and stated in addition that I would be executive director of the projected development drive.

With some intensity I told the faculty that I would rather leave the Seminary than to be saddled with the development program; my primary interests and commitments like theirs were academic. Without protest I had served as academic dean during the Seminary's beginnings when the assignment was arbitrarily thrust upon me. I had sacrificed research and writing time to promote the Mid-Century Rose Bowl Rally, and had just recently invested extra time in the Rose Bowl Easter Sunrise Service because Dr. Fuller was speaker and the Seminary would be publicized on the Mutual Broadcasting System. While I was willing to offer suggestions, actually directing the development drive was a totally different matter.

Despite my protests I was soon outlining and implementing procedures. Several secretaries worked full-time in an office equipped with telephones, files, typewriters and robotypers. We announced that the cornerstone of the new Charles E. Fuller building would contain a scroll bearing the names of Old Fashioned Revival Hour contributors from all parts of the world, and we solicited other gifts large and small. I visited the office staff daily to suggest further robotyper uses, helped them solicit mailing lists and draft appeal and acknowledgment letters. I declined, however, to approach individuals personally for funds. With contributions arriving daily, $127,500, almost half the needed construction balance, had been received by the end of summer. The Seminary at that time enrolled 219 students, all of whom were eager for more appropriate facilities. But when ground was to be broken in October government permission had not yet come for allocation of scarce post-War construction materials; hope faded that the building would be ready in the Fall of 1952.

While in Minneapolis for the Spring, 1951, Northwestern Schools lectures, I had gone to Mayo Clinic for a complete physical by Dr. Carl Morlock. Clinicians analyzed my intense migraines as tension-related. They also recommended stripping of troublesome varicose veins and a program of weight reduction. I arranged for veins surgery in June, 1952, a month or so before leaving on a five-week Winona Lake School of Theology "flying seminar" to the Holy Land and Near East. On return to Rochester, Minnesota, the following year, I learned that Dr. Morlock was chairman of the deacon board at First Baptist Church. He was gratified that in a year I had lost twenty-five pounds. He scheduled my clinical interview and surgery with a veins specialist, Dr. Karl Lofgren. Dr. Lofgren and a colleague, Dr. T. T. Meyers, had perfected the technique of stripping varicose veins—that is, removing them completely, rather than merely injecting or severing and tying them. I had hoped to probe my surgeon's spiritual convictions but felt our first meeting was somewhat inappropriate, although Dr. Morlock had intimated something about Dr. Lofgren's past or present interest in The Salvation Army.

On the morning of surgery after being wheeled into the operating theatre it occurred to me spontaneously as the doctor arrived to suggest offering a prayer. The arriving physician, whom I mistook for the surgeon, was actually the anesthesiologist and was somewhat taken aback by my proposal. But at that precise moment Dr. Lofgren himself entered and greeted me by name. To remove any embarrassment I remarked that I had just suggested offering prayer. "I'm heartily in favor of it," replied Lofgren; "please lead us." What I did not realize—and what would doubtless have deterred and intimidated me—was that behind opaque windows overlooking the operating theatre, visiting medics were observing this relatively new surgical technique and listening over the sound system to the surgeon's step-by-step comments. I closed my eyes and prayed. I thanked God for the gift of life, for the gift of medicine and for the gift of Christ our Savior, and asked his wisdom for doctors and nurses in this operation. Since such a petition seemed a bit selfish, I invoked God's help that day not only for surgeons and doctors and nurses and patients at the Clinic, but anywhere and everywhere! The prayer must have taken less than a minute, even if it seemed longer to me. As a few "amen's" were added here and there, the anesthesiologist went to work.

I am unsure just how many hours later a soft tapping on my foot awakened me. Dr. Lofgren was standing by my bed in a hospital room and smiling. "That prayer you offered," he said, returning to our last shared moment of consciousness, "greatly impressed me." Through it, in fact, he and I became fast friends; on numerous occasions I met in the Lofgrens's home to speak of Christian matters with their Mayo associates. Whenever Helga and I came to Rochester we were their guests and I often spoke at First Baptist Church where they are devout and active members.

A few days after surgery I was on my feet; six weeks later I was lecturing, as scheduled, on a flight seminar to Bible lands; within six months little evidence of surgery remained. Helga meanwhile drove from Pasadena with the children and her mother, who was nursing a broken arm. They left the morning after Helga had taught eighty people in a community Teacher Training course, and met me in Rochester on discharge from the Clinic. Together we drove to Winona Lake, Indiana, for the pre-flight orientation seminar on Saturday, July 26, in Billy Sunday Tabernacle on "Jerusalem and the Modern World." The four flying seminar faculty members were Dr. Edward J. Young, Dr. Arnold Shultz, Dr. John Huffman and myself.

We left Fort Wayne airport Monday morning aboard TWA on a schedule to Paris July 28–31, Rome July 31–August 3, Cairo August 3–7, Beirut August 7–8, Jerusalem–Jordan August 10–16, Jerusalem–Israel August 17–18, Athens August 19–23, Zürich August 24, Geneva

August 25 and London August 26–30. This group of eighty-two comprised the largest tour party to date to travel as a single unit to the Near East with touchdown in a dozen or more countries within thirty-five days.

The lecturers had prearranged responsibilities. My presentations were in Paris, Rome, Athens and Geneva. I also cabled a weekly column to the *Los Angeles Mirror.* In the noisy propeller-driven planes of those days one could hardly carry on an intelligent conversation with seatmates. It was really little disturbance to anyone that I put a portable typewriter to use in flight and in airports during immigration and customs delays. By tour's end I had completed all but the concluding chapter of *Glimpses of a Sacred Land* (published in 1953); the appendix contains the address I gave on Mars Hill. A Los Angeles businessman had placed an excellent motion picture camera at my disposal, and I photographed scenes that Westminster Films later edited for church showing under the same title as the book.

On my return to Fuller in September, 1952, another Los Angeles layman, an investments advisor, came to see me. Hugh Murchison was chairman of the Union Rescue Mission, directors and active supporters of many evangelical enterprises. He had bought a small hilltop site in a remote section of Los Angeles and planned to establish a low-powered radio station, KPOL, that would beam throughout California. He was eager to line up an agenda of features and participants. Would I take a fifteen-minute spot every Sunday, he asked, or two or three times a week, or daily, even if I needed to prerecord the broadcasts (and even if I could accept only for the first month)?

After checking available time slots I chose 7–7:15 A.M. just after the headline news. Titled "Let the Chips Fall," my broadcast opened and closed with fanfare by Fred Waring and His Pennsylvanians and the moving lyric, "For this is my country, to have and to hold." Usually I began with some timely news event that raised a moral or spiritual concern or pressing national problem, focused it clearly and after an appropriate hymn or musical number addressed the issue as if in conversation with the listeners.

The program went so well (I even had to join the American Federation of Radio Artists) that a Pasadena automobile agency offered to sponsor it. A. Lewis Shingler, a partner in Uptown Chevrolet Company, often drove with me at dawn to the studio to do the agency commercial; we not only became good friends, but for many years served as co-chairmen of the Rose Bowl Sunrise Service.

Now and then I conducted a personality interview. An attractive Christian secretary in her late twenties, on vacation from duties on General MacArthur's staff, mentioned on the air that she wished she could return to Japan as a missionary. I asked why she didn't do so. "Because Uncle Sam doesn't pay air fare for that kind of work," she responded. Scarcely had we gone off the air when a listener telephoned and volunteered to pay the flight costs. Mabel Hughes returned for several years of dedicated missionary service.

Years later Murchison and his partners sold KPOL for three million dollars. He promptly took a trip around the world and along the way invested his share of the profits in mission enterprises. One day he appeared in Virginia, where I lived as editor of *Christianity Today,* and asked, since I had shared in early launching of the station, what I now needed to set the cause ahead. I really had no needs, I said. But when he saw my decrepit typewriter he insisted that we go out and buy a new one, which we did.

I continued KPOL broadcasts until the summer of 1953 when I took a semester sabbatical from Fuller to compensate for research and writing time preempted by development drive duties. Scores of Americans traveled for graduate study to New College, Edinburgh, and I decided to spend the Fall semester in Auld Reekie. Our budget was still very tight, however, given monthly house payments and the burden of accumulating a good library. We could not afford to go abroad as a family. Helga continued to teach, scheduling classes to be able to see the youngsters off to school in the morning and be on hand when they returned. Paul was then eleven and Carol turning nine; both had church and community as well as school activities. Paul's schedule included a *Star-News* paper route, membership in Boys Club band and on Saturday mornings—we astoundedly discovered many years later—weekly stops at a barber shop to sell his place in line for a nickel to successive patrons. Carol was busy with piano lessons. Helga's mother was living with us as an ever-ready help and loving presence.

The World Evangelical Fellowship had chartered a flight to Geneva for a late July weeklong conference in Clarens. One participant, it developed, had to depart early for Europe, so I bought up the one-way vacancy. My special fare ticket, it turned out, required me to spend a week in Switzerland in conference dialogue as Clarens participants discussed the possibility of producing an international symposium on the doctrines of revelation and inspiration, a project that never materialized.

On arrival in Switzerland I walked the shores of Lake Geneva talking theology with Walter Marshall Horton, whom I had written about my brief stop in Geneva en route to Clarens. (My harrowing midnight experience of reaching Clarens from Geneva is recalled in David Enlow's book, *My Most Memorable Encounter with God* [1977].)

After the week in Clarens I made my way by train from Switzerland to Frankfurt, Wiesbaden, Bonn, Cologne and Amsterdam, stopping for a night in each city. In Wiesbaden I passed a shop where a magnificent old Rosenthal dinner service caught my eye. I bought it for a song, and stayed with the manager long enough to pack it securely in several boxes for sea freight. I hoped to surprise Helga, amid her burdens at home, by a periodic parcel. From Amsterdam I posted a *tafelkleed* that still drapes beautifully across our baby grand piano.

My stop in London was memorable in a way I would just as soon forget. In early afternoon I sauntered through Hyde Park, where scores of crusaders daily mount their soapboxes in behest of a hundred and one causes. Billy Graham had been there some weeks earlier when, accompanied by media coverage, he drew thousands of observers. But I was less known than even the unknown God of the Athenians. I listened momentarily here and there to some thumping radical or partisan until I happened on a father and son team who from a stepladder took turns exhorting listeners to put their hearts right with God. I commended them. "Do you have a word for your Lord?" asked the father. Introduced as "an American visitor" I somewhat reluctantly mounted the ladder to give my testimony about God's forgiving my sins and saving me. "Right now," I continued, "if you will repent and receive Christ as Savior, God will forgive your sins, too, and give you new life." At that a chorus of contraries erupted. "What God?" "What sins?" "What Christ?" "What life?" In mockery one man threw himself on the ground at the base of the ladder and mimicked, "God be merciful to me a sinner." I disengaged myself from my lofty perch as discreetly as possible and listened to the father and son a bit longer until I could saunter away unobserved. I paid no attention to two men walking nearby until I overheard one of them remark, "That blooming American didn't have very much to say, did he?" Graham's calling and mine, I mused, are very different, and I was willing to leave it that way.

I moved toward Scotland sensing how little I really knew of that nation's long history that stretched from the ancient Celts and Roman invasions through centuries of social and political tug of war to times of peerless contribution to religion, medicine, literature, education, music, art and much else. Almost everywhere in Edinburgh the past seemed to thrust itself impressively into the present.

I still remember my first view of Princess Street, and towering above it Edinburgh Castle. Nearby on the Mound stand Free Church College and New College, symbols of the division that befell Scottish Presbyterianism. Free Church College, committed to evangelical orthodoxy, was dwarfed by ecumenically oriented New College which, although a few conservative scholars survived, increasingly embraced a pluralistic theology as it sought to reflect newer trends. In ever increasing numbers New College was attracting Americans and some students from the Continent also for graduate study. Americans were easily identifiable by their pastel suits, flashy ties and by what some Scottish students called "their dazzling wives." By the end of the '50s Americans outnumbered Scots on campus by almost two to one, although the school was being criticized by Americans for whom cognitive concerns seemed less important than practical preparation for ministry.

I knew by reputation and made it a point to meet and stay in touch with the Free Church scholars R. A. Finlayson, the systematic theologian, and A. M. Renwick, church historian, who had reviewed my books favorably in Scottish journals. In nearby New College I sought out H. S. J. Burleigh ("Jake" some called him), the church historian and probably the most conservative faculty member. Among New College faculty at that time were Principal John Baillie, a liberal who was intellectually the most able theologian on campus, and Thomas F. Torrance whom students openly applauded for his resounding attacks on Protestant modernism. Torrance came from a prominent evangelical family but had been heavily influenced during studies with Karl Barth. At Edinburgh University he had been active in the Christian Union which in time divided over rival views of the Bible represented by evangelical orthodoxy and by a dialectical Barthian alternative preferred by Torrance. But whenever Torrance in the classroom attacked rationalistic Protestant modernism—which Barth in 1925 had already declared "dead" in Germany—students thumped their feet in approval. The New Testament professor was James Stewart, a devout and gifted preacher with an irenic and rather eclectic approach to Scripture. A more critically biased approach was evident in Old Testament courses offered by Norman W. Porteous and Oliver (Olly) Rankin, whose specialty was Wisdom Literature.

New College provided access to massive library holdings in a setting where I was free to audit whatever classes I preferred and pursue research as I wished. I regularly heard lectures by Baillie, Torrance and Stewart, and occasionally those by others. For the most part I focused my reading and research on the questions of revelation, religious epistemology and the doctrine of God.

Professors either walked to campus or came by bicycle or train. They wore clerical gray and ecclesiastical collars, and donned gowns for lectures. Classes were announced by the hammering of a huge brass gong that was mounted on a frame in the hallway and that reverberated loudly enough to raise the dead. The classrooms were dark and cold, the library even colder; by tradition the furnace malfunctioned for several weeks each winter. One of the Old Testament professors—I forget which—waited ten minutes for tardy students to arrive, then locked the classroom door. Professors or lecturers opened class with prayer and closed with a benediction; the Hebrew class opened with the Lord's Prayer in Hebrew.

American students were virtually the only ones bold or brash enough to raise questions during lectures. The only lecture I remember interrupting was one when Torrance, in answer to a young Scot's question about biblical authority, seemed to give a misleading reply.

At noon time faculty customarily sat at the ends of dining room tables and during the course of the meal discussed apparent lecture obscurities. Campus food was a common complaint, although thanksgiving was sung at the end of each meal. I seldom ate on campus, but did so one day to chat with Torrance after he had reiterated in class that God's self-revelation is self-accrediting and that no rational tests are applicable to it; in other words, to raise questions means that one has not really heard God since he is known only in obedient response. I asked Torrance how he would reply to a Buddhist or to some other metaphysician who made similar claims for a rival god. He said not a word. We shook hands and that concluded the only "conversation" I had with Torrance during my three-month stay in Edinburgh. I visited in Professor Stewart's home and dialogued with many professors, but not with Torrance.

The annual meeting of Free Church ministers was scheduled in Glasgow and Professor Finlayson, then nearing retirement, was moderator. He invited me as featured lecturer for an appraisal of contemporary theological trends. We traveled by train from Edinburgh to Glasgow, talking much of the way first about the Barthian erosion of scriptural authority in the Church of Scotland and then of Carl McIntire's recent visit and polemical effort to capture Free Church pastors for the International Council of Christian Churches. About 200 ministers arrived in Glasgow, and soon settled down for the program. Finlayson rattled off a list of my credentials and then absent-mindedly presented me as "Doctor Carl McIntire." The clergy erupted into uncontrollable laughter. When Finlayson realized his error, he pounded the gavel and then, after apologizing for the mistake, proceeded in all seriousness to introduce me as "Doctor Karl Barth."

I had one other case of mistaken identity. I had preached in Edinburgh at Charlotte Chapel, the great Baptist Church where Graham Scroggie had long pastored so effectively that even New College could not forego conferring an honorary doctorate on him. In time word got around that I might be available for preaching. One day I had a phone message from the chairman of the pulpit committee of Murchison Railway Mission confirming my coming on a certain Sunday night. The church, originally organized as a witness to rail employees living or overnighting in Edinburgh, was without a minister. Due to a mixup in directions, I arrived just as the service got underway. After the opening hymns and offering, the presiding elder announced "how delighted we all are to have with us tonight Dr. Charles E. Fuller of the Old Fashioned Revival Hour" and then, just before the message, to evidence the congregation's appreciation of the broadcasts heard weekly on "the wireless," asked that everyone sing "Heavenly Sunshine," a hallmark of Fuller's program. I knew at once that a colossal misunderstanding was underway. About seventy people were present—a rather large Sunday night attendance for a Church of Scotland parish—and none of whom presumably had ever seen or would ever see Charles Fuller. To have corrected the mistaken identity at this stage would have ruined the service. I prayed for special unction. Some of the worshipers may have thought that the wireless somewhat distorted my normal voice but many, I suspect, until this day think that they heard the great radio evangelist, and that he was not nearly as impressive at close range as at a distance.

For my first weeks in Edinburgh I had comfortable lodgings more than a mile from the campus at the Christian Guest House run by two women at 13 Mayfield Gardens. They served a typical hearty Scottish breakfast and always a "high tea" of scones and other snacks if one made it back to the hostel by late afternoon. Already the mid-September weather was penetratingly damp and cold. For "tuppence" I could take the tram to Princess Street. But in fair weather the brisk walk was a body-builder and I could browse along the way at antique or used book stores. To be nearer the College I then moved in with fellow Americans who had an apartment across the Meadows with a spare bedroom. For relaxation I went Friday or Saturday nights to the Gilbert and Sullivan and other stage presentations at nearby King's Theatre, where gallery seats cost two shillings sixpence, or 30 U.S. cents.

I wrote Helga twice weekly and heard from her as often. I mailed home parcels of used books although I had unfortunately arrived just too late to acquire G. T. Thomson's library which his widow had sold to Thin's for two shillings a volume. To whet Helga's appetite for some future trip to Scotland I also posted fabrics and some attractive used silver plate serving dishes and decorative brass pieces. Helga was not only teaching despite a pesky eye affliction but addressing teachers' conventions and providing Christian education direction at the Pasadena Mission Covenant Church. She was approached about writing the story of the Union Rescue Mission in Los Angeles, a book that subsequently appeared under the title *Mission on Main Street* (1955). Saturday afternoons she and the children spent at Brookside Park with other faculty families, including Bernard and Alta Ramm, Ed and Shirley Carnell and Everett and Arlene Harrison.

The big news that came from Pasadena was the dedication on September 22, 1953, of the Seminary's new building with superb lecture facilities at 135 North Oakland Avenue. Both Dr. Fuller and Dr. Ockenga spoke at the dedication. At about the same time "Highgate," as we called the Cravens estate after earlier disposal of the lower part of the property, was sold for more than $100,000.

Carnell wrote me he was disturbed by what he considered a "lukewarm reception" of his *A Philosophy of the Christian Religion* (1952). "After pouring the fruit of my philosophic labors into it, it has received little or no acclaim; at least not a measure of what I thought it was deserving in the light of the effort expended." He added: "There is a parochialism in evangelicalism from which I must withdraw. I trust that the fruit of this withdrawal will be a richness and breadth of comprehension that will serve as a new point of rallying for the evangelicals. . . . I want to command the attention of Tillich and Bennett; then I shall be in a better place to be of service to the evangelicals. We need prestige desperately."

Meanwhile a few of us in Scotland had two interesting contacts with Tillich. The first was in Aberdeen, where Tillich was giving as Gifford Lectures material later contained in the second volume of his *Systematic Theology* (1957); the other was when Tillich soon thereafter came to New College for a lecture.

Five of us Americans had set out from Edinburgh for Aberdeen in Dave Wallace's car. An Aberdonian, a Christian who worked in the city clerk's office, had invited us to spend a night at his home, and assured us that he and his mother had ample room. The drive through the heather-covered mountains was memorable but the main reason for our trip was to visit the divinity school of the University of Aberdeen. The mayor of Aberdeen welcomed us at high tea. Since at that time only seventeen students were enrolled in King's College, the arrival of us five was described as "the American invasion."

Aberdeen and its historic university are charming. But the frigid weather is another matter. I had been told that London was on a weather line with New York, Cambridge with Boston and Edinburgh with Toronto; that classed Aberdeen, I suspected, either with Nova Scotia or with Alaska. At any rate, when that night we retired I was chilled to the bone long before I reached the blankets. We were each given a heated towel-wrapped brick to tuck into our beds.

But earlier that evening we enjoyed a memorable dinner at Aberdeen's leading hotel. Learning incidentally that Tillich had come to town for the "Giffords" I wondered if perchance he was registered there, and indeed he was. Since only a slim audience had heard him on opening night, I wondered whether he might be available for dinner and phoned his room. Before long we were dining together and enjoying stimulating conversation. I asked Tillich about the lingering influence of Kant's philosophy on his outlook, especially the emphasis that we can make no objectively valid predications about God. Tillich, whose theology stresses existential analysis and ontological solutions, replied he was unaware of any debt to Kant. At that time virtually no one in Aberdeen seemed much interested in existentialism. Tillich's opening night attendance of twenty-five persons grew modestly from night to night, but Aberdonian intellectuals were not inclined to embrace his philosophy.

Some time later Tillich came to New College for an evening presentation, followed by a discussion, on "The Theological Problem in the Light of Existential Analysis." While attendance was higher than in Aberdeen, it was not large. The question period was almost disrupted—half the audience responding mirthfully and the other half in shock—when after a specially abstruse response an American visitor asked Tillich what he would say if a deathbed patient unexpectedly asked him how to be saved. I shall leave the story there.

In late October and early November the cold weather intensified, penetrating the high-ceilinged buildings. After an hour's reading in New College library my hands sometimes turned blue. During lunch hour the librarian graciously invited me to use an extra desk in his office which had a small heater. Sometimes I would study in the public library as an alternative. By mid-November, just two short weeks before returning to California, I invested in a heavy Harris tweed overcoat that I donned as often for inside New College library as for outside. But I had completed an immense amount of reading in areas of special interest, reflected on implications of the divergent positions held by modern authors, organized much of the material for ready access and was ready to return to students and research at Fuller's new facilities whose realization I had helped promote.

The return to California and to campus was exhilarating. Classes thrived in the new center and Fuller enrollment continued to climb. Carnell had grown extremely aloof to outside invitations, burrowed ever more deeply into Kierkegaard's writings, and felt that a program of lonely isolation would best ensure his highest contribution to Christian scholarship. Everett Harrison had more than 100 in his Life of Christ course. Students were pressing for additional reading courses and for more specialized study. Alongside my required course on Doctrine of God, I offered a seminar on the divine attributes, focusing first on divine love and righteousness. I preferred morning to late afternoon seminars, but the schedule was already preempted from 7 A.M. onward. So I inaugurated Fuller's first class at dawn, with ten students meeting at 6:10 A.M. Early one morning Pasadena police saw a chap with a heavy briefcase running along the street and decided to check things out. Pulling the cruiser curbside, the driver asked: "What's in that case?" "Books on God's love," came the reply. "Stop the kidding," said the driver; "let's have a look." When the student explained he was rushing to a six o'clock class on the nature of God, the police apologized.

After seven years as nonresident president, Ockenga in 1954 said that he definitely intended to move to Pasadena in the Fall. When he shared the momentous news, he and the faculty were dinner guests in our home, and Helga and I honored the occasion by asking him to write his name and the date on the underside of his chair. When he laughed this off, I myself inscribed the words: DR. OCKENGA'S ANNOUNCEMENT CHAIR, words that remain to this day. The *Pasadena Star-News* carried a banner headline in its second section announcing Ockenga's prospective coming.

Ockenga told me that Charles Fuller had offered to underwrite him, once he came, for six months or a year on television, and that if the program won its way Ockenga could continue the telecasts in the name of the Seminary; Fuller himself would continue the Old Fashioned Revival Hour on radio. An outstanding preacher, Ockenga's messages had doctrinal and apologetic power; I felt he could in time emerge as the Fulton Sheen of American Protestantism.

When Ockenga returned East to his family and to Park Street Church, he once again faced misgivings about moving to California, although Fuller faculty were unaware of this. When he returned for the Fall convocation further confirmation of his resident presidency was expected. The morning of convocation day Ockenga called me into his Seminary office to join him and Dr. Fuller. He would not be coming West after all, he said. It was imperative therefore that the Seminary announce someone else as a permanent resident president. He and Fuller were thinking of naming Dr. Carnell and wondered what I thought.

I was astonished, of course, at both items of information, and indicated why I thought Carnell should not be named president. First of all, Fuller would lose an astute scholar and writer and a popular teacher to administrative work in which he had no experience whatever, not to mention promotion and fund raising. Such experience, it seemed to me, was indispensable at this stage of the Seminary's existence.

And to select a president from within the faculty rather than from outside, I thought, could raise any number of problems.

Ockenga asked what alternatives I might propose from inside or outside the faculty. Inside, I noted, Charles Woodbridge (who was then at his prime) brought a heritage from Europe as well as America, had studied under both Harnack and Machen and knew the theological struggle long range, had pastored a large congregation, was widely known to many conference audiences and had numerous business and professional contacts that could be serviceable. I obviously had not reflected on the matter, I added, since I had expected Ockenga to come. But the best alternative option, it seemed to me, would be to turn outside, perhaps to Dr. Frank Gaebelein of The Stony Brook School, a respected educator and administrator. Ockenga then turned to me and said, "Well, we have decided to name Ed Carnell. I know that you two have been good friends for many years and that you will support him." What was there to say? A decision had already been reached on an issue presented to me as still open.

Fuller Seminary was by agreement at its founding to be a faculty-centered school, with full faculty involvement in relevant decisions. At the public convocation that night, Ockenga announced the appointment of Carnell as Fuller's first full-time resident president, and that he, Ockenga, would continue as chairman of the Board. Like me, Wilbur Smith had been preinformed. But Everett Harrison, although a member of the founding faculty, did not even know such a move was in prospect until he heard the announcement that night. All of us congratulated Carnell, of course, and wished him well.

The next morning Carnell came to my office. He said he knew that I had some reservations about his appointment but hoped he could count on my good will and friendship. I assured him that he could. He then brought up the matter of promotion and newspaper contacts. If he placed at my disposal a full-time secretary for whatever services I wished, would I then add promotional duties to my commitment? I indicated in good spirit that there were several reasons for not doing this and that I must decline. For one thing, adequate secretarial services, including typing of manuscripts, were already guaranteed to faculty when the Seminary was launched; for another, any discrimination in faculty availability of such services would raise problems with colleagues. More than that, I was eager to complete my volume on *Christian Personal Ethics,* and beyond that a work on Christian social ethics. As he himself had been, I was increasingly reluctant to take on further nonacademic commitments.

I was happy in my Fuller associations and relationships. Helga was involved in extended teaching commitments and the entire family was fully engaged in gratifying pursuits and interests. I carried forward research and writing on the margin of rewarding classroom opportunities. In the nature of the case Carnell was now often on the road, and we did not have as much time for cognitive discussion as in the past. The faculty as a whole had lost a certain amount of social cohesiveness and attempts at monthly get-togethers enjoyed only partial success. Everyone was engaged on personal projects and the original vision of a corporate literary impact faltered.

Early in the summer of 1955, after Carnell's first year as president, two inquiries came my way about enlarged evangelical literary output. One involved what became the *Contemporary Evangelical Thought* series of symposium volumes, the first of which appeared in 1957 under that specific title. Others continued to appear sporadically until the seventh and last volume in 1978, *Horizons of Science.* Lester Doniger whose Evangelical Book Club then had 20,000 members, stopped at my office one day and asked what kind of volume I thought might be serviceable to the evangelical constituency. Evangelicals needed something like Kepler's *Contemporary Liberal Thought,* I said, all the more since liberals exuded the impression that reason is preempted by liberal theology and that evangelicals are noncognitive. Reaching into his pocket, he handed me a signed contract, and told me to proceed. That was the beginning of *Contemporary Evangelical Thought.*

The other development was lively discussion of a new evangelical magazine that ultimately emerged as *Christianity Today.* My name had been mentioned as a possible editor, all the more after Wilbur Smith disavowed interest. But on June 5, 1955, Billy Graham wrote a letter to Nelson Bell posing three problems and shared a copy of it with Wilbur Smith, J. Howard Pew and me. Graham paid me tribute and thought the problems could be resolved. "I do not know any man in evangelical circles with whom I could agree theologically more than with Carl Henry. I do not believe that we could find a more dedicated, yielded, Spirit-filled, gracious man of God than Carl. I have profound respect for him. He has a great love for evangelism. . . ." Graham's threefold reservation, however, was equally clear: (1) Would I understand that the new magazine's prime objective would be not to reach or please American fundamentalists but to lead confused and bewildered liberals to accept the authority of Scripture? (2) Was I "too well known as a fundamentalist," thus inviting counterattack in those terms? Should the editor's name be concealed for a year or two or, in order to reach certain people, would I be willing temporarily to use an assumed name as did C. S. Lewis and J. B. Phillips? (3) Was I so intellectual that I "cannot be simple"? The magazine was not projected for seminary professors or university intellectuals, he stressed, but for the *Christian Century* readership. Graham nonetheless developed the possibility of my serving as editor-in-chief, along with Nelson Bell and Marcellus Kik as assistant editors.

I wrote Graham on June 20, acknowledging his letter with appreciation and noting that our paths had not crossed since the Mid-Century Rose Bowl Rally. Although Harold Lindsell was apparently endorsing my name, I said, I did not consider myself an applicant for the job. Dr. Bell had recently called on me at the Seminary and I had indicated to him three considerations that might well rule out my name: (1) I was convinced that an authoritative Scripture is the watershed of theological controversy. (2) I was convinced that Liberalism and Evangelicalism do not have equal right and dignity in the true Church. (3) I was convinced that American capitalism is not beyond Christian criticism. My reply to Graham added some impressions about the preconditions of a successful magazine, including some cautions—that it must not be an N.A.E. or even Billy Graham house organ, nor should it be committed to saying only bad things about the nonevangelicals it aims to win. I would be glad to meet with Graham, I wrote, to offer observations that might be helpful, but "I wish to assure you that I have no ambition to 'candidate' and urge you to turn elsewhere if God allows it."

On August 18 I wrote Graham that I had wrestled into the night recent proposals that the new magazine "introduce a sturdy theology only by degrees." I had grave doubts, I said, whether under such circumstances I should step out of my existing theological opportunities at Fuller. An irenic approach and effective strategy, I said, need not be pursued at the expense of theological lucidity. The magazine should be prepared to harvest as quickly as three months after seedtime. "The truth is still the indispensable factor in Christian apologetics; truth without love will usually be ignored," I wrote, "but love without the truth is not even real love."

Graham asked me to fly to North Carolina and to visit with him about the prospective magazine and other evangelical concerns. The ecumenical tide was running higher than ever; sentiment favoring a united Protestant church had climbed from 40 percent to 50 percent between 1940 and 1955, and 38 percent of the clergy thought the Bible contained legends and myths. Among subjects we discussed was the need for a great Christian university which Graham conceded to be "a *must*"; the new magazine could nurture interest in it, he thought. In answer to a specific question he assured me that I would have liberty to voice constructive criticism even of Graham crusades. A Labor Day meeting was being projected in New York City to discuss the whole venture.

Before the New York meeting Graham wrote a further letter. He thought the editors should not be on the Board of Trustees but that Nelson Bell "is in a slightly different category" because "so much of this magazine has been his vision and work until now and due to the fact that his ultimate responsibility will most likely be on the Board of Trustees." He was supporting Bell to be secretary of the Board, he added, because Bell could "become a liaison between the Board and its editors."

9

Christianity Today: The First Year

When I was asked early in 1955 if I might be interested in editing a new evangelical magazine that would give the liberally oriented *Christian Century* a run for its biases, I was reminded of a Spring day in 1938. Wheaton's dean of students, Dr. Wallace Emerson, asked three of us Seniors at dinner what we individually considered Christianity's biggest need. Sam Moffett, who mentioned Christianity's reinforcement in Asia, became a lifelong missionary to South Korea and author of a major work on the history of Asian Christianity. Dayton Roberts spoke of evangelical penetration in Latin America; he married Grace Strachan, daughter of the founder of Latin America Mission and gave lifetime missionary leadership in Costa Rica. I mentioned evangelical Christianity's need of a counterpart to *Christian Century,* although neither the vision nor the resources for such a venture was then in view.

That same year in China, medical missionary Dr. L. Nelson Bell, later Billy Graham's father-in-law, became increasingly troubled by the spiritual and theological deterioration of American Presbyterianism. Born in 1894, Bell had graduated from Medical College of Virginia and after graduate studies in surgery, became from 1916–1941 chief surgeon of the largest Presbyterian Hospital in China, Tsingkiangpu General. In June, 1935, he became indignant over the continuing ecumenical promotion of *Rethinking Missions* that demeaned Christian medical work in China as evangelistically coercive. In the booklet *Unscientific Thinking,* printed in China, Bell replied that *Rethinking*

Missions denied "the unique position of the Christian religion . . . that Christ is the one and only Saviour." Subsequently he was stirred by Dr. J. Gresham Machen's lectures on the widening drift from biblical orthodoxy. On return to Asheville, North Carolina, in October, 1941, he was on the surgical staff of all four local hospitals. He conversed and corresponded with leaders about the need for a conservative magazine in the Presbyterian Church in the United States. Those contacts rallied a board of directors that established the *Southern Presbyterian Journal* which promoted evangelical theology and delayed for decades a union of Southern and Northern Presbyterians.

On Christmas Day, 1954, Billy Graham, who had married Ruth Bell in 1943, visited in the Bell home and the men spoke of the need for an evangelical magazine rivaling the *Christian Century.* Within an hour they were charting its possibilities. With secretarial and travel funds from the Billy Graham Evangelistic Foundation Bell made contact with evangelical leaders—"almost a thousand—most of whom responded"—and promoted the idea. Among these was the Sun Oil magnate J. Howard Pew, who seemed generally but not specifically interested.

Graham said later that his vision for the new magazine—even the budget—came to him one night, about two in the morning. Soon thereafter he discussed it with Wilbur Smith at Fuller Seminary. Approached about the editorship, Smith was at first interested.

Later in 1955, convinced that the project was feasible, Graham and Bell went to Philadelphia and talked further with Pew. Contending that the venture was needed only if it "gets preachers back to preaching the Bible," Pew volunteered $150,000 a year for two years.

When Wilbur Smith had meanwhile decided against accepting the editorship, Graham talked about the need for an editor with Paul S. Rees, Harold Ockenga and others. Some suggested prospects were devout and gifted, but lacked either evangelical clarity, academic qualification or editorial experience. Along with numerous others I was asked, and consented, to serve as one of many contributing editors. If the venture is not theologically compromised, I noted, "it could be a tremendous boon for the evangelical cause. The fact that it aims to be (a) transcontinental, (b) interdenominational, (c) theologically affirmative, (d) socially aggressive and (e) irenic, is, humanly speaking, the needed note for the hour." Wilbur Smith meanwhile volunteered to me that he thought I had the training and the gifts to "make it go."

Apparently prodded by Nelson Bell or Billy Graham, Harold Lindsell asked about my possible interest in the "associate editorship." I replied that the project was still imaginary. "As of now, I have a call to a teaching ministry . . . which can hardly be contrasted with a hypothetical and problematical option. . . . An associate editorship could not be a spiritual option apart from a specifically designated coworker with whom one would share the labors of an effort." I added a specific comment about magazine content: its editorials, I said, "must be more virile and no less competent than those of the *Christian Century* or the journal will be mediocre."

By February, 1955, Dr. Bell was corresponding as "acting executive editor" about the direction and content of the projected magazine and shared a preliminary nine-page policy statement. The Rev. J. Marcellus Kik, minister of the Second Reformed Church in Little Falls, New Jersey, offered a five-page single-spaced proposal with many worthy suggestions. He urged that articles be of a seminary rather than Bible school level and stressed the need of both doctrinal and practical content.

I first met Bell, to whom Lindsell had relayed my comments, and met J. Howard Pew also, when they visited Fuller Seminary that month. We chatted briefly about both the theological and the politico-economic drift among many church leaders. Loosed from biblical verities, I remarked, even capitalism could become monstrous. Mr. Pew commented that if it did so, it would no longer be capitalism but would have collectivist features.

For its Chicago convention the National Association of Evangelicals scheduled me to speak on "Christianity and the Economic Crisis." Upon inquiry I gave *Christian Century* permission to print the remarks. But once my name became linked to a new evangelical magazine the *Century* opted out. The address then appeared in *Vital Speeches* for May 15, 1955, in *United Evangelical Action* for May 1 and 15, 1955, in *Facts Forum News* for January, 1956, and then also in *Christian Economics.* Nelson Bell wrote that it was "a *masterpiece*" that had done "the entire evangelical cause a real service."

Billy Graham, while conducting a crusade in Scotland, sent a letter on April 13, 1955, to Mr. Pew telling of conversions during his crusade, of the Scottish clergy's widespread disenchantment with liberal theology, and of renewed interest in biblical theology. He stressed the need of an intellectually competent evangelical magazine. He sent copies of his letter to Dr. Bell, Paul Rees, Harold Ockenga, Maxey Jarman, Howard Butt, Jerry Beavan, Walter Bennett, George Wilson and me. Graham proposed that a board of directors be organized for the new magazine. Although initially he said that he ought not himself to serve on the Board, Graham now felt he should be a part of "a silent non-published group of men who actually control the paper" and be chairman, at least temporarily. Of those who received the letter Wilson,

Bennett, Beavan and Bell were B.G.E.A.-related, Wilson being treasurer. Pew, Jarman and Butt were potential donors who already enthusiastically supported Graham's evangelistic crusades. Jarman was president of General Shoe Corporation, the world's second largest shoe manufacturer, and a leading Southern Baptist layman. Butt was vice-president of one of the South's largest supermarket chains, H. E. B. Stores. Both men had voiced interest in supporting the new effort. Beavan was the Graham organization's gifted campaign organizer and public relations man. Bennett, a Lutheran layman, directed advertising aspects of Graham's ministry.

The same letter proposed Bell, Ockenga and Rees, with Bell as chairman, as editorial and policy committee. The name *Christianity Today,* which for months topped Bell's letterhead, was now being urged as a permanent title. Publication, Graham thought, could perhaps begin in February or March, 1956, three or four months after his return to the States.

Early in July I received a letter from Graham, then in Europe, pursuing my possible interest as editor. I wrote that if he was still of the same mind when he returned, I would gladly discuss the matter. Meanwhile religious circles buzzed with rumor. Some denominationally related clergy, knowing that Fuller now rivaled denominational seminaries, voiced fears that the magazine might become too theologically aggressive and ecumenically disruptive; my association with it, some said, would mark the magazine as antidenominational since I had gone from Northern Baptist Seminary to an interdenominational campus. Others noted that some whose views were doctrinally gray were being urged as contributing editors. From the evangelical far right came still other complaints.

On August 18 I wrote Graham and Bell that unless the magazine from the outset combined an irenic spirit with theological integrity I could not justify stepping out of my theological responsibilities at Fuller. Later that month we met for exploratory conversations in North Carolina. Among other things we discussed relationships between the magazine and Wheaton College and Fuller Seminary, and decided to accept articles on the basis of merit and not of sentiment, and underscored the fact that during the magazine's first years the prestige and denominational standing of writers was especially important.

Present at the Labor Day meeting at the Hotel Statler in New York on September 5 were Beavan, Bell, Bennett, Butt, Jarman, Ockenga, Pew, Rees and also Wilson (whom Graham proposed for the Board). Also on hand were John Bolten, head of Bolta (plastics) Corporation and member of Ockenga's church; Dr. Cary N. Weisiger III, minister of Mt. Lebanon United Presbyterian Church near Pittsburgh;

Marcellus Kik and I. From the beginning it had been clear that the hour of opportunity had struck for a new evangelical magazine. Now the main concern was to fuse talent, resources and message.

After a short devotional by Dr. Rees, all of us prayed for divine guidance, blessing and help. An initial Board was then constituted comprised of Beavan, Bell, Bennett, Bolten, Butt, Jarman, Ockenga, Pew, Rees and Weisiger, with provision for additional members by majority vote. Henry, Kik and Bell were asked if they were available if funds were pledged for an initial year of experimental publication to begin sometime in 1956. Within a short time the Board elected an editorial staff comprised of me as editor, Kik as associate editor and Bell as executive editor. The Board voted that, beginning September 1, Henry and Kik were to receive $200 a month plus necessary secretarial help, and Bell $500 a month (since his participation would require a cutback of his medical practice), to compensate for time devoted to the magazine prior to our full-time engagement.

Ockenga was elected chairman of the Board, Rees vice-chairman and Bell secretary-treasurer. Bell was the only editor named to the executive committee (Ockenga, chairman; Bolten, Pew, Rees and Bell, secretary) and likewise to the editorial committee (Ockenga, chairman; Weisiger, Rees, Bell). Named to the business and finance committee were Pew, chairman; Jarman, Butt, Bolten, Bennett and Beaven, secretary. Pew offered to make $25,000 available immediately if the finance committee could match it before April 1.

October 1, 1956, was projected as a tentative date for the first issue, with a publications office to be opened about April 1, 1956. The name *Christianity Today* was approved. A small Machen magazine of about 2500 readers had borne that name some years earlier, but it was now defunct. The corporate name "Today's Publications, Publishers of Christianity Today" was approved with the same officers as for the Board of *Christianity Today.* The officers and editors were requested to decide location of the publication office. A budget of $11,400 was approved for the four remaining months of 1955 to cover salaries, secretarial services, postage and supplies, telephone, travel and miscellaneous. Board members were asked to prepare a list of outstanding clergymen supportive of the proposed magazine's objectives from whom a strong core of contributing editors might be named. The goal was precise: to articulate historic Christianity and its contemporary relevance primarily for the clergy and incidentally also for thoughtful lay leaders. The initial objective would be to reach 200,000 clergy in America and the English-speaking world.

When I began my final year at Fuller, I learned that Wilbur Smith was greatly disturbed about Marcellus Kik's *Revelation Twenty,* a book that aggressively promoted postmillenialism. Smith feared it might adversely stamp the magazine. He wanted nothing to do, he said, with a publication that encouraged the illusion that the world is progressing toward the millenium despite "two world wars, with the threat of atomic and hydrogen bombs hanging over us, and the powerful government of Russia . . . telling one-third of the population of the earth that God does not exist." A graduate of Hope College, Kik had attended Princeton Seminary for two years, and then graduated from Westminster Theological Seminary. A minister of the Reformed Church in America, he stood firmly for the unbroken inspiration and authority of Scripture, and was a champion of J. Gresham Machen and Oswald T. Allis. For thirteen years he had produced a small conservative magazine in the Canadian Presbyterian Church. The suggestions he had written to Dr. Bell included recommendations for such features as a master sermon series and a Text of the Month to alternate with a Bible Book of the Month essay. In addition to theoretical material he insisted on having practical helps as well. Both Bell and Ockenga had earlier agreed that he should be a member of the editorial staff. From the outset the editors agreed that the magazine should concentrate on major concerns and should reflect differences only subordinately. Wilbur Smith concurred and became identified as a contributing editor; from the very first issue he gave the magazine his solid support.

In mid-October Nelson Bell found some very desirable office space in Washington a block and a half from the White House. After Marcellus and I met him in Washington on November 9 to look at the floor plan, Nelson proceeded to Philadelphia where the next day the executive committee (Ockenga, Pew, Bolten and Bell; Rees absent) voted to locate *Christianity Today* on the tenth floor (1014–1021) of the Washington Building at the "World Corner" of New York and Pennsylvania Avenues under a five-year lease at $900 a month. The 3,147 square feet of space would be partitioned as the editors desired for occupancy February 1, when Marcellus would move to the Washington area.

Nelson, Marcellus and I each claimed one of the offices overlooking the Treasury Building and the White House. The Treasury Building was for me a daily reminder that I had once been offered a civil service job there as junior typist. The White House, just beyond, reminded us of Christianity's relevance for all facets of life, politics included, and also of the importance of church-state separation.

A sense of unity and candor, of camaraderie and mutual affection, sprang up between Nelson, Marcellus and me as we joined forces in this venture. We prayed for each other and for wisdom in planning and projection. We agreed to reach our decisions as fully as possible as a team, although I was to head the editorial staff and to bear final authority.

We were of very different backgrounds, gifts and temperaments. Nelson was a surgeon, albeit a devout layman and Southern gentleman. Like many gifted Christians, he was into more activities than any mortal could comfortably live with; despite early warning coronary attacks, he was determined to die "with his boots on." Whenever he came to Washington—at first three days every other week and finally two or three days every third week—he updated us on Billy Graham's crusades and on Southern Presbyterian developments. He came to the office early, and he worked late.

Marcellus drew up an impressive statement of magazine objectives. The executive committee charged us with working out an informal division of labor. Nelson's impression—and I shared it—was that "not even one member of the Board has the remotest idea of the *complexity* of our problems." Their "cold perspective," he wrote, "reduced to getting out a number of good articles and editorials and news reports" with little insight into the analysis, balance and judgment that each item requires.

"You men thrash out with me a plan that will leave you happy," I wrote Nelson and Marcellus. "Put enough starch in the title editor-in-chief [as I was originally to be known] to keep it from going flabby, without evasion of responsibilities, and to temper it enough to preserve all the dignity, stature and importance of two colleagues without whom I now feel the venture would be a nightmare and on whose shoulders I want to lean with the fullest confidence and sense of teamship." We agreed that we would together propose, evaluate and finally choose contributing editors, correspondents and authors as well as subjects of articles. We wrote each other almost daily, sometimes twice a day.

It was part of my work to correlate the names of contributing editors and correspondents, project the typography and layout, propose articles and prospective authors, enlist someone to prepare a style guide and someone to do proofreading. Marcellus supervised the acquisition of office furniture and furnishings, prepared a manuscript evaluation sheet, had charge of news reports, book reviews, Text of the Month and Bible Book of the Month features and was to maintain W.C.C., N.C.C. and New York denominational contacts. Nelson would keep in touch with the Board, promote the magazine among leading churchmen, be responsible for financial matters, oversee office staff and records and carry on general correspondence.

Nelson was still doing major surgery in mid-November—as many as five operations a week. ". . . Giving up a work I love so dearly," he wrote, "is like a fellow must feel on his first parachute jump. But the Lord gave up heaven for me." One week he performed an emergency operation on Sunday, two major surgeries on Monday and five additional operations on the remaining days. "I *love* this work," he wrote, and jested about setting up an operating room in the Washington offices. But he was suddenly overtaken by severe attacks of angina and was hospitalized for a week. To combine even a curtailed medical practice and certain writing chores for Billy Graham and magazine duties posed just too great a physical strain. "I feel that this was the Lord's doing to give me a clear conscience (humanly speaking) in giving up my practice," he wrote. On December 5 Nelson flew to Washington where the three of us finalized office layout and other matters. Six weeks later we again met for several days of conference and work; on January 23, while waiting to board a train for home, Nelson had an angina attack at Union Station.

His comment about vocational transition had touched a sensitive nerve; I too wished to remain professionally alive during the coming year at *Christianity Today.* At Fuller in the summer of 1955 and during the 1955–56 school year I worked feverishly to complete final chapters of my *Christian Personal Ethics.* As research aide I enlisted a seminary graduate awaiting chaplaincy appointment, Warner Hutchinson, and, except for a commencement address at Taylor University and a fifty-page essay on "Science and Religion" for the *Contemporary Evangelical Thought* symposium, concentrated on the ethics volume. Originally alongside *Christian Personal Ethics* I had hoped to produce a companion work on Christian Social Ethics as a followup to *The Uneasy Conscience of Modern Fundamentalism.* It was increasingly clear that the time at *Christianity Today* would delay that effort.

Because my associates lacked certain technical training in journalism and editing, more and more routines fell my way. More than I they also accommodated hurried statements of positions and relied on polemics rather than critical analysis.

During his hospitalization Nelson reflected further on refining our job descriptions. While the editors would function as a team, the Board had affirmed that the head of staff and final authority for the magazine is "the editor-in-chief, Dr. Carl F. H. Henry." To this Nelson now wanted to add two more proposals. First, we should affirm even more strongly that the minds and input of all three editors are essential to the best interest of the work. And second, he preferred that writing editorials be his primary responsibility.

When I replied to Nelson on November 30 I mentioned that I had forwarded to Harold Ockenga as Board chairman inquiries from friends of the magazine who wondered whether "the men who write the checks will dictate the editorial policy." "It is indispensable," I added, "to define the final authority for what appears in the magazine. . . . It should be clearly understood either that the editor-in-chief bears the final responsibility for what goes into the magazine, or that everything that goes into the magazine is chargeable equally in terms of responsibility to the editorial associates. I have indicated a readiness either way, but I do not want blame without authority, nor the contrary." Nelson had a special gift for short editorials, I observed, that should not be stifled. I considered the *Century*'s policy of longer editorials on special concerns a good one, however. In any event, I did not intend to allot more than one editorial an issue to each of the editors.

When *Time* magazine noted in December that Harold Fey had become executive editor of the *Century,* I wondered whether that was tantamount to serving as editor-in-chief. Nelson wrote: "I am not concerned as to what 'Executive Editor' may mean with the *Christian Century.* . . . In every publication I have looked up . . . the Executive Editor is below and subordinate to the Editor-in-Chief. . . . The title fits in with some of the promotional work I hope to do, particularly in raising funds. . . ." Nelson strongly reiterated that our titles be listed as editor-in-chief, associate editor and executive editor, in that order.

The matter was dropped until April 11, when Monsen/Los Angeles was in the final stages of producing plates for a promotional brochure. Nelson urged that my title of editor-in-chief be abbreviated to editor. Since the plates had in fact already been completed, the identification had to be routed out. All I wanted, I wrote Nelson, was "a title appropriate to the responsibilities, as understood by the whole staff. . . ."

On January 19, 1956, the Board met in Washington at the Willard Hotel with Ockenga, Weisiger, Rees, Pew, Jarman and Bell attending. Robert Lamont of First Presbyterian Church, Pittsburgh, was an invited guest and, together with Horace Hull, a prominent Memphis layman, was added to the Board. Marcellus and I were asked to join in Board discussion until the meeting went into executive session. I reported on editorial aspects. Mutuality prevails in the editorial staff, I noted; in case of uncertainty over inclusion or exclusion of material the decision is made by all the editors. The Board accepted the report, but for the record stated that it regards Dr. Henry "as final authority for that which appears in the magazine." The Board approved the editorial staff's recommendation that the printing contract be awarded to McCall Corporation and approved use of a paper stock the equivalent of the *Century*'s. It also voted to send the magazine to all ministers and ministerial students while at the same time vigorously soliciting paid subscriptions. It authorized payment for articles, encouraged dropping or curtailing issues during the summer vacation period, thought forty pages the ideal unless advertising required more and voted that free distribution in Britain or elsewhere abroad be contingent upon gifts designated for that purpose.

Despite our division of duties correspondence now far outran our energies. We needed an on-site business manager so that Nelson as treasurer could concentrate on soliciting gifts. I kept at a discreet distance from donor contacts; Nelson on the other hand eagerly interested them not only in *Christianity Today* but in other causes also.

Nelson's first proposed budget for all of 1956 was $200,901.69. Of this, $66,000 was for salaries, moving allowances and editorial, business and Board travel; $56,000 for printing seven issues of the magazine, $30,000 for promotion, $30,000 for office expenses, $117,700 for office equipment and $6,000 for research. His revised budget for 1956 was $241,823, indicating more and more unforeseen needs. By mid-April three $5000 gifts had come from John Bolten, Howard Butt and an anonymous source. Since capital expenses were mounting, Nelson asked Pew and others if they could advance at least part of the gifts pledged for September. By the end of April Nelson recomputed our budget at over $460,000 a year.

Given those circumstances, Nelson presented with little enthusiasm our need for a business manager who could also oversee advertising and promotion, a trained news editor in touch with a global network of correspondents and a managing editor to see the magazine from its writing stage through proofreading, printing and mailing (in lieu of a circulation manager).

The Board voted to combine the work of business manager and managing editor in one person. Russell Hitt of *Eternity* declined that role. I probed Larry Ward of Gospel Light Press in Glendale, California, who had been managing editor of *Christian Life* magazine and had direct mail subscription promotion experience. Ward indicated that the managing editorship would not appeal to him unless it were correlated with other duties such as circulation and/or news, or his duties overlapped those of managing editor and business manager, that is, advertising, circulation, promotion and supervision of production. On November 10 the executive committee invited Ward to come as business manager with these multi-faceted duties. It also voted that early in 1956 official public announcement be made of the magazine, its editors and publication offices.

Since publication date was nearing, the Board now set my salary at $12,000 from June 1, 1956, until June 1, 1957; since for the present

I commuted every other month from our home in Pasadena and lodged in Washington hotels, $300 per month was added for travel and living expenses. On average this broke down to $159.65 for hotel, $100 for meals and $40.35 for travel which by the cheapest excursion fare would allow a flight home to see my family every few months. I covered my own retirement plan. I had never, nor had Helga for that matter, made reimbursement the determining factor in vocational commitments, and I was not about to do so now.

For the eleven months prior to October, 1956, the first month of publication, the executive committee approved a budget of $50,000 to cover rent, salaries, travel, advertising and promotion, postage and miscellaneous.

In those days American Airlines offered a $168 round trip Los Angeles to Washington thirty-day ticket. Every other month after a week or ten days with Helga and the children I routinely booked the overnight Royal Coachman back to Washington. Because I traveled so much, Helga and I made sure we would always know where the other could be reached in case of emergency. Long distance calls were a luxury (we were still making house payments) and we simply entrusted one another to God's providence. That first Thanksgiving away from home was specially lonely. Early that morning when walking to the office I spotted a crumpled $5 bill in the overnight sidewalk litter. I telephoned home with special thanks and joy.

Marcellus had moved to Washington full-time on February 1 to establish a beachhead in the 1014 Washington Building offices and to implement operational requirements. He hired a highly qualified secretary, Carolyn Bateman, who served well for many years. (The usual secretarial scale then was $75 a week, with superior personnel getting $80.) I invited Irma Peterson, Fuller faculty secretary, to come to Washington, and she served the magazine expertly and devotedly for over two decades.

During the formative months, besides helping coordinate decisions on contributing editors and correspondents, and probing article possibilities, I conferred with Monsen of Los Angeles about a format appropriate to our specific objectives. We wanted type faces that would reflect our dedication to the biblical heritage as well as the magazine's contemporary relevance. When my colleagues saw the final sample they were enthusiastic; we used the approved typography and format for almost ten years until the July 17, 1964, issue.

Another of my responsibilities was to find a style editor to formulate a style guide. A Wheaton alumna, Joan Wise, for ten years a McGraw Hill style editor and now destined for its textbook division, prepared a guide that we distributed to contributing editors and others. Because of interest in our fledgling magazine she came to Washington Saturday mornings for copyediting.

But more energies than I had expected went into voluminous correspondence with prospective contributing editors and essayists. The final list, we agreed, must reflect both evangelical conscience and entrepreneurial strategy and should feature academicians whose publications reflected and confirmed their competency, whether on secular or denominational campuses. Most *Christian Century* news correspondents were members of divinity school faculties; we planned, however, to use leading pastors and on a six-month rotating basis. In evaluating prospective contributors our main concern was to win a hearing for evangelical orthodoxy from nonevangelical scholars, 95 percent of whom were in mainline ecumenically affiliated denominations. Which evangelical writers would they read? And which scholars could we count on for virile and challenging theological exposition? By mid-January, 1956, one in three persons solicited as contributing editors had responded affirmatively, world correspondents were being approved and correspondence about key essays was underway.

Although the Board had initially firmed the circulation goal at 200,000 (300,000 had been briefly discussed), with a live possibility of later adding a British edition, one Board member, as publication neared, thought we should print only 30,000 to 40,000 copies to begin with and on the least expensive newsprint. My commitment, I reminded Nelson, was made on the basis of a 200,000 distribution; I would find it difficult to justify my leave from Fuller on an 80–85 percent cutback. Graham offered to promote the magazine to his mailing list. Marcellus garnered over 70,000 names and addresses of the over 200,000 clergy to whom we would send the first issue or issues of the magazine.

At the end of May Nelson wrote from Montreat: "I am convinced that if we could get the right kind of publicity we could get a *million* subscriptions for *Christianity Today.*" We must write, he insisted, "so that the average layman and the not-too-brilliant pastor can understand what we mean." That had its point. But *Christianity Today*'s primary audience was to be every gospel minister in the English-speaking world. Although the new magazine was not to be a technical journal, its main target was not a lay audience. In a note from Honolulu in March Graham characterized *Christianity Today* as "the greatest single need in India and the other countries that we have visited" and added: "You are going to need the wisdom of Solomon, the patience of Job, the courage of Elijah and the faith of Abraham."

Some Board members were uncertain about the practicality of soliciting advance paid subscriptions. When Larry Ward came in April, with responsibility for circulation, he was understandably troubled about promoting paid subscriptions if free distribution would continue indefinitely. Ward suggested a mass mailing that would place promotional material into the hands of prospects.

There were other reasons for doing this. Hostile rumors were abroad, both left and right. The same article in the *Presbyterian Outlook* that misidentified me as president of Fuller Seminary also erroneously reported a subsidy of $400,000 by Mr. Pew. When reports circulated that Pew had founded *Christianity Today* to get revenge on the National Council of Churches, Graham advised Pew to withdraw from the Board to give the lie to such charges. We editors discouraged such reaction, however. Neither Pew's post on the Board nor his contributions should be despised, we held, as long as he was not the magazine's sole or dominant source of support. The *Century* ran an article by Reinhold Niebuhr critical of Graham, who was conducting an Oklahoma City crusade. Denominational leaders and publications castigated contributing editors for associating with our effort. The best reply to any and all charges, said Ward, would be to deliver the facts promptly into the hands of the clergy, and at the same time ask for paid subscriptions.

By mid-April Nelson was under such physical strain that he pushed increasingly for quick decisions. He had retired from surgical practice early in 1956 because of recurring cardiac problems. We urged him, if he had to cut back on magazine involvement, to concentrate primarily on financial matters. Since Mr. Pew felt it would be unwise to make a supplementary gift, additional funds would be needed from other sources. A statement was prepared that outlined our purposes and that invited outright gifts or underwriting blocs of subscriptions in various denominations. Marcellus's mailing list had grown to over 100,000 individual names; bulk copies, we agreed, would be sent to seminaries.

Given the wild rumors and the uncertain duration of free and paid circulation, Nelson, Marcellus and Larry, unknown to me, distributed a subscription appeal along with a four-page, magazine-size replica of the front page of our first issue. The masthead announcement included the editorial staff, contributing editors and correspondents, a $5 annual subscription rate and a tentative list of contents including key articles by specific authors scheduled for early issues. When this information reached me in Pasadena, I was stunned, since this release destroyed the valuable element of surprise regarding format, typography and content. But Nelson insisted that "it will whet the appetites of those who receive it" and "we should have distributed it earlier."

Six months later, on September 11, we conferred with the noted editor of *U.S. News and World Report,* David Lawrence, and his publishing director, John Sweet, and business manager, Anthony Gould. Because of his regard for Billy Graham, Lawrence had set aside two and a half hours to help us in launching our effort. His first question was: "What have you done to promote *Christianity Today*?" The eager reply was that we had extensively mailed a four-page facsimile listing forthcoming articles and authors. "That," Lawrence replied matter-of-factly, "was your first mistake." My colleagues seemed baffled. But in the next ten minutes we got a top-level lesson in public relations. "Your golden opportunity is evaporating right now," he said. "You must *sell the vision* before the magazine appears. Once the publication is out," he continued, "everyone who gets it will find something that disappoints his or her expectations. The great promotional opportunity is to *sell the idea;* once the magazine appears, to sell that vision will be three times as hard."

Lawrence also warned us that sample promotional literature is more costly than a promotional letter and less productive. He stressed that we needed more help with editorial, circulation and advertising skills. Since promotional costs usually offset circulation income, he told us to expect a deficit for the first three years.

We had delayed public announcement until after Easter, to correlate better with a promotional letter by Billy Graham and to be nearer the October publication date. Made by Billy Graham and me, the public announcement got a good press, including national coverage by George Cornell of Associated Press. But it touched off further criticism from the ecumenical left and from the independent right. Fundamentalism's John R. Rice complained in *Sword of the Lord* that the new magazine would be "slanted to the 'intellectual' viewpoint" while the ecumenical left gratuitously declared us to be pro-capitalist and anti-ecumenical.

May 11, 1956, was the last day of classes at Fuller and, once final exams were graded, I gave full attention to the magazine and the approaching monthend move to Washington for a year. After a decade as a member of the founding faculty, it was gratifying that colleagues granted a year's leave of absence in full expectation of my return. The student body dedicated its yearbook to me, and in addition the Senior class publicly read a generous resolution wishing me Godspeed in my new endeavor and urged "emphatically that Dr. Henry return to his professorial duties at Fuller Theological Seminary at the earliest practicable date."

American's seven-hour red-eye special arrived at Washington (National) well ahead of schedule at 6:45 A.M. on Tuesday, June 5. I went immediately to *Christianity Today*'s offices, washed and shaved, and had devotions. At day's end I registered for an experimental week at the Y.M.C.A. Wheaton classmate Richard Halverson, newly named director of International Christian Leadership, it happened, was to address the weekly lobby lounge supper. Dick and I later walked the Washington streets and prayed for God's anointing for our separate missions. Subsequently invited to dinner at I.C.L. Fellowship House, I learned that the first convert that in 1933 I had led to Christ, Al Graunke, had become one of that movement's stalwart leaders in Suffolk County on Long Island.

Thursday morning Nelson Bell was running a fever, so he made a reassuring visit to a local physician. I returned late in the day to the Y where, despite my request for a quieter room, a noisy roof garden dance gave me a throbbing headache. Thereafter I made the Parkside ($5 a day) my lodgings for the first year.

Two months before publication I urged that *Christianity Today* address the race problem, perhaps even in our first Christmas issue. In view of our somewhat differing perspectives, I proposed that each editor prepare a thousand-word statement, Nelson on "A Southern Physician Looks at the Race Problem," Marcellus on "A Northern Clergyman Looks at the Race Problem" and I on "An Evangelical Theologian Looks at the Race Problem." Nelson had written almost the entire statement carried on April 11, 1956, by the *Southern Presbyterian Journal* signed by forty-four outstanding men in the Presbyterian Church in the South. "It represents my own feelings in the matter. It is hard for you men in the North to realize," Nelson wrote me, "that our problem is in many parts of the South, one of *ratio,* not of race. Also, in many areas in the deep South, Negro children are so filthy, infected with disease and immoral, that white parents will not send their children to school with them. This is not true in the North, generally speaking, or in the West, where the Negroes are of a much higher economic status and also have much better educational backgrounds. . . . The matter will not be solved by a cold recourse to law."

Billy Graham, who had integrated his crusade choirs, agreed that the growing controversy over race should be addressed. But *Christianity Today* was not in the forefront of the race problem for several reasons. We were not consulted when ecumenical leaders made their moves. If the ecumenical effort was "Johnny come lately" in concern over national discrimination, evangelical engagement was admittedly "Johnny come later." For one thing, the magazine opposed the disrespect for law implicit in mob demonstration and resistance, when a single well-publicized protest could have thrown the issue into the courts where justice issues were to be resolved. We left the evaluation of Martin Luther King's call for racial justice to Nelson, who held that King preached not the gospel but a message of social change. Although we emphasized what liberal theology ignored, namely, the gospel's life-transforming power, we escalated it at times into a solvent sufficient for all social injustices. If legality without good will cannot inaugurate utopia, it can at least frustrate public injustice by imposing penalties on discrimination, not only by people at large but even by believers whose sanctification is incomplete. Finally, we saw the race problem—rightly, I think—as one dimension of a more comprehensive problem, and not as the cutting edge of a dramatic social reformation.

I reported to the Board meeting on September 13 that the main essays for the first two issues were in hand. Some 118 articles had been assigned subject to approval, I noted, but we desperately needed a production manager, a role that neither Marcellus nor Nelson could assume. "Some of us have been twelve hours a day at our desks," I said, "and more often than not, Saturdays as well." The multiplicity of other tasks denied the magazine, I said, the creative contribution of its own editors.

It was evident that our annual printing bill alone would run at least a quarter of a million dollars, and would be our biggest budget item. Typesetting would be done in Washington at McArdle Printing Company which would prepare and ship mats by overnight train to Dayton for next day press run and mailing by McCall Corporation.

At the September 13 meeting Nelson projected an annual budget of $493,820 for October 1, 1956, to October 1, 1957, and anticipated $125,000 from subscriptions, $156,000 from advertising and $213,000 from contributions. Of this last item Board members had pledged all but $50,000 still to be raised. Professionals at *U.S. News* had urged Nelson to add $120,000 for promotion and to fix the budget at $600,000; moreover, instead of anticipating $400,000 income, $230,000 would be more realistic. All subscription income ought to be set aside, they advised, for pursuing more subscriptions and renewals. This would mean raising $320,000 rather than $50,000 in additional gifts. Such a budget they identified with nothing more than "sheer survival." In fact David Lawrence urged Nelson to give the Board a budget figure of $1 million, and then show gratifying progress after the first year by using the $600,000 figure at that time.

Advertising was under pressure because the magazine was being launched toward the end of the budget year when many firms had already made alternative commitments. Without a publisher's representative—an additional expense—we could not gain access to mass media advertisers, who claimed that they already reached our target audience through established national newsmagazines. For all that, we had about $8,000 worth of advertising for the first issue, and fifty advertisers had purchased $20,000 worth of space in immediately subsequent issues.

As to circulation, Marcellus projected distribution of 275,000 copies of the first issue. McCall Corporation was already processing 190,000 names of ministers with more in the mails; 20,000 sample copies were intended for lay promotion, 40,000 copies would go to Billy Graham's list and 14,000 in bulk to seminaries. At that time *Moody Monthly*'s readership included only 13,500 ministers; *Presbyterian Life* and *Sunday School Times* each had about 6,000 clergy readers.

The first issue was scheduled to go to press on Monday, October 8, with a publication date and anticipated postal delivery a week later. This put us advantageously beyond the summer vacation season. In mid-September I learned from Ockenga that Mr. Pew wanted to see advance proofs of the first issue; Ockenga surmised this would not be a routine requirement and thought we should comply. In the past Mr. Pew had been "burned" so often by causes that promised one thing and delivered another—especially in N.C.C. contexts—that nothing would be lost, Ockenga observed, if we could satisfy and reassure him in this way.

I wrote Nelson Bell promptly. If there was no alternative, I said, I wanted him and Ockenga to know that the mailing of those advance proofs would also imply my impending resignation from *Christianity Today.* I would stay for a season rather than to embarrass the magazine at its very outset, I said, but I had no intention of editing a magazine without editorial freedom.

I was as yet unaware—and learned only many years later from copies of correspondence—that in July Mr. Pew had summoned Nelson to Philadelphia and suggested to him that Pew see all articles "prior to publication." Nelson told him that he would talk it over with the other editors. Instead Nelson wrote Pew on July 13 that "the editors, along with Billy and Harold [Ockenga], feel that this would be unwise, especially as there is already some wild talk and criticism with reference to your support of the magazine. If we can say that we are entirely free in our editorial policy and that no editorials and articles are submitted to any member of the Board prior to publication it will greatly strengthen our position." Nelson sent Ockenga a copy of his letter, noting that he had assured Mr. Pew that no article or editorial would appear which did not first meet with the approval of all three editors.

Mr. Pew replied by phone that he was "unwilling to accept that response." If he was to put money into the magazine, he said, he had a right to prior inspection of its contents, or he would not support it. He finally indicated that he would be satisfied if Howard Kershner of *Christian Economics* saw the material; he did not, however, wish other Board members to know about this. Without my consent or knowledge, Nelson accordingly sent materials for the first issue to Kershner.

After Ockenga's instructions to me to post advance proofs to all members of the Board, I wrote Nelson I was willing to comply but would resign. The fact is, I did not know what had happened during a luncheon that followed the September 13 Board meeting. At the conclusion of the meal Ockenga, who was seated with Pew and Bell (the only editor on the Board), announced without open discussion that the Board of Directors should "assume its full responsibilities for *Christianity Today,* and that this would involve submission of all articles and editorials to members of the Board before publication." Most members of the Board were unaware of the nuances.

After devotions the next morning, Nelson wrote "selected members of the Board" (Paul Rees, Robert Lamont, Cary Weisiger, Billy Graham and Jerry Beavan). This policy was practically impossible, he noted, and editorial responsibilities, moreover, had been "vested in the editors by the Board, with Dr. Henry as Editor-in-Chief." "The Board has the right to dismiss us for cause at any time," he added, "but it does not have the right to set itself up as a board of censors. I do not believe that any self-respecting editor could rightly submit to such an intolerably restrictive procedure."

Pew had restated his desire to Ockenga to see the material personally, to which Ockenga consented at luncheon. This line of action, then, was the basis of Ockenga's telephone directive to me. When I informed Nelson that I was obeying Ockenga's instructions by sending proofs to Ockenga for the whole Board, and was indicating my forthcoming resignation, Nelson did not tell me what had happened either in his July conference with Mr. Pew or at the Board luncheon. Nelson did indicate, however, that he and Marcellus also, so he felt, would sign any strong letter of protest to the Board that I might draft. The letter, signed by me, and then by Kik and Bell, read:

> TO THE BOARD:
>
> In submitting this copy for Board approval, the Editors feel that their sense of professional dignity is lowered to half mast. Men who bear in the sight of the public the responsibility for the published content cannot long be deprived of a commensurate authority without either deterioration of spirit or a departure to other work. In coming to CHRISTIANITY TODAY, the Editors did not regard themselves as salaried propagandists under censorship but as principled men under divine constraint. In championing

the freedoms which Christianity bears to men, they can only protest against the compromise (here involved) of liberties which inhere in a free evangelical press.

CARL F. H. HENRY
J. MARCELLUS KIK
L. NELSON BELL

When Nelson Bell phoned Billy Graham of my intention to resign, Graham called Ockenga, who in turn phoned me. He had heard from Billy, he said, that the editors were unhappy about sending proofs to the Board. Indeed so, I replied. That principle, we thought, had been settled at the initial Labor Day founders' meeting when editors were named. Ockenga seemed not to grasp what I meant. It would be "only a matter of the first few issues," he remarked; we must keep Pew happy in view of his substantial investment. The mistake was made, Ockenga added, by the expectation that we submit "everything" to the Board instead of "only the controversial articles and especially the editorials." That proposal, I countered, "places the ultimate responsibility for what appears in the Board and takes it away from the Editors." Ockenga once again indicated that "this would be only a temporary thing"; surely I knew him well enough, he added, to know that he was "a strategist in many of these things." I promised to send the material but under protest; he should know not only that my fingers were crossed about the whole matter, but also that correspondence was already in the mail.

The background for Pew's distrust, Nelson alleged in his letter to selected Board members (of which I knew nothing), stemmed from the fact that after the public announcement of *Christianity Today* the then editor of *Eternity* magazine told Mr. Pew that "Carl Henry is a socialist." The same calumny was repeated to him as well, said Bell. That charge was "pure fabrication . . . an absolute falsehood," Bell told Pew. In his letter to the "selected" Board members Bell indicated the two of us had talked about economic issues and "Carl takes the position that Capitalism and Labor *both* must come under the scrutiny of God and his holy laws—something with which all Christians should agree." I learned later from Pew himself that *Eternity* wanted Pew's substantial support and resented the founding of a new magazine. Our whole Board found *Eternity*'s critical editorial comment on the emergence of *Christianity Today* most disappointing.

Nelson concluded his letter to the Board "selectmen" by saying that "none of us is willing to have *Christianity Today* bought by any interests. . . . If this position entails a loss of certain financial support we will seek it elsewhere."

Meanwhile Billy Graham called Pew and told him that it would destroy the magazine if the editors had to submit advance proofs to the Board. The Board has power to fire an editor if it is displeased, he said; if it hires an editor, it should trust and support him. Mr. Pew agreed. The letter signed by the three editorial associates was therefore never sent.

This was the finest hour in my relationships with Nelson Bell and Marcellus Kik, and one of the finest with Billy Graham (though I did not contact him directly). Paul Rees wrote that he was dumbfounded at Ockenga's announcement. "I do not see how we can continue our joint enterprise as Board and editors unless we settle, once for all, the policy of granting normal editorial freedom and responsibility." Maxey Jarman wrote: "The trustees must place their complete confidence in the judgment of the Editors, realizing there are bound to be differences of opinion."

Nelson was in fact in a somewhat awkward position because he sporadically sent Mr. Pew material that he projected for the *Southern Presbyterian Journal.* Once *Christianity Today* was launched, he did not hesitate to read to Pew by phone some editorials that he was projecting for the magazine even before they crossed my desk.

At our prepublication press conference on October 12, we reported 15,000 advance subscribers. The magazine, I stressed, was not merely a Protestant effort to parallel the *Christian Century* but would creatively and relevantly articulate evangelical theology. Press coverage was highly gratifying. George Cornell's national AP column gave generous space, as did Religious News Service and many religion editors including Ken Dole of the *Washington Post and Times-Herald,* Casper Nannes of the *Washington Star-News* and Dan Thrapp of the *Los Angeles Times.* Paul Harvey mentioned the effort on the Mutual network coast-to-coast, *Newsweek* made it the lead religion article and *Time* carried a brief notice.

The *Century* shunned any mention of *Christianity Today.* Its first allusion was a reference in its February 20, 1957, issue to "a hard-core brand of Protestant fundamentalism . . . receiving large funds from reactionary economic and social interests." *Christianity and Crisis,* however, carried an editorial by John C. Bennett of Union Theological Seminary who further circulated the *Presbyterian Outlook*'s report that we were Pew-subsidized. Bennett wrote: "The editor is Dr. Carl F. H. Henry of Fuller Theological Seminary who represents a sophisticated and irenic theological conservatism. . . . He has written a book entitled *The Uneasy Conscience of Modern Fundamentalism.* . . ." Years later I found in a used book store Bennett's marked copy of *Uneasy Conscience* indicating what he approved and disapproved.

Our first published issue was dignified and attractive, its content and design showing some changes from the prematurely distributed sample brochure. The masthead listed Carl F. H. Henry, Editor; L. Nelson Bell, Executive Editor; J. Marcellus Kik, Associate Editor; Larry Ward, Managing Editor; and George Burnham, News Editor. Burnham, who for fifteen years had been with AP and with daily newspapers, and had covered Graham's crusades in Europe for more than 100 papers, joined us September 15 to develop our news reporting. In November these names were supplemented by that of Charles Claus, Business Manager, when production duties and the deluge of subscriptions preempted Larry Ward's energies and required someone to concentrate on advertising.

The magazine's first lead-off article, "Changing Climate of European Theology," was by the Dutch theologian G. C. Berkouwer. Next was an article by Billy Graham, "Biblical Authority in Evangelism," followed by my article on "The Fragility of Freedom in the West," and then an essay on "The Primary Task of the Church" by Addison H. Leitch, president of Pittsburgh-Xenia (United Presbyterian) Theological Seminary. Editorials began at the center spread; the first, "Why 'Christianity Today'?," reproduced the promotional brochure distributed previously. The news section bore the general caption: "Conflicts of the Gospel with Paganism." There were five book reviews, a quarterly feature titled "Current Religious Thought" submitted in this initial issue by Philip E. Hughes, one time secretary of the Church of England Church Society, and a page of letters to the editor under the general caption, "Eutychus and His Kin" (recalling the mope in Acts 20 who fell asleep during the apostle Paul's preaching). A short feature titled "Preacher in the Red" supplied a needed element of humor, later to be provided by a cartoonist. Marcellus Kik supplied the first Bible Book of the Month article, an exposition on the Gospel of Matthew. There were almost ten pages of advertising, mostly by publishers, and all of it—as *Time* magazine noted—"culturally constructive."

The masthead listed the names of 49 contributing editors and of 73 correspondents. They had been chosen from many hundreds of possibilities.

The initial contributing editors, listed in the magazine with their affiliations, included Oswald T. Allis, G. C. Berkouwer, Robert F. Boyd, Geoffrey W. Bromiley, F. F. Bruce, Gordon H. Clark, F. P. Copland Simmons, Earl L. Douglass, Edward L. R. Elson, William Fitch, C. Darby Fulton, Frank E. Gaebelein, John H. Gerstner, Billy Graham, Richard C. Halverson, William K. Harrison, C. Adrian Heaton, Philip E. Hughes, W. Boyd Hunt, Norman C. Hunt, Clyde S.

Kilby, W. Harry Jellema, Harold Kuhn, Robert J. Lamont, Roland O. Leavell, Pierre Marcel, Clarence E. MacCartney, Duke McCall, Samuel H. Moffett, Arthur J. Moore, J. Theodore Mueller, Roger Nicole, Harold John Ockenga, Stanley W. Olson, J. C. Pollock, Bernard Ramm, Paul S. Rees, W. Stanford Reid, William Childs Robinson, W. E. Sangster, Samuel M. Shoemaker, Wilbur M. Smith, Ned B. Stonehouse, John R. W. Stott, James G. S. S. Thomson, Cary N. Weisiger III, Faris D. Whitesell, Maurice A. P. Wood, Kyle M. Yates and Fred Young.

An early disappointment was my inability to enlist C. S. Lewis. I reached for him not as a contributing editor but rather for a monthly page, possibly in the format of a letter, that would appear opposite unsolicited letters to the editor. I had never met Lewis, though we had a bit of correspondence during the war years. My best access was the Anglican bishop A. W. Goodwin Hudson who had a London parish and now and then accompanied Lewis on his occasional presentations to Inter-Varsity meetings. Inter-Varsity used Lewis sparingly because he deviated at points from evangelical orthodoxy, but Lewis served Inter-Varsity if the invitation was convenient. In September I asked Goodwin Hudson, who had been a guest in our home, whether at the magazine's expense he would drive to Oxford, take Lewis to lunch, share our objectives and present Lewis with a written invitation to participate.

Lewis was not unsympathetic to our effort. But he insisted that the time had come for him to engage in theology only allusively through fiction as a medium. It was rumored that in recent weeks he had been bested in a theological exchange with G. E. M. Anscombe, and had decided thereafter not to engage in direct theological confrontation. "You may as well ask me to dance in a ballet, or to bowl for England," he told Goodwin Hudson. Some years later, the *Century* carried a theological piece by Lewis, reprinted I believe from an overseas source. I wrote Lewis reminding him that his theological witness was more consonant with *Christianity Today* than with that of *Century.* "If I have done anything to help their cause," Lewis wrote me, "I am sorry."

We ran articles by former modernist or neoorthodox clergy who had moved toward evangelical orthodoxy. Tom Allan, leader of the "Tell Scotland" movement, told the General Assembly that he had concluded that there are "not five theories of the atonement, but one—that is, that Jesus Christ died for our sins." Many churchmen in Scotland disagreed, he added, but "their churches are empty."

As bags of correspondence reached our offices it became obvious that job descriptions needed refinement and change. We had added

Bill Clemmer for proofreading. Now Nelson approved the hiring of appropriately experienced staff wives at nominal wages. During this my first year, while I was on leave from Fuller, Helga remained in Pasadena with the children, Paul, fourteen, and Carol, twelve. She was under contract as associate professor of education at Pasadena College which now approached her about becoming dean of women. But a memorandum from Nelson reiterated that if we moved East as a family Helga should serve as an editorial aide in revising manuscripts for publication.

At the November 7 Board meeting we reported that 22,827 subscriptions had been entered and an additional 2,000 were being processed, totaling 24,827. More than 4,000 were for three years. I emphasized the risk of illogical subscribers: "The larger the proportion of lay readership," I remarked, "the greater would be the pressures to transform *Christianity Today* into a sort of *Christian Life* or *Moody Monthly,* contrary to our objective."

I also told the Board that "the Editor is now so overwhelmed with the ebb and flow of other responsibilities that in the past four months he was able to complete two contributions for the magazine only by getting away from Washington"—a routine that David Lawrence followed at *U.S. News.* The following week I wrote Paul Rees that the editorial phase of our effort was "woefully understaffed," and mentioned incidentally what I had shared with the Board a week earlier: "The situation at *Christianity Today* now demands twelve to fourteen hours a day, plus my Saturdays, and leaves me without time for the creative or the reflective life." I was declining out-of-town lectures strategically important for the magazine, since office absence for a day or two would accumulate a mountain of unanswered mail.

Larry Ward and I had complete physical checkups, each coping with arrhythmia under the pressure of responsibilities from which there seemed to be no relief. Larry had hoped in spare time to write a Civil War historical novel, but issue-to-issue burdens left him with sleepless nights, and he soon urged us to get full-time staffers in production and circulation. Not many months would pass before he would return to the West Coast, serving there as our advertising representative while he inaugurated a new magazine launched by Bob Pierce for World Vision.

I phoned Billy Graham in November to relay my impression that, although the current budget estimated our needs at $8,000 a month beyond assured income, in my opinion a figure of $15,000 was more realistic.

Nelson and Marcellus gave their utmost to our common task. Many practical gains were traceable to their efforts and suggestions. Yet I never foresaw the heavy pressures on time and spirit that engulfed us all. There was never enough editorial help. Nelson's limited visits coped with accumulated articles submitted for publication, and Marcellus's time was channeled largely to routine but essential features. We shared in projecting future articles, but the editing and processing of accepted materials fell to me.

Marcellus's editorial experience had been with a small Canadian periodical. In view of his preaching experience, we channeled to him material that dealt with practical and pastoral concerns of ministry. He supervised general staff procedures as well. Coverage of NCC and WCC activities he considered his special province, yet he lacked the time actually to attend.

Nelson handled much of the critical correspondence, bore the burdens of secretary and treasurer of the Board and sought financial contributions, as well as shared editorial concerns. His broken presence made my office involvement doubly necessary, and restricted opportunities for editorial participation in out-of-city academic and ministerial dialogues. Not only had prospects vanished for time off, but I was now spending Sunday afternoons struggling to prepare something worthy for the current issue.

During the initial year *Christianity Today* carried articles by Tom Allan, Oswald T. Allis, H. H. Barnette, Andrew W. Blackwood, G. W. Bromiley, F. F. Bruce, Edward John Carnell, Gordon H. Clark, F. P. Copland Simmons, L. David Cowie, Joseph M. Dawson, Peter Eldersveld, Elisabeth Elliot, Edward L. R. Elson, Frank E. Gaebelein, John H. Gerstner, Richard C. Halverson, Everett F. Harrison, Gen. William K. Harrison, Paul Harvey, S. Richey Kamm, James L. Kelso, Senator William F. Knowland, Harold Kuhn, George Ladd, Calvin D. Linton, Ernest C. Manning, Bruce M. Metzger, J. Theodore Mueller, John Murray, Roger Nicole, Paul S. Rees, W. Stanford Reid, William Childs Robinson, Andrew K. Rule, W. E. Sangster, W. Graham Scroggie, Samuel M. Shoemaker, Wilbur M. Smith, George Stob, Ned B. Stonehouse, R. V. G. Tasker, Robert A. Traina, Faris D. Whitesell, G. Brillenburg Wurth, Edward J. Young and many others, including the editors and those already mentioned as sharing in the very first issue, Berkouwer, Graham and Leitch.

At the outset not many people volunteered essays. We solicited articles from evangelicals in mainline denominations, not because we were precommitted to ecumenism but because writers in the independent churches might give the magazine an anti-ecumenical cast that would hinder our outreach. Evangelicals on ecumenical frontiers were usually more aware, moreover, of current theological issues. To preserve reader interest we shortened essays from 3000 to 2000 and in some cases even to 1500 words.

I spent Christmas, 1956, in Pasadena. Now in her twentieth year of teaching, Helga, besides her classroom work, was supervising cadet teachers in the city schools. The children were attending Culter Christian Academy in Los Angeles, Paul as a high school sophomore and Carol an eighth-grader. Carol had been almost a straight-A student as long as we could remember. Music was a special interest; agile at the piano, she was chapel pianist, chorus accompanist and the automatic music resource in any emergency. She moved rapidly as well in violin. Paul, ever gregarious and people-oriented, played both piano and specially the trombone and participated in two bands. Both youngsters professed Christ as Savior and were active in church life.

We were stunned at 1956 yearend by *Christianity Today*'s financial pressures. More major donors had not been forthcoming, advertising was $48,000 below projections, postal costs staggering. The next Board agenda would discuss the magazine's very survival as much as its future hopes. Other than to make funding a prayer concern, I was determined not to feel personally responsible for it. Raising money was not my calling, and our half-million dollar budget would not intimidate me. God owned the cattle on a thousand hills no less than the oil that Sunoco pumped. My job was to make each issue of *Christianity Today* so worthwhile that if suspension of the magazine became inevitable we could still rejoice over the evangelical witness of its lifespan, however short. No national magazine, I was convinced, not even *Time* or *Fortune,* had a more urgent message than ours.

At the January, 1957, convention of Evangelical Press Association, Professor Kenneth Butler of Medill School of Journalism (Northwestern University) paid the new magazine gratifying tribute. The type faces we had chosen, he said, "present a character which is pristine, full of tradition and quiet dignity. . . . Everything is handled with exquisite good taste, even if subdued. Headlines are well written. . . . Body type is equally distinguished, highly legible and beautiful. Type size, leading and elements of spacing are handled in good taste. . . . Good writing and careful selection of subject matter is here everywhere present which, to thoughtful readers, may overcome the lack of color and zest in physical presentation." Since *Christianity Today* was founded to be a *thought* magazine, we considered this evaluation high praise indeed.

Evangelical scholars in Britain and the Continent, and in Africa, Asia and Australasia as well, shared ever more conspicuously in the effort. *Time* magazine commented that *Christianity Today* reflects not the parochial viewpoint of the Bible belt, but rather an international, transdenominational scholarship that undergirds the evangelical perspective.

With a decision pending in the Spring of 1957 about my continuing at *Christianity Today* I reassessed my leave of absence from Fuller.

Smith, Harrison, Archer and Lindsell were urging my return. The A.A.T.S. had withheld expected accreditation, and for the first time student applications showed a marked decline. The Seminary seemed to be moving toward faculty and staff attrition and outside gifts were lagging. For all that, no theologically conservative faculty was more productive, and the idea of a corporate center of evangelical research and writing was still sound, enhanced by the eight-hour semester teaching load and two months each summer for study, research and production. Yet there were glimmers of faculty conflict that might frustrate cooperative efforts and larger impact. Several professors were nearing retirement; some were restive. Lindsell assured me these problems were temporary and that he had no plans to leave. Although Fuller Foundation had curtailed its giving, Pew had given $150,000.

On February 2, 1957, I reminded Ockenga that I was on a year's leave from Fuller and must inform the school on March 1 about my intentions for September. "If I were seriously to consider *Christianity Today* as a permanent alternative," I wrote, "there would have to be a definition of areas of responsibility, authority and liberty; at present these are unsatisfactorily nebulous. What is at stake for me is a life work."

I had vexing doubts about the situation at *Christianity Today.* Arbitrary decisions and actions by the Board chairman, Board vacillation about staff authority and responsibility, overwork and curtailed opportunity for creative contribution because of inadequate personnel had riddled our first year. Under these circumstances the joy and freedom of an academic life seemed far preferable.

The previous night I had written Nelson about my disposition to return to Fuller in the Fall unless the Board intended to maintain a circulation of 160,000, unless I had "overall authority" for magazine policy and unless as a Board member I was answerable to the whole Board and not to individual members. Nelson's feelings were hurt by my suggestion that the implications of his title as "executive editor" be clarified. He offered to step aside entirely. I intended nothing of the sort, of course. But the complexity of interrelationships between Nelson and Board members and his privileged committee roles within the Board seemed often to undermine or at least threaten the spirit and implementation of our founding modus operandi. I agreed with him that our editorial relationships were in large measure "triplicate." But we differed increasingly over editorials. Nelson preferred many short ones which he could produce with enviable speed. His productivity outran the magazine's capacity to absorb them. I wanted longer, more analytical editorials as well. Additionally I questioned at times whether all editorials ought to appear anonymously.

Beginning with the June 10, 1957, issue we assigned Nelson a monthly page, "A Layman and His Faith." A sermonic, doctrinal and practical feature, it promoted spiritual awakening and evangelistic earnestness, and voiced concerns of the laity about churches absorbed in socio-political matters. It was a readable and popular feature that lent itself to ready quotation from the pulpit.

Mr. Pew pressed for regularly scheduled articles on the great doctrines of the Bible, and all of us concurred. Evangelicals would never convert professional churchmen like Bishop G. Bromley Oxnam and Eugene Carson Blake, Pew felt. But ordinary preachers knew that spiritual power rests in authentic Christianity alone. Pew suggested a private meeting of a dozen leading ministers, including those on the Board, for suggestions of content that they would welcome. I hoped and expected that Ockenga and other clergy on the Board would volunteer essays, but few did.

At the February 7, 1957, Board meeting, we reported that our paid circulation of just under 35,000 paralleled that of the *Century.* The Board voted to cut the magazine print order to 160,000 per issue for the next three years, thus reducing the budget to $39,000 a month.

The first nine issues had made plain the emphasis of the magazine: in theology, conservative and biblical, without provincialism; in evangelism, promotive of personal decision in view of Bible doctrine; in ecclesiastical affairs, cooperative while disapproving ecumenical inclusivism; in social concerns, stressing Christianity's relevance to culture and the arts without falling into a social gospel; in economics, partisan to responsible free enterprise over Marxist collectivism while rejecting secular materialism; in socio-political affairs, exhibiting the connection of human freedom and rights with the Christian revelation; in all things, charity coupled with faith and hope.

"Across the land, and in lands beyond," I told the Board, "men of loyal evangelical persuasion in many denominations relay to us their gratitude that their sense of loneliness in evangelical witness seems to be lifted away by this effort. Do not deprive yourselves of the joy of reading their unsolicited letters. They belong to that scattered army of evangelical workers to whom it is our task to give leadership and courage."

"The Board will need to decide after this year of beginnings," I noted, "whether it regards as permanently ideal the present division of authority, or whether *Christianity Today* would be advantaged through an editor-in-chief bearing both a full authority and responsibility for content. Editorial integrity requires a strict balancing of responsibility and authority."

The Board requested me "to assume the position of Editor-in-Chief on the basis of a permanent relationship" and if I accepted, that Harold

Ockenga ask Fuller Seminary to extend its leave of absence. It defined the title Editor "as meaning Editor-in-Chief" and stipulated that "full and final responsibility for all that appears in the magazine rests with the Editor-in-Chief" who "shall have complete freedom in the selection of all subjects and material to be handled and full responsibility for their appearance in the publication." Marcellus and I were both elected to the Board, and the Board also authorized employment of an editorial assistant.

I asked Carnell for an extension of leave to devote another year to *Christianity Today.* "If alternative leadership were in sight for the months immediately ahead," I wrote, "I would return gladly to my teaching." My decision was not taken for financial gain, I noted, since the magazine provided neither retirement benefits nor ministerial housing deduction; and it would cost $2500 to enroll both children in a boarding school. For a year Helga and I would face adjustment to rental living in Washington and my treasured and valuable library would stay behind while we leased our comfortable Pasadena home. No less important, Helga would lose her teaching income and her teaching career would likely come to an end.

After I received my Fuller leave extension, Lindsell shared misgivings about certain developments at the Seminary. Disenchanted over Carnell's elevation to the presidency, Woodbridge left his post in church history and was downgrading the school. The financial situation was weakening; unless Carnell assumed responsibility for raising money, Lindsell surmised, "he will have to call it quits."

As the 1957 fall semester approached, Woodbridge had resigned, Ladd was on sabbatical, Clarence Roddy had not fully recovered from a heart attack, Rebecca Price was seriously ill with an inoperable brain tumor and I was on leave.

"*Christianity Today* has a great future," Lindsell wrote subsequently. "Considering the type of magazine I doubt that you can expect a circulation of, say, 100,000. But it will have an influence which cannot be calculated. The future of the magazine depends on the sagacity of the editor and his ability to steer a clear course. Keep at it!" Ockenga had concurred, he added, that Henry "had done a bang up job at *Christianity Today*" and were I to return to Fuller "he did not have the faintest idea who could possibly fill the spot in Washington."

Perhaps by virtue of long years in leadership roles Ockenga exercised what he himself called an ability to place men in strategic places. He mentioned Bob Lamont at First Presbyterian of Pittsburgh, Alan Redpath at Moody Memorial Church and Carl Henry at *Christianity Today!* The Carnell presidency at Fuller was another instance. What in time demolished Carnell was deployment to administration for which he was unprepared and more specifically to fund-raising which he found repulsive. Declining health and recurring tensions overtook him until in May, 1959, he resigned his position. Granted a sabbatical until January 4, 1960, he then resumed full-time professorship in apologetics.

Once again but without success Fuller trustees pressed Ockenga to take the presidency. Gordon College was also wanting him as president, an alignment that would not uproot his family and also allowed continued associations at Park Street Church. Meanwhile Ockenga talked with Addison Leitch at Pittsburgh-Xenia about the Fuller presidency, but Leitch was loathe to leave a denominational seminary for an interdenominational $200,000 deficit. Ockenga had increasingly considered Lindsell indispensable to Fuller, but there was little trustee enthusiasm and Lindsell expressed disinterest in the presidency; Gordon trustees were meanwhile probing Lindsell about coming East. In October, 1959, Ockenga told the Fuller faculty that no presidential possibility was as yet in view and that financial problems were the reason. For all that, Fuller enrollment had rebounded. As things developed, after a two-year futile search to replace Carnell, Ockenga in 1961 once again became nonresident president until Fuller's leadership fell to David Hubbard.

At *Christianity Today* in the Spring of 1957 we learned something about publishing intrigue. Composition was being done in Washington by McArdle Printing Company and printing in Dayton by McCall Corporation. To us it was irrelevant that Walter McArdle was a prominent Roman Catholic layman honored by the Vatican, as long as his company fulfilled its contractual agreements. One day McCall Corporation phoned us to say they had been threatened by a lawsuit if our next issue contained a projected advertisement that included a statement about the Roman Catholic Church. I asked our production department for a page proof, but the proofs of that material had not as yet reached us from McArdle. What happened, we learned, was that a Roman lay brother typesetter who therefore had advance knowledge of *Christianity Today* content, was sharing information with outside Catholic agencies, and doing so before proofs were returned to our own staff. That was the end of our business with McArdle.

That same year, interestingly, I was making fruitful contacts with Catholic intellectuals. Along with Gustave Weigel, the gifted Jesuit apologist at Woodstock College then in Maryland, I was invited as observer at the Oberlin Faith and Order Conference late in the Summer of 1957. The main difference was that WCC paid his expenses but left me as the evangelical observer to pay my own—a matter of independence that I did not regret, but of discrimination that I did. Weigel favorably reviewed significant evangelical books, including my own, commending them to Catholic scholars interested in contemporary Protestant thought but enamored of liberalism and neoorthodoxy. Weigel seemed perplexed that when the U.S. State Department sent abroad teams of exchange speakers on morality and religion the Protestant appointees seemed routinely to be nonevangelical. He invited me to Woodstock to address 300 Jesuit priests in training, most of them for the Philippines. We met periodically for lunch in Washington to discuss theological trends and assess influential theologians.

By the Spring of 1957 our publication costs ran $20,490 an issue, an operating loss of $15,740 per issue given income of $2,000 from circulation and $2,750 from advertising. We had used up subscription funds—contrary to the counsel of *U.S. News*—for current expenses, so there was no reserve for a renewal effort. Board members had pledged to seek donors, but few were forthcoming. We needed more staff but could hardly guarantee even the modest salaries that the Board approved. Nelson's concentration was on fund-raising correspondence duties and I was writing almost nothing for the magazine. Would I then serve the overall cause better, I asked, if in September, 1957, I resigned as editor to become associate editor on half-time and half-salary, not to return to teaching but to shape essays and editorials to notch ahead our evangelical witness?

At the May 28 Board meeting I reported that we were two-thirds of the way through the initial year of publication and had already surpassed the paid circulation of such long-established periodicals as the *Christian Century* and *Eternity*. We had elicited from a neutral observer, the managing editor of *Look*, in remarks made to Associated Church Press, the accolade that "among the so-called think magazines, *Christianity Today* is most stimulating." These gains were made, I added, although we had "not one key individual on the editorial, advertising or circulation side previously associated with a first-rate religious magazine," and a salary scale, moreover, that discouraged prospects from joining us as editorial assistants.

The magazine had been soundly established with an intellectual dignity and theological earnestness that promoted meaningful conversation with liberal and neoorthodox ministers. The time had now come, I noted, for some aggressive moves. Three maneuvers were in immediate prospect: (1) *Christianity Today* in June and July would abridge four lectures on "Dare We Revive the Modernist-Fundamentalist Conflict?" that I was to deliver first at Northern Baptist Theological Seminary and then at Calvin College to the Christian Reformed Ministers Institute; (2) the August 19 issue, in advance of the WCC study sessions on "The Unity We Seek," would carry a symposium by contributing editors from large denominations; (3) in the Fall we would launch a series of articles by scholars not frictionally identified with the Fundamentalist movement on crucial christological concerns and would also enlist international scholars for a theological series on revelation and inspiration.

The outcome was highly gratifying. For one thing, the two-volume work on *American Christianity* by H. Shelton Smith, Robert T. Handy and Lefferts A. Loetscher (Scribner's, 1963) devoted almost ten pages to quoting and summarizing the material on "Dare We Revive the Modernist-Fundamentalist Conflict?" and considered it as significant for the evangelical thrust in the second half of the twentieth century as was J. Gresham Machen's *Christianity and Liberalism* (1923) in the forepart of the century; it quoted both sources selectively and extensively. For another, the World Council of Churches in its section on "Doctrinal Consensus and Conflict" invited me as a consultant in sessions on "The Unity We Seek." The wife of Charles Clayton Morrison, a former editor of the *Century* (who regretted the *Century*'s move to the left of his own views), phoned to express appreciation of *Christianity Today*'s scholarly level and good spirit. A university professor from one of the most prestigious Ivy League schools posted congratulations—not for publication—and added: "I read it quite continually and value its witness. Do not imagine I am alone in this among faculty and students. . . ." Conservative scholars who had carefully watched the effort without committal—Bruce Metzger of Princeton among them—now began to contribute.

Scarcely a week passed but I reminded editorial associates and staff of our awesome opportunity and responsibility. Not even Billy Graham, I stressed, spoke to 160,000 Protestant ministers every fortnight. We began the second year of publication in October with 38,000 paid subscribers, some 4,000 beyond the *Century.* We expected a letter that Graham would circularize in the Fall to lift us above the 50,000 mark, since response to the magazine continued to be overwhelmingly favorable, and advertising was now notably on the upturn. We lacked a professional circulation manager, yet we were restless to reach 80,000 paid since that would entitle us to second class mailing privileges on the basis of a total 160,000 circulation.

10

Beyond an Impressive Launch

Billy Graham's Madison Square Garden crusade in the Summer of 1957 cumulatively drew two million persons, and recorded 50,000 "decisions for Christ." For the opening night I took a Washington-New York train and invited Charlie Claus, our new business manager, to come along. We spoke about spiritual things, and he asked about my own conversion. When Graham gave a public invitation that night, Claus was the first to step out and commit himself to Christ.

The *Century* saw fit to devalue Graham's crusades, and this in turn divided Protestant ecumenists over the imperative of evangelism. Crusade literature tables offered and produced thousands of six-month introductory subscriptions to *Christianity Today.* The magazine carried full crusade coverage, as well as an editorial assessment.

Exhausted from the year's strains, Helga joined me in New York for June 19 departure on a five-week motorcoach tour in Europe sponsored by the Arlington, Virginia, County Educational Association. She brought word of having rented our Pasadena home for the school year of September 1 to June 15 to a visiting California Institute of Technology professor from Sweden. We now trusted God to indicate whether on our return to buy property in the Washington area and to enroll the youngsters nearby in high school, or to rent and enroll them at a distant boarding school. Through the weeks of travel we prayed frequently for Paul and Carol, whose letters indicated full awareness that they might never return to what for many years had been home. Helga's sabbatical from Pasadena College would now mean a year of gratuitous literary work—editing manuscripts for *Christianity Today* and for symposium volumes and hopefully some creative work of her own.

When we returned to Washington we canvassed housing and school possibilities, opted to rent small furnished quarters near *Christianity Today* offices and to enroll the children, if they welcomed the idea, at Ben Lippen Academy in Asheville, North Carolina.

I covered the office during staff vacations in August. By the end of that month, paid subscribers numbered 38,250. That figure not only put us well ahead of the *Century* but was only a fourth of our total mailing. In a single fortnight I had two hours with the religion editor of *Time,* lunch with the religion editor of *Newsweek* and left for Oberlin as an invited evangelical consultant to World Council study sessions on "The Unity We Seek."

Helga meanwhile drove the children cross-country, enrolled them in Ben Lippen and then came on to Washington. We lived temporarily in Allies Inn established near Pennsylvania and 17th St., N.W., by General Pershing's widow after World War I (but razed in recent years for new construction) and then in Monmouth Apartments (later also razed for World Bank facilities).

In the final issue of its first year the magazine included an index of contents, a major editorial on Oberlin Faith and Order and an essay on "The Drive for IMC-WCC Merger" assessing the ecumenical assimilation of the International Missionary Conference. From influential sources came direct and indirect assurances that the magazine was "on target." Clarence Hall of *Christian Herald* wrote: "You have the right pattern for a magazine of your type. . . . Stay with it." The American Association of Theological Schools listed *Christianity Today* along with established journals in its annual index of religious publications important for reading and research. The *Index to Religious Periodicals* issued by the American Theological Library Association announced that it would include articles from *Christianity Today.* The editor of *Time* remarked that *Christianity Today* had brought to the evangelical cause a surprising and impressive range of international scholarship diffused through many denominations.

We began our second year in October, 1957, with articles by Andrew W. Blackwood of Princeton on the deity of Christ, G. C. Berkouwer of Free University of Amsterdam on the prevalent temptation to theological relativism, Tom Allan of Scotland on the role of the laity, James Stewart of New College, Edinburgh, on Christ's kingship over history and Billy Graham's sermon on "The Marks of a Christian." The editorial section republished our "Declaration of Principles." Subsequent issues featured timely essays not only by independent evangelical giants like Clyde W. Taylor of the National Association of Evangelicals, Paul Wooley of Westminster Theological Seminary, J. Theodore Mueller of Concordia Seminary (Lutheran), St. Louis, Gordon H. Clark of Butler University, Wilbur M. Smith and Edward John Carnell of Fuller, Martyn Lloyd-Jones of London's Westminster Chapel, V. Raymond Edman of Wheaton Graduate School and Bernard Ramm who was then abroad on leave from Baylor University School of Religion, but by ecumenical churchmen also like Samuel M. Shoemaker, Alexander Schmemann, Edward L. R. Elson, Walter H. Judd, and scholars like Geoffrey W. Bromiley, Donald J. Wiseman, Calvin D. Linton, William Childs Robinson, Oscar Cullmann, James I. Packer and many others. Marcellus Kik contributed a clever essay on "The King's Existential Garments." Earl L. Douglass, whose Sunday school lessons appeared in many hundreds of newspapers, told of his renewed confidence in the virgin birth of Christ. J. Edgar Hoover, director of the F.B.I., discussed America's moral climate and the importance of a spiritual impact on youth.

Our first news editor, George Burnham, wanted at yearend to return to secular press coverage. David E. Kucharsky's coming as news editor at the beginning of 1958 provided an outstanding news section. Kucharsky had prepared United Press radio news and bulletins in Pittsburgh. Now in our magazine he brought to the attention of secular editors and religious radio newscasts important and quotable material. *Christianity Today* soon became the nation's most frequently and widely quoted religious magazine. Television camera crews periodically trucked their cables and lights into the office for comment on controversial church issues.

Early in February, 1958, I addressed the Monday noon Student Forum at Union Theological Seminary in New York City on "Revelation and the Bible" and engaged in spirited dialogue. The Forum's correspondent invited me, assertedly, as "the most articulate exponent" of "right-wing Protestantism," for a 45-minute lecture to be followed by questions from a panel, and then a luncheon discussion. East coast weather predictions were bleak. I flew from Washington late Saturday on what proved to be the last flight given clearance to land in a blinding snowstorm at LaGuardia, and spoke the next day at Calvary Baptist Church. Late Monday forenoon I took the subway to Broadway and 120th Street and went as requested to President Van Dusen's office just before noon, since he wished to escort me to the lecture room. When we entered just before noon we found a meager half dozen students. Van Dusen was visibly embarrassed, while I did my best to take matters in stride. Then a student explained that everyone had moved to the chapel because the room became too crowded.

The chapel was in fact filled to overflowing, and in the rear section I could make out the visage of a few Union professors, most prominently Reinhold Niebuhr. The student sponsors set up recorders to capture the address and dialogue. My remarks were published in *Christianity Today* in the June 9 and 23, 1958, issues. The ten-minute spirited dialogue concerned mainly the legitimacy of higher criticism. I commented that something is surely askew when seminarians are more persuaded of the existence of J, E, P and D—whom no one has seen—than of the biblical writers to whom the Judeo-Christian witness attributes the sacred writings. At luncheon a pro-Niebuhrian student asked whether it is not a manifestation of human pride to insist on biblical inerrancy. It might no less be a matter of human pride, I replied, to insist on the Bible's errancy.

Word came unexpectedly that my father at the age of 72 had died of cancer on February 7, 1959, and I attended the funeral on Long Island. When I had visited him some time earlier, we talked about family and spiritual matters. But I was unable to move our conversation spiritually beyond his insistence that he had forgiveness of sins and hope for heaven because as a Lutheran he had been baptized as an infant. His second wife, Mae, had arranged a high requium mass in St. John of God Roman Catholic Church. At the interment in the church cemetery the presiding priest delayed the committal ceremony for 45 minutes because Father was not a member of that parish nor of any Catholic church. It was a sad day.

During our first one-and-a-half-years of publication *Christianity Today* lost a managing editor, news editor and two editorial associates, due less to dissatisfaction than to job offers with more guarantee of permanence, and in a few cases because our staff needs required greater competence than most religious publications. This turnover necessitated reorientation and training of new help, and placed still more burdens on the core staff. Some competent editorial associates we drafted for only a month, or a summer vacation, or in Peter de Visser's case, for a year.

At yearend Fuller Seminary had received full accreditation. Both faculty and students were urging me to return. I was still inwardly drawn to seminary life with its carefully monitored hours for teaching, research and writing, and its three-month summer respite and sabbatical prospects.

The next magazine Board meeting was scheduled after the February 28 deadline on which Fuller needed final word over whether after August 31, 1958, *Christianity Today* or Fuller would become my fixed base. Would the Board be open, I asked, to a modified teaching load alongside the editorship? "In the event the Board thinks it best to secure another Editor, I shall make the transition with glad heart once again to the campus. . . . Either a full-time or part-time connection with the Seminary will guarantee my own best creative work for *Christianity Today.*" The magazine ought not, I said, be deprived of the creative and reflective leadership of its own editors.

Conversions from complimentary to paid subscriptions were lagging because ministers discovered that some colleagues continued to receive the magazine even if they did not pay for it. Some Board members thought that the cost (including salaries) involved in securing and processing paid subscriptions argued for a totally free distribution. The editors contended, however, that permanent free distribution would affect the perception of the magazine's worth and would also permanently forego any possibility of more economical second class mailing privileges. Worse yet, our decision not to carry certain kinds of ads had decreased advertising income; some issues didn't cover advertising staff travel costs, let alone salary.

At the same time, the magazine's editorial impact accelerated. At its June 5, 1958, meeting the Board received the 87-page findings of a survey by Opinion Research Corporation of Princeton which showed *Christianity Today* topping all other religious magazines in a poll of clergy reading preferences. *Christianity Today,* the poll indicated, was now the most widely and most completely and most regularly read Protestant magazine. United States Information Agency libraries around the world began to display it alongside the *Century.* My mail involved frequent exchanges with liberals and neoorthodox clergy, with far left ecumenists and far right fundamentalists, with professors who lauded the magazine or who welcomed it merely for parallel reading, with clergy who wanted counsel about what seminaries and colleges they or their sons and daughters might most advantageously attend and with students on many campuses. Reflective conservatives lauded the note of critical evangelical self-appraisal. One doctoral candidate put it this way: "As a conservative you have done what fundamentalists have fought tooth and nail—introduced self-criticism. . . . Such a willingness to judge ourselves is not only basic to our making an impact on our contemporaries, but it is indispensable for presenting ourselves worthily before the Lord."

Gradually we acquired editorial and production assistance that promised better days. In June, 1958, I introduced to the Board not only news editor Gene Kucharsky but also Frank Farrell who had come as editorial associate. Board members discussed the urgent need for a business manager, a managing editor and a circulation manager. Individual Board members pledged $100,000 of the $125,000 needed to finish the year in the black.

For all that, we frequently gained one worker only to lose another. Farrell's coming coincided with Peter de Visser's return to Eerdmans, which now left us for months without a managing editor. An honors student at Wheaton and Fuller, and holding his doctorate from New College, Edinburgh, Farrell brought a theological point of view to convention coverage and special events. He enhanced manuscript evaluation and handled the letters page. He worked slowly and deliberately, and had an astonishing capacity for overlooking deadlines, but he produced material of cognitive worth and literary brilliance, and always submitted in final form. Bill Clemmer's transition to the Navigators meanwhile left unfilled layout and production needs. Except for Kucharsky, whose news duties demanded his full time, I noted to the Board that I had not a single aide with technical experience in the production phase of the editorial effort, including manuscript revision, copy mark-up for composition, layout and so on. For such chores I passed over participation in strategic conferences and spent Saturdays in the office collaborating with part-time editorial or production help, and would even interrupt my summer vacation in Pasadena to spend ten additional days every other month in the office.

Once a third year of publication to begin in October, 1958, was assured, and the magazine's continuance was clearly in view, Board members pressed for my permanent commitment. Fuller had extended its faculty leave to three years, but requested final word by December 31, 1958. I had accepted *Christianity Today*'s earlier invitation with a rider that dissolved the agreement if personal creative opportunities remained unrealized by the end of 1958.

To attest "its esteem and affection," as Nelson Bell put it, the Board now in June, 1958, offered, effective immediately, a three-year contract at a salary of $15,000 with some supplemental benefits, and approved a $300 monthly reimbursement for Helga's work in research or revision, to be done either in the office or at home, but on condition that full-time residence in Washington first be established. It approved also a three-month summer leave to be used as I wished, provided staff covered all phases of my work. I was to continue for three years, residing in the Washington area except for three months annually.

The decision was one of deep personal struggle. It was burdened by a telegram from Fuller students stating that as tomorrow's leaders they needed the comprehensive and persuasive Christian world-view that I championed. Letters from established Christian leaders argued on the other hand that it would be irreparable loss to the magazine were I not to remain. Andrew Blackwood of Princeton and many others urged that I stay with *Christianity Today* for the sake of the larger cause. Billy Graham wrote: "I do not have enough adjectives to describe how pleased I am with the progress of *Christianity Today.* . . . It is nothing less than phenomenal. . . . Certainly there can be no doubt in your mind but what this was God's place for you. I am convinced that there is no single ministry in the nation today that carries with it such responsibility and opportunity as yours."

The magazine was in fact beginning to set an evangelical agenda, rather than merely reacting to ecumenical or radical initiatives. Foreign scholars now routinely contributed essays no less than American scholars not previously in the forefront of evangelical witness. Not only was *Christianity Today* the most frequently quoted religious journal, but the secular press also dubbed me—doubtless to the evangelist's rightful embarrassment—"the thinking man's Billy Graham." Yet alongside Graham the magazine was indeed providing a second line of national reinforcement of evangelical perspectives. Gleason Archer, who hoped I might return to Fuller, nonetheless conceded: "Something is being done through your magazine which has not been done before in this century, and the whole Protestant scene in America has been profoundly affected by its astonishing success."

On every hand there was evidence of evangelical penetration. Commander Lamb of A. J. Holman Company, one of the nation's oldest Bible publishing houses, consulted me early in 1958 about how that firm might best observe its centennial, and then implemented my suggestion that the Holman Study Bible be issued in correlation with a three-volume work, *The Biblical Expositor,* involving evangelical scholars from twenty denominations on four continents.

In May I flew to New York for a conference with denominational leaders on church-state problems. Eugene Carson Blake introduced me as spokesman for "the independent evangelicals." I disavowed his "gracious exaggeration" and also reminded participants that *Christianity Today* spoke even more pointedly for evangelicals inside the ecumenical denominations than for the independents. After return to Washington duties I backtracked to New York for a Fund for the Republic seminar on "Religion in a Democracy." Returning for a long, hard week in Washington, I then flew to New York to join Frank Gaebelein of The Stony Brook School for a private conference with Nelson Rockefeller about a Rockefeller Foundation project concerning the lost sense of national purpose and the need to identify and recover national goals.

Nelson Bell commented in August, 1958, that with our contemplated staff additions we have "sufficient staff to put out a weekly." Hopefully, the Board's approval of James DeForest Murch's coming from *United Evangelical Action*—albeit at 65 and in his retirement years—would in September, at the threshold of our third year of publication, temporarily round out actual staff needs. Nelson's own vacation in Asheville and mine in Pasadena had in fact been almost entirely preempted by magazine concerns. Marcellus was pressing for a three-year contract, in part because of such loose suggestions that we might be overstaffing, and in part because some of my notes written under pressure may have offended him. Nelson and Marcellus were unaccustomed to blunt memos that editorial offices consider routine, and I was too frayed at times to sense that some written exchanges, made necessary by the fact that all three of us were seldom in Washington at the same time, might be considered testy and abrasive. I had forewarned Nelson that his newly abridged schedule of three or four days in Washington every third week, due to his physical condition, might involve times when we would not see each other for a month and a half, since I might be away precisely on his preferred dates.

I had indicated that with the coming of a managing editor in September we must recanvass the assignment of editorial duties in the light of staff abilities and preferences. Marcellus had carried a full load and done it well, but his lack of experience in copyreading, markup and production supervision had left me to police his own work. I reminded Nelson and Marcellus that they had borne many burdens without which the magazine could not have existed. I assured Nelson of my esteem for him as "a Christian gentleman and Christian colleague" and that it could only be "a blow to the enterprise and to me personally if he were to diminish his interest and activity." Looked at merely from the standpoint of my own vocational security, I added, Nelson was my closest link to Billy Graham, and had contacts with the financial sources supporting the magazine; from the standpoint of propriety, moreover, he had explored the magazine's feasibility from the very first and given his life to it; from the standpoint of personal contribution, furthermore, no one worked (despite a coronary) with such efficiency, providing an effective link to lay readers and constituting an irreplaceable tie to the Board. For me, it would be easier to step out if Nelson did, not easier to continue. In reaching for a technically competent staff it was really the need for my own involvement in magazine routines that I was aiming to replace, and not others'.

Three problems nonetheless surfaced and resurfaced at *Christianity Today.* One was the emerging tension between those who understood Mr. Pew's vision for a thought magazine essentially for the clergy, and later evangelism-oriented trustees who saw the magazine as an opportunity to enlist a large lay readership. Fearing that the magazine would be read "by intellectuals only," Nelson thought editorial writing should be his prime responsibility. Despite our assignment to him, alone of all the editors, of a monthly signed page, he continued to criticize longer-range editorials and "cold analytic" articles on which, he felt, there could be little divine blessing.

Another tension pertained to editorial authority and responsibility. Nelson had assumed the title "acting executive editor" during the magazine's earliest planning stages and permanently retained the executive editorship—"window dressing to attract funds," he called it. After I was solicited to come as editor-in-chief, he considered the title ostentatious; I was amenable to the alternative of editor so long as ultimate editorial authority was not at stake. Nelson's proposal that all editors together share responsibility for accepting and rejecting content seemed a good policy, especially at the magazine's beginnings. But Billy Graham's original proposal included Nelson Bell as the only editor to serve on the Board, albeit in his role as secretary-treasurer. Once the magazine began publication, the Board added Marcellus and me also to its ranks, but Nelson alone was named to the executive committee. Later he suggested that the presence of editors on the Board frustrates its evaluation of editorial performance; he favored the non-Board status of editors, although he would remain on the Board for other reasons. The Board continued to include Marcellus and me in its ranks, although Nelson remained on the executive committee which, as it developed across the years, had power of life and death over an editor.

Nelson's role as secretary-treasurer was a golden asset in keeping potential donors abreast of the magazine's needs, but it was also a leaden liability in interpreting staff shortages. His insight into editorial staff requirements was understandably limited and in view of budget deficits he presented the case for staff additions with little enthusiasm. Since neither the executive editor nor the associate editor had backgrounds in professional journalism, I continually bore an overload of responsibilities. My first twenty months as editor had allowed practically no opportunity to advance such concerns as social ethics and religious epistemology, not even on weekends, because office duties ordinarily not an editor's domain virtually cancelled the time necessary for reflection. At the same time I was aware of Nelson's close links to Pew and to Graham which made him a ready channel for their complaints and preferences. The Board knew from my handling of the very first issue that I was not prone to compromise the editorship. Nelson saw his greatest contribution to be in person-to-person relationships, a role in which he considered me deficient, he said, because I was both a "brilliant intellectual" and "perfectionist" and not pliable enough.

By September our full editorial staff was to be in view—Bell, Kik, Kucharsky, Farrell, Murch and myself. But Murch had to delay his coming for family reasons. Further help came through Marian Caine who concentrated on manuscript revision. John Johansson, a retired minister and skillful proofreader, came as production manager and prepared the annual index. A New Jersey businessman, Clair Burcaw, came as advertising promotion director in late September to replace Charlie Claus who had moved to a Chicago agency.

A prod toward greater financial help came in November, 1958, when the Internal Revenue Service approved *Christianity Today*'s application for tax exemption, retroactive to the date of incorporation. Pew considered the magazine "the most important project in America." The political and economic future of America, he stressed, depend upon the nation's spiritual welfare. He would cover up to half of the deficit after subscription and advertising income were deducted—in short, $150,000 a year; with income pledged by other sources, the magazine would need to attract another $74,000 to meet its $500,000 budget. But Pew would join in, he said, only if circulation was not dropped under 160,000.

Just as the Summer of '58 granted to me in Pasadena had shriveled under the encroachment of Washington duties, so now expectations of a more creative Fall soon evaporated. Whatever program the Board accommodated, practical realities required my Washington participation. Dr. Murch delayed his arrival until mid-October and when J. D.—as we called him—did come, he found a nonwriting role difficult to accept and earlier commitments chipped away at his office presence.

I still pondered the attractions of returning to campus life. The Fuller option offered research time, critical reflection and writing in an established professional routine, an annual vacation and cumulative sabbatical time, happy social relationships, preservation of Helga's college and other teaching, continuity of our family as a unit, a good family church situation, a fine cultural environment and a home we treasured for location, charm and comfort. More than that, Fuller had a circle of competent and accessible scholars, just enlarged by the coming in historical theology of Geoffrey Bromiley, whom I had first interested in Fuller when in 1957 I preached for him in St. Thomas Episcopal Church in Edinburgh.

The Washington option, on the other hand, offered an immediate outreach to 160,000 readers and a direct impact for evangelical perspectives perhaps on a national or even international front. There was, however, some divergence within the Board over the magazine's cognitive level, a problem worsened by adding trustees with donor potential but not specially committed as were the magazine founders to a publication intended mainly for clergy and reflective laity.

Financially the differences between Fuller and *Christianity Today* were not great, all things considered. But *Christianity Today* provided no formal contract, no tenure and security, no employer retirement benefits; continuing there meant, moreover, delay if not sacrifice of a volume on Christian social ethics and/or on the doctrine of God.

There was one further but unpublicized reason for preferring Fuller, one that Helga and I had committed confidently to God's providence. Years earlier, during my first complete physical exam, Mayo Clinic had discovered hip joint deformities; specialists foresaw the live possibility of my spending future years in a wheelchair. "If ever you choose between a desk job and work that involves much movement and travel," a specialist counseled, "take the desk job and you'll be less likely to run into trouble."

Now throughout Christmas holidays the alternatives confronted our entire family. We charted what each option implied for the family as a whole and for each individual person. We discounted any considerations of compensation, convenience and comfort. The day after Christmas I wrote Nelson: "Never in all my life have I gone through a valley like this one, though I have had important decisions to make—turning down a college presidency, a seminary presidency, a seminary deanship and so forth, each of them in turn to give myself to the academic priorities of research and the classroom. The opportunities of *Christianity Today* (and you know how great I think they are) attract me in terms of Christian vocation far less than the desire to step back into professorial life toward which all my training has been directed. . . . I am ready to put to death the attachments to Fuller if that be God's will, but even to this moment I am not persuaded about the mind of Christ in the matter, and face the future with *Christianity Today* only as a matter of resignation. God can transcend that if he speaks the word and it is his word and will we want."

Letters arrived continually from those who hoped I would remain at *Christianity Today.* They came from theologians, administrators, authors and even publishers. William B. Eerdmans, Jr., wrote: "You have done a tremendous job." Correspondence reflected the entire evangelical spectrum: Harold B. Kuhn of Asbury Theological Seminary, Henry Stob of Calvin Theological Seminary, J. Theodore Mueller of Concordia Seminary (Missouri Synod), Roger Nicole of Gordon Divinity School, W. T. Purkiser of Nazarene Theological Seminary, John Gerstner of Pittsburgh-Xenia, Faris Whitesell of Northern Baptist Theological Seminary, Rufus Jones of Conservative Baptist Home Mission Society and others.

We went to prayer as a family the night of December 29, determined to wait before God until he had opened and closed doors. That prayer time reversed my inner expectations; it retired the intimate professional ties that for more than a decade had bound me to Fuller. Cost what it may, we were convinced about continuing at *Christianity Today* and that the family should join in that commitment. In the Spring Helga would terminate her teaching; in the Fall we would establish residency in the East.

On December 30, 1958, I wrote Harold Ockenga, severing the link to Fuller, and proposed that he, Bell and I have breakfast at the Willard to discuss moderating some of the difficulties at *Christianity Today.* I phoned Billy Graham; Nelson wrote that he was "thrilled and thankful" for the decision.

By yearend 1958 advertising totaled $55,352 and much space was already contracted for the new year. In a total circulation of 160,000, paid subscriptions numbered over 30,000. An estimated three to five persons read each copy. Roland Kuniholm accepted our invitation to be circulation manager. We were eager now to get our evangelical missile fully into orbit for still greater impact.

Our third year of operations, October 13, 1958, to October 12, 1959, had begun with an interview with Billy Graham on "The Evangelical World Prospect." Issue after issue carried articles by well-known Christians, among them William G. Pollard of Oak Ridge Institute of Nuclear Studies, Ronald C. Doll of New York University, Otto Michel of Tübingen University, Harvard's Pitirim A. Sorokin, Princeton's Otto A. Piper, Fuller's Edward John Carnell and J. Edgar Hoover of the F.B.I., and even an article by Eugene Carson Blake on "Tax Exemption and the Churches." Cornelius Van Til wrote on "What of the New Barth?" and Geoffrey Bromiley on "Barth: A Contemporary Appraisal." There were regular contributors, like Berkouwer, Packer, Linton, Robinson, Kuhn, Ladd, Ramm and Tenney. A feature on outer space exploration included comments by Barth, Brunner, Cullmann, Niebuhr, Tillich, along with those of evangelical theologians. The main news section initiated use of pictures that covered Graham crusades as well as major ecumenical events. Comments by the magazine's 50 contributing editors made up the yearend editorial that assessed the national and world situations.

The January 19 and February 7, 1959, issues carried a two-part article, "Perspective for Social Action," and the latter issue also a lead editorial on "Race Tensions and Social Change." Other later editorials discussed "Brotherhood for a Week," "Theology in Ecumenical Affairs," "The Resurrection and Modern Life." We still lacked timely short editorials on late-breaking events of religious importance, but the *Century*'s weekly rather than fortnightly appearance with a much lower print order worked to its advantage. Our new production schedule, however, now held open in every issue both a late news page and a late editorial page to be prepared just before final deadline.

At its first 1959 meeting the Fuller faculty adopted a resolution† in appreciation of my years at the Seminary, voiced continuing interest in the success of *Christianity Today* and invited me to deliver the 1963 Payton Lectures. To honor *Christianity Today* and secondarily me, Los Angeles businessman W. C. Jones underwrote an April 3 banquet at the Statler-Hilton for 250 guests. Dr. Wilbur Smith, featured speaker, gave a characteristically moving address that Radio Station KPOL later rebroadcast. Throughout the banquet Helga sat on a well-concealed goose-down pillow; while answering the phone in processing banquet R.S.V.P.s she had slipped on a newly waxed floor.

The magazine's acceptance throughout evangelical ranks continued. During my Pasadena visit I gathered three distinguished evangelical theologians—H. Orton Wiley of Pasadena College, Geoffrey Bromiley of Fuller and Roger Nicole of Gordon-Conwell—for a spirited dialogue that *Christianity Today* carried on the doctrine of divine election. In it a Nazarene, an Anglican and a Baptist shared agreements and differences in a way that illuminated one of Christianity's most controversial doctrines. The National Association of Evangelicals, although once highly apprehensive lest *Christianity Today* prove directly competitive with *United Evangelical Action,* now recognized that we brought to the evangelical cause a powerfully articulate voice, and did so in a wider denominational context.

The editors were increasingly in demand as speakers and dialogue participants, something we encouraged insofar as it was strategic for the magazine. Nelson carried a remarkably heavy schedule, including a Sunday Men's Bible Class in Asheville which became an Adult Bible Class of 1500 members as part of the Montreat summer conference programs. But when our work-week engagements disadvantaged office production we charted guidelines that limited absences to magazine promotive involvements.

When the family moved East, Helga voluntarily assisted me at home with manuscript revision that we had hoped Murch would carry. I

---

† Noting that I was "a member of the faculty . . . for twelve years and also a charter member, . . . an indefatigable worker, a keen defender of the orthodox faith, a discerning observer of the times, an author of note, a friend of students and a fellow companion of this Faculty," the resolution expressed the Fuller faculty's "love and devotion, its sense of appreciation for his splendid service, its recognition of the strategic impact he has made by his long and honored association with the Seminary, its heartfelt prayers for the success of his new undertaking and its firm and warm hope that the Holy Spirit of God will endue him with greater power for service in our age to the end that the Lord of the Church may be glorified in and through him."

still got to the office by 7:30 A.M., having scanned the *Washington Post* during a breakfast of coffee and blueberry muffins at Chamberlin's Cafeteria (819 15th St., N.W.) and used that early time frame for dictating replies to important mail. After staff gathered at 9 A.M. for Bible reading, devotional comments, prayers of thanksgiving and for special needs, we went to work. The day after each new issue appeared the editors met to evaluate and criticize, and to finalize the next issue with its special features and editorial assignments.

The Summer of 1959 was in numerous ways momentous. I took part in my first World Vision pastors' conference in Asia, coordinating my vacation with a complete change of environment and activity. Even so, I enlisted knowledgeable correspondents in numerous places, arranged for redistribution of yearend bulk shipments of the magazine to English-speaking missionaries and Asian seminarians who would be specially interested in the projected "Christianity and World Religions" issue and also airmailed timely news articles from lands in which we ministered.

Comprising the team that Bob Pierce led across the Orient were Paul Rees, Dick Halverson, Bishop Enrique Sobrepena (chairman of the Southeast Asia Christian Council) and Kung Chik Han, founding minister of the famed Young Nak Presbyterian Church in Seoul, Korea. The six-week itinerary from June 30 to August 15 involved five major conferences in Malaya, Burma, Thailand and the Philippines, with short rest breaks in Singapore and Hong Kong.

Just before the Asian venture, Helga joined me in Washington early in June for two weeks of house-hunting. Carol and high school senior Paul insisted that they could take care of themselves and in addition keep our Pasadena premises presentable for three days of open-house scheduled by our real estate agent. Helga returned in time for Rose Bowl ceremonies, at which Paul was honored as "outstanding junior [R.O.T.C.] cadet." She brought word, moreover, that we had bought a house in Arlington, Virginia, for Fall occupancy. I had a week at home with Helga and the children who during my flight to Asia would be left alone to sell the Pasadena home, prepare for moving and hold yard sales before my mid-August return.

Bob Pierce and I were to fly to Asia from Los Angeles via Japan, where in Osaka Pierce was to address a converts' meeting a month after his break-through crusade there. A cable from Don Hoke, president of Japan Christian College, urged me to stop in Tokyo to give four lectures on that campus, and then the dedicatory address for Japan Bible Seminary newly formed by Akira Hatori, Junichi Funaki and Hoke. Hatori, one of my former Fuller students, had already become a prominent Japanese evangelist. After these engagements

Pierce and I continued on July 4 to Osaka, where through an interpreter I spoke extemporaneously for ten minutes to a restless overflow crowd of 3,000 people. Meanwhile Bob made his way from inside the auditorium to an exterior balcony for better access to the outside gathering.

Our schedule carried us next to Manila. There I addressed an International Christian Leadership breakfast and linked up with Halverson and Rees who had arrived from Los Angeles to join us for flight to Singapore en route to programmed meetings in Malaya. Tropical heat and humidity took its toll even upon seasoned travelers. Exhausted by his Osaka crusade, Bob Pierce dropped out for the next week. Jack Conner, the young musician whose marimba fascinated many Asians, suffered a heart attack in Burma. In Thailand I put in at Bangkok Christian Hospital for a half-hour of heat therapy to relieve severe back pain from lugging heavy baggage. For a brief rest the team tried a round of golf at the Philippine mountain resort of Baguio, but shortness of breath felled me on the first hole. Back to my hotel room I went to rest before preaching that night. Such experiences were flipside aspects of our transnational, transracial and transcultural mission.

Helga and the teenagers, besides writing me almost daily, coped with sale of the house, suitcase survival as furnishings were sold, not to mention a car that had sprung a radiator leak. Upon returning from Asia I spent a week in Pasadena, but soon took off again for a long-scheduled minister's conference in Pensacola, Florida.

Toward the end of August Helga and the children in three days drove from Pasadena to Arlington. Crossing the Virginia state line had buoyed their weary spirits. But coping now with speeding, tailgating drivers on historic two-lane, no-passing roads was another matter. Thinking the particular shoulder area simply overgrown with weeds, Helga pulled over to get rid of the impatient driver behind her. Into the ditch she went, and Carol in the back seat was promptly buried under bags and baggage. Paul thumbed a ride for help in the nearby village and soon returned with a tow truck that extricated them—shaken but unhurt—for the remaining 25 miles. They arrived at our Arlington home-to-be, 2373 North Kenmore Street, about 4 P.M. on August 31, Carol's birthday. Irma, my ever-thoughtful secretary, had a birthday cake waiting. The four-level, three-bedroom house cost $31,950, toward which we applied the $23,500 cash received for our much more substantial and commodious Pasadena residence. But located as it was on a quiet cul-de-sac, and facing a small city park and specially only 12–15 minutes' driving time to both the heart of Washington and National Airport, it proved an excellent choice.

In September Paul took off for Wheaton College, checking the footlocker which he had safely transported cross-country, only to have Greyhound forsake it in Chicago. Carol entered Washington-Lee High School in Arlington as a Junior. The high school had just admitted its first blacks—two in number—and by way of caution cancelled the year's social activities. Helga [born in Africa] had to clarify her racial status before Carol was admitted. Arlington had a long way to go in race relations, but it was poised to move much more quickly than many persons thought.

We settled in quickly. Though fully weary as I, Helga largely inherited the task of "unboxing" belongings. Ed Carnell, who had resigned Fuller's presidency, wanted to occupy my former office, so my books were hurriedly parceled by students without presorting and shipped—about a hundred boxes—to *Christianity Today.* Twenty more boxes went to Arlington. For economy and relaxation, we both enrolled for a week-night adult education class in woodworking. I built so many bookcases to house my volumes at home that the instructor wondered whether Sears, Roebuck had me under contract. Helga made a footstool.

The next Board meeting, on September 10 in New York, impressed me again that the men who stood behind the magazine were men of big vision and stout heart. While there, Billy Graham asked me to accompany him to Germany for six weeks in 1960 for theological lectures on the edge of his evangelistic meetings.

Two developments confronted us at the beginning of the magazine's fourth year in October, 1959. For one thing, Nelson felt he must curtail the time he gave to fund raising for the magazine, and expectations that Mr. Pew might set up a supportive foundation seemed to me highly presumptuous. For another, Billy Graham proposed the yearend launching by B.G.E.A. of a new magazine, *Decision,* aimed specially at the laity and at ministers interested in evangelism. *Decision* was to be mailed free to the entire Graham list. Postponement of its introductory issue to October, 1960, enabled us to lend-lease Sherwood Wirt, the projected editor, as an interim editorial associate at *Christianity Today.*

Our Board was not pledged to maintain free distribution beyond October, 1959. The annual budget was $580,000. Advertising income had reached $100,000 a year. We anticipated that in another year our paid circulation would double the *Century*'s. But Board members had not attracted supplemental outside support. One Board member made a loan to the magazine.

Our fourth anniversary issue (October 12, 1959) led off with the Bromiley-Nicole-Wiley dialogue on divine election and included news editor Kucharsky's coverage of Khruschev's tour of America. Kucharsky had been the only representative of the religious press among the 250 international journalists who accompanied the Russian visitor. The same issue featured 25 prestigious theologians and philosophers in a symposium on "Christendom's Key Issue," and set the stage for subsequent essays by Emil Brunner, Otto Dibelius, Edward L. R. Elson, Cyrus H. Gordon, Russell Kirk, Charles Malik, Otto Piper, Andrew K. Rule, along with more routine contributors such as Berkouwer, Bruce, Carnell, Linton, Mueller and Tenney. Gordon's article on "Higher Critics and Forbidden Fruit," leading off the November 23 issue, was widely quoted.

Nelson left for Los Angeles in November to address the National Association of Evangelicals and in December continued to Korea to represent the Board of World Missions of the Presbyterian Church, U.S., in resolving a problem apparently provoked by Carl McIntire in the Korean Presbyterian Church. He hoped to be home for Christmas.

So heavy was correspondence that I seemed at times to be the only member of the editorial team coping with it. Sometimes months passed before Marcellus—struggling against the same time pressures that I faced—would submit an article or editorial of his own, and some of this material lacked organization, substance or artistry. Some Board members felt the associate editorship must be notched up. I determined to risk personal exhaustion rather than to require the resignation of a founder-colleague. On November 17, however, Marcellus notified me that he had tendered his resignation to the Board effective December 31, but would leave on December 15—in just a month—in view of unused vacation time. He planned to complete some private literary projects, one being a Reformation study that specially interested Mr. Pew and on which Philip Hughes was also engaged. At the turn of the year Murch informed us that he, too, would leave in mid-April, 1961, for larger writing opportunities. Thereupon *Christianity Today* enlisted Calvin Bulthuis of Eerdmans as managing editor.

At the annual dinner for staff and their wives a few weeks before Christmas at Arlington Tea House, and to which we invited also the Washington religious press, we introduced the magazine's staff. Present on editorial side besides myself were Kucharsky, Farrell and Wirt, all highly gifted, and Murch whom we were losing but would have been glad to retain as managing editor. Clair Burcaw on the business side and Roland Kuniholm in circulation also brought strength to the effort. Other faithful workers like John Johannson and Marian Caine covered proofreading and copy-editing. Burcaw had raised 1959 advertising income to $90,000. The prospect of replacing Wirt and Marcellus Kik, and of adjusting to Nelson's curtailed participation, had but one consoling aspect: to get away from the office I no longer needed to fly West, but could escape to nearby Arlington.

There were moments when we gladly would have posted "For Sale" outside our Virginia home if the alternative had been anything but divine disobedience. In contrast to California, the Washington area seemed in some ways a land of dry and barren tradition. As for the weather, especially in summer, we soon learned why certain diplomats considered it a hardship area. Helga specially missed the cooperative interdenominational life of vigorous evangelical churches. Dedicated and devout, strong of spirit yet flexible, she was reconciled to the loss of her professional opportunities without being resentful. I was secretly burdened, because I felt that the magazine had not kept its assurances to enlist her gifts. I spared her details of my concerns at *Christianity Today* except for what we ought mutually to share in prayer, and our children were aware only of the positive aspects of my work. When Helga asked what special vocation remained for her, she saw our teenage children as a continuing sphere of ministry, and lightening my literary load, as present priorities. She wrote and sent our annual Christmas letter to a list that grew from 300 to 400 to almost 500. In addition she started graduate studies at George Washington University for a possible doctorate.

Late in January, 1960, on the edge of the Evangelical Press Association conference in Minneapolis, I spent a weekend with medics at Mayo Clinic who the previous September had counseled me to cut back my work load. Migraine and vertigo were now less frequent, but physical exhaustion required my departure from the office at two thirty in the afternoon for uninterrupted work; since I came in at 7:30, in part to avoid the traffic, I still put in full days. One week Kucharsky and I bore the entire office load—Bell was on his second trip to Korea, Murch in the West for a Christian Church consultation, Wirt in South Dakota, Farrell on an out-of-town assignment and Johanson ill. March brought word that Nelson was taking codeine for sub-sternal stress. He avoided going to a cardiologist for fear he would be hospitalized. But his discomfort continued. He was confined for a week and told that the pain was apparently due to the passage of a small arterial clot.

The magazine's impact continued to demand my personal involvement on academic, ecumenical and cultural frontiers in addition to faithful editorial engagement and projection. In a single week in April, 1960, I spoke in Biblical Seminary and Eastern Baptist Seminary chapels, recorded two radio addresses to be carried on forty-three stations, met for breakfast with editor Dan Poling of the *Christian Herald*, took part in an NBC network panel, prepared for our Board meeting and readied plans thereafter to leave for a week in Colombia with a World Vision team.

Almost every issue we received letters from unanticipated sources who applauded the magazine—professors on ecumenically oriented campuses, denominational leaders reaching for more theological or evangelistic earnestness, pastors who felt isolated in their denominational contexts. George Cornell's national AP column referred to *Christianity Today* as "comparatively new" and yet as "already influential" and characterized it as scholarly—"a sort of intellectual voice of conservative, Evangelical Protestantism" and now "a counterpart of the widely respected liberal weekly," the fifty-year-old *Christian Century.* Kenneth Dole, religion editor of the *Washington Post,* paid tribute to "the brilliantly edited evangelical magazine published here," even if he said it symbolizes "the new fundamentalism." Dole was a Universalist, albeit a theist. He sought to be meticulously fair in his religion coverage. The president of a Southern religious college volunteered that, of the evangelical forces in the United States, *Christianity Today* now exercised the greatest regulatory influence.

Top level confidential meetings of Christian leaders had launched into the conversation stage the possibility of a great Christian university in the metropolitan New York City area. My lead-off editorial essay titled "Do We Need a Christian University?" in the May 9, 1960, issue brought to light some of the remarkable talk circulating among certain evangelical academics and was quoted by *The New York Times* and by Paul Harvey and others on national media.

I surmised to evangelical editors in Minneapolis that for reasons other than his religion Democrats would not nominate John F. Kennedy for president. ABC and NBC networks declared, gratuitously, that *Christianity Today* had taken a stand against a Catholic president. Television variety show host Ed Sullivan resented our occasional reference to "Romanism"—in distinction from Protestantism—and made a snide comment about *Christianity Today* in his syndicated *New York Daily News* column.

With an explosive political campaign in prospect, I reminded the editorial staff that we wanted objective presentation and a good conscience in the arena of religion-and-politics. "CT is not devoted to the election of a particular presidential candidate; we want to keep the magazine above all parties, programs and personalities" and to "see the issues squarely in terms of principle."

Invited by the Fair Campaign Practices Committee I met for two days of dialogue with eighteen persons chaired by Charles Taft, son of President Taft and brother of the late Senator Robert Taft. Roman Catholic participants included Monsignor Lalley of Boston, editor of

The Pilot; Monsignor Higgins of the National Catholic Welfare Conference; and Gustave Weigel, the Jesuit theologian. Jews were represented by leaders of the National Council of Christians and Jews and by rabbis from Orthodox, Conservative and Reform wings. Protestants present were Arid Olsen of the National Council of Churches, Emmanuel Carlson of the Baptist Joint Affairs Committee, Winthrop Hudson of Colgate-Rochester Divinity School and I.

Catholic participants were aggressive and had a well-knit and confusing strategy. Protestants divided into those who found the answer to all problems in religious pluralism, those who feared that one who spoke his mind would be considered a maverick, and a fool like myself who said what I believed. Although a board member of that group, Carlson did not even defend Protestants and Other Americans United when it came under fire. And I didn't learn, until I got a letter from him a week later, that Hudson shared my anxieties.

The major agreement—which hardly justified luncheon through luncheon sessions—was that a candidate's religion has a relevant bearing on politics, and that a political campaign should not be made the occasion for condemning him for his religion, but only of raising the religious question at its points of relevance to political matters.

Catholic participants held that Senator John F. Kennedy had answered all church-state questions, yet that Protestants reraise them as if they were unanswered; that Protestants view Roman Catholicism only in terms of Spanish Christianity; that Protestants misinterpret Catholic politics in the United States in terms of long past papal pronouncements. Catholics also emphasized that Kennedy opposed federal aid to private schools on grounds of church-state separation. Moreover, they singled out as offensive an article in *Christianity Today* by Stanley Lowell titled, "Protestants, Catholics and Politics," in which without mentioning that President Eisenhower had a Protestant minister on his staff, Lowell warned that priests and nuns would swarm through the White House if a Catholic became president.

When the matter of an ambassador to the Vatican came up, Taft indicated that a number of informed leaders believed that the amount of useful information available from the Vatican is exaggerated, and that any significant information could be secured from Switzerland or some other country where the Vatican has an ambassador.

I asked the group point-blank, and Father Higgins especially, if my own presentation came across as bigotry. After a bit of purgatorial silence, I was assured that it was a legitimate contribution to the dialogue. The reason I asked, I said, was that Ed Sullivan in his syndicated column had branded as "hateful bigotry" an editorial titled "Bigotry or Smear?" that took the same tack. The Catholics then said, "Well, you can't escape all that sort of thing." So I indicated that, appealing to graciousness and fair play, Sullivan had sent a six-page letter as a reply to an "Open Letter to Ed Sullivan" that we carried from Glenn L. Archer, the highly respected executive director of Protestants and Other Americans United. I stated our willingness to publish it as a move toward fair practices—on condition that we be given a reciprocal opportunity to reply in Sullivan's syndicated column, "Little Old New York," that appeared in the *New York Daily News* and 100 other papers. Word got back to Sullivan and the material appeared both in the *Daily News* and in *Christianity Today.*

The Democratic National Convention, which was to begin July 11, was now likely to nominate Kennedy for president. We had received a moving essay titled "A Catholic for President?" by a former Roman Catholic priest who had become a Protestant minister. The essay was typeset on June 22 and proofread, ready for publication whenever stipulated. A decision had to be made very promptly about its use in the magazine and Nelson was not available.

I was to fly to Latin America for a four-day World Vision pastors' conference May 9–13 in Medellin, Colombia, that incidentally would afford an up-to-date glimpse of what religious liberties and evangelistic prerogatives a Catholic political order preserved there. I bequeathed to Nelson therefore the decision on whether to run the political essay, since we had long gravitated political contacts in Washington to him. I was to leave for Europe, moreover, on August 11 for a major Graham-sponsored consultation on evangelism on August 16–18 in Montreaux, Switzerland, where a hundred invited delegates were to assess the world situation in anticipation of Graham crusades in Switzerland and Germany the next five weeks. All issues interacting with the presidential election would necessarily go into magazine production before I returned from the commitment I had earlier made to Graham for ministerial meetings in Berne, Lausanne and Basel. In my absence, I indicated, Nelson should take both editorial and newsside responsibility for all politically related material since he was most aware of the Board's view of how extensive the magazine's involvement should be.

Some Board members thought we should engage in the debate over whether the Democrats should nominate Kennedy, some thought we ought to become involved only if a Kennedy-Nixon campaign eventuated. The *Century* endorsed Kennedy and some feared that if elected Kennedy would void the tax exempt status of *Christianity Today* and other evangelical magazines. Our lawyers warned that political involvement of any kind might endanger *Christianity Today*'s tax status.

In April, 1960, I was told just after the *Century* had endorsed

Kennedy that Richard Nixon wanted me to visit with him in his office on Capitol Hill. We chatted for about an hour. Nixon left me with two overarching impressions: first, that as a teenager he had made a personal decision for Christ during one of Aimie Semple McPherson's meetings; second, that he better than anyone else discerned the nature of the communist threat and recognized that communism is a malignant force in the world. One would never have prognosticated from that conversation either the events of Watergate or the new era of relationships with Red China. Although he did not say it in so many words, Nixon clearly hoped that *Christianity Today* would endorse his candidacy, to offset the *Century*'s endorsement of Kennedy. At the conclusion of the interview I thanked him. As we shook hands I said, "Mr. Nixon, *Christianity Today* has set a high standard, and whoever rises to that standard will inherit its influence." During my years the magazine endorsed no candidate, of whatever party, although a successor, in a personal Editor's Note, publicly indicated his support for Nixon.

At the April Board meeting I reported that in less than four years we had in every way reached a plane of equality with the *Century,* whether measured by paid circulation, appraisals by neutral sources or network invitations to the editor to appear on national programs. Lou Cassels, religion editor of UPI, declined an invitation to the *Century* staff to develop a news section rivaling *Christianity Today*'s.

I also informed the Board that to overcome fatigue I needed to get away for a year when my agreement with the magazine expired on September 30, 1961. I did not want to rehearse office pressures again to the Board. I would like to go abroad, I indicated, to stay abreast of current theological and other trends. The Board should be free, I said, to choose a permanent editor by way of replacement, or on the other hand to name an acting editor, in which case I would return. I stressed that whoever was invited should come for the Summer of 1961 to get some grasp of magazine routines. Ockenga pressed me to stay until June, 1962, to which I reluctantly agreed. But I increasingly needed physical rest even more than time off for reflection and creative writing.

While covering summer routines I additionally prepared for the ministerial addresses in Europe on the drift of contemporary theology. Helga had been invited to come along because of her facility in German, which she had taught to college and seminary students. But that evaporated. She was determined, for one thing, to be accessible to her brother Carl Ronald who was fighting for his life against leukemia. She was equally constrained to seize one of the last opportunities to fellowship with and influence our children before Paul's return to Wheaton and

Carol's last year in high school. On the afternoon of August 11 she and Paul and Carol drove me to Washington (National) Airport for the first leg of my New York–Amsterdam flight; we would not meet again for more than two months. At monthend Helga drove both Carol and Paul to Wheaton, in order to give Carol a glimpse of the campus, and then returned with her to Arlington. In a happy turn of events, Carol was invited to join the junior staff of the Alexandria School of Music to teach ten hours of piano weekly beginning that Fall.

I proceeded to Montreaux for Graham's pre-Crusade consultation with evangelical leaders. Clyde Taylor presented a global survey of missions and evangelism. Bob Pierce observed that "our children will live in a nonwhite world before Jesus comes," something for which the American church, at least, had no plan. Graham warned that "The whole church is going to go through a great period of suffering and persecution. . . . The church will either be repentant or rebellious. . . . I don't think the church in America is going to repent. Thousands of professing Christians," he added, "will desert the camp." Festo Kivengere of Uganda said we need The Reviver more than revival. Tom Allan, former chairman of the "Tell Scotland" movement and member of the WCC department of evangelism, reviewed his recovery from Protestant liberalism, and Graham's ministry in Scotland. I perceived a sense of both heavy burden and evangelical opportunity. But I saw little emphasis on the war of ideas, little concern for the university world, for doctrinally powerful literature or for the world of work. Stacey Woods and I walked the streets of Montreaux late into the night speaking of the neglected campuses and the forfeited world of modern learning.

Next we moved on for Graham's crusades that carried to Switzerland and Germany the evangelistic thrust that for ten years had captured headlines in the United States. Multitudes who had stopped attending church came to listen. In Germany cumulative audiences ran 700,000—some 25,000 made public decisions. Graham had asked me to address ministerial meetings because few clergymen other than an evangelical minority turned out for crusade meetings; nonevangelical pastors tended to dismiss the meetings as simplistic. Ministerial meetings assessing the theological drift, Graham felt, might serve as a bridge. I had consented if Graham promised not to attend, since the clergy would obviously want to hear him instead.

In these forums it became evident that the German scene offered no magazine comparable to *Christianity Today.* Some spoke of the special need of such an evangelical witness at this theological transition time, when the theological initiative of Barth and Brunner had been broken and Bultmann was becoming a rallying force for young intellectuals. "If Bultmann prevails," one spokesman said, "we shall have a renaissance of liberalism." The largely nonevangelical scholarship of German divinity faculties had nullified the biblical commitment of Continental pulpits, channeled mediating scholars to influential teaching posts and intimidated the beleaguered evangelicals.

Graham's two-day crusades in Berne, Basel and Lausanne each drew over 25,000 for the most extensive mass meetings in Swiss history. He had drawn larger attendances in earlier one-night meetings, but the week-long Hamburg crusade would now mark his largest cumulative turnout to date in Europe. Night meetings in West Berlin also drew a total attendance of 22,000, some 2,000 coming from East Berlin despite communist hostility.

More significantly, the West Berlin campaign attracted 25,000 students, the largest assembly of young people gathered before or since the Reformation for a single religious service and the largest meeting of youth that Graham had addressed. This response was all the more noteworthy because both Lutheran and Reformed churches tended to postpone personal spiritual decision to the piety of the middle years.

I addressed the Berlin student meeting for ten minutes before Graham's message, and spoke to two meetings of 400 pastors and Christian workers from West and East Berlin, as well as to a ministers' meeting in the Hamburg Cathedral, and to 1,200 high school students in Essen in the industrial Ruhr Valley. In all, I spoke to 1,200 clergy and full-time workers in French-speaking and German-speaking Switzerland and to about 1,200 in Germany.

When theologically conservative pastors learned of its growing impact and that *Christianity Today* was considering a British edition, they probed the possibility of a German edition also, a possibility that John Bolten, Graham and I thought should be explored. When asked by Graham for his reaction to the notion of a German edition, Bishop Hanns Lilje of Hanover, who attended the opening night of the Berlin crusade, reacted positively. But Lilje noted that conservative forces in Lutheran and Reformed circles would need to be enlisted, since only one in ten ministers was in the so-called "free churches."

Lilje had already left Berlin when I learned about this exchange. I dictated a letter stating our goals, suggesting that a German edition have twenty contributing editors from Germany alongside those already listed from Britain and some from the United States. Our European contributing editors already included Berkouwer of the Netherlands, Marcel from France and Bruce, Hughes, Tasker and Wiseman from England. My inclination was to enlist among others from Germany, I added, Bishop Lilje, Bishop Dibelius, Prof. Adolph

Koeberle and Prof. Otto Michel of Tuebingen, Prof. Hans Rohrbach of Mainz, Prof. Edmund Schlinck of Heidelberg, Prof. Ernst Kinder of Muenster, Prof. Johannes Schneider of Humboldt University of Berlin, Prof. Martin Metzger or Dr. Hans Luckey of Hamburg Baptist Seminary and perhaps Evangelist Willie Busch. Other German scholars might also contribute articles, especially conservatives like Bergmann, Burki, Deitenbach, Rienecker, Ruloff and Schmidt. What was Lilje's reaction, I asked, and what editors and essayists would he himself propose? Should we not also ask the German Evangelical Alliance for suggestions?

I stressed the need for swift beginnings. German theology was again at a turning time, and a move was underway to the left of Barth and Brunner toward Bultmann that threatened resurgence of the old liberalism in a subtle, highly romanticized form. Some scholars were already at work to frustrate the resurgent Bultmannism. Transitions in formative theological positions usually occur but once in a generation, I noted; once fixed, new positions force scholars to resist and counter their influence for decades. "This is the time to move into the vacuum," I wrote, "with a solidly evangelical thrust, across denominational lines, in a constructive ecumenical spirit, pleading the cause of biblical theology, biblical ethics, biblical evangelism, and creating new respect for the authority of Scripture."

I phoned Lilje in Hanover in hopes of meeting him there. But he had already left to lecture on a remote Danish island accessible only by ferry from Copenhagen. In hopes of striking a providential contact, and I did, I arranged my return via Copenhagen. Lilje and I explored my list of possible European contributors; to mine he added the names of Joachim Bieneck, Peter Brunner, Leonhard Goppelt, Joachim Jeremias and Karl Rengstorf. The German Evangelical Alliance suggested the names of Dibelius, Koeberle, Michel, Schneider, Weber, Busch, Lilje, Bergmann, Luckey, Metzger, Bishop Wunderlich and Frey.

Preliminary inquiries showed that a German edition of 25,000 copies could reach 14,000 "state church" (or peoples' church) pastors in West Germany and German-speaking Switzerland, 1,700 "free church" pastors, as well as 300 theology professors and lecturers in German universities and teacher training colleges, 3,000 teachers of religion in high schools and 1,150 church deacons. On a monthly (rather than fortnightly) basis, such an edition would cost $71,000, including modest offices in Wuppertal and Geneva. Bolten and Graham each indicated a willingness to underwrite $20,000 during the first year. We had earlier inquired into the availability of Harold Kuhn of Asbury Theological Seminary, who knew the German scene well, as special associate editor in Washington to coordinate and oversee the project. Pew approved the additional salary if we proceeded.

With Bolten's and Graham's encouragement I commissioned Brockhaus Verlag in Wuppertal, a leading evangelical publishing house, to prepare a master list of names and addresses of all German Protestant clergy for prompt conversion to address plates. We also prepared preliminary magazine cover projections of *Christentum Heute.* Appropriate articles from the American and/or British editions would be translated into German, while desired articles from *Christentum Heute* would be translated into English for Anglo-American use. Brockhaus Verlag promised free office space in Wuppertal. I mentioned to Graham and Bolten that if we "go ahead," I would feel "morally obligated to get it successfully underway; . . . if we wait . . . we may find ourselves confronted by the law of diminishing returns—both in respect to ecclesiastical enthusiasm and theological opportunity." They agreed. The *Christianity Today* Board met on November 3. I reported that although *Christianity Today* was influentially defining the evangelical position and bracing American evangelicals against the dominant theological tide, "we have thus far not decisively directed nor influenced the content of contemporary theology. One reason for this," I added, "is the unchallenged leadership and influence of the German theologians whose positions we now encounter only after they have become entrenched." The Board was intrigued by Graham's report of the crusades in Switzerland and Germany, and exhilarated by the wider recognition accumulating to *Christianity Today.* The possibility of a German edition—for all the added burdens it would place upon an already overburdened staff—was exciting.

But the question soon arose whether German sources would share the cost of the effort and to what extent. Many felt strongly that a German edition was desirable but were troubled by the continuing need for funds for the American effort. *Christianity Today* was finishing out 1960 with an overall budget of $672,848, of which advertising and subscriptions covered $273,420, leaving about $400,000 to be raised by Board contributions. Would the German Evangelical Alliance preliminarily underwrite the cost of sending one issue to all the clergy? The Alliance itself survived by prayer and piety; its main cooperative effort was an annual day of prayer and the sponsorship of occasional evangelistic crusades. Could we, moreover, really expect financial assistance from ecumenically oriented agencies? Would German laymen rally to the opportunity? The Board was within $19,000 of agreeing to proceed with a German edition when it decided to postpone a final verdict for six months until April, 1961. Even if the final decision were yes, that delay nonetheless precluded any publication before January, 1962.

To me the next Board meeting in November was ineffective. Some arrived the night before but had to leave by 10:30 A.M.; others arrived at 10:30 and had to leave at 1 P.M. Still others came not primarily in the interest of *Christianity Today* but to pursue other causes. Only one Board member pledged financial support if we proceeded with the German project. Graham, Bolten, Beavan and I were named a committee to report back in the Spring. Meanwhile we put a hold on completing a clergy mailing list. In the interim the German edition of *Entscheidung* (*Decision*) appeared in order to reinforce results of the Graham crusades. *Christianity Today* meanwhile carried four essays on the religious drift of German Protestantism titled "Wintertime in European Theology."

The plain fact was that German laymen lacked sufficient vision to help underwrite such an effort aimed at theological renewal. Many German laymen probably reflected the mood of their pastors: theology divides, evangelism unites. They little suspected that apart from biblical theology evangelism soon clouds and conceals the gospel.

From the outset *Christianity Today* had a concern also for English-speaking clergy outside the United States. Through Marcellus Kik's personal interest a free distribution went to 3,725 Canadian clergy of whom almost 2,000 became permanent subscribers. Short-term free distributions were made on the edge of Graham crusades both in Britain and Australasia, though the cost of foreign mailings and delayed delivery worked against paid subscriptions. After my participation in pastors' conferences in the Orient, World Vision underwrote 450 subscriptions to key English-speaking Christian leaders in Asia.

Also from its beginnings the magazine aimed to reinforce evangelical vitalities in Britain, where conservative intellectual and academic strength was largely uncoordinated. The executive committee had voted as early as November, 1956, that for the present we would not, however, employ a British editor, but simply enlist contributing editors and correspondents. Philip Hughes, former secretary of the Church Society of the Church of England, became one of our several Anglican contributing editors. Because British subscribers could not send funds out of the country, we secured Marshall, Morgan and Scott as British agents, but with rather meager results, possibly because they considered *Christianity Today* competitive with their own publications. Evangelical forces had acquired *The Church of England Newspaper,* but it was already in financial need. When Sherwood Wirt left us to edit *Decision,* our Board enlisted Hughes, by then editor of *The Churchman,* to come to Washington for a stint as editorial associate beginning October 24, 1960. Meanwhile we explored prospects for a British edition and opening our own office on London's historic Fleet Street by the Spring of 1961. In view of Graham's enlarging ministries in Britain, both Graham and Jerry Beavan encouraged this possibility.

To accelerate interest I had stopped in Britain early in October on my homeward trip from Copenhagen to address clergy in London, Manchester and Glasgow. The three meetings were remarkably diverse.

In London some seventy ministers, all theologically conservative, gathered under the auspices of the British Evangelical Alliance for my appraisal of and dialogue over the current theological scene.

After London came Glasgow, where onetime socialist and ex-liberal Tom Allan hosted ministers in St. George's Tron. Allan had invited me at Montreaux, saying he would encourage nonevangelicals to attend. While I knew the overall British theological situation quite well, I was unsure of the present stance of John Macquarrie, lecturer in systematic theology at Trinity College, Glasgow. As the queue for the British Airlines London–Glasgow flight inched forward, I noted a chap ahead of me apparently reading a paperback about myth. After he checked in I commented obliquely that he seemed to be enjoyably absorbed in a detective story. "No," he chuckled, "I'm a theologian and it's about religion." He was John Macquarrie, reading a volume about Bultmann's theology. As seatmates on the flight we talked theology all the way; the hour provided helpful orientation about the Scottish theological scene. Later we exchanged some of our books by mail. About twenty-five clergy attended, only a few among them theologically evangelical. Discussion was lively but in good spirit.

I continued to Manchester, where the Graham committee had scheduled me to address clergy several weeks prior to Billy's crusade there. The forty ministers who convened covered a theological span from conservative to neoorthodox. Their interest in theology appeared at low ebb; they looked to evangelism to cure the church's ills.

Despite the mixed situation, I found lively interest in a British edition of *Christianity Today.* Some leaders anticipated 5,000 paid subscribers in short order. The British Evangelical Alliance offered to circularize its clergy list. Graham's upcoming Manchester crusade could consolidate the magazine's opportunities. The option to proceed would now rest on Board decision.

When staff gathered for the annual Christmas dinner on December 15, Philip Hughes and Mrs. Hughes were among the participants. Our main personnel at that time included Bell, Burcaw, Farrell, Kucharsky, Kuniholm, Murch and myself. The second echelon included Llewellyn Buntyn, Marian Caine, Clyde Freed, John Johansson, Mabel Miller and, in addition, secretarial and subsidiary staff.

The Board had thus far been unable to find a replacement if I took a sabbatical. Anticipating approval, Graham suggested that at stipulated salaries I choose an associate or assistant editor, a research editor, enlist Helga as literary assistant and as soon as such auxiliary personnel enabled, go on leave for however long was necessary. In hopes that by the December Board meeting things would level out, I decided to bide my time. The Board generously suggested (without my asking) an $18,000 salary with some insurance and retirement benefits, and three months for travel, writing and other activities that would inevitably involve benefits to the magazine. Ockenga indicated that the Board would make my life commitment a precondition of underwriting a year's leave. But the need for technically qualified staff was unresolved, and I rejected any built-in guarantee of returning unless and until I knew the staff personnel and resources.

We had too little skilled staff when we began, and we still had far too little; possible recruits lacked demanding vocational experience or were laden with pre-existing secondary commitments. We needed a successor to Kik, and to Murch who in March would move on. Helga was volunteering a third of her time at home on manuscript revision. Short-term help brought temporary office relief, but perpetuated long-term needs. January, 1961, meant Philip Hughes's return to London, where we would involve him another way, and Sherwood Wirt's departure to launch *Decision.* Kucharsky and Farrell were high assets, and we advanced Farrell to assistant editor. Nelson at best was now in the office every other week, helping with the bottomless pit of accumulating mail and pursuing financial as well as editorial matters. He was in telephone touch with Pew, he said, "almost every day—sometimes several times a day." Editorial continuity devolved wholly on me.

Frank Gaebelein, who reportedly would retire soon from The Stony Brook School, indicated an earliest availability date of June, 1962. Billy Graham had suggested as a possible editorial assistant Harold Lindsell, an ardent Graham booster who had convictional courage, but Lindsell, although unhappy at Fuller, had already committed himself for the following academic year. I indicated to Ockenga that the Board should either add an associate editor in the summer of 1961 who might benefit from a few months of apprenticeship, or arrange for a temporary fill-in from September, 1961, to June, 1962, when Gaebelein might perchance come as senior editor.

After a span of silence Ockenga wrote in mid-March, 1961, from Africa where he was spending six weeks. Although recognizing that my three-year contract would expire on September 30, 1961, he nonetheless was troubled by my "apparent willingness to leave *Christianity Today* for a year's rest and change, regardless of whether the work was adequately covered, and regardless of any commitment to return.

. . . These are times when personal considerations and preferences must be subordinated to an overwhelming need. . . . I do not see how you can leave *Christianity Today* with an unsolved dilemma. . . . The magazine is the best sounding board you will ever have."

In his reply Ockenga acknowledged that the now expiring contract had indicated that once we moved East Helga's literary gifts would be enlisted on staff for editorial revision. She had in fact discontinued college and seminary teaching in Pasadena for an expressly stipulated *Christianity Today* staff alternative. But she accepted the breach of contract in good spirit and enrolled instead for graduate studies at George Washington University, while helping voluntarily for long hours at home without compensation when magazine pressures were at their peak. Ockenga now proposed that the mistake be rectified and that she be hired promptly. I replied that she currently had new teaching offers from a college and from a seminary that required her decision within a month, and that I myself was in conversations to be finalized April 15 for a post with McGraw Hill which would preserve a fixed work week. We were also considering renting our home in the Fall, when both our son and daughter would be in college.

Wilbur Smith wrote from Fuller: "I well know that you are doing the work of three men and everyone else knows it. What mystifies me is that your Board of Trustees does not seriously concern itself with getting adequate help for you. . . ." Yet Smith urged me to reverse my desire to leave the magazine. "No one anywhere in North America . . . can edit *Christianity Today* with anywhere near the brilliance with which you have edited it since its foundation. . . . You know more evangelical leaders and liberals too than any other man on our side of the road and what is more, you have their confidence and you are able to get them to work for you."

Graham wrote a moving four-page letter that reached me a few days before the April 12 Board meeting. He had "read and reread" my report to the Board and was "somewhat stunned"; my decision to resign, he commented, would be "somewhat of a shock to us all." *Christianity Today* had "far surpassed" his "earliest and fondest dreams . . . largely due" to my editorial leadership. He too constantly suffered "battle fatigue" and times of "deepest despondency and discouragement that could be attributed only to Satanic influences." *Christianity Today* would "survive the jolt and shock of your resignation," he said, but in a hand-written footnote he added: "*You must not leave Christianity Today* but I will not *beg* you to stay." "If you make your resignation stick, I shall feel a personal hurt and disappointment, because I will feel that a mighty warrior has deserted in time of battle. . . . I believe God's plan for your life is to be Editor of *Christianity*

Today. . . . All these years of preparation in journalism, in theology, philosophy, et cetera, prepared you in a unique way for this responsibility. . . . There are few men that I love and admire as I do you."

Graham offered an agenda of practical solutions: Six months' leave beginning September 1 for meditation and study; salary scale adjustment so *Christianity Today* can attract two associate editors of the calibre of Harold Lindsell, Sherwood Wirt or Aiken Taylor; Helga to assist editorially at a satisfactory salary; relatively few office hours, and these for soliciting articles and deciding which go into the magazine; several short vacations a year but avoiding travel engagements marginal to *Christianity Today*. It was, in brief, a prescription for an editorial millennium, but I had doubts that it would or could be fulfilled this side of the Lord's return.

Ockenga came late to the April 12 Board meeting at the Warwick Hotel in Philadelphia, but Graham attended and, in fact, doubtless was the decisive influence. I noted to the Board that virtually every issue of the magazine now carried top names and first-rate essays; that the ablest evangelical homileticians were selecting and evaluating our sermon series; that evangelical theologians in all major denominations were writing on basic Christian doctrines; that we had given perspective on the European transition from neoorthodoxy to neoliberalism; that five major publishing houses had approached us about book reproduction of magazine content; that major papers like the *New York World Telegram* had reprinted editorial material; that eighteen religious broadcasters now routinely used our news section for radio material and credited the magazine; that *Christianity Today* was widely regarded as the most regulative influence for the evangelical view in contemporary Protestantism; and that ecumenical leaders frequently invited the editor to conferences or activities as if the magazine constituted a major Protestant denomination.

I indicated to the Board that evangelical penetration in depth requires five facets: (1) evangelistic breakthrough (already achieved by Graham's ministry); (2) a thought magazine concerned with theology and formulating evangelical strategy (*Christianity Today*); (3) textbook literature to challenge the secular academic mindset; (4) a cooperative research community of scholars and writers elaborating the Christian world-life view, not least of all the doctrine of the church; and (5) a breakthrough in evangelical social action.

I shared with the Board my "firm conviction that next to Dr. Graham's evangelistic penetration across denominational lines, the evangelical movement today has no more powerful propaganda instrument than *Christianity Today*." "It is important," I added, "that new staff members at the helm of this venture shall not simply exploit the magazine as a larger platform for their other interests, but that they earn the privilege of prominent identification through dedication to the magazine's priorities."

By these emphases I sought to bequeath a comprehensive vision, so that, were this my finale as editor, some facets of my dream of a better and higher evangelical future might survive. The Board sensed, I think, that it would be an unprofitable and time-consuming matter to engage in a discussion of staff possibilities. Its one question was: Would I stay permanently if I had a blank check to get what staff personnel I needed, and then take a paid sabbatical as soon as feasible, even if that might mean late in 1962?

Graham presented and moved resolutions to implement much of the millennial agenda about which he had written me: the Editor to search out and employ a top-flight editorial associate at $15,000, an editorial assistant at $9,000, a research assistant at $5,200, and to enlist Mrs. Henry for revision and other editorial aid at $500 a month; editorial time for rest, reading and creative writing; outside contacts that strengthen the magazine and enhance its prestige. Pew asked whether this met the Editor's problems and I replied that "it does, provided the staff can be found. Then we will be in business." The Board also offered to raise my salary, but I declined, to reinforce the point that my complaint was not monetary. The Board also named an executive committee (Ockenga, chairman; Pew, Bell, Weisiger and Lamont) and an editorial committee (Weisiger, chairman; Baker, Lamont, Fulton, Beavan) to convene as necessary between semiannual Board meetings.

I was between Scylla and Charybdis. No Board could do more, yet no problem seemed so incapable of satisfactory solution. For the good of the magazine, come what may, I felt I must stay, rather than see it wither. The day after the Board meeting I lunched with Èmile Cailliet, an intimate friend of Frank Gaebelein, who cautioned that it would be wrong to pressure Gaebelein to come to *Christianity Today* as senior editor if we expected him to make the magazine his priority since at retirement age any gifted man has long postponed projects that he needs to complete. At the end of April came word from North Carolina that Nelson had undergone surgery and would be out for six weeks.

Ockenga wrote: "I rejoice that you have had the issues resolved in relationship to *Christianity Today*. . . . It is my understanding that you have a blank check to get the personnel to help you with the work. Surely if you cannot find an associate or assistant, we shall never be able to supplant you at any future time. I sincerely hope you can find the help you need. . . . With best wishes to you, and rejoicing in your permanent relationship to *Christianity Today*. . . ."

I declined many speaking engagements, especially those that conflicted with production deadlines and favoring those involving campus interaction. This nurtured the cerebral competence required of an editor and it provided an opportunity both to learn and to shape the climate of thought and discussion. In March I addressed an N.A.E. convention luncheon in Grand Rapids (the religion editor of the *Grand Rapids Press* called it the one "really prophetic address" of the convention) and then the Calvin Theological Seminary student body. I shared also with Cornelius Van Til in an academic panel sponsored by Westminster Theological Seminary on Barth's theology, and in April addressed the American Association of Evangelical Students in Springfield, Missouri, in a gathering attended also by our son Paul, who was their "political awareness" chairman. In May I went to New York for a trial recording for the NBC network of five thirteen-minute weekly radio reports on religion prepared by Gene Kucharsky and narrated by me. But after leaping two of the five hurdles I botched it, and never pursued such a possibility again; migraines enervated me, and voice control was poor.

We had now established a British office on London's famous "newspaper row," Fleet Street, with Philip Hughes serving for the time being as British editorial associate and Gervase Duffield, Cambridge graduate and Anglican layman, as London manager. I would soon have an unforeseen opportunity to survey the effort the first week of June.

The Israeli embassy's press office invited me as editor of *Christianity Today* to make a ten-day trip to Israel—which would permit stopover in London—for informed assessment of developments in Israel. For two years the embassy had made that offer, and assured me of access to leaders and authorities, but I demurred lest an acceptance would somehow compromise me. Now the Israeli government invited a group of twenty or more journalists to make the all-expense-paid trip the latter part of May. As the only invited religion reporter I did not want to risk a charge of distorting what I observed. I told the embassy that I would feel more comfortable if invitations went also to Kenneth Wilson of *Christian Herald* and Sherwood Wirt of *Decision.* From May 18–31 the three of us accordingly not only learned much about modern Israel, attended the Eichmann trial, met confidentially with evangelical Christian workers who gave an account of the gospel witness in Israel and identified restrictions on their freedom to evangelize, but also walked again where Jesus walked. I wrote four articles on that experience for *Christianity Today.*

On return from Israel I stopped in London the first week of June to assess the recently opened *Christianity Today* Fleet Street office. After helping shape the July 31, 1961, issue devoted to "Britain: A Mission Field," I took British Rail to Cambridge to meet the gifted Scot, J. D. Douglas, former lecturer in church history at University of St. Andrews and currently librarian at Tyndale House. I enlisted him as British editorial associate and found him to be one of the ablest assets *Christianity Today* ever had. Back in London I spent time with Donald Wiseman, Assistant Keeper at the British Museum of the Department of Western Asiatic Antiquities.

Meanwhile in Washington no firm prospect had yet emerged for either an associate editor or an editorial associate in September. We thereupon engaged Helga, who had declined teaching invitations, for part-time help in June and then as full-time literary assistant. That June I received the Wheaton College outstanding alumnus award and shortly thereafter shared in a national NBC Frontiers of Faith panel and in local television discussions as well. Ray Scherer and an NBC crew invaded the offices with klieg lights for a network interview on the church in social action.

When the Board in 1961 finally approved a full editorial staff, it was clear that *Christianity Today* was at last perceived as in a league of its own, and not merely as a bigger and better something else. Some Board members, however, thought that not over 5 percent of the ministerial recipients understood the content. I replied I would like to see a marked copy to learn which specific pages were so unintelligible.

Theological interest quickened in the aftermath of my articles on changes in European theology ("Has Winter Come Again?: Theological Transition in Europe," Nov. 21, 1960; "Wintertime in European Theology," Dec. 5, 1960 and Jan. 2, 1961 and Jan. 16, 1961). While some Americans engaged in ecumenical dialogue were calling for greater attention to the views of Barth and Brunner, we broke the news that Bultmann had captured the initiative in Germany and that, in fact, even a post-Bultmannian revolt was clearly underway. In this framework we projected a week-long conference of evangelical scholars at Union Theological Seminary, New York, at the end of June, 1961. It issued in the volume *Jesus of Nazareth: Savior and Lord* in the Contemporary Evangelical Thought series and provided numerous articles for the magazine.

Mail from appreciative clergy continued. One Presbyterian minister wrote that during the past five years nothing in America had created respect for orthodox Christianity as had *Christianity Today.* A Unitarian minister wrote: "I take forty magazines but *Christianity Today* is one of the two that I read from cover to cover." Another avowed liberal put it this way: "It is now necessary to read *Christianity Today*, even though grudgingly." A liberal academician wrote: "I am amazed at the erudition, scholarship and editorial efficiency of *Christianity Today.*" Ned B. Stonehouse, New Testament scholar at Westminster, commended the continuing confrontation of readers with the great theological issues and the refusal to minimize or shelve such concerns on the ground that they are important only for so-called intellectuals. The Education Department of Calvin College passed a resolution commending the magazine and its editor for a special issue devoted to Christian education. A clergyman in the Philippines wrote: "My son, . . . a liberal minister, has come to appreciate more fully the articles in your magazine. He is amazed that your contributors are very well acquainted with the writings of the liberal, neoorthodox and existentialist theologians. . . . His forceful preaching is now based and oriented with the Bible."

For July and August, 1961, we added Harold Lindsell as a summer editorial associate. In September we added James Daane as continuing editorial associate. Minister of First Christian Reformed Church of Los Angeles, Daane had spent a post-graduate year under Berkouwer at Free University of Amsterdam after earning his Ph.D. in theology and philosophy of religion at Princeton. At the same time J. D. Douglas, ordained in the Church of Scotland and our Scottish Editorial Associate, became British Editorial Associate alongside Anglican Philip Hughes. Advertising and paid circulation continued to increase. Our masthead throughout the fifth year of publication carried the reminder: This Issue Exceeds 172,500 Copies.

Our October 31, 1961, anniversary issue, beginning the sixth year, carried a news feature in which twenty-five theologians identified America's false gods. The material was widely quoted by *The New York Times* and many other daily newspapers. Shortly thereafter I interviewed Charles Malik, former chairman of the United Nations General Assembly, in a significant appraisal of contemporary moral, spiritual and political tensions. Titled "A Civilization at Bay," it appeared in the November 24 issue.

Nelson Bell urged me to cover the New Delhi assembly of the World Council of Churches scheduled at yearend, since I had been at Oberlin and Cleveland and other important ecumenical conferences. I took with me hundreds of copies of a fresh issue of the magazine that analyzed the views and commitments of American delegates. Jerry Beavan and I then distributed them in India through the participants' hotel mail boxes. The issue infuriated Eugene Carson Blake but Matthew Spinka of Hartford Theological Seminary and others declared it excellent.

I promptly cabled magazine coverage when on the very first day of meetings American ecumenical engineers integrated the International Missionary Council into the WCC. On the second day, the Russian Orthodox Church was received into the WCC. But I had been in Delhi but a few days when urgent word from Nelson Bell implored me to return immediately to Washington. The staff of *Christianity Today,* he cabled, harbored a communist. When I shared the message with Jerry Beavan, who was in India preparing for Graham's post-Assembly Christian witness, he exploded with laughter. We agreed to wait out the situation. The problem was as we had surmised: Jim Daane, like many Christian Reformed scholars, harbored personal sympathy for Dutch socialism. But he was not brought to *Christianity Today* to expound it, nor was he sympathetic to communism.

After cabling stories for two successive issues I stopped in Hong Kong at the Grand Hotel ($8.50 a day for room and meals) to snatch a few days of uninterrupted rest. Knowledgeable tourists often came to the Grand for its English breakfast. One morning when I bowed my head for grace a nearby patron approached my table. "Pardon me," he said, "I take it you are an American and a Christian." "I own it gladly," I replied, and shook hands with Cleo Shook, then Far East program director of the U.S. Peace Corps. We became lifelong friends.

Aided by an upturn of advertising and circulation income, we ended 1961 in the best financial condition to date. Other magazines applauded and commended our witness. In its January, 1962, issue, *Christian Herald* featured a dialogue in which Reinhold Niebuhr and I gave contrasting answers to the question, "Who Is My Brother's Keeper?" Niebuhr hailed the welfare state as an implementation of the Christian love-commandment, while I contended that "the 'Santa Claus' state which penalizes solvent taxpayers to preserve the insolvent undermines many of the Judeo-Christian virtues." I declined many speaking invitations. I did, however, accept the February 28–March 2, 1962, Tharp Lectures at New Orleans Baptist Theological Seminary and one on March 5 at Biblical Seminary of New York that was included in *Christianity and World Revolution,* edited by Ed Rian, and Spring convocation lectures in Sioux Falls at North American Baptist Seminary on March 13–14 where participants were snowbound. But my major opportunity that year was the Easter sunrise sermon on April 22 in the Pasadena Rose Bowl.

When Karl Barth came to America for a few lectures at University of Chicago Divinity School and Princeton Theological Seminary, George Washington University made a belated effort to bring him to the nation's capital. Barth was weary, but volunteered to come for an hour's question-answer dialogue. The university invited 200 religious leaders to a luncheon honoring Barth at which guests were invited to stand, identify themselves and pose a question. A Jesuit scholar from either Catholic University or Georgetown voiced the first question. Aware that the initial queries often set the mood for all subsequent discussion, I asked the next question. Identifying myself as "Carl Henry, editor of *Christianity Today,*" I continued: "The question, Dr. Barth, concerns the historical factuality of the resurrection of Jesus." I pointed to the press table and noted the presence of leading religion editors or reporters representing United Press, Religious News Service, *Washington Post, Washington Star* and other media. If these journalists had their present duties in the time of Jesus, I asked, was the resurrection of such a nature that covering some aspect of it would have fallen into their area of responsibility? "Was it news," I asked, "in the sense that the man in the street understands news?"

Barth became angry. Pointing at me, and recalling my identification, he asked: "Did you say Christianity *Today* or Christianity *Yesterday?*" The audience—largely nonevangelical professors and clergy—roared with delight. When countered unexpectedly in this way, one often reaches for a Scripture verse. So I replied, assuredly out of biblical context, "*Yesterday, today* and *forever.*" When further laughter subsided, Barth took up the challenge: "And what of the virgin birth? Would the photographers come and take pictures of it?" he asked. Jesus, he continued, appeared only to believers and not to the world. Barth correlated the reality of the resurrection only with personal faith.

Later, UPI religion reporter Lou Cassels remarked, "We got Barth's '*Nein!*' " For Barth, the resurrection of Jesus did not occur in the kind of history accessible to historians. Religious News Service and other media echoed my "encounter with Barth." But at the end of the hour Barth added a gracious apology. He was not fully happy, he said, with the way he had responded to some questions, and particularly about the way he had referred to *Christianity Today.* Some years later when Barth wrote his *Evangelical Theology: An Introduction,* he commented in the preface that he could go neither the way of *Christian Century* nor the way of *Christianity Today.*

The July 13, 1962, issue of *Time* led off its religion page with an article that in several ways was a tribute to *Christianity Today.* Noting that 140,657 Protestant churchmen got it free while only 38,208 paid for it, *Time* observed that most readers on the free list would probably pay for it rather than lose it. "It is a magazine of evangelical Christianity that tries to make traditional Protestant theology clear and interesting—and nearly always succeeds." The magazine had become "indispensable—if often irritating—reading in manses and seminaries across the U.S." *Washington Post* columnist Kenneth Dole meanwhile declared the editor "as erudite as he is articulate." The professional media judgment was that the magazine was on target in its efforts to reach a literate readership.

We devoted our July 20 number to "Christianity in Free Europe," with J. D. Douglas contributing the background essay on "The First Nineteen Centuries." The overall conclusion was that Europe is a vast mission field, and that Free Europe was in spiritual decline.

James Boice joined us in July and August of 1962 for summer vacation relief help, a week before Harold Lindsell was to come in mid-August for a month. I learned that Lindsell had been forced to interrupt an overseas teaching mission in Japan because of complete exhaustion provoked in part by the work demands at Fuller during the illness of both Carnell and Archer. "I simply could not continue to teach or do anything," he wrote; "I could hardly hold my head up." Instead of coming to Washington he and his wife returned directly to California, where a physician promptly hospitalized him for nervous exhaustion and pneumonia.

Throughout much of 1962 we featured sermons by leading overseas clergy including Bishop Dibelius, James Stewart, Leon Morris, Ermanno Rostan and others. We had announced an award of more than $1000 for the five best original sermons expounding the biblical view of man's final destiny. In all we received about 250 sermons from respondents in the United States and 10 foreign countries. That year I was voted into Washington's intellectually prestigious Cosmos Club where a retired rear admiral, Theodore Lonnquest, and a distinguished economist, Dr. Elgin Groseclose, asked me to lead a weekly breakfast Bible study. At University of Wisconsin/Madison I addressed some 200 Inter-Varsity Christian Fellowship faculty associates, and at the University of Illinois Y.M.C.A. about 200 faculty members at a luncheon forum. One Urbana professor called it "the boldest, most direct presentation of evangelical Christianity heard by the faculty in many years."

Nelson's trip to Japan and the Far East for the Presbyterian Church in the U.S. (South) necessitated his absence from the September 11 Board meeting. He wrote the Board how pleasantly surprised he was to find *Christianity Today* being read with avid interest by expatriots and others. He encouraged the Board to approve a sabbatical for me "of at least six months" beginning in the Summer of 1963. Graham attended the meeting and was gratified to learn that his promotional letter had added 7,000 new subscribers. There had been preliminary conversations with Frank Gaebelein, moreover, who would be retiring from The Stony Brook School in March at the age of 64, about the possibility of his coming to *Christianity Today* as senior editor in the Summer or Fall of 1963. In view was a three-year contract with a one-year exploratory option involving three, four or five days of work a week. Gaebelein indicated on November 30, 1962, that he was minded to accept the call to *Christianity Today* for a year beginning September, 1963, but with the proviso that when I returned from sabbatical he could decide about continuance. He wanted the matter of title to be left open, so that he and Ockenga could discuss it further. As it developed, Gaebelein pressed for designation as co-editor.

The magazine began its seventh year on October 12, 1962, coincidentally with the opening of the Vatican Council, and we devoted an entire issue to "Rome and the Protestants." Subsequent issues carried reports from Vatican City by J. D. Douglas, who attended from London. Photo coverage of Graham's Latin American crusades appeared in November. In December Frank Farrell reported on an NCC-sponsored conference on religio-economic concerns held in Pittsburgh. The yearend issue focused on Christianity and communism.

For a year I had felt the need of a sabbatical in our now present seventh publication year.

Lindsell felt that his seminary situation had deteriorated considerably after the Fuller board meeting on December 3, 1962. "It has come to the place where I must leave—sooner or later," he wrote. "And sooner may be better than later." Edward Johnson, head of Financial Federation and longtime friend of Lindsell's, had resigned from the Fuller board. Ockenga seemed no longer able to exert decisive influence. Assured by Ockenga of a sabbatical leave, Lindsell asked whether Gaebelein was already committed to *Christianity Today* and indicated his own interest in coming as associate editor in September, 1963.

As it was, James Daane was committed to the editorial staff only through August, 1963. Were he to opt for a teaching alternative, as seemed likely, a door would be open for both Gaebelein and Lindsell. On December 12 I wrote the Board about Lindsell's availability and recommended an invitation. Lindsell and his wife planned a world cruise overlapping his Fuller sabbatical in the spring quarter. Their hope was to leave for London at the end of March and to arrive in Washington in mid-August, 1963, to begin full-time association with *Christianity Today.*

The Board greeted my letter with cautious waiting. Fuller Seminary was in considerable disarray. At a faculty planning retreat in December, 1962, Dan Fuller's presentation on Scripture infuriated Wilbur Smith, the most influential member of the founding faculty and personal friend of Dan's father. Charles Fuller later seized the transcript and kept it inaccessibly stored in the offices of the Gospel Broadcasting Association. Nelson Bell wrote Lindsell asking whether he ought not remain at Fuller "during this critical period in the hope that the situation might be recovered."

Early in January, 1963, Fuller trustees reaffirmed the Seminary's commitment to biblical inerrancy and asked faculty members to do so also. Dan Fuller insisted in the trustee meeting that Scripture contains error. David Hubbard made a strong statement minimizing the areas in debate. Charles Fuller firmly supported both his son and Hubbard. One of the trustees, Charles Pitts, resigned.

Billy Graham's presence was highly important, but as things progressed he did not carry the day. Fuller trustees discussed presidential possibilities. Hubbard vigorously pursued the presidency and David Weyerhauser, Larry Kulp and H. J. Taylor met with him privately. Weyerhauser had also discussed possible presidential nominees with President John Mackay of Princeton and former President Ed Rian of Biblical Seminary of New York. Weyerhauser and Kulp pushed aggressively for a mediating view of Scripture and for Hubbard as president. Graham told Ockenga at day's end that Ockenga must by all means come as resident president to save the Seminary he had founded. Ockenga said he would come but, after a telephone call to Boston, said his final answer would come within five days. Lindsell talked to Ockenga about a *Christianity Today* connection.

Early in February, 1963, Dan Fuller announced to the faculty Hubbard's acceptance of the presidency effective September, 1963, with the proviso that he also receive a tenured professorship. At that point Ockenga approved Lindsell's coming to *Christianity Today* as associate editor beginning September, 1964. When Lindsell wrote me, he said the magazine had made "amazing progress . . . from nothing to a place of strategic importance in a few short years. . . . I hope you will do nothing that will sever your relationship. . . . The fact that we will be working together again affords no small measure of delight."

Graham said he would support Hubbard only if Ockenga remained as chairman of the Fuller board and if Carl Henry came on the board since it included no theologian. Ockenga invited me to join the Fuller board but without mentioning that Hubbard had already been approached as president. All was well at Fuller, he said; board and faculty were now united, the faculty who remained agreed with the statement of faith and those who did not were leaving. I informed Graham that there was little point in my coming on the Fuller board, since the crucial decisions had already been made.

Gaebelein confirmed his coming in 1963, Lindsell his in 1964; both men, I told Ockenga, would be a high asset to the magazine.

With speaking engagements scheduled in Tokyo, Hong Kong, Singapore and Hawaii, the Lindsells sailed on their spring sabbatical in March, 1963. Before Lindsell left, Ockenga mentioned to Lindsell that Pew wanted Ockenga to "stay and fight the thing through at Fuller"; to this Ockenga added that his hand would be greatly strengthened if Lindsell stayed on.

Ockenga was elected Fuller board chairman in May, when three new trustees were added, but he was not named chairman of the executive committee, which was now the key post. Reports persisted that eight to ten of the faculty and trustees, including Weyerhauser who was a chief donor, would leave if the Seminary maintained inerrancy. Deeply perturbed, Wilbur Smith sought in protest to annul, but in vain, the bequest of his vast library to Fuller, and to give it instead to Trinity Evangelical Divinity School, where he shortly became visiting professor; there he was soon joined by Old Testament professor Gleason Archer, Ockenga's one-time assistant at Park Street Church. Lindsell meanwhile put a world tour between himself and Pasadena, for health reasons. He bypassed the August, 1963, editorial relief work in Washington, and invested an additional year at Fuller.

Simultaneously with the book's publication, *Christianity Today* led off the first issue of 1963 with a segment from Barth's new work on *Evangelical Theology.* With the new year we added Carol Friedley, as gifted a copy editor as any editor might wish. And we announced the appointment as publisher of Wilbur D. Benedict, who had served Curtis Publishing Company for thirty-four years and had most recently managed *Presbyterian Life*'s Philadelphia regional advertising office. He had charge of all noneditorial facets of our effort, including advertising, circulation and promotion.

In the second January issue we carried a feature interview with William F. Albright, "Toward a More Conservative View."

Nelson shared with the Board an evangelical minister's letter stating that he and his friends "never cease to marvel at the phenomenon of *Christianity Today* which arose (as far as we could see) out of thin air and became almost immediately the finest, most provocative and certainly the most courageous of Protestant periodicals." Not long thereafter came the news that Nelson had suffered a slight stroke that impaired his left hand and at times his speech. He had tried to ignore it, but had to cancel speaking engagements for the Presbyterian Board of World Missions. Asheville doctors referred him to Mayo Clinic, where forty years earlier he had been a visiting fellow. He had not disclosed to us that several months earlier he had caught his foot on a landing, cartwheeled down seven stairs and struck his head on a concrete floor; the resulting blood clot caused severe headaches. Mayo doctors anticipated full recovery, but ordered a complete two-to-three-month rest after which he promptly returned to the typewriter.

Early in 1963 Bill Gold's "District Line" feature in the *Washington Post* listed me among public figures observing January 22 as their birthday. It was my fiftieth, and it came in the midst of a bitterly cold winter. Earlier in the month I had flown to Texas for an exchange with Methodist professors and pastors on the issue of the church and social concerns. Next came Buffalo for an N.A.E. executive board meeting, then Newark, New Jersey, in 10-degree weather to address Protestant chaplains at Fort Dix; and finally a hurried junket to Boston for a Gordon College trustees' meeting. In February I was religious emphasis week speaker at Oklahoma Baptist University. But that month I capitulated to Asian flu, which grounded me for sustained work only on manuscripts. In May I gave the Payton Lectures at Fuller on *Aspects of Christian Social Ethics,* and at monthend the commencement address at Asbury Theological Seminary. In June came commencement addresses at Malone College and Seattle-Pacific College. The latter conferred my first honorary degree, doctor of literature, for "your excellent scholastic career as an evangelical scholar who respects the divinity of Christ and regards the Bible as truly inspired."†

From Seattle to Chicago I took the overnight flight to attend Paul's graduation from Wheaton as a political science major. Helga drove from Virginia. Paul wanted us to meet a young lady from Winnipeg, Canada, a psychology and piano major. We found Karen Borthistle, a junior, to be an intelligent, charming girl with a warm evangelical dedication and spirit. We enthusiastically approved the couple's desire to become engaged. We thought it specially providential, in fact, that Paul, who in August would begin two years' service in Africa with the Peace Corps, would have a captive heart to encourage him and to return to.

Immediately after commencement our entire family and Karen waved Paul off for a summer orientation course at Syracuse University. On September 4 Paul flew to Africa. To mark the day and to remember Karen's and our family's days together in Virginia, days of mutual entrustment of one another to God's keeping and promises, Helga

† The citation continued: "Your dream for a great evangelical university bringing scholars of repute from all over the world is well known to the academic community in America. It is our faith that one day your dream will come true. You have stimulated many students to become scholars in your work as Professor of the Philosophy of Religion at Northern Baptist Theological Seminary, and as Professor of Theology and Christian Philosophy at Fuller Theological Seminary. We honor you for your excellent editorial work. . . . You are best known to all of us now as Editor of *Christianity Today,* America's leading conservative Christian magazine."

baked a cake inscribed with the word EBENEZER. On September 6 Helga again drove the long trip to Wheaton, taking Carol and Karen. She then hurried back to Washington to pack for nine months' absence and to prepare our home for interim occupancy by the Gaebeleins.

After the Wheaton commencement I participated at an Army War College seminar in Carlisle Barracks, Pennsylvania, and went to Indiana to address graduating seniors at Anderson College. There Helga met me by car, after first seeing Carol off from Wheaton for Summer geology studies in the Black Hills. We then drove back to Washington for a major *Christianity Today* interview with Bishop Otto Dibelius of Berlin. Dibelius was relieved and gratified by the experience, especially since, as his aide later confided, the Bishop had been warned that we were of the radical conservative fringe. Several summer television opportunities emerged; in one, I dialogued with Martin Marty of the *Century* and others in an hour-long NBC special, "The Quiet Revolution," that focused on the church's social involvement. From July 12–26 I attended the World Council Faith and Order Conference in Montreal as advisor, following up my participation some years earlier as observer at the Oberlin conference.

Ockenga had asked me late in August to outline a proposal that would happily maintain my relationship to *Christianity Today.* Trinity Evangelical Divinity School was projecting a quality seminary under the leadership of Kenneth Kantzer, who had headed Wheaton's Division of Bible and Philosophy. Trinity offered me eight months of teaching and four months for research, writing and travel, plus a semester every other year on full salary to complete academic projects; beyond that, the offer included my being the chairman of the Department of Christian Philosophy and Apologetics and, in addition, a teaching role for Helga at Trinity College. Although I had turned down the invitation for September, 1963, Ockenga had learned that Trinity had renewed its offer for either full-time or part-time identification effective September, 1964. Bethel Seminary also inquired about my possible interest in the vice presidency and deanship. Gordon offered posts to both Helga and me. Return to *Christianity Today* after my sabbatical seemed problematical. Seven years, I felt, was long enough to cope with fifteen-hour days. I talked privately with Nelson and indicated that I was probing an alternative, but assured him that, however long it took, I would see that a proper transition was made to Gaebelein.

By the end of September Gaebelein had overcome the physical problems that delayed his coming, but could assume at first only part-time duties. He was a devout and analytical Bible student and expositor, an educator of high regard and well-respected literary craftsman of numerous books and articles. In many ways he was a Renaissance man—cosmopolitan, well-traveled, an able conversationalist, a fine pianist, a connoisseur of the arts, a lover of books, sportsman and mountain climber. After his duties as headmaster that involved him seven days a week, he now looked forward to relaxed Saturdays and Sundays. Within a few weeks he was accumulating take-home work and take-home pressures.

Nelson came on October 2 for a periodic visit during which the three of us visited at lunch. I indicated to Gaebelein, in fairness, that I had several academic options, including preliminary inquiry from New Orleans Baptist Theological Seminary. My final decision, I said, would be given to Ockenga in February, 1964, while I was abroad on my nine-month sabbatical. Gaebelein suggested that *Christianity Today* should annually assure me two months for writing and a month for vacation, but that if it did so, the co-editor should have similar guarantees.

Lindsell had predicated his interest in joining the editorial staff on the assumption of my continuance. Ockenga wrote him that "there is no reason to think Carl will not continue unless he elects to do otherwise." I was reluctant, however, to make futile demands upon the Board. The Board, I felt, simply could not fulfill whatever guarantees of staff help it approved in principle. I was allowing two hard-earned doctorates to rust, several half-completed books (in which earlier summers had been partly invested) to mold and was foregoing the creative writing that distinguishes a good editor from a lobbyist.

Paid circulation now stood at 64,000 and we considered 100,000 a live prospect. In the weeks before my sabbatical began in mid-October, letters kept coming from Christian leaders urging my ultimate return to *Christianity Today,* whatever the cost. Charles W. Koller, president emeritus of Northern Baptist Theological Seminary, wrote: "While any seminary would be fortunate to have you as Professor of Theology and Philosophy, I am not sure whether it would be good kingdom economy for you to terminate your service as Editor. You have done a monumental work there, and your magazine is esteemed by conservatives and liberals alike. To me, the magazine is quite irreplaceable; I wonder if someone else would carry it forward in the same stride. . . . If you were twins, I could wish that one would remain as Editor, and the other as Professor. . . ." The magazine staff urged that I delay a decision until a year after both Gaebelein and possibly Lindsell were in place. Adding to my vocational struggle were letters from ministers who, under the magazine's influence, had moved from liberalism or neoorthodoxy to an evangelical stance. An Indiana clergyman, graduate of DePauw and of Chicago Theological

Seminary, who was "steeped in the liberal tradition," was so impressed by "the scholarly acumen of *Christianity Today* as an evangelical witness" that he asked what divinity school he might encourage his son to attend. "I would like my son to reverse my experience" (the theological journey from conservative Christianity to liberalism), he added. A graduate student at U.C.L.A. wrote that amid the current theological and philosophical confusion *Christianity Today* had become "exciting . . . 'must reading' for any university student. . . . I for one find your treatment intelligent, comprehensive, penetrating. . . ."

But the best news of all was a letter received just before I flew to Europe on October 13. It was from H. Shelton Smith, who after teaching at Yale had gone to Duke as professor of American religious thought and director of graduate studies in religion. A past president of the American Society of Church History and of the American Theological Society, Smith, along with Robert T. Handy, Professor of Church History at Union Theological Seminary, and Lefferts A. Loetscher, Professor of American Church History at Princeton Theological Seminary, authored what some scholars regarded as the most important book in American Christianity yet published, the two-volume work *American Christianity: An Historical Interpretation with Representative Documents.* The first volume covered the period before 1820, and the second volume, the years 1820–1920. A copy of the second volume, just published by Scribner's, Smith wrote, was on its way. Loetscher had done the chapter covering theological conflict in the first half of the twentieth century, and quoted extensively from Machen's *Christianity and Liberalism* as a decisively influential conservative work; moving this sweep of events ahead into the second half of the century, Smith quoted just as extensively from my *Christianity Today* series, "Dare We Renew the Modernist–Fundamentalist Conflict?" (June 10–July 22, 1957) and identified it as an equally formative evangelical contribution.

11

A Workaholic's Sabbatical

Our travel included air, train, bus and steamer transportation to twenty-one countries, with departure on Sunday, October 13, 1963, from New York, and return to Washington on Saturday, July 4, 1964, well before my mid-July resumption of magazine duties. We scheduled Portugal, Liberia, Nigeria, Cameroun, Brazzaville, Congo, South Africa, Rhodesia, Kenya, Egypt, Lebanon, Syria, Jordan, Israel, Greece, Italy, France, Spain, Switzerland, Austria, Germany, Denmark, Sweden, Norway, the Netherlands, England and Scotland. In some places we stayed only a few days, in others a week or two.

The itinerary projected conversations with evangelicals, intellectual encounter, an overview of theological trends as well as a week with our Peace Corps son in Africa, prayer and meditation, rest and recreation, and companionship with Helga.

At Idlewild airport I took a person-to-person good-bye call through Pan American from Carol, now a Junior at Wheaton, while Helga policed our luggage in the check-in line.

PORTUGAL. The crowded flight to Lisbon was uneventful and we established ourselves in the Hotel Eduardo VII set among beautiful gardens at the fringe of the city but convenient to the mid-town Metro that often took us where the action is. Already we were in another world. Women and children proudly balanced trays of fish or boxes of live chickens or produce atop their heads. In stall after stall of the sprawling market, people hawked their wares. Fruits and vegetables ranged in artful rows; skinned hogs' heads and other meats hung from nails. Nearby piles of entrails bespoke brisk business. Black-garbed widows and barefooted children leaned from pastel-stuccoed houses that clung to the city's seven hills. Everywhere laundry whipped from balconies. Outdoor bird cages and even monkeys here and there added to the view. Women hurried to and from housework that netted $1.50 a day or less; men lounged in cafes, sipping wine and talking by the hour.

Missionary friends reviewed signs of spiritual hunger amid the country's pervasive Catholic formalism. After meeting with 35 Pentecostal ministers in Lisbon we drove 200 miles north to Oporto. Massive traffic jams of pedestrians, oxen, burros, trucks and bicycles, complicated the move through colorful fishing villages along the way where racks of sardines dried in the sun and Phoenician-style boats bobbed at seaside. At village wells blindfolded donkeys trotted round and round drawing water. Bustling markets offered the usual rabbits, pigeons, geese and eels, plus Portugal's famous pottery and glassware. Olive orchards, cork tree groves, rice paddies and endless vineyards comprised the more distant landscape. We noted, as we drove along, secluded centuries-old universities and monasteries.

Once at our Oporto destination, a layman's four-story villa overlooking the ocean, I spoke to 35 ministers, businessmen and other Christian workers who had gathered to hear and share about Christian opportunities.

Returning to Lisbon I addressed other Christian workers before proceeding by train for three-and-a-half hours to Leiria. Here, with Wheaton alumnus and long-time missionary Sam Faircloth translating into Portuguese, I lectured to 200 young people, including seminarians.

Scheduled rest days back in Lisbon were unexpectedly thwarted. Among other problems was that of an unexpected package. A solicitous American had belatedly sent us a large assortment of vitamins that the Washington staff, in turn, forwarded. Now we not only lost half a day convincing authorities that no drugs were involved, but also paid a steep customs charge. Another frustrating experience involved a diplomatic matter. In Washington the South African Embassy had hedged on granting an entry permit to a clergyman-journalist. But after billing me for a cablegram to Pretoria the Embassy evasively promised final clearance in Lisbon. As it now developed, the Lisbon office had no information.

LIBERIA. Having taken our first anti-malaria pills to supplement earlier yellow fever shots, we proceeded to Monrovia, capital of Africa's oldest republic, yet a city of unbelievable squalor. We arrived the night of October 28 in a driving rain. Paul was waiting. For an hour we drove, better slogged, though muddy roads to the welcome oceanfront compound of Sudan Interior Mission's radio station ELWA. From this site powerful beams broadcast news, music and above all the gospel and Bible study courses across much of Africa and even beyond. In addition, hospital, school, chapel and other services ministered in many ways.

Paul, while on a three-day work break, shared our quarters and brought us up-to-date on his Peace Corps life. He watched bemused as we jumped over inch-long roaches and sand crabs that he had already learned to ignore. The Peace Corps had assigned Paul to reorganize the postal service where mail delivery lagged months, even years, and parcels, some of them addressed to missionaries, deteriorated in dusty corners. He observed how exploitation by whites that blacks protested in America was found in Liberia also, except that blacks in power were disadvantaging fellow blacks.

Besides fellowshiping with ELWA workers and local pastors, we met friends serving VOA and UNESCO. At City Hall I addressed the Monrovia Fellowship of Christian Leaders, a branch of International Christian Leadership to which John Cordel, British M.P., had recently spoken, and then met several government dignitaries. We saw the vast Firestone rubber plantation and journeyed up-country to President Tubman's zoo before visiting various missionaries including the Bowers family, Mrs. Bowers being Virginia McQuilkin of the revered McQuilkins, and Helga's Wheaton classmate.

Committing ourselves mutually to God's keeping, Paul and we exchanged good-byes.

NIGERIA. Helga and I flew on to Lagos, where Harold Fuller, editor of *Africa Challenge,* met us on arrival November 2. At our assigned Sudan Interior Mission guest house we lunched on native "chop," then proceeded to University of Lagos Medical School for an Inter-Varsity squash party. It was hosted by a brilliant faculty member, Dr. Ishaya Audu, a third generation believer whose grandfather was the first Muslim in northern Nigeria to convert to Christianity.

At our S.I.M. quarters in suburban Yaba we thankfully escaped the noisy and raucous day and night throngs of capital city Lagos. Unrest and struggle amid the growing population in this age-old seaport city left one grateful for the impact of missionaries across the years. After preaching at an indigenous church and then to a dedicated body of S.I.M. workers, I met with missionary leaders to project a special Africa missions issue to appear late in July, 1964, in *Christianity Today.*

The day before departure on an early morning flight to Cameroun on Tuesday, November 5, I learned that the Nigerian immigration office processed visas to South Africa. Rushing there a half-hour before closing time, I discovered that we needed two residents of Nigeria to vouch for us. Resident missionary friends zoomed through the dense traffic and reached the embassy with only minutes to spare. So visas withheld in Washington and Lisbon were granted us by blacks in Nigeria.

CAMEROUN. Next came our first major tour within our sabbatical, the visit to West Cameroun, even as the Holy Land would in time be another. Here Helga's pioneer missionary parents had invested almost thirty years between 1899 and 1935, and here Helga was born in 1915, youngest of Carl and Hedwig Bender's six children.

We had prayed that the trip would refresh details of Helga's childhood. William Rentz of the Soppo Baptist Teacher Training College met us at Tiko airport. On the road en route to Soppo, Helga's birthplace, we met Esaso Woleta, once a houseboy at the mission compound where among his duties he carried Helga on his shoulders to safeguard her from possible dangers. Gleefully he recalled those early years, speaking in German to verify his identity.

Sango and Nyango Bender were remembered well both in the Victoria and Douala areas where mission work had begun, as well as at the subsequently developed inland stations. Learning of Helga's visit, converts walked many miles from many villages to recite past associations with her parents. Some had trekked with Sango Bender through the jungle or had maneuvered dugout canoes through mangrove swamps; some had learned their carpentry, bricklaying and other trades from him. Some recalled occasions of correction and discipline. Converts, national teachers, evangelists and deacons remembered mealtimes in the early years when Sango joined them in their smoky huts to scoop "chop" with his fingers from the common pot. Still others mentioned Nyango's training in housekeeping, sewing and healthcare, and her own ever-ready nursing of their disease-plagued bodies. And the Benders' fluency in tribal languages was always a special key to mutual understanding.

Some had helped build Bender Memorial Church that Sango had conceived, designed and implemented, but not as a memorial. In its final stages of construction, he slipped and fell while at work on the belltower. But it was dread black water fever that subsequently took his life. Some of the workers had seen him fall, had prayed at his bedside and had seen him die; some had dug his grave at the church's cornerstone and laid him to rest.

Second, third and even fourth generation believers—many reached for Christ by workers trained by the Benders—came to greet Helga at the special celebration service. Hours of singing (in English, German and tribal dialects), tributes by young and old and speeches by Helga and me were followed by a moving rededication service at Sango Bender's grave site. As the church bells tolled, we gathered to read again the unpretentious marker inscribed: "He fought a good fight, he finished his course, he kept the faith." Later at a fellowship hour, Sarah, who had lived with the Benders and was now president of the Ladies Society, voiced a shared feeling: "We thank our heavenly Father that he has brought you safely home."

We met government officials in Buea and then boarded a seven-passenger "grasshopper" at Tiko airport for Bamenda. From here we drove 600 miles by Landrover to the interior areas, stopping at chapels and at medical installations. We visited the large Mbingo leprosarium compound where Wheaton alumnus Dr. Gene Stockdale was the only medic; on my return to the States I was able to attract a modest grant from the Pew Foundation for an electricity generator. At the Mbem maternity center twin boys were born about the time we arrived and were named Carl and Henry; another newcomer was named Helga. I shared at the Bamunko Bible Conference and then at Ndu, where 2,000 Camerounians met for four hours while my message was translated by my former Northern Seminary student, Elmer Strauss, into pidgin English and then by others into four tribal dialects. At Kumba a bow-and-arrow and spear-equipped nightwatch guarded our uneasy sleep.

After a stint in terrorist-pocketed East Cameroun where burned villages and impaled skulls evidenced rebel warfare, we turned toward Victoria. The veranda of Saker College guesthouse faced the harbor where Helga's parents often embarked or disembarked and where Alfred Saker in 1858 arrived from Fernando Po to establish Victoria city and its first Baptist church where her father, too, had often preached. Helga and I both spoke there.

We proceeded to Douala where Saker had carried on his major work and had an extra day before the dawn flight to Congo. We had heard about Douala's reputation for thievery, even in the French-speaking Catholic mission where we stayed. While guests ate in the dining salon, we learned, rooms on occasion were pilfered. We were uneasy about losing clothing for all seasons as well as mementos and gifts we had acquired. Adding to our restless sleep were the world's hungriest mosquitoes, undeterred even by mosquito nets. A fierce tropical thunderstorm burst overhead during the night; lightning incessantly struck with unsparing fury. The mission's prearranged taxi failed to appear at 5 A.M. to get us to the airport. Thieves and pickpockets, we had been forewarned, plied the alleys around us. But there was nothing else to do: leaving passport, wallet and travel tickets with Helga, I ventured into the black tropical night and flagged the first transport I could find.

BRAZZAVILLE. En route to Leopoldville we flew to Brazzaville where we stayed in the Swedish mission, true to its tradition of comfort and wholesome food. The national president, we learned, was an evangelical believer. At the French church service we met Gilbert and Ginger Ward of Virginia, he with the American Embassy and she active with Laubach Literacy, who gave us a tour of the city before we moved on. The ferry crossing on the lily-choked Congo, we learned, was sometimes disrupted by rowdy porters; some did, indeed, try to scoop up our luggage but we held them off.

CONGO. Impressively modern, Leopoldville seemed to be "in order." But it had only recently weathered revolutions and residents spoke of our "uneasy ghost town" as colonial controls eroded. Malaria was again a problem. For all that, Leopoldville was the most modern city in Africa we had seen so far. Its beautiful buildings bore clear evidence of former European colonial regimes. But the economy was bad and shops seemed empty. We paused at the Stanley monument, visited the university and stopped at the ivory market for a few trinkets.

At the Union Mission House (Central Rest Home) we lodged quite close to the inner city and within access of mission-related personnel. I preached Sunday morning at the English service in the British Baptist Missionary Society chapel. At night we met in a restaurant for discussion with thirty missionaries and workers who shared distressing stories of the Congo revolution's impact on mission work.

All along the way—in Lisbon, Monrovia, Lagos, Cameroun and now Congo—former Wheaton, Northern and Fuller students were eager for news about evangelical advances in America and at the same time enlisted our prayers and help in behalf of their own witness.

SOUTH AFRICA. South Africa would expose us next to yet another distinctive culture. Upon after-midnight arrival at Johannesburg airport I held my breath at the immigration desk, but our Lagos visas were unquestioned. Just before dawn on Thursday, November 21, we signed into the Astor Hotel. Our private bath, twin-bed room, with balcony and window view of King George Street, cost $7.70 a day for two including sumptuous breakfasts that Helga was disposed to make her main meal. In its seventy-five years Johannesburg had become a busy metropolis of a million people living in modern European or American style, except for apartheid. The end of November was midsummer—children splashed in pools, flowers bloomed everywhere.

The *Christianity Today* staff had presented me with a small radio transistor that we turned on for international news at our six o'clock wakeup. That Friday, November 22, we were stunned. BBC world news led off with "President Kennedy has been assassinated." Few details were as yet available other than that Dallas was the setting. Curiously, BBC added that Kennedy's right wing critics were thought to be involved—the more remarkable since Lyndon Johnson suspected Marxist implications.

Whites and blacks remained separated on the Johannesburg streets. But as we sauntered along, a young black broke from the crowd and asked if we were Americans. Baffled by Kennedy's assassination, he asked: "What hope is there for us, if this happens in America?"

I sought perspective on South Africa's race problem from many Christians and alerted *Christianity Today* to expect a news report. The Washington staff was performing valiantly. Gene Kucharsky had just closed out a new issue and was having lunch with the Washington correspondent for *Time* when news broke of Kennedy's death. Putting a "stop" on the magazine, the staff worked into the evening on a new lead editorial to produce an issue that reached readers simultaneously with *Time* and *Newsweek* and beat the *Century. Time*'s December 30 issue carried complimentary references to *Christianity Today* and "the evangelical undertow."

Harold Ockenga wrote me in Johannesburg that the Board, at its November 6 meeting, voiced pleasure over reader interest and the rising number of paid subscriptions. Criticisms were but two: some articles were too philosophical and heavy, and we gave too much space to hostile views before refuting them. Ockenga himself felt that the essay on analytic philosophy by Alvin Plantinga belonged in a philosophy journal. I should know, moreover, he added, that the Board urged me to use my sabbatical for "spiritual, mental and physical refreshment" rather than for travel, speaking or writing. "Settle down in some beautiful and relaxing place for three months," Ockenga exhorted.

By Monday, November 26, we were more relaxed than we had been for years. We started out for nowhere, browsing in department stores and antique shops. In the afternoon we listened intently to the broadcast of Kennedy's funeral. Later in the week we walked to the planetarium for a lecture on the star of Bethlehem that I later ran in *Christianity Today.* Next day we went our separate ways and I returned to an antique shop to bargain for a handsome centerpiece, a beautiful quadruple plated six-tray Victorian epergne. At first I hid it under the bed for a later mailed surprise, but finally shared the happy find with Helga, who admired it every bit as much as I did. We posted it well boxed but it arrived home smashed to smithereens.

Our last Sunday in Johannesburg I preached to a "coloured church" pastored by Don Aeschliman, former Fuller student serving under

The Evangelical Alliance Mission. The communion service I conducted, I was told, was the first in which both coloureds and whites shared. We later met for dinner at the Aeschliman home and fellowship with many missionary families. On Tuesday the Aeschlimans took us to the airport, driving through Bantu locations and non-white developments. To friends in South Africa and friends abroad I indicated that "I am wholly unconvinced that the policy of the South African government can succeed as more than a temporary expedient. Its weakness is twofold: it sunders the body of humanity and it sunders the body of Christ."

The magazine's stand on racial issues came into debate during my sabbatical. Much perturbed over the civil rights bill passed by the House, Nelson wrote that "Frank Gaebelein wanted to come out with an editorial backing this particular bill but I persuaded him against it." Reflecting confidence that only spiritual conversion could change social conditions, Bell gave an enthusiastic report of Graham's crusade in Birmingham where 35,000 nonsegregated people attended and half the choir of 3,500 were blacks. Graham was commended for his early integration of crusade choirs even by *The New York Times* and *Washington Post.* But left in the air was the question of equal rights before the law of all citizens irrespective of color. When Lyndon Johnson later signed the civil rights bill I sent a handwritten letter on *Christianity Today* stationery saying it was his finest hour. Later we assigned Frank Gaebelein to cover the Selma episode, where he voluntarily joined some reporters in the march. This action invited staff criticism not because Gaebelein was unfree to indicate his personal convictions, but because our unwritten code was that reporters of an event should not become public partisans.

RHODESIA. We stayed in Salisbury in the old wing of the Meikle's with only a day and a half to sample the charming British-flavored city. After breakfast we strolled through the nearby business section before shops opened. A middle-aged man and a teenage boy seemed to tag a half block behind us. Finally, as we stopped for a traffic light, the man called out, "Are you Carl Henry, by any chance?" It was Orla Blair, my Wheaton '38 classmate, whom I had not seen since graduation. He had gone to Southern Rhodesia as a missionary under TEAM and served in a remote area several hours' drive from Salisbury. That day he had come to Salisbury to meet his wife who had undergone surgery and was due back on a morning flight.

Word went out to the Christian community and that noon I addressed local ministers. In the evening we joined the Don Hoyts for supper before some fifteen missionaries arrived for fellowship and to sing pre-season Christmas carols. Next day, after tea with Bill and

Joyce Warner who shared their vision of a Christian university in Salisbury, Don Hoyt took us to our late night B.O.A.C. flight to Kenya.

KENYA. We arrived at midnight in Nairobi on December 5 and left just after midnight the following day. Due to internal problems in Sudan, we could not get visas to stop off in Khartoum. Lynn Ashley, secretary of British and Foreign Bible Society, checked us into the Brunner (formerly Queen's) Hotel. Nairobi was brightly decorated for the nation's upcoming Uhuru or independence day. John Mpaayei, assistant secretary of the Bible Society, reviewed emerging spiritual developments in Kenya as he drove us the next day to the well-known national animal preserve. Back at the Brunner we packed for our flight, but first had dinner. We unobtrusively offered grace, only to have a guest at a nearby table inquire who we were. Thus we met the Tengborns, Lutheran missionaries in Tanganyika on holiday in Kenya. They were *Christianity Today* fans and insisted on driving us to our midnight flight.

EGYPT. The trip to Egypt, aboard Central African Airways, was long and hard. Reaching Cairo at dawn on December 7, we took the B.O.A.C. limo to the inner city. There, to outwit devious cab drivers, we took the second class public tram for an unforgettable, never-to-be-repeated ride to the Mena House in Gaza, at the end of the line near the great pyramids. For eight cents each, including extra assessment for luggage, we had a firsthand in-depth exposure to people and places.

Our bedroom at the Mena House looked out on the pyramids, on the Sphinx and on the passing parade of camels and their drivers. We walked to the pyramids, which I had first seen on my Winona Lake lecture tour. When a camel padded unheard behind her and licked her hair, Helga developed a sudden aversion to the beasts, although she eventually hazarded a camel ride.

We then went inside the Queen's chamber. As the passage got smaller and smaller, my back and hip problem required me to proceed on "all fours." Soon it became so humid that I stretched out momentarily on my back, but then could not right myself to proceed. Helga feared I was having a heart attack. Eventually I managed the ordeal, and to finish off the day, toured the temple near the Sphinx.

In the inner city the great Cairo Museum, displaying the contents of King Tutankhamen's tomb and countless items of both archaeological and biblical interest fascinated us for hours. We also saw Cairo by night and, in the El Musky market, bought a treasured 42-inch square leather hassock.

Room accommodations and meals at Mena House were good, but

the eerie Moorish atmosphere unnerved Helga, as fez-capped, white-robed personnel emerged suddenly to view from behind long draperies or soundlessly vanished through them. Equally disconcerting were masses of people pushing and fighting their way through the cluttered streets of the squalid inner city. Street vendors hounded tourists on every hand. The Arab way of doing business—asking double the value, and then indulging in a fiery verbal exchange before settling for half the asking price—dismayed her. But the last straw came one night at dinner. We had been wondering how and why waiters appeared mysteriously to serve a next course when we had barely finished the last bite of the previous one. Then Helga saw him: from the uppermost balcony another of those long-robed turbaned characters was watching us to the last mouthful and signaling the waiters below. That did it; Helga construed the maneuvers not as efficiency of service but as yet another invasion of privacy. We moved ahead by two days our flight to Beirut, seeing "Nasser Village," the old section of Cairo, on the way to the airport.

LEBANON. We asked the taxi driver to take us near Hagazian College. When we got out to exchange money we found ourselves precisely where we hoped to stay, namely, the Austrian Pension (Myrton House), a few doors from the campus.

Next morning we walked in downright chilly weather to the blue Mediterranean, thrilled also by views of distant snow-capped Mount Lebanon. Beirut promised to be a highlight of our journey. Then one of the world's beautiful cities, it was a thriving metropolis hosting tourists from around the globe. Since Israel and Lebanon were economically the most developed countries in the area, one easily gained the impression that in case of military threat they would stand as allies against a common enemy.

We invited President and Mrs. John Markarian of Hagazian to lunch and with them attended the annual Christmas carol sing—in Arabic and English—at the American University. At the Southern Baptist Arab Theological Seminary I spoke in chapel and taught a theology class and then lunched with the acting president, David King, and met John Watts, newly named president of Ruschlikon Seminary near Zürich. Sunday night I preached in Beirut's Southern Baptist Church.

During the week a 5½-hour round trip taxi ride shared with others provided a leisurely visit to the ancient ruins at Baalbek. We also viewed the ruins of the ancient biblical cities of Tyre and Sidon and observed the archaeological exhuming of a mummy.

SYRIA. On December 18 we left early on the three-hour drive to Damascus, the oldest still standing city in the world. Along the way we snapped pictures of Mount Hermon (the Mount of Transfiguration). We signed into the Grand Hotel, then walked through the bazaars where in small shops craftsmen hammered copper and brass and finished wood inlay products. We continued to Straight Street and the house of Ananias. We were moved anew by the significance of the Damascus road event for Saul of Tarsus and through him for the moral and spiritual fortunes of the world, though many Syrians seemed oblivious to it. We viewed also the wall where through a window Paul was let down in a basket.

Our first meal at the hotel—eggplant pâté followed by steamed brains—was intended as gourmet fare, but unaccustomed to such cuisine we requested egg omelette instead. The Grand Hotel, it developed, employed a one-man porter, elevator operator, bartender, gift shop clerk, cook and waiter, although someone else functioned as chambermaid. We tried to recall who had first recommended the Grand, but in vain, and fortunately so for whoever it was.

JORDAN. December 20 we boarded a service taxi leaving for Amman. Our fellow-passengers were a soldier and two novitiates from Rome going to Jerusalem. Maneuvering the car as if he were wrestling with demons, our driver nonetheless held the road around countless hairpin turns. At one point he squeaked the car between a donkey and its escort. Clearing the Syrian-Jordanian checkpoint we passed by the archaeological excavations in progress at Jerash and continued through the barren, rocky mountains where Arabs still live as in biblical times. At last we reached Amman, Jordan's capital city. There former Fuller students John and Marian Ferwerda met us and drove us to the Philadelphia Hotel, located across from ruins of an old Roman stadium. That evening, at the Arab Evangelical Church, pastor-missionary Don Whitman translated my message. Later evangelical leaders showed me their airmailed edition of *Time* (December 20 issue). The religion page carried my picture and an article on "The Evangelical Undertow" that credited evangelicals with striving for a "consistent, logical theology," and mentioned Van Til and me as exemplifying their best-known writers.

Awakened at sunrise by the Muslim call to prayer, relayed over powerful loudspeakers, we continued after breakfast to Jerusalem/Jordan. The trip was steeped in the emotive power of biblical contexts—the Jordan River where John the Baptist immersed Jesus and learned that the Nazarene was the Son of God; the Dead Sea; Jericho in the distance; the first glimpses of Jerusalem, the city set on Mount Zion; the drive past Bethlehem and through Bethany. The sacred sites carried a forceful reminder that Christianity is a religion of historical revelation and that Jesus Christ was historically manifested in the same history as that of the Herods and of Pilate.

We lodged at the new Jordan-side Y.M.C.A. in Jerusalem. From there we could walk to the American Colony where I had stayed previously, to the Mennonite Refugee Complex, and to an archaeology study center where Gleason Archer, Old Testament scholar at Fuller, had come for part of his sabbatical research.

The Y asked me to bring the Christmas Sunday sermon at its chapel. Later we walked the few blocks from the Y to the Garden Tomb, and through the Damascus Gate into the Old City, and finally to and through the Church of the Holy Sepulchre, which many archaeologists consider the probable site of Jesus' burial and resurrection. After dinner we took a city bus and spent a time of meditation on the Mount of Olives which biblical prophecy associates with the Lord's return.

Monday was our detailed tour of the Old City area including the Dome of the Rock, the Wailing Wall, Hezekiah's aqueduct, the Pool of Bethesda and the fourteen stations of the Via Dolorosa enshrined by Catholic tradition.

On the day before Christmas we watched from the roof of the Jordan Y while perhaps 3,000 Arabs filed one by one from the Israeli side through the Mandelbaum Gate to spend an allotted thirty-six hours with relatives and friends in Jordan. The American flag fluttering from the American Embassy near the Gate communicated its own message. But the day's highlight lay ahead. Promptly at 4:30 P.M. 1,000 Christians left by busloads for Bethlehem and the Y.M.C.A. Christmas Eve English and Arabic service and carol sing at Shepherd's Field. A choir of blind children sang, Dr. Roland Brown of Chicago brought the message and Gleason Archer and I also participated. Afterward in the nearby cave everyone joined in a shepherd's supper of filled pita bread. As we left the evening stars were already shining.

Since we had no decorated Christmas tree, we tucked the many cards received from friends into the louvre doors of our hotel room closet. We were doubly nostalgic, for this was the first Christmas without Paul and Carol; Paul was in Liberia and Carol on holiday vacation in Pasadena with the Lindsells. At midnight the bells chimed across the way at St. George's Cathedral, and camels in the distance "bellered" in response.

Once again we watched Israeli Arabs filtering through the Mandelbaum Gate, this time in the opposite direction, for another year's separation—even by mail—from loved ones. We fellowshiped with workers at the Menno Relief Center, and the following day joined John Ferwerda to drive from Amman to view the Cave of Machpelah in Hebron where the patriarchal greats are buried, and to visit famous glass and pottery works. We stopped, on return, at Baraka tuberculosis sanatorium where Wheaton classmate Eleanor Soltau had already ministered for two decades. Then we went also to the Church of the Nativity in Bethlehem, before driving to Ramalah, where the boy Jesus was missed by his parents as they journeyed to the temple, and to Bethel with its many Old Testament associations. Finally we went to Emmaus from where one can glimpse Lydda and even Tel Aviv on the Mediterranean.

ISRAEL. On December 27 we ourselves moved through the Mandelbaum Gate with its barbed wire barriers, were checked by both Jordanian and Israeli officers and entered Israel. The well-known Y.M.C.A. there was a disappointment compared to its Jordan-side counterpart. On the Jewish sabbath we attended morning services at the Southern Baptist Church whose pastor, Robert Lindsay, in later years lost an arm when he walked through a mined Israeli field, and whose church later was burned down by Israelis. After lunch we visited G. Douglas Young at the American Institute of Holy Land Studies, and on Sunday attended Christian and Missionary Alliance services before lunching on shishlik (shish kebab) with Dr. Chaim Wardi, the Israeli government's liaison for religious affairs.

By December 30, our last full day in Jerusalem-Israel, it had begun to snow. With a tour group we visited the holocaust museum, the tomb of David, the tombs of the Sanhedrin and Hebrew University.

On the last day of 1963, we boarded the 7 A.M. train for Haifa via Tel Aviv, where we were met by *Christianity Today*'s news correspondent, Dr. Dwight Baker of the Baptist Convention. Dwight drove us to view the excavations underway at Beth Shearim and then to the shores of Galilee. After a fish dinner, we visited Capernaum, Mount Tabor and looked down on the Valley of Megiddo. New Year's Eve lodgings, where we had a bedroom view of Mount Carmel, were in a German hospice run by nuns of the Catholic Order of St. Charles. Our quarters were undeniably simple but spotless. We heard ships in Haifa's harbor blow their stacks and shoot cannon to welcome in the New Year.

GALILEE. New Year's Day, 1964, we shared a picnic lunch with Dwight and Emma Baker at Caesarea on the Mediterranean where excavations and restorations were underway. As we walked along the shoreline Helga and I found three rust-encrusted Roman coins. Next day we stopped at the Megiddo excavations and, after first touring Cana, continued to Nazareth where early in January Pope Paul VI was to speak at the Church of the Annunciation. We also saw the traditional Nazareth site of the synagogue where Jesus had begun his ministry by reading from Isaiah 61:1–2. After dinner with evangelical leaders I spoke for Baptist Pastor Faud Saknini at his Thursday evening prayer meeting.

After the night with Southern Baptist missionary James Smith and his family, we took the early bus from Nazareth to Tel Aviv. We planned to fly to Athens that morning, but since *Christianity Today* asked that I cover the approaching papal visit we extended our Holy Land visit a week. Meanwhile with the Chandler Laniers we drove from Tel Aviv to Joppa (Jaffe) to see Simon the Tanner's house, the shoreline where Jonah embarked to Tarshish and other biblical sites. We then went by train to Haifa for a house Bible study that Jewish believers conducted by candlelight to avoid provocation of hostility.

When we returned to Nazareth on January 4 the temperature plunged very low; we wondered how cold the nights may well have been for Mary and Joseph and Jesus whose lodgings were hardly as comfortable as ours at the Grand New Hotel. Against the biting cold outside and even frigid hotel conditions I wore three pairs of socks.

Sunday at daylight the curious throng began gathering for the papal visit. While Helga looked on from the hotel, I set out at eight for the Church of the Annunciation to join the international press entourage to cover the event. As the papal procession moved through Nazareth's crowded main street, some irreverent observers suggested that the Holy Father should have been suspended in a basket on a guywire stretched the length of the avenue; that way everyone could get at least a glimpse of him. Others wept as if Jesus himself had returned for a visit to his home town.

In my first few months on sabbatical I had projected a special missions issue on Africa for June, 1964; supplied news reports on religious developments on that Continent; assisted in covering the papal visit to Palestine. Now Athens, where the West begins, lay ahead, and in an exclusive interview there I would cover the Greek Orthodox challenge to Rome's claim of papal supremacy.

ATHENS. We arrived in Athens on Monday, January 6, and lodged two blocks from the downtown Olympic Airlines terminal at the comfortable Alexiou. Although Athens was rainy and colder than we expected, we sauntered to the Acropolis and to the Archaeological Museum, at a curbside stand sampled souflaki, one of the many delicious Greek pastries, and at night shared a large broiled fish served complete with head and mournful eyes.

Later in the week we went to Pireaus, the seaport of Athens, and the next day with friends journeyed by bus to Sounian on the Aegean Sea.

Among mail that awaited us in Athens was a letter from Harold Ockenga dated January 8. In it he indicated the *Christianity Today* Board's desire that I retain leadership as editor-in-chief. The Board expressly guaranteed a month's vacation and beyond that six weeks annually for study, teaching, lecturing, conference participation or whatever; periodic production or editing of my theological books, moreover, it considered highly desirable. Gaebelein and Lindsell were to relieve me of most office routines, but I was to accept only strategic out-of-town engagements. An executive committee, said Ockenga, would be available to discuss any other needs. "We want you at *C.T.*," he stressed.

This was as forthright a letter as I had ever received from Ockenga and I welcomed it. The magazine had, at the time of my sabbatical, almost four times the *Century*'s paid circulation yet had merely tapped its larger possibilities. Our overall circulation was about 210,000 copies per issue, and it was remarkable that so many paid their way to assure uninterrupted arrival. I wrote Ockenga on January 15 that I would try to make the magazine option work. This presupposed, I noted, Gaebelein's full-time continuance and Lindsell's actual arrival in the Fall of '64.

A severe snowstorm had blanketed Athens the day of departure for Rome and we waited until Alitalia finally shifted us to a TWA flight.

ROME. The sun shone brightly when we arrived, belying the cold weather. We made our way to the Italian Bible Institute where Royal and Elizabeth Peck awaited us. Next morning we visited the Coliseum, Forum, Arch of Hadrian and finally the Mamertine Prison where in stunned silence we contemplated the great apostle Paul's imprisonment in those stifling quarters. Several days later the Pecks gathered missionaries from three continents, including us, for dinner.

After speaking several times in chapel at the Bible Institute, I arranged for a month's rail pass to other parts of Italy. Naples was the first of our many stops at which we had made no room reservation.

NAPLES. Once we arrived in Naples, we went to nearby Biblio Centro, the Conservative Baptist missionary headquarters that had translated some of my work. Learning from workers there about pensions that faced the sea, we took a street car to the Bay of Penelope. Within fifteen minutes we found a quiet fifth floor pension with fully as good a view, if not better, as many of the noisy disco hotels.

Naples was alive with cultural and archaeological interest, and not least of all the music of men like Verdi and Rossini. Among our first prowls was that in "Brass Street," where craftsmen produce world-famous marble-based scales and other items. We walked through parks and along the shore to observe seafront activities. We had devotions by the shorefront. Hours were spent in the archaeological museum and in art galleries on the Capidomonte.

Reserving our room for return from a side trip to other areas, we took the train to Pompei to see the ruins of the playboy capital of ancient Rome. Beautiful Salerno, Amalfi and Sorrento were next on our list. At Sorrento's back street woodworking inlay shops we watched artisans fashion exquisite furniture and smaller specialties, and later also visited Correale Museum and reviewed a bit of World War II history.

We then took the ferry to Capri. The weather had turned bitter cold, the sea too rough to explore the Blue Grotto. We made the best of traversing narrow hilly and rocky paths to see what we could, had early supper and prepared for bed. Over her pajamas Helga wore her Harris tweed coat, donned a scarf and hat and a pair of my sox and gloves. Our visit to Capri was hardly what we expected; it was good that Sorrento had for a time at least exhausted our romantic propensities.

After an additional day or two in Naples and environs we entrained for Rome and farewells to the Pecks.

FLORENCE. On February 3 we were bound for Florence where we had no advance reservations and had told no one we were coming. We located a third-floor pension a short walk from the railroad station, but it was undergoing renovation; the proprietor referred us to the locanda on the next floor. We decided to check it out, since a locanda is one grade below a pension simply because it provides no meals. Shown a huge, warm room with two double beds, a davenport and lounge chair, and perhaps a hundred English-language paperbacks, we accepted it without ado, slipped out for window-shopping, enjoyed a *prezzo fizzo* meal at a neighborhood restaurant and returned. I began reading *Advise and Consent,* which I had not ventured before, and almost finished it by midnight.

The next morning we covered the usual "must sees": Chapel of the Medicis, the Baptistry, Duoma church and Bell Tower, postponing the Uffizi Gallery until after lunch. No end of bookstores, antique shops and art galleries beckoned us. At one stop we bought a white marble hand holding a pen poised for writing.

It rained Thursday morning so I went out alone for book covers and other small leather items. When I returned at noon, Helga greeted me with: "Guess who was here—in a big black Cadillac that could hardly squeeze through the alley—and came up to our locanda!" "You're kidding," I retorted. The calling card she handed me bore the name of the U.S. Vice Consul in Florence, Richard Martin. "We're invited to dinner tonight," Helga added. "How did the consulate get our name and address?" I queried. Then the story unfolded. A devout Christian and subscriber to *Christianity Today,* the deputy consul when in Rome the previous day happened into Royal Peck, who mentioned our having gone to Florence but who had no idea where we were staying. The consul thereupon alerted Florence police to notify the consulate (298276) when my passport showed up at the hotel registries. At an inner city hotel that evening the Martins entertained the entire evangelical missionary community along with Helga and me for dinner. That Helga and I had "missionary lodgings" specially pleased the Christian workers.

On our last full day in Florence, we toured the Pitti Gallery, went to the Restaurante il Pagione with its blazing fire for our last *prezzo fizzo* meal of broiled chicken, vegetables and fresh fruit, then wandered aimlessly back to our pleasant warm locanda room to ready for morning departure.

Arriving in Pisa by train on Saturday we covered the usual tourist sites, walked to the Arno River area where in 1955 we had stayed with an educators' tour group, bought some beautifully colored alabaster eggs, wandered through the market and called it a day.

After brief stops once again in Rome and Salerno we continued by train along the Mediterranean coast to Messina and Taormina, crossing into Sicily by train ferry. We taxied from the train station to the Pension Bodia Vecchio with its sunset view of the sea and at dusk of glowing Mount Etna. Taormina was as charming as a picture postcard, and invited leisurely walks, browsing here and there, and willing compliance with siesta hours. At an afternoon concert in a former palace we heard eighteen mandolins, two guitars, a bass viol and a kettle drum try a repertoire of Brahms, Mozart and Rimsky-Korsakov. One morning we took the local train to Randazzo to view at close range fiery Mount Etna that had recently erupted. After several days in Palermo where we again looked out on the Mediterranean and distant mountains we boarded the early Palermo-Naples-Rome train to move northward and eventually west on our European course.

This time at the Italian Bible Institute we joined a former Fuller student teaching theology at Seeheim, Germany, and a dozen other guests being entertained by Lynn and Bernie Oxenham. Once again I spoke in chapel and later addressed a Christian Literature Conference.

Our final stops in Italy were in Genoa and San Remo before we proceeded to Monte Carlo.

MONTE CARLO. Our month-long Italian rail pass had served us well. Now in Monte Carlo where Trans-World Radio staffer David Carlson met us I taught the adult Sunday school class the following morning. Speaker at the morning service that followed was Chaplain Stewart Robinson of the U.S. Sixth Fleet's Flagship *Springfield* who invited us to tour the ship. After later participating in an afternoon service we toured the impressive Trans-World Radio facilities and learned something about recording and broadcasting techniques. During a power outage there we were trapped in an elevator between floors for thirty minutes.

FRANCE. That Sunday morning in wet, blustery cold weather I had waited half an hour for a tardy driver at a designated pickup spot. Now on Monday an inflamed throat and chills kept me in bed thinking positive anti-flu thoughts.

The Hotel Univers in Nice where we stayed served breakfast in bed—magnificent croissants, butter and jam and piping hot pots of coffee or tea. To anticipate Maurice the waiter's coming, Helga customarily tidied up the room and after primping herself into relative attractiveness, jumped back into bed. That Monday morning of my indisposition she ventured, after breakfast, through driving rain to a pharmacy. The clerk gladly sold her needed medications but also tricked her by giving old instead of new francs in change. In all, I spent almost five days in bed in the longest stint of illness in many years. Helga meanwhile explored the Old City, had our ninety-day Eurail passes stamped and made reservations for travel to Marseilles.

By Trans-Europe Express we reached Marseilles, associated with "The Count of Monte Cristo," in two and a half hours, and were soon lodged in the Splendide Hotel. At the Alhambra we had delicious potâge, chou fleur au gratin, coq au vin, crêpe confiture. Later we were introduced to the city's delectable bouillabaisse. But Marseilles appeared grim and uninspired, except for lovers who seemed undeterred by anything and anybody.

SPAIN. We entrained for Barcelona, where I spoke the next afternoon, March 5, in the Baptist Church, and the day following in the Baptist seminary chapel, before we entrained anew for the Spanish capital.

In Madrid we went to the delightful Carlos V Hotel, even if we were surprised by the 9–11 P.M. dinner schedule. Special activities included a half day at the world-famous Prado and at the Royal Palace, and finally a visit to the Rastro (flea market) where we bought a gorgeously crafted silver on copper vase with an iris design.

Somewhat perplexing was a letter from *Christianity Today* mentioning a brief stop at the office by our son, whom we presumed to be in Liberia. A next-day letter from Paul told of his reassignment to Ethiopia after a Peace Corps conference in Washington. Before yearend Paul had intimated that Peace Corps workers in Liberia faced administrative resistance in their effort to resolve postal problems. We cautioned that caustic criticism might complicate his relationships and encouraged him to make the best of the situation. The Peace Corps director in Liberia seemed content if appointees simply put in time;

the American ambassador, on the verge of a new assignment, chose not to intervene. Paul protested to Washington and was summoned home. The routine procedure in such circumstances was to stand by superior officers and to terminate an unhappy worker. Paul had the foresight to arm himself with supportive letters from United Nations personnel, American University professors in Monrovia and others. When his judgment was questioned, he produced the correspondence. He was reassigned to Ethiopia for the second year of his term and worked congenially outside Addis Ababa both as a teacher and on a high school construction crew.

In a meeting at the Spanish Seminary with Christian leaders including José Cardona, secretary of the Evangelical Defense Commission, we discussed limitations on Protestant rights. The Spanish government was gradually easing restrictions on the 30,000 Protestants despite some vigorous behind-the-scenes hierarchical opposition.

We left Madrid on March 17 for Bordeaux as our ultimate destination, arriving en route at 9 P.M. at the Spanish-French border city of Hendaye where we stayed the night. The 9:55 A.M. train next morning to Bordeaux would connect with one to Limoges, the French city renowned for porcelain and enamels. But we had scarcely left Hendaye when we noticed a train steward doing an unusually brisk business peddling French newspapers. I noticed large headlines about a national rail strike that had immobilized France. Since we were on a moving train headed for Bordeaux, I waylaid a conductor who indicated that only international trains like ours were being permitted to function. If we detrained at Bordeaux, he said, we would be without further train service until the strike ended, and that—he assured us—might be never. Since our train was going through to Paris and we had Eurail passes, we could continue without additional arrangements to Paris, where we preferred to be stranded, if stranded we must be.

FRANCE. We reached Paris in drenching rain, to news that Metro employees had struck, there was a massive traffic snarl and hotels were crowded. We took a conductorless Metro to Gare du L'Est where I left Helga in a sheltered doorway with our baggage. A half hour later I returned with reservations for the last available room at tiny Les Voyageurs Hotel.

We had lovely days in Paris. Despite the morning rain, we went to the Arch de Triomphe and strolled the Champs Elysee hand in hand as if we were back in college days. Next day we walked along the Left Bank and in a cozy café shared a Chateaubriand steak, a rare treat. After an afternoon at the Louvre and a quick self-service snack, we decided to walk to Mont-Martre as darkness fell. But when light rain turned into a downpour, we stepped into an antique shop where two proprietors were taking inventory and invited us to look around. We told them we specially admired a matching pair of silver-plated fruit bowls with heavy-glass inserts, but warned that our offer would be taken as an insult. They laughed, insisting that any offer is better than nothing. When they heard our price the manager fell backwards to the floor as if shot through the heart. His assistant came running to assure us, hilariously, that it was not the first time his partner had been felled without a gun. We made profuse apologies, only to see the manager revive promptly, carry the bowls to the counter and carefully pack them for us with his best wishes.

SWITZERLAND. The Paris stopover had replaced a scheduled brief visit to Limoges and another to Geneva. To recover our itinerary, we left Paris on Saturday evening for Basel aboard TEE (Trans-Europe Express) where James and Linda Boice met us and accompanied us to the Hotel Vogt Flügelrad. An honors student on a Princeton scholarship, Jim was completing his doctorate in New Testament under Oscar Cullmann. He had worked on *Christianity Today*'s summer staff and we hoped he would permanently join our ranks. After Sunday service in the Anglican church, we had dinner and spent the afternoon at the Boices in theological dialogue with Basel seminarians.

We took TEE to Zürich and stayed at the *alkohol-frei* Augustinerhof on St. Petersstrasse. Accommodations were spotless, and innkeepers highly hospitable in Switzerland, Austria and Germany; goose-down quilts and pillows added to overnight comfort.

We took the train to Ruschlikon to visit the Baptist Seminary and had dinner with Dr. and Mrs. John Watts whom we had seen last in Beirut and then in Jerusalem. The following day I returned there for a theology lecture.

On Wednesday I spent an hour with Emil Brunner, talking theology as we walked the streets of Zürich. I asked him who was currently king of the European theological scene. "Bultmann ist jetzt König," he said tartly, adding in English, "but not for long!" "Why not?" I asked. "Because Bultmann thins out the gospel too much," he protested. I paused a few moments and began again. "About your own view," I said to Brunner, "have you changed your mind about the virgin birth of Jesus?" "Ach," he said, "it's myth, it's myth." It was clear that Brunner not only stood to the left of Barth on numerous issues, but that he no more than Barth adhered to a consistent religious epistemology that could escape the Bultmannian defection from evangelical orthodoxy. Brunner was a man of courage, a scholar who recognized the peril of communism; he emphasized the need of personal decision and called believers to invest vocational gifts christianly. But despite all his emphasis on general as well as special divine disclosure, the theory of revelation on which he insisted vulnerably divorced faith and reason and weakened the gospel by internalizing its miraculous aspects. In the afternoon we called in Zollikon on devout believers, Mr. and Mrs. Alfred Hirs; he had been treasurer of Switzerland and their son later was to hold an active role in international banking.

AUSTRIA. Our early Thursday trip to Innsbruck was an unforgettable ride through Swiss mountains. Innsbruck itself was cold and rainy, and the view even from our fourth floor window was disappointing. Since weather predictions were unpromising, we cut short our stay and left next morning for Salzburg. The scenic trip through ski country—Worgl, Kitzbühl, Zell am See—was breathtaking.

In Salzburg we opted for the convenient Pension Sandwirt near the Bahnhof, and enjoyed its piping hot German soups and specialties, from *Fleischstrudelsuppe* to *Rindfleisch mit Nockerl* (Spätzle). We routinely walked the mile to the Altstadt, heard the Glockenspiel, passed Mozart's birthplace, walked through the Mirabel Gardens and attended on opening night the Salzburg Marionettes in their astonishing presentation of Mozart's "Magic Flute."

Easter Sunday we heard an excellent message at the Evangelical (Lutheran) Church where worshipers filled the sanctuary and were standing. Easter Monday was a holiday and we entrained at 11 A.M. for Vienna, arriving in midafternoon in the city so exhilaratingly associated with the names of Beethoven, Haydn, Mozart, Schubert, Mahler, Strauss and others. One third of this city of 1½ million people had been damaged or destroyed in World War II; even our hotel had been subsequently rebuilt.

We walked to the Domplatz, returned for our evening meal at a neighborhood restaurant that served delectable *Rindsuppe mit Leberknödl, Fleischgulyas mit Nockerl* and *Apfelstrudel.* The friendly Austrians seemed never to talk with anybody without the initial and concluding greetings, "*Grüsz Gott!*" and "*Auf Wiederschauen!*" Tuesday was migraine day—due neither to exhaustion nor to work pressures but to the damp cold—yet we walked the entire *Haupt Lindstrasse* in a relaxed way. Wednesday I visited the secretary of the Evangelical Alliance. Then we went to the Mariahilferstrasse area and bought prints for framing and watched women gardeners at work in the many city parks. Thursday we joined a three-hour tour of the city. We visited Schönbrunn Palace and walked through 45 of its 1440 rooms. There Mozart played his first concert when he was six; Kennedy and Khruschev ate in the reception room during their 1960 talks. We saw the Opera House, Strauss's salon and his memorial (he composed *Blue Danube* and other popular numbers in Vienna) in the Stadtpark. Helga took a memorable ride on the world's biggest ferris wheel, built in 1879; instead of sitting in seats the riders occupy cabins in which as many as 20 people can stand and roam about as the huge contraption makes its rounds.

A note from Nelson Bell indicated that at the end of March *Christianity Today* had 95,922 paid subscriptions of which 3,210 went to the British Isles and the Continent; the magazine now hoped to reach 100,000 paid during April. Nelson indicated that he was about to leave for a fortnight in Korea in connection with Presbyterian missionary concerns.

GERMANY. We arose before dawn on Friday, April 4, and from the Westbahnhof took the early train to Munich via Salzburg. Saturday we toured city sights in Germany's third largest metropolis (after Berlin and Hamburg). Founded by monks and now 70 percent Catholic, it was 45 percent damaged during World War II when its art treasures were stored in the Austrian salt mines. The swinging city boasts 13 beer factories, the oldest going back to 1328, and months in advance of *Oktoberfest* its inhabitants eagerly anticipate its 16 days of beer-drinking and other festivities.

Next stop was Nürnberg, which strikingly combines the medieval and the modern and is famous for the Nazi war trials. We were in Hans Sachs and Albert Dürer country. We attended Sunday service at St. Lorenz-Kirche where about 100 confirmands dressed in black received their first communion. Our ample Sunday dinner at Nürnberger Hof (*Hühnersuppe, Gefüllte Kalbsbrust, Rohklos, Salat, Eis*—that is, chicken soup, stuffed veal breast, potato dumpling, salad and sherbet) cost well under a dollar.

While Helga roamed around Nürnberg I went to Erlangen on Monday to meet professors at the historic Lutheran divinity faculty. In the afternoon Helga and I joined forces to visit Nürnberg Castle, Dürer Haus and various monuments. Then we drifted to the antique shops, bought used porcelain and silver items and walked and talked about our years together and our future hopes. In midweek we took the train to Stuttgart and made the Tübingen connection. The rail trip through the Nürnberg area's snow-decked forests to the fruitlands near Stuttgart was rewarding and relaxing. We found Tübingen in many ways a medieval city, especially in its older, well-preserved sections. I met the next morning with several of the divinity faculty.

On April 10 we went by train and bus to Seeheim to visit the Bibelschule (German Bible Institute) where my former Fuller student Wilfred Naujoks was teaching. I spoke in chapel and lectured in several classes. In the afternoon we drove to Mainz. There I interviewed humanist Manfred Mezger who reduces love of God to love of man, and also Herbert Braun who stands on the death-of-God left of Rudolf

Bultmann. Continuing to Worms we saw the imposing Luther memorial and the place where the Reformer bore his courageous witness before the Diet. I also met with Wolfhart Pannenberg in his nearby apartment; together we talked about the connection of revelation with revealed truths on which American evangelicals insist. Pannenberg was unfamiliar with B. B. Warfield's classic work on *The Inspiration and Authority of the Bible* which I commended.

After the Seeheim stopover the Naujokses drove us to Heidelberg, where Helga and I spent ten memorable days. For the first time in many months I shed my overcoat. We strolled through the city, noting many changes since our 1957 visit. After German services at Heilige Geist Kirche, we phoned Colonel John Scroggs of the SHAFE (Supreme Headquarters Allied Forces-Europe) command in Paris and Heidelberg who confirmed my commitments at the military post for the following weekend.

The three intervening days I spent at Marburg and Göttingen campuses to gain perspective on the changing frontiers of European theology. The more I spoke with theologians and New Testament scholars, the more apparent it became that a major shift was in process, one of which few Americans were aware. The numerous interviews that lay ahead in Germany would yield an important series of essays that *Christianity Today* would carry on my return to the States.

In Marburg the faculty secretary indicated that Herr Professor Bultmann was in town but had not been on campus. When my phone calls were unanswered I ventured to Bultmann's home located in the highest part of the city on Calvinstrasse near the Schloss—somewhat inappropriately, I mused, for one who had demythologized both Calvin and the third heaven. I knocked, but to no avail, first at the front door and then at the back. From across the street a neighbor called, "Wen suchst du?" "Herr Bultmann," I replied. "Er ist nicht zu Hause," she answered. "Wo ist er?" I asked. "In Wiesbaden. Er sucht eine Kur." To this point my German had been adequate but now I was in trouble. I misunderstood the neighbor lady to say that Bultmann was looking for "eine Kuh," that is, a cow. Why in the world, I wondered, would Bultmann be in Wiesbaden looking for a cow? "Wo [where] in Wiesbaden?" I asked. "Im Goldenen Brunnen Hotel," was the answer. Then the light dawned: Wiesbaden is famed for its mineral springs and curative baths; Bultmann, not well, had gone there in quest of a cure.

I returned to Marburg university and interviewed New Testament scholar Ernst Fuchs at length about the multiplying divisions at German theological frontiers, then signed into a pension near the *Bahnhof* to make an early train to Göttingen. There I contacted the American

Dutch Reformed theologian Eugene Osterhaven, who was completing his doctorate under Otto Weber. After an hour's drive to a mountain retreat where Weber was engaged on a writing project we dialogued about and assessed theological tensions in Germany.

Next morning I phoned Bultmann, whom I had never met, but he was not in his Wiesbaden hotel room; I was told to try again just before noon. I took the train to Frankfurt and from there just before noon when I was to board the Wiesbaden connection called again. Bultmann had already left for the dining room. I left word that an American writer and theologian had tried twice to reach him by phone and that I was traveling to Wiesbaden specially to see him; I would arrive early in the afternoon in hopes of conversing with him briefly.

My message had not been delivered, however, because Bultmann had left word that he was not well and did not wish to be disturbed. Not unlike prayer, a few well-placed coins can sometimes move mountains. A willing waiter delivered the phone message to Bultmann who was still in the dining area. As Bultmann and his wife emerged, the waiter presented my card and indicated I was just outside in the lobby. Bultmann really looked unwell. I explained that I had interviewed a whole spectrum of Continental scholars from Brunner and Pannenburg to Fuchs and Mezger, and that I was eager that a series of essays in *Christianity Today* would represent him fairly.

Bultmann produced his card, and on it scribbled "Sieben Uhr. Weinhaus Rille"—that is, 7 P.M. at one of Wiesbaden's old winehouses. Frau Bultmann accompanied him and for about an hour we talked theology. After the Bultmanns had ordered their wine and I *Traubensaft,* I got the conversation moving by asking: "Who are the *echt* [genuine] Bultmannians today?" "They are all *echt* Bultmannians," he briskly retorted, speaking of Germany's leading New Testament scholars. "Even Herbert Braun and Manfred Mezger?" I asked—thus raising the death of God question. Bultmann straightened up and emphasized: "If they imply that I do not think that God is real they do not know what they are talking about."

The conversation was then underway in earnest. We spoke of the post-Bultmannian revolt paced by Ernst Käsemann, and the diversity of views held by scholars who felt that it was time to advance beyond Bultmann. But Bultmann remained adamant: it was he, not they, who represented the future of New Testament studies.

Two impressions still remain. One is that whenever I conversed with Karl Barth I had the clear sense that, however flawed was Barth's dialectical theology, I was in the presence of a believer in the gospel. Bultmann, by contrast, had demythologized the gospel, and seemed to lack the joy and buoyancy of Christian faith, at least in this, my only meeting with him. A second impression concerns Bultmann's dehistoricizing of the Gospel accounts of Jesus of Nazareth. Bultmann regarded the Gospel miracles as myth; what is factual, he held, is that Jesus lived and died and taught in parables. When I raised this subject, Bultmann—then in quest of a personal bodily cure—added that what may also belong to historical fact rather than to myth is that "Jesus healed the sick."

On my return to Heidelberg Helga and I had dinner with chaplains and their wives at the U.S. Army base, and with several officers and their wives, before I addressed the Sunday morning service at Patrick Henry Village chapel; in late afternoon I spoke at a special young people's meeting. The second Sunday in Heidelberg I preached at Mark Twain Village Air Force chapel. Afterward we joined the Scroggses, Chaplain Kermit and Lynne Johnson, and others, to exchange convictions about spiritual conditions in Europe, before we met with Heidelberg University students for discussion at the Johnson home. Later I spoke to Senior High School young people at the base. The following morning, our last in Heidelberg, we received a wealth of mail, including a letter that Paul had posted in Paris en route to his new Peace Corps assignment in Addis Ababa, Ethiopia.

That day we left for Frankfurt. We dined that evening at the Officers Club with Colonel Harold Kennedy, former Sunday school superintendent at Cherrydale Baptist Church located near us in Arlington, and with chaplains and other officers stationed at the base. We took an early train to Wiesbaden next morning to continue by Rhine steamer to Bonn.

At Bonn I contacted university professors before we retired at our hotel where a nightclub blared through the hours until 4 A.M. As we thought about home we remembered that Carol was giving her Junior piano recital at Wheaton that same night. Paul had sent her a monetary gift and we had sent flowers and arranged for an after-recital party. Carol's next letter told of her successful performance. Too, she had been invited to be assistant housemother during intersession and the first term of summer school.

Our schedule had called for but a single day each in Frankfurt, Bonn, Cologne and Hanover. Hamburg promised a longer stay. Mail awaited us at the Hotel Pension St. Vitter including a glowing analysis of Carol's recital by Reginald Gerig, her major professor. Paul's first letter from Ethiopia told in high spirit of his assignment to teach history and English on the secondary level in Lekempt, a small town twenty-five miles from Addis Ababa.

In Hamburg I spent our entire first day with university professors, among them Helmut Thielicke who shared impressions of the changing climate of European theology.

On another full day we toured the city and then browsed in antique shops. In the last hour before an auction house closed for the week we bought 26 pieces of cobalt and gilt-edged Rosenthal porcelain and arranged for shipment. The day ended with a trip to the harbor area (Helga's parents had shipped out and returned here to and from Africa) for an evening walk that terminated unexpectedly at Hamburg's infamous *Reeperbahn.* Sunday we attended Dr. Heitmüller's Evangelical Church where that day an annual youth festival of 22 churches attracted 4,000 persons under the age of 30.

Little over two months now remained of my sabbatical abroad. On Monday, April 27, we arrived by train in Copenhagen, Denmark, an hour's ferry trip from Puttgarden. On our first evening's exploratory walk from the Missionshotellet Anneks we gravitated almost by instinct to antique shops and found a magnificent platform centerpiece which we wrapped in now unneeded winter clothing and mailed home.

It was a four-hour trip from Copenhagen to Malmo, Sweden, and an additional train trip to Lund. When I telephoned Professor Anders Nygren he invited us to join in a midafternoon family birthday celebration after which he and I would talk theology. Nygren was specially pleased because I was familiar not only with his published works available in English, but that I was also well versed in his unpublished doctoral dissertation on the religious a priori. When I was teaching a course on religious epistemology at Fuller, I had for several Saturdays engaged a Los Angeles Swedish Covenant pastor to translate the dissertation to me. Nygren and I spent an hour talking about theological developments in Sweden as they contrasted with the situation in the rest of Europe.

It turned cold and light snow was falling, so we had time in Lund only for a quick glimpse of the city and to purchase a few ruby glass bobeches. Next morning we took the train to Stockholm, charmed by the scenic landscape along the way with its many lakes and pine and birch forests. We checked into the Hotel Serena, and ate across the square at Margaret's Cooking School, a well-known establishment that served meals prepared by trainees. Learning that Walpurgis Night festivities—folk dancing, singing, fireworks and bonfires—were in process to celebrate the arrival of Spring, we hiked to Skansen to join the throng.

The next day, May 1, was a traditional European holiday. Everything closed down for political parades. Sweden's King and Queen rode at the head of the procession that had in tow a variety of demonstrations (mostly by middle-aged and older people representing Laborites of the Social Democratic Party) for a shorter work week, for the United Nations and against the bomb and South African apartheid. Police carried swords or sticks, but no guns. The spectators seldom showed any emotion. Airplanes overhead advertised cigarettes and hair cream. For part of the day I went to Uppsala to visit at the university with New Testament professors Birgar Gerhardsson and Harald Riesenfeld to get their reading of current Swedish theology. Many Scandinavian theologians were still somewhat intimidated by logical positivism. Gerhardsson and Riesenfeld were trying to break their preoccupation with merely descriptive theology that avoided normative judgments.

Sleet and cold our last day in Stockholm prompted us to stay indoors for reflection and correspondence, and for packing for the following day's departure. The whole nine-hour rail trip to Ostersund in northern Sweden was memorable for miles of forests and numerous lakes, some still frozen over or dusted with snow. We stayed the one night in Hotel Linden, observing ruddy, happy skiers.

NORWAY. Our 6 A.M. train soon crossed into Norway with its scenery rivaling that of the Alps and, where fjords are concerned, of Scotland. As we approached Trondheim we talked about my revered Northern Seminary church history professor, Peder Stiansen, who had lived here. We walked the city until after 9 P.M.; darkness did not descend until shortly before midnight. Before moving on to Oslo I visited the local newspaper office and told the editors what a gifted historian Trondheim had given us in America. The paper front-paged my tribute to Stiansen.

Still fascinated by the waterfalls, ice-crested lakes, snow-covered trees and fifteen-foot snow fences protecting cozy hillside homes, we reached Oslo by train at 10:30 P.M. People were still enjoying bright daylight. The next day I once again sought out university professors before we indulged in touring art galleries and visiting tourist attractions. Painters like Munch, Dahl, Fearnley and Sörenson had become well-known for depicting the country's landscapes as well as its people and their struggles. At Frogner Park we viewed Vigeland's controversial statues, and at the Open Air Museum, remarkable reminders of Viking prowess in past centuries.

DENMARK. Our schedule now called for return to Copenhagen by way of train to Helsingfor, Sweden, and ferry from there to Helsingor, Denmark. After revisiting some of our previous haunts we added an exposure to Tivoli with its cultural attractions as well as more popular features like a Russian fleet brass band, vaudeville and even a flea circus.

Since the next day was Mother's Day we joined a special round trip train and ferry excursion to Denmark's second city, Aarhus, a twelve-hour trip that covered a considerable part of the country. The following day meant return to Hamburg.

GERMANY. Hamburg in early May was remarkably warm. Sailboats dotted the bay; lilacs and tulips and rhododendrons were in full bloom. We walked and talked without plan or purpose—just relaxed. We couldn't resist returning to the auction house where we had bought cobalt dinner plates and, indeed, found another dozen. That night we decided—even if it was a considerable trip—to go the next day to Selb near the east German border to visit the Rosenthal porcelain factory to compensate for our failure to get to Limoges. Our three-month Eurail ticket lent itself readily to such sudden inspirations. We left Hamburg on a 7 A.M. train and, making necessary changes, reached Selb at 8 P.M. From here, one of the porcelain centers of the world, we could look across the hills into the East Zone; trains to and from Leipzig and Dresden pulled into the nearby *Bahnhof.* Next morning we learned that not only Rosenthal, but also Hutschenreuther, Heinrich, Krautheim and other porcelain factories were headquartered in Selb. We were as much gratified as disappointed to learn that the Rosenthal library did not list the magnificent very old dinner service that I had discovered years before in Wiesbaden. Its massive platters and other serving pieces as well as dinner and luncheon settings depict different scenes in the very proper courtship of two lovers. We returned to Hamburg for a move to Nürnberg and beyond. Because we learned that 4,000 persons were about to descend on Nürnberg for a Sudeten celebration, we left that city sooner than planned and headed for Zürich to begin two weeks in Switzerland. On our train was an elderly couple who narrated their trials in East Prussia under the Czechs and Russians until American soldiers facilitated their escape. They spoke gratefully of the Care parcels that in those years had kept them alive.

SWITZERLAND. After a one-day side trip to Basel from Zürich we went to Lucerne for several rainy days. Finally we boarded lake transport to Stannsstad. From there a funicular trolley took us through flower-decked mountain meadows to Engelberg, a charming haven 3,000 feet above sea level. Helga and I had been to Engelberg in 1957. The spacious Terrace Hotel, where we then stayed, had since been purchased by a private club for exclusive use by its members. The small Eden Hotel, where we now stayed, likewise offered breathtaking views in every direction. We meditated on God's glory reflected in nature, and on his goodnesses to us through the years.

At Interlaken, where next we tarried, we looked out each day on the "Jungfrau." In that mountain air the brilliance of blooms in the flower clock and the echoing clarity of the city orchestra built fond memories.

A side trip to busy and cosmopolitan Geneva was an abrupt change. Of special interest was the Reformation Monument to Farrel, Calvin, Beza and Knox, with its side plaques honoring also Luther and Zwingli.

From Interlaken we journeyed finally to Montreaux. Of course, we visited the Castle of Chillon on Lake Geneva, immortalized by the poet Byron.

Then came Aigle where Francis Schaeffer met us and we taxied together to L'Abri at Villars where we stayed overnight in challenging double-decker bunk beds. I had little trouble persuading Helga to take the upper berth. I wrote an extensive and appreciative report on Schaeffer's "mission in the mountains," assessing it as a significant spiritual clinic. *Christianity Today* carried my coverage of L'Abri in the July 3, 1964, news section, and several years later carried also an essay by Schaeffer.

Then it was off to Lausanne, and by bus to Institut Emmaus at Vevey to visit Dr. and Mrs. René Pache.

From the beginning of my sabbatical I had projected interviews in Basel with both Barth and Cullmann and asked Jim Boice, who had my travel schedule, to keep me informed. A telegram now brought good news and bad: APPOINTMENT WITH BARTH SATURDAY MORNING 11:00. CULLMANN IN PARIS. Helga and I boarded separate trains; I went first to Lausanne for an appointment while Helga went directly to Basel, where we ultimately met at the Bahnhof. We joined the Boices and a number of their friends for supper.

May 30 was Helga's forty-ninth birthday—her last, she insisted—and after my interview with Barth we met in the park for ice cream and fresh strawberries. That night the Boices joined us for cordon bleu at dinner in the Walliser Kanne; Jim and Linda brought red roses and Frey chocolates, Basel's best. Two bachelors at a nearby table drank a toast to Helga, announcing that only a remarkable wife would get roses and chocolates on her birthday (in Switzerland, they joked, wives get something practical, like a new toothbrush).

THE NETHERLANDS. Boarding TEE once again, we headed now for Amsterdam by way of Strasbourg, Metz, Brussels and Rotterdam. We reached our hotel along one of the canals about 10:15 P.M. It was Helga's first introduction to Holland's steep narrow stairs and tiny hotel rooms.

Invigorated by the distinctive Dutch breakfast of sausage, ham, cheese, various breads and good coffee, we visited Rembrandt Studio the next day. Helga bought a Dutch dunes scene by A. A. van de Wal, professor at the Amsterdam Academy of Arts, while I bought an Alps scene by Toon Koster, who was painting a large mural for the Dutch government. Interspersed with strolls along Leidesstraat and Kalverstraat, despite chilly and damp weather, I made reservations for our flight to London and the later July 4 transatlantic flight to New York. I also interviewed Professor G. C. Berkouwer of Free University. Then, just before dusk, we took the Rundfahrt at 8:30 P.M. for one more launch trip through the canals and to the sea. Sometime during our city wanderings my goose-down pillow—which I took along on the sabbatical—vanished from the hotel room; I had forgotten my morning ritual that day of locking it in my suitcase. Otherwise all our goods were intact.

On June 5 KLM flew us to London, where at Heathrow Airport J. D. Douglas of *Christianity Today*'s London office welcomed us.

ENGLAND. We had seen much of London on earlier trips, but one never exhausts the city's attractions and surprises. Next day was the twentieth anniversary of D-Day. I took Helga to the Silver Vaults, where many of Britain's choice treasures were first stored underground during the Luftwaffe attacks. This time at the British Museum we made it a point to see the Rosetta Stone and the special Shakespeare exhibit, and in addition heard a lecture on Greek antiquities.

I addressed an Evangelical Alliance luncheon and then greeted staff members at the *Christianity Today* office. In addition to lesser tourist attractions we spent time once again at the National Gallery, and at night saw "The Sound of Music" on Leicester Square. Like many Americans we made the rounds, among other places Selfridge's, Hyde Park, Picadilly Circus, Trafalgar Square, Foyle's bookstore. Sunday we walked from our lodgings in the Bloomsbury area to All Soul's Church, Langham Place, where John Stott preached.

British Rail took us comfortably to Oxford where I visited Dr. James Packer. In the Town Hall we attended the world premiere of David Swann's new opera based on C. S. Lewis's *Perelandra.* The orchestration was superb. Remarkably, we were seated next to Mary Ruth Howes of American Inter-Varsity editorial staff who, in the strange providence of God, would twelve years later be the book editor at Word Books to implement the initial volumes of *God, Revelation and Authority.*

Helga preceded me to Stratford-on-Avon where, when I later joined her, she had standing room tickets for that evening's tremendous 3½-hour production of *King Henry IV.* The following day we went to Manchester, where I met Dr. F. F. Bruce. Helga went on ahead to Carlisle, where she met my later train.

SCOTLAND. June 19 we arrived by train in Edinburgh in a mixed weather welcome of sunshine, rain, furious winds and hail. From well-located Craigholme Hotel we had ready access to many places of special interest and to transportation as well, if needed. Dr. Norman Hunt of Edinburgh University and his wife Lorna drove us through Sir Walter Scott country and entertained us in their home.

Sunday at Charlotte Chapel our American friend, Paul Rees of World Vision and a *Christianity Today* Board member, was guest preacher. In the afternoon I met with university students at the Hunts while Helga readied for a solo departure the next day to Inverness and other points north and west in a week of sightseeing. During her week's absence I remained in Edinburgh for conferences about theological conditions and trends with scholars at both Free Church College and New College.

Helga enjoyed stays at the Isle of Skye, Applecross, Mallaig, Fort William and Glasgow, negotiating from place to place as each situation required by train, bus, ferry, mail boat and freighter. Except for prearranged hospitality in one place, she determined each day's accommodations as she went along. She'd do it again, any time, was her verdict. Among special highlights was a day at David Livingston's birthplace outside Glasgow to see and read his diaries and view other mementos of his life.

When Helga returned to Edinburgh we scheduled a final week in Cambridge and London, with return to New York on July 4 on Pan American. We spent the night on Long Island with Howard and Johanna Albert, my sister and brother-in-law, with whom I had left our car almost nine months earlier. Next day, July 5, marked the long drive from New York to Arlington, Virginia, and the end of one fascinating chapter and the beginning of another.

During my sabbatical year I had traversed much of Africa, the Middle East and Europe. I had interviewed leading theologians and New Testament scholars, had made personal contact with many of the magazine's fifty contributing editors, interpreted our effort to correspondents abroad, and made the magazine known to scores of leaders whose convictions were not evangelical as an academically respectable effort whose circulation now ran about 210,000 copies an issue. In the course of my international travels I had written timely news features or articles on evangelical effort in Portugal, the struggle for Protestant rights in Spain, South Africa's race dilemma, student religious exposure in Europe and a comprehensive series to begin in the September 11, 1964, issue on the theological situation in Europe which indicated not only that Barthian neoorthodoxy but also Bultmannian existentialism had passed its peak, and that neo-Bultmannian scholars were at serious odds with each other in a new transition time for contemporary European theology.

What I did not know—and did not learn until many years later—was that a proposal to end my editorship was made during my absence. For one thing, Nelson Bell wrote me on March 17, 1964, complaining that Gaebelein's editorial approach was not basically theological. A

Board meeting scheduled in April was reset for June 25 to assure maximal attendance. Nelson Bell indicated to my secretary that I need not return early since I would concur with a projected outline of important theological emphases, noting that "Billy and some of the others feel . . . it is necessary to take the offensive more" in respect to National Council of Churches positions. At its June 25 meeting the Board voted to reconvene in New York on July 8, after my return. Nelson wrote me that "there were real storm clouds on the horizon which could have seriously affected the magazine. A crisis had arisen which should never have happened, and would not had you been here. . . . In view of your arrival home on the 4th of July the Board voted to adjourn to meet again the 8th. . . ."

In all of this there was no mention of what Frank Gaebelein subsequently told me a few years before his death. The controversy concerned an article by Mr. Pew that *Christianity Today* carried in the July 3 issue just before my return. It discussed the Church and politico-economic affairs and was specially critical of the United Presbyterian Church. Mr. Pew thought it should be featured as the leading article and apparently had the enthusiasm of Nelson Bell and some other Board members. Gaebelein thought it unwise to use it as the lead-off article, not necessarily because he disagreed with content or emphasis, but for strategic purposes. To do so, Gaebelein held, would revive misconceptions that the magazine was Mr. Pew's mouthpiece; moreover, since its criticism specifically had the United Presbyterian Church in view, it might better be used in a subordinate position. Some Board members rallied to Pew. At a luncheon at which Gaebelein remained adamant, Gaebelein said that he thought he was acting on the same editorial instinct that would guide Carl Henry. At that juncture, Gaebelein told me in the early 1980s, Pew turned and said to Billy Graham, "We've got to get rid of Carl."

12

Berlin / 1966

The unprecedented World Congress on Evangelism rallied 1,200 evangelists and evangelism directors to West Berlin from more than 100 nations under the banner, "One Race, One Gospel, One Task," from October 25–November 4, 1966. The daily sessions, translated into English, French, German and Spanish, were held in the *Kongresshalle* near the Berlin wall which at Brandenburg Gate stands eight-feet thick. The focus on the Church's unfinished world task brought into view the indispensable concerns of evangelism, theology and social concern.

The Berlin Congress, and the form it took, eventuated from a conversation in the rear of a taxicab in Washington, D.C., early in 1964. Billy Graham phoned to say he had just visited in the White House with President Lyndon Johnson, and he wondered whether I might join him on his way to National Airport. His taxicab picked me up at the Washington Building and we spoke of his long-standing desire for a global conference on evangelism. He feared that such an event would be dismissed as organizationally promotive if the Billy Graham Evangelistic Association sponsored it. *Christianity Today* could sponsor it, I proposed, as a tenth anniversary project. In that event, he replied, I should be chairman. Only on condition, I replied, that Graham would be honorary chairman.

A planning committee met in New York on September 14–15, 1964, to implement the venture under *Christianity Today* sponsorship. Two years of intricate planning followed. Committeemen met periodically in Washington, New York, Chicago, London and Berlin. Clyde Taylor, George Wilson, Walter Smyth and Stan Mooneyham had previously met informally along with Robert Evans of Greater European Mission and Robert Van Kampen, Wheaton publisher, to discuss possibilities of a major evangelism conference in Rome or Copenhagen. But when I became Congress chairman, this executive committee approved Berlin as the locale, set precise dates and named Mooneyham as Congress coordinator, Victor Nelson as assistant and Gil Stricklin of B.G.E.A. as director of information. In our Washington offices I immediately enlisted a third secretary exclusively for Congress correspondence.

As coordinator, Mooneyham bore the heavy burden of setting up *Kongresshalle* offices in January, 1966. There he maintained on-site liaison with German and other European participants; implemented Pan Am charter reservations on jets from Tokyo, Beirut, Chicago, New York and London; negotiated hotel and pension lodgings for 1,200 participants; supervised translation of papers into the four Congress languages. Victor Nelson of the Graham headquarters and his staff processed reservations and anticipated registration procedures.

Meanwhile the delegate invitations committee, meeting periodically in Washington, set national quotas and worked through the names of recognized foreign evangelists. The program committee simultaneously projected morning Bible studies, position papers, panel discussions, news-windows on the nations and evening addresses. The several committees coped with many individuals who aspired to come as delegates or whose friends nominated them as speakers. Since a ceiling of 100 was placed on participants from the United States, we inevitably alienated some. Evangelists discouraged invitations to theologians ("they don't know how to lead souls to Christ") and theologians to evangelists ("they are doctrinally anemic"); a few of the invited participants unfortunately turned their inclusion into an official worldwide endorsement of their organizations and on that basis solicited funds. Helga meanwhile began English translation, for distribution to the Berlin participants, of Paulus Scharpff's German text on the *History of Evangelism.*

The conflict in ecumenical circles that pitted social action priorities against evangelism was at that time already running at high tide. In January, 1966, the parish and community life director of the NCC's Division of Christian Life and Mission warned American Baptist ministers that Graham's "traditional evangelism" offers "too narrow a view of conversion" and poses "a danger to the Kingdom of God."

Graham meanwhile had scheduled an evangelistic crusade in Berlin from September 23–30, just prior to the Congress. Early in April I got a disconcerting transatlantic phone call from Berlin.

The NCC at that time had seventeen ecumenical "fraternal workers" in Berlin. These "fraternal workers"—American, Dutch and French—were engaged in church and social work. As couriers between East and West they had access across the Berlin wall that was denied even to the Berlin clergy. To the chagrin of many West Berlin pastors, most of these couriers viewed the church's mission in secular political terms and tilted politically left. Some were prone to dismiss evangelistic efforts as spurious and counterfeit.

In direct attacks on Graham's projected crusade, and indirect criticism of the Congress, some of these ecumenical aides classified "the evangelistic type" along with Nazi Christians who by insisting that the Church concentrate on "traditional" concerns betrayed the cause of justice. Those reluctant to engage the Church in social revolution these "fraternal" workers depicted as "misleading evangelists" and traitors to Christ's cause. Graham was even alleged to occupy a White House office where he helped to shape President Johnson's war effort in Vietnam.

Background materials were appearing simultaneously for the WCC World Conference on Church and Society, scheduled July 12–16, 1966, in Geneva. Critics noted the ecumenical bias toward socialist theory, and its murky evaluation of the role of revolution in advancing social change. Ecclesiastical discussion unavoidably set in sharp contrast the WCC Geneva world conference and the Berlin World Congress.

An official of the National Council of Churches now sent a letter that Berlin fraternal workers used to promote clergy suspicion and distrust of the World Congress. The letter had apparently been solicited by Robert Starbuck, a worker under supervision of the United Church of Christ's board of homeland ministries but assigned by NCC and stationed for ten years in Berlin. The letter, from Dr. Robert Spike, then executive director of the NCC Commission on Religion and Race, and later head of the University of Chicago's ministerial doctorate program, declared—with no restrictions on use—that Graham is "immunized from all encounter with the real problems human beings are facing." Moreover, Spike branded Graham's evangelism "artificial." Spike added that through close associations in the White House he had learned that President Johnson was "using Mr. Graham." American churchmen were pained, he concluded, by the prospect that conservative European churches would now similarly "use" him.

Such propaganda confused churchmen at a time when ecumenical assemblies were appealing for church union and periodically holding out an olive branch to "conservative evangelicals." Stan Mooneyham urged that I keep my schedule flexible enough to fly on short notice to confer with key Berlin clergy. While dates were being probed, I emphasized that the vocal radical vanguard's misrepresentations should be counterbalanced by several facts: many of *Christianity Today*'s contributing editors were leaders in ecumenically affiliated churches; the magazine featured an interview with Bishop Otto Dibelius when he was a member of the WCC central committee, and had used articles submitted by Dr. Eugene Carson Blake and Dr. Eugene L. Smith; we carried feature stories that readily quoted key German and other theologians; I was an invited observer at the Oberlin and Montreal faith and order conferences, and was soon to address the upcoming annual meeting of the U.S. Committee of the WCC. To oppose the World Congress on the edge of quasi-official criticism was therefore to promote the bias of partisans hostile to personal evangelism and evangelical orthodoxy.

In the next weeks the controversy went underground. Ecumenical activists were preoccupied first with the WCC Geneva conference and then with summer vacations. In Washington we readied issues of *Christianity Today* that would give readers access to the position papers and to succinct news reports almost simultaneously with the Congress. The magazine also sponsored a prize hymn competition, the award going to Anne Ortlund's *Macedonia* ("The vision of a dying world. . . ."), for which Henry S. Cutler composed music. It appeared in the July 8 issue of *Christianity Today,* well in advance of the Congress. Copies of an issue published virtually on the eve of the Congress were flown to Berlin and distributed to participants.

Helga preceded me on a transatlantic flight, and took along late manuscripts for editing in London; on my flight abroad I worked on my Congress comments. From London we flew together to Amsterdam and then after a few days to Berlin on Friday, October 14, two days before the opening of Graham's crusade.

West Berlin had 3.3 million inhabitants, more than thrice the population of East Berlin. I had been there for several committee meetings and to view the oyster-shaped *Kongresshalle* erected with private American funds after World War II, but this was Helga's first visit. We went to lodgings I had reserved in Pension d'Este, which offered a twin-bedded room with large work space and comfortable facilities just two or three blocks from Graham team headquarters in the Hilton-Ambassador. We were aware that many Congress participants would be crowded into less comfortable lodgings. Upset to discover we had not checked into the Hilton, Stan Mooneyham transferred us so we would be immediately at hand to meet local dignitaries, the press or Congress committees.

Graham's October 16–23 crusade provided Berlin churches with a week-long show window on mass evangelism in a land where 96 percent of the people were mainly inactive church members (50 percent Protestant, 45 percent Catholic and 1 percent free church). It nourished rumors to the East zone that gave new heart to believers there. It also disarmed the ugly effort of ecumenical aides to discredit both Crusade and Congress as being a front for a political *status quo* that would have accommodated Hitler's Auschwitz.

Graham spoke nightly in the twin-tiered *Deutschlandhalle* whose 13,000 seats filled up for the final meeting but drew respectable crowds also on nights when the rain was so chilly local Christians lent overcoats to Third World visitors who possessed none. Border restrictions kept most East Berliners from attending; their lives were restricted by barbed-wire fences; concrete and steel barriers; guards in observation towers or prowling about with submachine guns; searchlights; dogs and warning devices; military police delays at the Checkpoint Charlie border crossing. Berlin's Bishop Kurt Scharf extended opening night greetings. Bishop Dibelius paid a closing night tribute to the Crusade. Privately he informed us that as a member he had without success urged the WCC Central Committee of 100 to commend Graham as a model for mass evangelism and to throw its influence behind him.

The approaching end of Graham's crusade and the soon-to-be Congress meant frequent executive committee meetings. Every meal now became a work-session with one or another subgroup. The Congress Hall would accommodate only 1,300—1,100 delegates, 100 observers, 100 press. Wives who came with delegates, pastors who came uninvited in hope of admission, had to be excluded. Clyde Taylor's wife Ruth, Vonette Bright and Helga implemented a train tour of Europe for interested wives, who along the way were heralded as women evangelists. During this trip Vonette introduced the group to the "four spiritual laws." Apart from this "flight of the gals" I could usually find Helga working long hours in the Congress Hall checking English manuscripts and German-English translations, collating materials and otherwise assisting staff. If perchance she was absent, I knew she had wandered off to "antique alley" to admire old German porcelain and silver in shops to which I had introduced her, and where we invited owners and clerks to attend the Graham crusade.

No one worked more strenuously or more skillfully for the success of the Congress than did Stan Mooneyham. He coordinated special bus schedules with the arrival of charter flights at Templehof airport, confirmed the readiness of lodgings, arranged for transport to and from daily Congress Hall meetings. He supervised preparation of the arresting exhibit that confronted every entrant, a towering thirty-foot world population clock that ticked audibly with each passing second and dramatized the addition during the ten-day gathering of two million new-born to the earth's inhabitants.

I made it a point to get to Templehof Airport to meet arriving jet charters. For many travelers it was a first flight, even a first trip beyond their own country's borders. Auca Indians stomped on the concrete surfaces, amazed that earth's crust could get so hard. All gave God glory for safe flight; many told of prayer meetings aboard; most ached for a good night's sleep.

Registration proceeded all day until evening dinner at the *Kongresshalle.* The executive committee, meeting daily for breakfast, asked me to make my remarks early, just before the evening mass prayer service, rather than at the morning opening. That gave us a good trial run of lights and sound, provided a cushion for unforeseen delays and created a little extra time for a surprise feature the opening morning.

In my twenty-minute comments I spoke of the need not only of evangelists and of theologians, but of theologian-evangelists and evangelist-theologians. I emphasized also that the God of the Bible is the God both "of justice and of justification." The Christian evangelist, I said, has a message doubly relevant to the modern scene: "he knows that *justice* is due to all because a just God created man in his holy image, and he knows that all men need *justification* because the Holy Creator sees us as rebellious sinners." Those whom the early Christians touched, I added, acknowledged them to be "a new race of men. Will it be said of us: They came to Berlin pondering their individual tasks in a world out of joint; they returned like a host from heaven, unable to stifle their praise of Christ, their thousand tongues swelling into a single mighty voice, and their lives glowing with the radiance of messengers from another world?"

Next morning I accompanied Stan Mooneyham to Templehof Airport to welcome Emperor Haile Selassie, the born-again Ethiopian ruler who had consented to share his Christian testimony with the Congress. Stan had flown to Addis Ababa some weeks earlier to invite his participation. Selassie, 75, was titular head of the Ethiopian Orthodox Church which traced its beginnings to conversion of the Ethiopian eunuch depicted in the book of Acts. During his long reign he wrote Ethiopia's first constitution and abolished slavery.

When the press learned suddenly that the Ethiopian emperor was arriving, German government officials were stunned, since governments conventionally arrange visits of foreign rulers and are responsible for their safety. Addis Ababa confirmed that the monarch was on his way. When Selassie arrived, the West Berlin political protocol system out of Mayor Willy Brandt's office took over. It virtually ignored Congress officials who had arranged the visit. Ecumenical churchmen who had previously shown little interest in the Congress now pressed forward to be publicly photographed as among Selassie's eager welcomers. We were assigned places in the greeting line below all local government and ecclesiastical functionaries. That noon city officials hosted an official luncheon reception in Mayor Brandt's offices for Graham and leaders of the Congress. Graham was not invited to sit on the dais, that spot being reserved for a Berlin churchman.

Only at the end of the "political day" was Emperor Selassie turned over to Congress leaders. But not a single one of the local officials who had been so publicly conspicuous through the day appeared in the *Kongresshalle* when Graham presented the Emperor. In his remarks Selassie threw his weight behind religious liberty and declared it "our prime duty to preach the gospel of grace to all our fellow men and women."

One of the Congress's most important subgroup sessions, in my view, was a luncheon for educators who were invited to discuss the need to address intellectual concerns. It contemplated the spiritual openness of many students (on some American campuses several hundred students were being won to Christ in a single year), the important future role of present Third World university students, the large numbers of unreached college and university students (estimated at 5 million on 2,500 U.S. campuses alone) not enrolled in evangelical schools. It discussed also the desirability of a great evangelical university comparable to Hebrew University of Jerusalem and Georgetown University or Catholic University of America in Washington.

I had hoped to interest Graham in a world student congress, or in a week-long conference in England or for all Britain; such a gathering might feature simultaneous meetings by and with professors and by and with students, but in the evening all participants would attend Graham's larger sessions.

But Graham had established an effective crusade pattern and members of his team were reluctant to see him involved in anything that might detour his ministry. A great sense of urgency nonetheless marked the Berlin educators' luncheon where, Oral Roberts said, he made his decision to launch a university.

The Congress also went out of its way to reassure evangelicals who for one reason or another were critical of the Berlin effort. Martyn Lloyd-Jones, distinguished successor to G. Campbell Morgan at Westminster Chapel, contended that revival of the churches is a necessary prelude to effective evangelism, and withheld his cooperation during Graham's periodic crusades in London. Graham invited him to Berlin as an unpublicized observer, and he came. Lloyd-Jones never questioned Graham's sincerity or his sense of divine call, and applauded much that he heard and saw. But he did not change his view, although he differed in a gentlemanly way.

Another critic was Carl McIntire, head of the International Council of Christian Churches, who attracted press publicity by labeling the Congress "soft on communism" much as ecumenical aides had branded it as soft on Hitlerism. McIntire flew to Berlin to demonstrate against the Congress. He announced that he would begin at the Berlin wall and lead a procession of protest to the Congress Hall. In what *The New York Times* attributed to me as "a rarely acerbic statement," I told the press that if McIntire was really intent on a protest against communism he should begin at the Congress Hall, march to the Berlin wall and keep on marching into the East zone.

The spiritual drama unfolding daily inside the *Kongresshalle* generated immense enthusiasm. The interracial company of Christian witnesses from around the globe (Hungary and Yugoslavia alone represented Eastern Europe because of communist refusal to grant visas) exhibited the spectacular diversity of the Christian outreach and reflected the divergent fortunes of its leaders. Contrasted with earlier world missionary congresses, these delegates were not mainly church administrators ensconced in comfortable offices but nationals actively fulfilling the evangelistic mandate in over 100 nations. Represented were the ancient Mar Thoma Church of India, claiming to go back to the first-century apostle Thomas, and Auca Indians from Latin America whose recent, growing church had risen from the blood of missionary martyrs.

The secular press had initially voiced doubts about the event's media merit. But for evangelical Christianity the Congress yielded a conspicuous media breakthrough, even as it propelled numerous Third World participants into the age of nuclear and space-age evangelism in a world of mass communications. *The New York Times* carried daily reports, Religious News Service covered it comparably to Vatican II and the 1966 Geneva Church and Society conference; Vatican radio took notice. Scores of American dailies carried front-page coverage, and the religious press gave extended space.

The October 28 issue of *Christianity Today,* which reached readers simultaneously with the opening of the Congress, carried the six position papers that prepared for thirty-six panels (each with four participants) preliminary to an hour of spontaneous discussion. The papers and presenters were: "The Authority for Evangelism," by Johannes Schneider, dean of the theological faculty of Berlin University and formerly on the Humboldt University faculty in East Berlin; "The Theology of Evangelism," by Harold Ockenga, whose Park Street

Church annually raised a million-dollar missionary budget; "Hindrances to Evangelism in the Church," by Walter Künneth, professor of Systematic Theology at Erlangen University; "Obstacles to Evangelism in the World," by Harold B. Kuhn, professor of philosophy of religion at Asbury Theological Seminary; "Methods of Personal Evangelism," by Richard C. Halverson, executive director of International Christian Leadership; and "Methods of Group Evangelism," by Anglican Bishop A. W. Goodwin Hudson of London. To my delight, since I was influential in choosing the theological spokesmen, Schneider's address elicited a standing ovation. Coordinating evangelism with biblical theology as its normative ground, he launched the evangelistic mandate against the Western world's materialistic preoccupations and modern theological novelties such as Bultmann's existentialism. Some of Berlin's 500 Lutheran pastors, even some of its free church pastors, had been deeply influenced by Bultmann's call for demythologizing the Bible.

Besides Graham, evening speakers included Anglican Bishop Chandu Ray of Pakistan, a convert from Buddhism; Dr. Kung Chik Han, minister in Seoul, Korea, of the world's largest Presbyterian Church; Gerhard Bergmann, German evangelist; and Fernando Vangioni, Latin American evangelist. National unrest in Nigeria at the last moment prevented Dr. Ishaya Audu, medical educator who had just become chancellor of Ahmadu Bello University, from delivering his address in person. Han's intensely powerful message on Zechariah 4:6 ("By My Spirit") left a holy hush over the entire Congress Hall. Many delegates were in tears as they boarded waiting buses for return to their lodgings. Dr. Helen Kim, president of Seoul Christian Women's University, whom I recognized in the throng, observed: "In Korea we would just stay on to pray through the night." Many delegates held late night prayer meetings in their hotels and pensions.

The Congress's one dramatic eruption into the public life of West Berlin came on Reformation Sunday. Originally I had proposed a bus trip to Luther's Wittenberg, but East German authorities refused permission. Instead, a parade of international delegates moved through West Berlin from Wittenberg Square to the Kaiser Wilhelm Memorial Church where more than 10,000 Christians joined the 1,200 Congress participants for an outdoor service addressed briefly by Graham and Dibelius. The unfurled flags of 100 nations and the presence of Christian converts who were now serving as dedicated evangelists in all parts of the world sent a surge of joy and encouragement through the throng of believers.

Congress participants were invited without regard to ecumenical orientation. The objective was not to forge some semantic statement of organizational commonalities, but rather to constitute a global vanguard for universal evangelism in fulfillment of the Great Commission. In contrast to many ecumenical gatherings, where editorial committees reflected on anticipated public proclamations even before the program was underway, Berlin kept its word that no statement would be issued unless by spontaneous demand of the delegates. The Congress shaped a mood in which evangelicals sensed their larger need of each other and of mutual encouragement and enrichment. While it put theology and social concern within its purview alongside evangelism, its role was that of stimulating discussion and reflection rather than of issuing preconceived pronouncements. A short 1,000-word declaration was adopted by acclamation on the closing day, before Graham conducted a service of prayer and consecration prior to the recessional. Even the secular press sensed among evangelical attendees a confluence of conviction and effort that promised to overcome competitive individualism without resorting to new bureaucratic structures. Berlin was therefore a milestone for the evangelical image. It further lifted the movement above the parochialism that prevailed in the aftermath of the liberal-fundamentalist conflict. Evangelicals wanted the world and the world press to know that evangelical soul-winning is unfinished business. Berlin defined evangelism as uniquely proclamation, and it disowned "all theology and criticism that refuses to bring itself under the divine authority of Holy Scripture, and all traditionalism which weakens that authority by adding to the Word of God."

One strong Congress subsection criticized the doctrine of universal salvation that had become prevalent in conciliar theology. Berlin exposed the speculative philosophy that underlay pluralistic ecumenism. It sketched tenets of the theology of evangelism which for a whole decade would give direction to the unleashing of evangelical dynamisms worldwide. If *Christianity Today* had already attested the existence of an international, interdenominational body of scholars who support biblical theology, then Berlin exhibited additionally the fact that despite ecumenical redefinition of the Christian mission a global vanguard remained fully as dedicated to New Testament evangelism as the early Christians had been.

In his *The Battle for World Evangelism* (1978) Arthur P. Johnston evaluates the Berlin Congress as "one of the most remarkable evangelical events in modern Christian history" and commends its programmed content for "the clear, unconfused, dynamic and biblical simplicity that had propelled a revival of historic evangelicalism in North America. . . . A biblical 'freshness' seemed to dissipate the dense clouds of theological ambiguity, scholasticism and equivocation so characteristic of Western assemblies" (*ibid.*, pp. 157 f.).

Those who criticize Berlin for not providing more theological structure, or for not focusing more fully on social concerns, do so from the standpoint of later ecclesiastical developments. They underestimate also its achievement of bringing together the disparate worldwide evangelistic forces to focus as a single body on the Church's priority task. Berlin necessarily had to brush in broad strokes lest it confuse more than illumine. Lacunae attributed to Berlin, such as the distinction between missions and mission, were addressed in subsections where at times frank and open disagreement emerged. Yet some topics seemed in need of more conspicuous treatment by evangelicals whose main context was Western ecumenism.

By no means was the only visibility to which the Congress was destined confined to the *Kongresshalle* where the central drama occurred involving the over 1,000 delegates from 100 countries. *Christianity Today,* as already noted, simultaneously brought essay, editorial and news commentary that provided a vast readership the next best option to being there. Consequently tens of thousands of American churches were indirectly involved in the Congress proceedings. But there was still another goal: post-Congress book publication of all Congress addresses and of the essence of all panel discussions and commentary, to be mailed to each delegate as part of the registration package. The attractive two-volume work, *One Race, One Gospel, One Task,* issued by World Wide Books, made Congress proceedings available in permanent form to seminary and mission field libraries everywhere.

Before we faced the task of editing post-Congress materials, we stayed behind in Berlin to check last-minute changes by speakers, to update translations, to see delegates safely aboard their flights, to dispatch letters of appreciation and in minor ways to assist Stan Mooneyham and Victor Nelson in an orderly closedown of *Kongresshalle* offices. Then, with what seemed a half ton of manuscripts, Stan and I and our wives boarded a flight to Barcelona and then to Palma, for an off-season week on Majorca. We went to the island's remote resort of Formentor. There, after early breakfast until a late luncheon that signaled an afternoon free for relaxation, we steadily pored over and edited Congress materials for prompt publication.

I commented one day that I thought I had worn out a pair of pants in Berlin and its related committee meetings. If so, divine providence compensated. One beautiful afternoon on Majorca we drove to Inca, where I found some of the most magnificent woolen fabric I've ever seen for a man's suit. A local tailor promised a next day fitting. Mr. Joy (pronounced Hoy) was less than five feet tall, and had to stand on a chair for measuring and fitting me. The cost, for material and tailoring, was $51. That suit has been one of my favorites; on occasion it still reminds me of the hazards of accepting a committee assignment.

Lecturer-at-Large World Vision, 1974-'86

13

Correspondence

Pew, Henry, Ockenga, Bell

Mr. Pew wrote me periodically, and more frequently from Spring, 1966, onward. On March 15 he asked by telegram whether, and if so when, we planned to use either of two articles he had relayed to us. I replied that for the May 13 issue prior to the United Presbyterians' General Assembly we had scheduled a criticism of the proposed New Confession.

In my response I observed that we indirectly harm our own cause if, in respect to the social relevance of the gospel, we emphasize only that the institutional church not become politically and economically involved. "There is a social relevance of the gospel," I wrote, "and individual Christians ought to be politically engaged to the limit of their competence. . . . The evangelical movement at its moments of greatest historical impact has been a force for social righteousness." We should not lock up individual Christians to only liberal publications for guidance they desperately need, I added, for young evangelicals seeking careers in political science are then unwittingly encouraged to think that the only "Christian view" is what liberal journals espouse. Moreover, by withholding our voice we tend to give credence to modernist propaganda that evangelicals are not interested in social justice but only in evangelism.

Pew agreed that these emphases were complementary and not antithetical. But for twenty years, he said, he had resisted what is objectionable, namely, efforts to make the state a servant of the church for purposes of promoting an alien ideology. Some time later Pew suggested that we carry an article on the position on economic and political matters of the Early Church, the Church Fathers, the Reformation and the Westminster divines, a theme on which Pew himself had in fact addressed the National Council of United Presbyterian Men a year earlier.

I was convinced that the upcoming 1966 World Congress on Evangelism in Berlin should devote a plenary session to the social relevance of the gospel; the Congress committee asked Dr. Harold Kuhn of Asbury Theological Seminary to address the subject. I then asked Pew if he would address the Berlin gathering—Billy Graham had spoken to him about the Congress at some length—on the primacy of evangelism. In my letter I also included information about the projected Institute for Advanced Christian Studies; Graham had mentioned IFACS to him, thinking that Pew might someday perhaps bequeath his Ardmore mansion to serve the Institute. *Christianity Today,* I added, would carry an editorial in the May 13 issue on the Institute's possibilities. The venture, I noted, would be a modest fallback from the former vision of a Christian university and that Lilly Endowment, to initiate the venture, might grant $100,000 over a three-year period.

While he favored the founding of such an Institute, Pew replied, his burden was for a refresher course for ministers three or four years out of seminary that would discourage aspirations for ecclesiastical and political power. To that objective he would devote "as much time, money and energy as possible." The thrust of the World Congress on Evangelism, he wrote, should be that "the Church has no jurisdiction in economic and political affairs. Continuance of the present trend," he added, spells "the end of Protestantism as a spiritual and ecclesiastical institution."

We agreed, I responded, that the church should not engage in day-to-day political and economic matters, but rather at the level of spiritual and moral principle. But a full range of evangelical goals, I suggested, requires a variety of platforms. We should not seek all ends from any one means; in short, we should not try to get from *Christianity Today* all objectives of *Christian Economics,* for example, which Christian Freedom Foundation had established twenty years earlier to promote free enterprise, or try to get from the Berlin World Congress on Evangelism all the objectives of *Christianity Today.* Would the suggested refresher course confront young ministers early enough in their educational process? The Institute for Advanced Christian Studies and beyond that, a Christian university, would carry more weight, I felt. "I'm not going to tell you what to speak on in Berlin," I concluded, "but I myself am wholly convinced that your remarks will carry a great deal more power and long-range influence if you give a layman's plea for evangelism than if you merely protest against politico-economic involvement."

"Your dedication and integrity, I have never questioned," he responded. "When your convictions are diametrically opposed to those I hold, one of us must be wrong. Twenty years ago, I realized that the liberals had obtained control of the machinery of many of the largest Protestant denominations; that they sought, above everything else, to exercise control over the lives and activities of people; that they were prepared to exploit Christianity in order to promote their own ideological concepts; and that they would accomplish their objectives by creating a power bloc to dominate the State." *Christianity Today,* he noted, was organized with the primary objective of supporting "the Scripture as the very Word of God" and "may well be proud of its achievements. Today the issue is out in the open for everyone to see. It is the Church seeking political and economic power. I would hope," he concluded, "that the keynote of the Berlin Conference would be 'Does the church have jurisdiction in economic and political affairs?' . . . No contribution . . . I could make . . . would be of any real value excepting that having to do with church involvement with outside affairs. And even here I would hope that someone else . . . could do this better than I could."

I expressed regret that my letter was disspiriting, since my intention was to give "an overview of our whole evangelical predicament facing the last third of the twentieth century." Unless a power grab by "ecclesiastical politicians" is stopped, I concurred, the evangelical effort in these next decades will be "first tolerated and then combatted" and in the end perhaps will face persecution. "But we can win that battle and still lose the war," I added. We must "rally evangelicals together for the fulfillment of Christ's mandate and all the legitimate related tasks. . . . More than any man I know, you have made a dedicated and costly contribution to the evangelical cause in our time. I shudder to think, for example, what would be the strategic stance of the movement today were it not for this decade of *Christianity Today.* I fear we would be split a dozen ways. The important thing now is to hold together an army for a massive impact. And our best asset is the very spiritual dynamic that the ecumenical planners seem almost characteristically to pass over. . . . I hope you will go to Berlin. . . ."

Pew had sent Graham a copy of my letter of April 9 and his April 13 reply. Graham answered that he was "delighted" at my clearcut vision for "an overall evangelical strategy during the next few years." Various evangelical gatherings including the Berlin world conference and Graham's later London Crusade would contribute vastly, Graham remarked, "toward galvanizing a unity among evangelicals. . . . We are already in the majority—but it is our tragic disunity that keeps us from having a stronger voice in the church councils."

Graham emphasized that the Berlin Congress would concentrate primarily on evangelism and missions, but that Pew's concern "most certainly should be brought out . . . but in the context of evangelism. . . . Evangelicals are so divided . . . at the present time that about the only thing they will unite on is evangelism."

Two weeks later I commended Pew for his article in the May, 1966, *Reader's Digest* titled "Should the Church 'Meddle' in Civil Affairs?" the more so because it moved from the authority of the Bible to evangelistic mission and political action, in that order. I referred to my remarks at Buck Hill Falls to the American Committee of the World Council of Churches (subsequently carried in the May 27, 1966, issue of *Christianity Today*). I noted also that the World Congress committee had met at the end of April and was inviting him to address the morning session October 31 on "The Obstacles to Evangelism in the World." After this, together with Negro evangelist Howard Jones and Latin American evangelist Florentino Santana of Puerto Rico, he would serve on a panel to which listeners could then respond.

In his letter of June 23 Pew shared the conviction that the battle against the proposed 1967 Presbyterian Confession "has been lost insofar as the ministers are concerned." The proposed revision, he protested, was "almost as bad" as the unrevised version; its misconception of the church's role in economic, social and political affairs constituted it "an evil document." His effort to get the clergy "thinking straight," he feared, was doomed. "It now appears that . . . the only hope of preserving the fundamental principles on which Christianity has been builded is by having an informed laity."

Pew was right, I replied, that many ecumenical leaders compromise the full authority of the Bible and are preoccupied with social revolution. The July 8 issue would contain a preview of WCC meetings scheduled in Geneva. The ecclesiological crisis involves lay leadership as fully as the clergy, I agreed. Clergy cannot get from their denominational leaders a firm commitment to historic standards yet, even if the high commitments are diluted, wish to remain in their churches. A recent poll had indicated that 74 percent of the ministers in the United States wanted to be known neither as liberal nor as neoorthodox, I noted, but rather as fundamentalist or conservative, although many had reservations about biblical inerrancy. The present process of seminary education multiplies the number of those open to ecumenical inclusivism. It was imperative to reach not only the clergy but lay leaders also and college and university students who must contend against rationalistic attacks on their faith. Evangelical ministers and evangelical laymen need each other, and the enlarging lay subscribership to *Christianity Today* as a thought journal was encouraging.

Pew suggested a special issue for lay readers and I concurred. I mentioned that Dr. George Bird, for thirty years head of the graduate division of the School of Journalism at Syracuse University, had characterized *Christianity Today* as on the threshold of its greatest opportunities. Bird grades the magazine "A+ on its first ten years, in which it came from nonexistence to preeminence in its field," I reported, and "he thinks that in the next ten years we ought to shoot for 500,000 paid circulation and take the lead away from *Time* and *Newsweek* in the interpretation of American religious life."

While I shared much of Pew's assessment of the church-and-world situation, I nonetheless questioned two of his inferences: that his investments in evangelical education and in *Christianity Today* in particular were underproductive, and that the present turn of history bodes only despair. I closed with a paragraph about our personal relationship: "Mr. Pew, you are the wealthiest man I know and one of the most reflective laymen I know, as well as a man of eminence in the business world and a humble believer. I have in common with you the last and greatest of these distinctions, but not the others, but there is one fact about my relationship to *Christianity Today* that has given me full courage across these years to speak the truth in our relationships and to be moved by nothing else—and that is the fact that I have never really hung up my hat here in Washington but have renewed my relationship to journalism rather than to education year by year. . . . I know that in the last analysis God will judge you, and he will judge me, for the special stewardship that he has entrusted to each of us, and that it is only his verdict that is finally important."

Pew wondered if I really comprehended his burden, namely, that extreme liberals control the major denominations, that while most ministers held views contrary to many denominational leaders they were unwilling to oppose the hierarchy for fear of reprisal, and that now only an awakened laity could save the church. Most of the laity, he lamented, look upon their clergy as sacrosanct, do not know the issues and pretty much do whatever their minister asks. "Only by awakening the laity can this trend be stopped. How to do it is a problem."

Pew's next letters were thematically similar. He had declined the World Congress invitation. I urged him to reconsider. The principal cause of denominational deterioration, he reiterated, was the "evil intent of our church leaders to take the church out of its ecclesiastical and spiritual field and involve it in the whole gamut of human affairs." His 1966 Christmas card bore this message: "When the Church as a corporate body takes a position on a controversial, secular subject, those who are opposed to the position taken by the Church will question the competency of the Church to speak with authority on ecclesiastical subjects. This fundamental truth was recognized by Christ, the Apostles, the Early Church, the Reformers, the Westminster divines, and our own Church Fathers."

Shortly thereafter Nelson Bell sent me a letter of which he had sent copies to Ockenga and Graham. He urged that before the January 12, 1967, Board meeting, I join Ockenga and Graham in conference with Mr. Pew, by telephone if in no other way. Again critical of editorials, Bell feared that our chief supporters would forsake the magazine. He mentioned especially Mr. Pew and Maxey Jarman. The Graham association, moreover, would need in 1967 to limit its support.

Pew's concern was to end the Church's political meddling. Bell had an intuition, he said, that Pew may come to the Board meeting with an ultimatum. He himself, Bell said, was coming more and more to share Pew's view that "the objective of current church leaders is to get power in their hands and then to dictate to the State." A conference before the Board meeting, Bell felt, would prepare us "to satisfy these men who have a right to be satisfied if they are to continue their support. The concessions do not have to be large, but I firmly believe they will have to be there. . . . B.G.E.A., Mr. Pew and Mr. Jarman are the ones without whom we would not exist. We cannot cavalierly dismiss their position, for they deserve to be heard."

I replied on December 31 that I would take a $1,000 cut in salary since after the Board meeting we would probably have to review the budget. Billy Graham had just assured me that he would attend the January Board meeting, I said, and "I find that Billy does not immediately identify himself emotionally with all criticisms of the magazine, even within the Board, but has a wonderful capacity for objectivity."

The January 6 issue, just out, was in fact the first to which I had contributed any editorials since returning from abroad. Quoting my editorial, Religious News Service said that *Christianity Today* virtually accused ecumenical spokesmen of duplicity in their subtle distinction between "speaking to the Church" and "speaking for the Church." "Anything stronger than that," I told Bell, "will destroy our opportunities as a magazine—and perhaps the executive editor could do it in good conscience, but I can't." Our escalating criticism of NCC-WCC involvement in politico-economic matters stirred deep resentment among clergy favorable to the ecumenical hierarchy, and brought ugly letters.

At the Board meeting, Mr. Pew called attention to Alice Widener's article on "The Gospel of Revolution," a lengthy analysis of official documents of the WCC issued at the 1966 Conference on Church and Society, carried by *Barron's* after it appeared in the magazine *U.S.A.* David Baker urged that we reprint Widener's article in *Christianity Today.* After *Barron's* vouched for the integrity of *U.S.A.* we talked with the author and decided to reprint the essay in our February 17, 1967, issue with permission, and in its original unabridged form. It was the longest article *Christianity Today* ever carried, and required adding extra pages.

No sooner had the article appeared than both friends and foes assailed it. Persuaded that the essay contained some factual errors, I remarked in a mixed group that I was personally sorry we had run it, because my policy was to condemn on principle and not on prejudice. Pew wrote that while he "would not have had the temerity to write an article for public distribution which went as far as did the article written by Alice Widener, nevertheless I think it is difficult to exaggerate the evils involved."

In late September, 1967, I indicated the need nonetheless to be increasingly critical of the ecumenical movement's apparent openness to revolutionary violence, and proposed that we run an address Pew had given on "The Power of the Gospel Throughout History." But Pew negated the idea because he was still delivering this address; in any case, he added, "it seems to me that it is a mistake for you to carry anything I have written."

Toward the end of January, 1968, Pew wrote to commend us on the January 5 issue. A concluding paragraph in Richard J. Mouw's article disturbed him, however, for in it Mouw expressed the conviction that the church must often take a stand on economic, social and political issues. Over against this, Pew commended Billy Graham's sermon in the following issue about the inherent evil of church involvement in economic, social and political affairs. Unlike Protestantism's accommodation of communism, Pew observed, the Catholic Church, instead of making that church a "socio-political organization . . . seems to be moving further to the right." Mouw's essay, I wrote in reply, had clearly stated that the church cannot offer legislative or military specifics, and is on safer ground, moreover, when it voices a negative verdict on the status quo. I assured Pew that *Christianity Today*'s commitment on Christianity and social action had not changed from its original stand and listed the five tenets of our position:

1. The Bible is critically relevant to the whole of modern life and culture—the socio-political arena included.

2. The institutional church has no mandate, jurisdiction or competence to endorse political legislation or military tactics or economic specifics in the name of Christ.

3. The institutional church is divinely obliged to proclaim God's entire revelation, including the standards or commandments by which men and nations are to be finally judged, and by which they ought now to live and maintain social stability.

4. The political achievement of a better society is the task of all citizens, and individual Christians ought to be politically engaged to the limit of their competence and opportunity.

5. The Bible limits the proper activity of both government and church for divinely stipulated objectives—the former, the preservation of justice and order, and the latter, the moral-spiritual task of evangelizing the earth.

Thereafter I received only infrequent correspondence; little if any of that pertained to the church in politics.

Bell, Ockenga, Henry

Alongside the exchange with Mr. Pew I also corresponded with Harold Ockenga. On January 4, 1967, I indicated that both Pew and Jarman had periodically urged that *Christianity Today* "should strike more bluntly at NCC-WCC affairs."

A Religious News Service report, I pointed out, charged a *Christianity Today* editorial with virtually accusing the NCC of duplicity, when we insisted that the ecumenical distinction between "speaking to" and "speaking for" the churches was merely a semantic ploy. "I do not see how much further one can go," I added, "and still retain a hearing from those we wish to reach."

I noted Nelson Bell's longstanding preference for short editorials. After giving him a full page to say what he wanted, we additionally accommodated his short editorials. He composed still others, without prior consultation, sometimes mailing them in just after a deadline. Others of his editorials would be dictated by telephone from Asheville to one of the secretaries, and after being transcribed appeared on my desk the following day with instructions that if unusable in the magazine they be sent promptly to the *Southern Presbyterian Journal.* Bell on occasion informed Mr. Pew in advance of editorials that he was submitting.

Like Bell before him, Ockenga proposed a telephone conference call between himself, Pew, Graham and me "because Mr. Pew is really giving us something of an ultimatum in reference to his support." The conference call never eventuated. Instead, Graham attended the January Board meeting after staying the previous night with Pew, who had been home only a few days from a brief hospital confinement. It was important to preserve Pew's support, Graham said, unless this compromised our deepest theological convictions. Graham thought it would forestall much of the criticism if we disapproved the corporate Church's involvement in politics and economics but supported the right of individual churchmen to do so. Graham also thought I might need to become somewhat involved in fund-raising for the magazine just as he was for B.G.E.A. efforts; this would mean closer personal relationships with large donors. That task I had earlier left to Nelson Bell, who was now cutting back his efforts.

Early in April, 1967, I had a ten-day commitment in Canada, sometimes speaking four times a day. After the Board had approved a special Canadian centennial issue, we had established a beachhead office in Toronto, in part because of Berlin Congress-generated enthusiasm. Although Canadian evangelicals hesitated about underwriting a Canadian edition, paid circulation in Canada rose to 7,000 subscribers.

My conviction mounted that the years 1967–75 were crucial for evangelical destinies in America. Billy Graham had shown revived interest in a Christian university to train evangelists as Harvard originally did. Unable to attract funds to secure Philadelphia-area properties, the Institute for Advanced Christian Studies was now probing Midwest alternatives for a research center. Through a Lilly Endowment grant *Christianity Today* convened a mainline Consultation of Christian Scholars attended by such luminaries as Alvin Plantinga. I suggested to the Board that an evangelical World Student Congress in 1970 or 1971 would strategically climax the World Congress on Evangelism. Luther, Calvin, Zwingli and other leaders of the Protestant Reformation, I reminded Board members, were university-trained scholars who gave intellectual guidance to the evangelical movement.

I toyed with the idea of applying to Lilly Endowment for a $12,000 eight-month research grant that might accommodate my magazine relationship as editor-at-large. In that context the Board, if it preferred, could name either another editor or acting editor. Our working staff was now at peak efficiency, although Harold Lindsell indicated that he preferred Christian college teaching to editorial work. When Wheaton offered Lindsell a favored faculty contract with half time for writing, he was off and running. Gene Kucharsky functioned efficiently as associate editor, Bob Cleath as editorial associate, Dick Ostling as news editor and Jim Boice had the potential for acting editor. Gaebelein had left us to complete creative literary effort of his own, and Jim Daane had accepted a teaching post at Fuller. Because of family health problems Frank Farrell had moved to California with Gospel Light Press before returning to teaching.

As a matter of courtesy I wrote Ockenga in April in order to keep him informed of the remote possibility of a Lilly grant. If perchance it materialized, I noted, it would not alter my magazine duties or relationships for a year-and-a-half; any Board action at this point would be premature. Ockenga was leaving for two weeks in Latin and South America and instructed me to alert the executive committee (Ockenga, Pew, Weisiger, Lamont and Bell). His first impression was that "we ought to keep you in connection with the magazine" even if I were to get a "three-year research and writing grant."

At the May Board meeting I reported having addressed student programs on various campuses (Mount Holyoke College, University of Miami, University of British Columbia, University of Calgary, Wabash College, Alma College, Western Maryland College), ministerial associations in five cities and several seminary chapels. Our paid circulation had soared to an all-time high of 163,000. The Board granted its executive committee power to work out editorial relationships, if, indeed, a research grant emerged that the editor accepted.

Ockenga was not at the Board meeting because of a virus. I was stunned on May 17, 1967, by a highly critical letter from him. Certain staff members and trustees had conveyed to him, he said, that "a tremendous amount of your time has been devoted to evangelical undertakings which are outside the scope of *Christianity Today.* This, I am told, has had a deleterious effect upon the staff. Personally, I know that . . . many activities you engage in are beneficial to . . . the magazine but I hope even though you are in a transition period you will feel that the work of the magazine comes first." I replied sadly that such a report could have come only from someone woefully misinformed about editorial staff morale. "The magazine is currently at its peak of influence, its paid circulation was never higher, we have never had a more efficient and effective team and if we can find the right successor to Harold Lindsell, we shall be operating at full potential." I mentioned Ockenga's letter to Nelson Bell, who said his remarks to Ockenga had been misunderstood and exaggerated, and that he would rectify matters.

On May 27 Bell himself wrote a somewhat enigmatic letter, the significance of which I did not really grasp. Ockenga had told him in March, said Bell, that I had written both him and Graham of a desire "to be freed from your editorial responsibilities in the Fall of 1968." The reference, I assumed, was to a sabbatical or to a research leave. Bell added that he and Billy Graham had jointly prepared a Board resolution of generous financial provision for what "you can continue to do for *Christianity Today* in the future." Although a copy had been sent to Ockenga and Weisiger for presentation at the May Board meeting, this was never done because Billy could not wait over and Ockenga was absent. "As this resolution has not been considered by the Executive Committee," Bell's letter continued, "I do not feel free to send you a copy. . . . The resolution we have suggested is one you would always be glad to refer back to with a sense of being appreciated."

Nelson added that he planned to come to Washington the following week. When he came, he gave no inkling that he was already proposing the termination of my editorship to the executive committee, and apparently with Billy Graham's concurrence.

On July 18 came an even more startling and bewildering letter. Writing "as Chairman of the Board of *Christianity Today,*" Ockenga stated that the executive committee had met in Philadelphia the third week of June to consider my "intention to return to the academic field if and when the proper opening comes"; a full Board meeting was scheduled for September 21. Then came the bombshell: "The Executive Committee agreed unanimously to relieve you of all editorial responsibility not later than July 1, 1968. Provision was made that your salary was to be paid in full for the year 1968 and the remuneration after 1968 was to be made commensurate with your services to the magazine."

Ockenga referred to the July 21 editorial in *Christianity Today* that reported the founding of the Institute for Advanced Christian Studies through a $100,000 Lilly Endowment matching grant for underwriting of research scholars and added: "We respect your sense of calling to this new field." Copies went to the remaining members of the executive committee, namely Pew, Bell, Weisiger and Lamont.

I replied promptly asking in effect whether Ockenga was telling me circuitously that I had been fired. The IFACS editorial stated, I pointed out, that the development of IFACS was in other hands than mine. Moreover, the selection committee would make no decision on unrelated applications for a Lilly research grant before January, 1968. Even if I qualified, I said, the grant would not be available until January, 1969. It was at Ockenga's behest, I added, that I had informed the executive committee of a remote possibility, but my correspondence was in no way a notice of resignation. "Does the Executive Committee mean," I asked, that July 1, 1968, is "the latest date that a resignation is feasible, or that I am, as of this notification, being requested to retire from the editorship?"

Next I sent a note to Bob Lamont: "Harold's letter is ambiguous, precisely where it needs clarity, and I would value a note of interpretation. Does he mean, in short, that I'm 'fired' . . . and if so, surely a reason must be given (e.g., moral blemish, theological weakness, politico-economic flabbiness, or whatever), or is Harold saying something else?"

From friends on three continents came letters saying they had heard that *Christianity Today* was looking for a new editor, and wondered what this implied. Nelson Bell, who had telephoned me in Washington several times a week, had become uncommunicative.

When I went home to Arlington the night Ockenga's letter arrived, I waited until after dinner to mention the matter to Helga. "You know," I said, "that we have talked often of returning to the campus. Today something happened that we can look at two ways. One is that God providentially opened a door to return sooner than we had planned. The other way of looking at it is that I have been 'fired.' "

Helga was then giving almost as many hours to the magazine as I. She did not know whether to laugh or cry, but did neither: we could trust God in "all things." When my son Paul heard the news, his comment was unforgettable: "Thank God, Dad," he said, "that you are no longer beholden to the evangelical establishment."

On August 14, I wrote Ockenga that three weeks had passed without any response to my inquiry. "In the meantime the ambiguity weighs heavily on me," I indicated. Replies were overdue regarding *Christianity Today* coverage of the upcoming WCC Uppsala assembly, about an invitation to debate Geneva commitments on Church and Society at a high-level ecumenical session in Bossey, Switzerland, from July 22–28, 1968, about sharing in the Malone consultation with NCC-WCC leaders in which our magazine had annually been involved, and about a joint consultation of Christian Medical Society and *Christianity Today* (already approved by the Board) for which former Supreme Court Justice Tom Clark had consented to be honorary chairman.

In the meantime IFACS received a legal opinion that no scholars serving as Board members could receive research grants without jeopardizing the organization's tax exemption privileges. I had not in any case anticipated any grant from IFACS, nor did I ever seek one.

Harold Lindsell had indicated his intention, before taking up Wheaton duties, of vacationing in New Hampshire in August about the same time that Ockenga and Lamont did so. I wrote him, sending greetings to the Lamonts. I remarked additionally: "I have been coping with spiritual suffocation lately—the sort of personal upheaval that adds nausea to migraine. . . . I'm on the uncertain end, apparently, of some Board committee decisions; one or another Board member comments on them to others (even from London I had an inquiry weeks before there was any intimation to me) and I'm in no position to confirm or deny reports, because I can get no clear reading of the situation, or even a bare acknowledgment of inquiries." My plans, I added, "are now more tenuous than for twenty years."

Lindsell replied on August 9 that he had chatted with Lamont and would be playing golf with "H.J.O." the next day and would "sketch me in." I was "not one whit worried about the future," I told Lindsell, but was deeply distressed by "my inability to get a candid reading of a decision" apparently made by Ockenga and the executive committee without conference after I had served eleven years as editor. "I wrote Harold Ockenga a half-month ago and have not had even the courtesy of a reply." A hurried note from Lindsell dated August 10 read: "Saw H.J.O. He is writing you about the whole situation. Failure to reply due to vacation."

On August 15 Ockenga wrote a quite impersonal letter, saying: "I have been 100% behind you and I still hope that you will stay permanently with *Christianity Today*. . . . The whole board had hoped that you would carry on, giving your full and foremost commitment to *Christianity Today*. We all understood, however, that it was your desire in the Fall of 1968 to be relieved in order to return to the academic field. It was on this presumption that we acted. However, we have a full board meeting on the 21st of September and I will be glad to have the whole situation reviewed at that time and thoroughly clarified. I think it would be foolish for us to have a meeting of the Executive Committee in the interim."

"From your letter of Aug. 15," I replied to Ockenga, "I can only assume that the Executive Committee acted with power to terminate my relationship as editor on July 1, 1969. The unexpected announcement of termination reached me almost a month ago. . . . After ten years of service, my relationship to the magazine was not only summarily ended without consultation or reason, but in the absence of a resignation and without agreement on public announcement. . . . Information was leaked to some Christian leaders (from whom I had inquiry) before a letter dated July 18 reached me almost a month after the Executive Committee's action. Even so, the letter of dismissal was not even marked confidential, and was opened and read by secretarial staff before it came to me."

"I'll submit my routine report to the September Board meeting," I added, "and bow to the Executive Committee's notice. . . . I wish *Christianity Today* and its board well, and hope the magazine soars to new heights."

Cary Weisiger sent me an end-of-August note of regret. He asked, "Is it too late to clarify what you want and what we should do as a board?" I replied warmly and appreciatively, but noted that I would bow to the executive committee's notice of termination. "Any other course, I am persuaded, would simply divide the Board and even the Executive Committee, and leave permanent scars. The well-being of *Christianity Today* is more important than my immediate future." But I noted that "a termination of services in the absence of a resignation not only interrupts employment, insurance programs and pension plan, but regrettably evaporates whatever direct service an employee can be to a cause in whatever years remain. What influence is left to an editor whose job is terminated unilaterally?"

My first word from Nelson Bell, dated August 26, was a form letter, an agenda to Board members about the September 21 meeting in Philadelphia in Mr. Pew's office. Ockenga wrote asking if I could meet with him in Boston before the Board meeting. Two items, I indicated, could be discussed helpfully before the Board meeting: first, agreement on a date for public announcement of termination, and second, agreement that the July 5, 1968, issue would be the last for which I would bear responsibility. "I prefer a delayed public announcement," I said, "not simply to minimize personal embarrassment (since I am committed to no alternative employment, submitted no resignation and can supply no reason for termination) but for another reason. It would evaporate the present editorial power of the magazine into an interim thrust if such an announcement were made with ten months to go."

On Nelson's visit to the Washington office early in September he was reluctant to discuss anything in advance of the Philadelphia Board meeting. He was even disinclined to indicate whether he had participated in the executive committee meeting in June. I wrote briefly on September 8: "It looks as if what started out twelve years ago as a great adventure has drawn to a close for me. . . . This has been a Summer of heavy burden." On September 12, Nelson wrote, seeking to explain the executive committee action as a decision about succession that I had forced by my expressed interest in alternatives. The fact was that I had privately corresponded with Ockenga about indefinite possibilities, and expressly indicated that Board action would be premature.

I acknowledged Bell's letter, pointing out that the Board had received no resignation of mine; that Ockenga's termination notice was not suspended on Board confirmation; that I got no reply to any immediate inquiry asking an executive committee member whether Harold's letter meant that I was fired as of July 1, 1968; and that I was consequently bowing to the executive committee's dismissal notice.

Minor surgery at George Washington University Hospital for a deviated septum ruled out an advance Boston visit by me to Ockenga, so I suggested we meet before the Board meeting either at breakfast or the previous night. At the Warwick Hotel, the night before the September Board meeting, Nelson Bell walked unexpectedly into the restaurant and joined Ockenga and me for coffee. "I thought," he said, "that you were committed to an alternative, and that this was the action you wanted us to take." "Nelson," I replied, "for twelve years you have picked up the phone and called me whenever there was the slightest question about anything. Why didn't you just pick up the phone and call me?"

14

A Dark Day in September

As usual, my editor's report along with other staff reports was mailed to members in advance of the Board meeting on September 21, 1967. The October 13 issue, I noted, would begin the magazine's twelfth year. Its influence is "at an all-time high." Its "reasoned support" of biblical theology, Christian evangelism and freedom under God, and its opposition to the Church's involvement in political specifics, I added, has escaped "a reactionary image" and "gained nationwide respect."

I reported that Harold Lindsell had accepted an invitation to Wheaton College as professor of Bible on a reduced teaching schedule that permitted time for research and writing. I recommended promotion of Jim Boice and Bob Cleath to assistant editorships. Magazine size was now routinely scheduled at forty-eight pages, I noted, except where heavy book or educational advertising or the annual index disadvantaged essay and editorial content.

Then I acknowledged "Dr. Ockenga's letter of July 18 relaying the Executive Committee's designation of a terminal date of my editorial services." Two related Board actions were now called for, I noted: confirmation that the July 5 issue would be the last to carry my name on the masthead as editor, and stipulation of a date for public release of news of editorial termination.

Speculation about my future work, I indicated, would be presumptive. IFACS had too many imponderables, and my role as one of the directors was secondary. Legal counsel had determined that tax exemption could be jeopardized if IFACS directors received grants. This warning, I added, might indicate also that salaried staff members [like Nelson Bell and myself] should not be *Christianity Today* Board members. I accordingly submitted my own resignation from the Board, aware also that such severance would "promote freer discussion of future editorial direction and policy." I then tributed lay leaders whose vision and generosity had brought the magazine into being and clergy who had lent their names and support despite adverse ecumenical pressures. "It has been a holy privilege to steer this magazine since its founding, and I shall wish for it a continuing impact for the evangelical faith in these critical times. My goal between now and the completion of my tenure will continue to be the production of the best evangelical journal of which we are capable."

At the proper time in the Board meeting, I mentioned that all Board members had routinely received advance copies of my report, and that unless the Board preferred otherwise, we might proceed directly to action on upgrading Boice and Cleath, on a termination announcement date and perhaps on the matter of staff membership on the Board.

"Further discussion of Dr. Ockenga's letter and the Executive Committee action," I said, "would not, I believe, set ahead the cause of the magazine. It is better that embarrassment fall upon me without embarrassing others and possibly dividing the Board on some issues. So I urge you simply to note that I am bowing to the Executive Committee's termination notice and then to proceed with matters that grow out of this severance." I emphasized again my "appreciation of these years together in the service of Jesus Christ. I honor the generosity of the laymen who have made this magazine their stewardship, and the support of fellow ministers of the gospel who have given of their time."

There was a span of silence. Since numerous staff members were present, the Board decided to dispose of all other business and then go into executive session with me alone.

Ockenga as Board chairman then made a brief remark indicating that the word "termination" was misleading; the Executive Committee, he suggested, had acted reluctantly in fulfilling my own desires. Nelson Bell intruded the same thought.

I had anticipated such diversion and presented simply for the record a memorandum as to why the July 18 letter permitted no other interpretation but dismissal. I determined at all costs to be a Christian gentleman; that determination, I felt, included the propriety of assessing what had occurred. "Mrs. Henry and I are reconciled to dismissal, both psychologically and spiritually," I commented, "although I must say the hurt has been deep."

Although I did not say so, the worst blow was not involuntary termination after twelve years of sacrificial labor. It was nullification of the opportunity to negotiate constructive alternatives while I still had a prestigious base. Possibilities of teaching in a state university religion department, of going to a major publishing house as religion editor or even of recanvassing seminary or evangelical college teaching options, could only be adversely shadowed by leaks to religious leaders that *Christianity Today* was looking for a successor to a lame-duck editor. Jim Douglas heard the report in London, Sherwood Wirt heard it in Asia and it was known in Wheaton and elsewhere.

Ockenga called on me to indicate why I thought his letter of July 18 implied irrevocable termination. I noted that it had been preceded by his May 17 letter in which as Board chairman he had questioned—apparently on the basis of prejudicial information—my vocational commitment to the magazine. The very next letter to come from Dr. Ockenga was his July 18 dismissal letter, in the absence of any conversation, call or correspondence with me. The termination notice was conveyed as coming from the whole Board for which Dr. Ockenga expressly spoke as chairman. Moreover, it specified as the severance date not July 1, 1969, but a date "not later than" July 1, 1969. Dr. Ockenga's expressed hope that this official action would not alter our personal regard for each other, obviously anticipated my personal disappointment over the action. News was leaked to others before word came to me. Information did not reach me until about a month after the executive committee meeting. The dismissal letter was not marked confidential and was read by secretarial staff before I got it.

Dr. Ockenga and I had a standing gentlemen's agreement, I noted, that there would be a year's notice in the event of severance, and his letter could therefore be readily interpreted as expressing the Board's disengagement.

"I am wholly convinced, at this stage," I indicated to the Board, "that the course that holds the least embarrassment is simply to concur in the Executive Committee's action and in my submission to Dr. Ockenga's notification of July 18. While I would have preferred that severance, when and if it came, should not come in this way, I want to show the marks of Christian grace in it, and not to injure the Lord's cause. I hope you consider my statement in the Board report in good spirit, for I intend it that way with all my heart."

Cary Weisiger asked whether it had been my intention to go to academic work. I answered: "Yes, if and when the right option opened. I hoped that our mutual trust was such that, in that event, we could shape the transition so that both the magazine's and the editor's interests would be preserved." Bob Lamont said, "Dr. Henry has for some years indicated his preference for an academic alternative." Kenneth

Keyes said: "Dr. Henry plans to go to an alternative and much as we regret to lose him we should proceed to find a new editor." Harold Ockenga said, "We failed. Instead of referring our action to the Board, we misunderstood it as official action, and we took it not in consultation with Carl but we acted only in view of correspondence."

Some Board members clearly were confused over the executive committee's action and even some members of that committee seemed perplexed. I withdrew from the Board meeting but was later asked to return. The entire Board, I was told, held me personally and my work as editor in highest esteem, and there had clearly been a sad and colossal misunderstanding. The Board was ready unanimously to confirm me in the editorship of *Christianity Today* if I would make that commitment my life vocation.

I thanked the Board for this expression of confidence. But for two reasons I must decline, I said, for the good of the magazine. First, the Board's proposal attached to the editorship a rider which would permanently preclude a consideration of alternatives, a requirement not previously appended to the editorship. More important, however, was the second consideration: in view of the Board's apparent reversal of a position taken by the Board president and by the executive committee, I could never again recapture relationships to certain influential Board members that had existed prior to these events. (I had no heart for coping further with Ezekiel-like wheels-within-wheels procedures and relationships.) For the good of *Christianity Today* and of its Board I felt it personally necessary therefore to bow to the mandate of the executive committee.

During lunchtime Cary Weisiger, a member of the executive committee, asked to see me alone. It was evident, he said, that a gross injustice had been done. What, if anything, might now be done to undo it? Did I have any intimation about future plans? Could *Christianity Today* somehow reinforce these? Could the magazine make evident its support and approval of my work?

I indicated that my whole vocational future was now uncertain, but that Helga and I considered going abroad for a year or two, perhaps to Cambridge, in order to put as much distance as possible between ourselves and the *Christianity Today* scene, and to concentrate on writing a needed work on the doctrine of God. "I couldn't possibly come up with a proposal," I said, "but if the magazine has a proposal of editor-at-large possibilities, or a research grant, or some coordination of these, that is another matter."

The Board proposed a two-year research grant for study and writing from June 1, 1968, in the area of current theological developments, and a coordinate loosely defined relationship as editor-at-large. Details were to be shaped with me by the publisher, Wilbur Benedict, and also Ockenga, before the December 7 Board meeting. Weisiger pressed for a statement of resignation to avoid giving "a false impression of Board motives" but I refused thus to gloss the facts.

On the way from the hotel to the September 21 Board meeting, Nelson Bell had handed me a sealed letter from Billy Graham that I could not conveniently open until after the meeting. Dated September 19, he expressed regret that he could not attend. He had learned only the previous evening, he said, of differences between me and the executive committee, and concluded there was a "colossal misunderstanding." Ockenga's letter was not a "dismissal," he said. "I am prepared to personally support you as editor of *Christianity Today*—or as leader in the new School of Advanced Theological Studies. . . . Whatever transpires at the Board meeting today, I hope there will be no break in the close friendship and fellowship you and I enjoy." Graham added further comments about my gifts and contributions. But the core of the letter was that "every member of the Board, including Mr. Pew, will want you to stay if you feel that this is the Lord's leadership in your life"—but at an express price of being more deskbound. "I have felt for a long time that [you] accepted so many speaking and writing commitments that had little to do with *Christianity Today*. . . . There will have to be a very clear understanding between you and the Board relative to other commitments."

I was glad that I had not read the letter earlier. For Graham was right that I carried too heavy a load, and perhaps was at times not discriminating enough in accepting speaking invitations. But he now apparently shared Nelson's concept that desk presence served the magazine more than frontier involvement. Not faced was the need for professionally skilled aides, and the importance of creative interaction and dialogue that advanced evangelical penetration.

After the Board meeting I wrote Graham that "it was a high act of devotion and interest" that he channeled a letter to me at the Board meeting, and that I value "your words and counsel." "I think the Board members will agree that I helped in good spirit to extract the Board from a highly uncomfortable and embarrassing situation into which the Executive Committee had led it. If Nelson had simply chatted with me, telephoned me or dropped me a line, indicating that he was instigating the meeting, and for what purpose, I would have saved them all later regrets.

"My philosophy of editorship for these years," I added, "has been to launch *Christianity Today* squarely into the orbit of the *Christian Century* and to establish an evangelical thought journal of maximal power and prestige. . . . Your own interest, and your readiness to make the World Congress on Evangelism its tenth anniversary project, gave both *Christianity Today* and me as its editor wide visibility, and I am grateful, and shall always be, for your devotion to Christ and friendship to me.

"In the matter of outside engagements," I added, "I am in a very awkward situation . . . because of Nelson Bell's direct line to you, Mr. Pew and Harold Ockenga. . . . I have operated explicitly on the editorial philosophy of maximal personal involvement at the frontiers, and I have generously kept the guide rules carefully spelled out by Harold Ockenga in correspondence across the years. Nelson, on the other hand, has been committed to a philosophy of a desk-bound editorship, and has pressured the Board chairman to criticize my supposedly inadequate vocational fulfillment and supposed neglect of magazine duties. Nelson told the Board that he had been misinformed, but in the interim not a few Board members have had the benefit of his critical impressions. The verdict on an editor's use of time ought to be in terms of the magazine product. If along the way I misjudged the importance of a three- or four-day engagement, charity might have counted it as vacation time (of which I've had none this Summer). . . .

"Now we look to the future. I am as free after July 1 as Abraham leaving Ur of the Chaldees for a promised land, and hope in my next and perhaps last decade of influence to make a major evangelical contribution at the frontiers of contemporary theology."

A handwritten note from Graham solicitously inquired about my possible interest in a five-year B.G.E.A. grant that would free me completely for original work. I responded that his interest staggered me, but that I was obliged to wait for details of *Christianity Today*'s proposal of a modest stipend as editor-at-large combined with a limited research grant. "If the Board intends this only as a temporary promotional expedient," I added, "and not as an ongoing arrangement (to be dissolved only by mutual agreement) I'll not be interested at all."

When on October 4 I received minutes of the September 21 Board meeting, I noticed they did not include my invited supplemental remarks concerning the executive committee's action. I protested to Nelson Bell, who ascribed the omission to oversight; the material was sent out the following week.

Christianity Today projected a $7250 annual research grant for two years and a $7250 annual editor-at-large compensation which, apart from secretarial help, would meet basic needs. Graham suggested in a phone call that my "release" from *Christianity Today* freed me for a leadership role in international consultations and would be a stepping stone to a fuller world contribution; he volunteered a B.G.E.A. travel card that would enable me to maintain mobility to international conferences and to academic centers helpful to my research and writing. But I had little need for travel assistance once I left *Christianity Today* since beginning with the U.S. Congress on Evangelism in 1970 I was very seldom on the invited participants' list for international and national evangelism conferences.

On October 14 Ockenga wrote that the editor-at-large commitment involved a permanent relationship to the magazine "on the same footing as that of the rest of the staff." It was important, he said, that an announcement be made as soon as possible "to prevent the rise of rumors." By that time reports had already come to me from different sources that G. Aiken Taylor, editor of *The Presbyterian Journal,* had been approached to succeed me as editor. To them I replied that I had tendered no resignation, and had made no commitment alternative to *Christianity Today.* I indicated to Ockenga that I was prepared to carry a magazine announcement as early as January.

In October I also addressed the 20 faculty members and 200 students at Perkins School of Theology (Southern Methodist University) on Christian theology and social revolution. Before yearend I addressed the Evangelical Theological Society at the University of Toronto on "Where Is Modern Theology Going?"—an address carried by *Christianity Today.*

My absence from the December 7, 1967, meeting, because of a long-standing commitment to leaders of the Texas Baptist Convention, was the only Board meeting I missed since the first gathering in New York on Labor Day, 1955. I submitted my customary written report, however; it noted among other things that beginning with the upcoming January 5, 1968, issue, *Reader's Guide* would selectively index *Christianity Today* essays. Such listing meant still greater outreach of the magazine through 17,000 public libraries that subscribed to the *Guide* and considered the magazines it indexed to be of both maximal general and research importance. I reported also about *Christianity Today*'s annual religious journalism fellowship that we had inaugurated in cooperation with the Washington Journalism Center; it was paying handsome evangelical dividends: Russell Chandler, our current fellow, had just been invited by the *Louisville Courier* as religion editor.

Held in Mr. Pew's office in Philadelphia, the December 7 meeting was attended by Baker, Bell, Bolten, Brett, Fulton, Jarman, Johnson, Lamont, Ockenga, Pew and Ralston Smith. Graham and several others sent regrets. My report was read by Wilbur Benedict, our publisher. Roland Kuniholm, circulation manager, reported that all free clergy mailings were being discontinued with the current issue, and that paid subscriptions now totaled 154,305 with a 1968 objective of 175,000 paid.

The editorial "Somehow, Let's Get Together" which appeared in *Christianity Today* as a plea for evangelical unity, I reported, had drawn the largest response of any editorial in the magazine's history. It resulted in two meetings of denominational leaders looking hopefully toward a simultaneous and cooperative evangelistic effort across America in 1973. When I informed Graham of the immense response from pastors and leaders in virtually all denominations, we invited a representative group for an unstructured all-day meeting at Marriott/Key Bridge in Arlington, Virginia. We expected that only a handful would attend, but the response was staggering. Leaders in denominations both represented and unrepresented in N.A.E. and NCC spoke in a preliminary way of what would become the Key '73 undertaking as a national effort. I thought it important that prospective magazine leadership carry forward this breakthrough.

In planning 1968, I chose July as a vacation month. Thereafter, I indicated to the Board, I would begin a new span of theological research and writing. Whenever Ockenga had definitively formulated the details of a two-year research grant and a permanent role as editor-at-large I would consider it. I would accommodate announcement of termination of my editorship as early in the new year as benefited the magazine. "My record of vocational transition in both the secular and Christian world—from newspaper editing to Northern Baptist Seminary to Fuller Seminary to *Christianity Today*—has been without blemish," I said, "and I would like to leave *Christianity Today* with positive memories."

In a New Year's Resolution appearing as an Editor's Note in the January 5, 1968, issue, I announced termination as of July 1, 1968, and my intention to "give these next years to theological research and writing" on the doctrine of God. The wording was deliberately ambiguous, to accommodate both the involuntary termination of my editorship and a voluntary departure on my part to pursue personal projects.

Secular newspapers noted that under my editorship *Christianity Today* had become the most effective evangelical thought journal on the contemporary scene; it had garnered more than 150,000 paid subscribers and become the religious periodical most often quoted in the secular press. *The New York Times* carried a five-column headline on its story; *The Washington Post* and *The Evening Star* carried prominent features; the *Northern Virginia Sun* did likewise, describing *Chris-*

tianity Today as "the world's largest interdenominational thought journal."

On January 22, I would be fifty-four. I knew that beyond the years of formal education one seldom expects more than four or five decades of professional contribution. I had behind me almost a decade of collegiate, graduate and postgraduate studies, a decade of teaching in the Midwest, a decade of teaching in California and more than a decade of editorship in Washington. I was unsure what the future now held.

15

The Search for an Editor

Hardly had the September 21 (1967) Board meeting concluded but that names were being proposed for a new editor. A pall of concern hung over the Washington office. Colleagues greeted with skepticism Board statements that I had voluntarily resigned. Since I could have stayed for life had I wished, this positive aspect was what we chose to publicize in news releases. Nelson Bell submitted a suggested terminal statement to be carried in *Christianity Today* as a Board announcement. The Board's prime interest now was to find, if possible, an evangelical more than generally critical of ecumenical politicization, friendly to the Graham enterprises, committed to being desk-bound in view of Nelson Bell's lessened on-site participation and ready to wield an unsparing pen.

Bell's candidate for editor, it developed, was first Addison Leitch, who was uninterested, and then G. Aiken Taylor, a Southern Presbyterian with a doctorate in Christian education and for some years editor of *The Presbyterian Journal.* He indicated that he did not even think of Taylor as a possibility "until Billy called me from Honolulu, and . . . the next week two other men on the Executive Committee brought in his name, and another said, 'I have had him in the back of my mind'. . . ." Mr. Pew was apparently very pleased and Ockenga was gratified.

When the editorial staff heard reports that the executive committee was considering Taylor as editor, they were dismayed. Since Ockenga on September 26 had written, "We need your wisdom about a successor and I hope you will not feel reluctant to give us any advice you have," I told him that any one of my associates—Kucharsky, Cleath, Boice or Ostling—would be a preferable choice. I urged Ockenga himself to leave Park Street Church and to come to the editorship of *Christianity Today* as a larger opportunity. Such appointment would maintain continuity with the founders and would be eminently satisfactory to Pew, who had earlier offered him the presidency of Christian Freedom Foundation. Certain Gordon trustees were simultaneously championing Ockenga for the presidency of Gordon college and seminary.

Reporting for the executive committee at the December 7 Board meeting, Ockenga nominated Taylor to become editor once I became editor-at-large in the Fall of 1968. Numerous Board members were absent and most of those present were unaware until an hour before adjournment that the executive committee contemplated naming Ockenga editor-in-chief. After probing Ockenga's availability as editor, the Board unanimously elected Taylor as editor and Ockenga editor-in-chief on a part-time in-office basis; Ockenga's name was to lead off the masthead. The next Board meeting was set for May 16, 1968, with emphasis that the date be altered only in case of "a dire emergency."

As news of the Philadelphia decisions emerged, the editorial staff became restive. Ockenga and Taylor planned to travel to Washington for a mid-month conference with individual staff members. But severe bronchitis cancelled Ockenga's trip to Washington. News editor Dick Ostling then phoned Ockenga and set up an appointment in Boston for Ostling, Boice, Cleath and Kucharsky on December 15, and they spent two hours with Ockenga at Park Street Church. Ostling assured him first that the visit did not relate to my severance from the magazine, since that was now considered a *fait accompli.* Nor had the men come to deliver an ultimatum. Their concern was Taylor's impending editorship. They wanted Ockenga to know that if Taylor came as editor all but two of the editorial staff—four key members among them—would leave *Christianity Today.* There were reservations about Taylor's specific adequacies for the *Christianity Today* post. The magazine was known, they indicated, for a certain balanced editorial philosophy and overall temperament that must not be sacrificed. Questioned also was the propriety of an editorial arrangement under which an editor-in-chief would not actually function as an editor. At the end of the candid exchange Ockenga phoned the executive committee and on December 19 he sent a telegram to all Board members:

PROBLEMS AT CHRISTIANITY TODAY CAUSED SEVERAL BOARD MEMBERS TO BELIEVE AN EMERGENCY MEETING OF THE ENTIRE BOARD TO BE

NECESSARY. I AM CALLING MEETING FOR 9AM THURSDAY JANUARY 4TH IN WASHINGTON OFFICE. IMPERATIVE THAT WE HAVE FULL ATTENDANCE DUE TO IMPORTANCE. ADVISEMENT OF YOUR INTENTION TO COME WILL BE APPRECIATED. HAROLD J. OCKENGA, PARK STREET CHURCH BOSTON

In a mid-month letter I summarized these developments to Lindsell who at Wheaton had already learned of the proposed Ockenga–Taylor editorial linkage. While I was not involved in the Boston visit, I said, I had nonetheless written Ockenga on December 19 about a related concern: "Nothing would destroy the twelve-year accumulated editorial integrity of our effort more than to announce to the world that the Chairman of the Board is to serve the magazine also as Editor-in-Chief. An editor's independence and moral conscience even in relationship to his own Board," I wrote, "is an indispensable asset in the journalistic field." It was for that reason, I reminded Ockenga, that I had at the founding of the magazine resisted his desire to send the magazine's page proofs to Mr. Pew. I told Ockenga that his name could appear on the masthead before July 1 only if he removed me or if Ockenga resigned as Board chairman. To coalesce the directive functions of the Board and the role of editor-in-chief in one person, I indicated, destroyed editorial freedom in relation to the Board, and would surely gratify observers unfriendly to conservative causes.

Lindsell found it "hard to believe that H.J.O. would allow himself to become editor-in-chief for it can do nothing but hurt the magazine—especially if he continues as chairman of the Board."

It became clear that the forces in control of *Christianity Today* now wanted more aggressive denunciation of ecumenical perspectives, less reflective and more lay-oriented content and larger integration of Board and editorial policy. The remaining editorial staff wondered about continued professional freedom.

When Aiken Taylor came to Washington for the January 4, 1968, meeting, he expected to be confirmed as editor. He returned to North Carolina aware that he was now but one possibility among others, however, in a highly confused search process in which Harold Ockenga was emerging as top alternative. Ockenga, Jarman, Graham, Bell, Butt, Bolten, Fulton and Hobbs attended the meeting; Lamont, Keyes and Weisiger were ill, Rees was on his way to India. Pew and Engstrom also had prior commitments.

For most of January, 1968, especially after the January 4 Board meeting, Ockenga weighed the possibility of full-time editorship. Still vigorous at 63, he also pondered opening opportunities at Gordon where he could perhaps shape a great Christian university. He asked me privately about my summer plans and whether I really wanted to "relinquish the editorship." I replied in a letter dated January 18.

My name would drop out as editor with the July 5 issue, as agreed by the Board, I said, but I would stay on beyond that date through August or mid-September, if necessary, to help integrate a successor. But I had no desire to regain an editorship that the executive committee had taken away. "The Board knows my emphasis—an established intellectual level, critical dialogue with other views and a reasoned assessment of ecumenism. . . . It would be unfair and wrong to involve me in a further relationship that the Board really doesn't want and would be tempted to reverse or revise in a year or two, at its convenience."

Time magazine ran a religion page feature titled "Mr. Inside" in its January 15 issue, referring to Billy Graham and to me as "the Mr. Outside and Mr. Inside of conservative Protestantism." Editorial chores had become "a miserable routine," it quoted me, and I planned instead to move more broadly into "the modern theological scrap." *Time* affirmed that "Henry has emerged as the arbiter in defining and defending conservative Protestantism," and it echoed Graham's tribute: "He is intellectually the most eminent of conservative theologians. I would say he's been the professor and I've been the student."

Graham meanwhile asked Kucharsky to explore the editorial staff's suggestions for a successor-editor. Kucharsky himself proposed Bernard Ramm, Leighton Ford, Samuel H. Moffett and Sherwood Wirt, in that order; others suggested Calvin Linton, J. D. Douglas and Oswald C. J. Hoffmann. When the executive committee met at monthend, Ockenga reiterated his unavailability for full-time editorship, but continued his interest in a two-day per issue part-time role. The executive committee now declared "part-time editorship" unacceptable.

A special meeting of the Board was then called for February 7 in Palm Beach, Florida, at the home of John Bolten. Dr. David Baker, Pew's son-in-law, now vice chairman of the Board, presided. Ockenga was in Asia; Pew, Jarman, Pitts, Elmer Engstrom, Weisiger and Keyes were also absent. Present were Baker, Bell, Walter Bennett, Bolten, Butt, Fulton, Graham, Hobbs, Johnson, Lamont, Rees, Ralston Smith and I as a silent participant. It was important, Graham said, to get an editor not only with journalistic experience but one acceptable to Mr. Pew. He had cleared the name of Harold Lindsell with the executive committee, and with all but a few Board members. Graham indicated my long-standing acquaintance with Lindsell and enlistment of him as associate editor, Lindsell's firm commitment to biblical inerrancy, his numerous writings, his administrative experience at Fuller Seminary where, as Graham put it, he really earned the presidency that was given to someone else. I [Henry] would doubtless be amenable to being an editor-at-large in that context, Graham volunteered.

Paul Rees then raised a point that—as somebody put it later—

"detoured" the Board for two hours. He noted first that at the end of the September 21 meeting Pew spoke at some length to the effect that if his contributions were to continue, Henry's successor must become more aggressive editorially regarding the Church's politico-economic involvement. Bell's minutes of that meeting, Rees noted, did not fully reflect Pew's remarks; clarification was needed of what Pew's insistence implied for a new editor.

Lamont noted that the Presbyterian Lay Committee, with Pew's consent, had moderated its position from disapproval of all ecclesiastical social pronouncements to (1) the right of individual Christians and ministers to hold their own views, while (2) the Church must speak only on a biblical basis. What the Bible does, in fact, undergird, Lamont noted, is a value judgment, hence this matter is a slippery issue.

How, Rees wanted to know, does this alteration in respect to the Presbyterian Lay Committee relate to Pew's view that Henry's emphases were not aggressive enough? It was "the degree of hitting the thing in *Christianity Today,* " Bell replied; Pew never withdrew support of Henry's editorship, but thought his criticism should be "sharper." Baker said that no change in policy was indicated by Pew's statements.

Why, then, Rees asked, did Pew think that under Henry's leadership the issues were not aggressively emphasized, at a time, moreover, when "in evangelical circles not a few men of our own persuasion thought that *Christianity Today* already was indulging in excessive criticism, and when the Board might be expected therefore to defend Henry's position and to commend it rather than to reflect Mr. Pew's concerns?"

When asked what all this had to do with the discussion of the nominee, Rees replied that he wanted to know in advance what is implied "in assurances that a new editor will become 'more aggressive' in editorial policy, and that the Board must approve him in these terms."

Lamont remarked: "That's why we backed off from Aiken Taylor!" and Bolten commented: "But Mr. Pew would have accepted Taylor as the Number One man." Edward Johnson—long a friend of Lindsell's at Fuller—then added that the nominee proposed by Graham would "perpetuate what the magazine has done; the initiative to leave was taken by Carl Henry, and hence we need a successor."

Still a member since the Board had not acted on my resignation from its ranks, I had nonetheless determined to remain silent unless asked. But at this point I spoke up: "You know that not I, but Nelson Bell, took the initiative regarding the termination date for my editorship."

Graham said that "Dr. Henry and Mr. Pew should have 'gotten together more often.' Their situation was complicated by 'go-betweens.' " Mr. Pew, he said, would have continued to support Henry but felt Henry should criticize Church involvement "more fully and more often."

At that point I ventured into the dialogue. "I came resolved to speak only if the Board invited me. This is still my intention. But if the Board at this point wishes a three-to-five minute statement on *Christianity Today*'s strategic stance on church and society issues, and the problems related to this, I'll be glad to give it."

Mr. Pew's concern, Bolten replied, is that the Church's involvement "requires a more aggressive criticism"; he wants *Christianity Today* to be "a wall" between the churches and ecumenical pronouncements. Bell commented: "I have known Mr. Pew for many years. On different days he will say different things."

Lamont returned to the point: "Paul Rees wants to know—and that's proper—if we are changing the job description for the editor."

Bell replied: "No Board members want a radical change."

Baker said he wanted to hear from Henry on magazine policy.

"First," I began, "no evangelical magazine has defined the evangelical alternative to ecumenical patterns on Church and Society with more critical power and precision than *Christianity Today.* I would be surprised," I said, "if the proposed editor needs to add clarity and/or depth to these positions." ["*Christianity Today,*" Lamont interjected, "made it possible for us to 'live with' evangelical criticisms as respectable positions."] "Secondly," I continued, "*Christianity Today* cannot 'win' by escalating editorial policy to a plane of polemics and propaganda; on that basis we would soon forfeit dialogue with the ecumenical leaders and churches. Third, the one level at which *Christianity Today* could have strengthened the attack—and I was wholly ready—would have been through essays from influential evangelicals in NCC-related denominations, including our own Board members, but these have not been forthcoming across these ten past years. If these criticisms now come from an editor or from essayists outside the ecumenical churches, they will be shrugged off as what may be expected from such sources."

Ralston Smith, who had moved from First Presbyterian Church of Oklahoma City to become *Christianity Today*'s fund-raiser, commented: "The Board should not nullify the significance of Mr. Pew's comments in September. He requested the closing thirty minutes to present his views. He has been dissatisfied with some things stated and some things unstated by the magazine and is impatient. Furthermore, our constituency is increasingly asking whether the change in editorship is related to a move further to the right; if so, one donor has said he will not repeat his contribution."

Bell protested: "Gentlemen, I have now written down so many

notes and the remarks are getting quite long. I think it would be well not to try to include all that we have said in the minutes. Mr. Pew would find some of this quite confusing."

"I have no objection whatever to Mr. Pew's reading the discussion and whatever I have said," replied Rees, "but I am not opposed to deleting extended comments."

"We do Mr. Pew a disservice," Graham remarked, "if we imply that he has tried to exert pressure on the Board."

Rees interrupted: "But you, Billy Graham, were not even at the September meeting of the Board and did not hear Mr. Pew's statement. What bearing does his statement have on our invitation to a particular editor?"

Johnson countered: "We have not given Mr. Pew the 'proxies' and control."

Wayte Fulton spoke up: "If we invited Eugene Carson Blake as editor Mr. Pew would be less than enthusiastic. [Laughter] He will go for the recommendation of the Executive Committee, and since Dr. Henry invited Dr. Lindsell as associate editor, he would after three years of experience be more able. By the way, was the name of Ed Clowney considered?"

Lamont replied: "Clowney would not have left some of us denominationally comfortable, although he is less a problem than Aiken Taylor. Westminster Seminary exists on the premise that the United Presbyterian Church is apostate. Clowney's name was considered by the Executive Committee. I have known Harold and Marion Lindsell for thirty years," he continued, "and I feel Harold would be an excellent choice."

Baker asked: "Can we have Dr. Henry's view of Dr. Lindsell as editor?"

I would reply, I said, not in relation to the strategic objectives of the magazine, but rather of Lindsell as a person. "I have known him since college days, and as a good scholar; he was best man at my wedding; he has administrative ability and—as was said—really 'earned the presidency of Fuller' even if he did not get it; he has preaching gifts and is popular with the laity; he made biblical inerrancy an issue in the faculty conflict at Fuller, though this important commitment must not be made the sole issue in the magazine's enlistment of participants; he served us well in the capacity of associate editor in the special context of our existing staff balances. I did indicate to Dr. Ockenga—and still stand with that judgment—that Dr. Gaebelein and I both felt that he was 'too hurried a spirit' to make us a directive editor—but it is possible that full-time office presence and burdens would lessen this. . . . If he is the Board's choice I would accept the research grant and continue as editor-at-large at least for a time."

Ed Johnson immediately moved that debate be closed and that the Board support the nomination of Lindsell as editor. Lamont seconded Graham's nomination. One member voiced reservations but the vote was made unanimous by subsequent resolution. Graham and Lamont were to phone Lindsell.

Lamont then asked if I once again would clarify my situation in view of my sense of call that led the Board to seek a successor.

"Put that way, let me repeat—what seems not to get into the minutes," I replied, "that the Executive Committee did not involve me in conversations either with regard to a terminal date for my editorship or to the selection of a successor; it acted not on my initiative but on Dr. Bell's. My own announcement of resignation came at yearend after the Board had already approached a new editor. I have been quite willing to regard the Executive Committee's action in the most favorable light as motivated by a misunderstanding rather than as taken in deference to pressures for a new editor. In the announcement about my plans all this should be clear. All questions about right-wing escalation I have suspended for judgment upon the identity of the new editor, and whether this involves a discernible shift in editorial view is something I have told the news media they will need to judge and discover for themselves."

Both Lamont and Graham commented that the executive committee acted on the impression that it was fulfilling my wishes. I would make no further statement, I replied. "I have simply stated the situation as the facts appeared to me."

"Then," said Lamont, "we shall simply have to agree to disagree and remain Christian friends."

"There is no question that Dr. Henry has publicly handled the matter in a very commendable way," Baker commented. "Shall we expect a reply from Dr. Lindsell in two weeks? And what do we do if he does not come?"

At that point I indicated that Helga and I were going to Cambridge in mid-September. I had responded affirmatively to Ockenga's inquiry, however, whether although my editorship would conclude publicly with the July 5 issue, I would serve in a background directive role through the summer if that were helpful. The Board unanimously expressed its appreciation.

I had first invited Lindsell during his Fuller years to *Christianity Today* as summer editorial associate in 1961. I indicated that we would gladly add him in time as an associate editor. Apart from handling correspondence and evaluating manuscripts, his major task was to probe 100 key ministers on the Blake-Pike plan for church union which had just overwhelmingly passed the UP-USA General Assembly. Lindsell served again during August, 1962, after Harold Kuhn's help in July. In December, 1962, he wrote that disconcerting faculty changes impelled him to seriously consider alternatives to his deanship at Fuller. Billy Graham, Bob Lamont and Mr. Pew favored Lindsell's coming, and I indicated this to Ockenga, and recommended that he be called as associate editor effective September 1, 1964. We welcomed him full-time that Fall. His two-part essay, "Who Are the Evangelicals?" which I had suggested, identified biblical inerrancy as a normative evangelical doctrine even if not all evangelicals subscribe to it.

In addition to the magazine Lindsell was soon also expending his energies in outside engagements. An effective and well-liked preacher, he accepted more and more church, conference and other commitments. His *Christianity Today* affiliation enhanced his position in independent circles. His name was in the hat for leadership of N.A.E., on the list of candidates for the Gordon College deanship, Metropolitan Baptist Church of Washington wanted him as pastor and President Hudson Armerding discussed with him a Wheaton faculty post as Professor of Bible.

Lindsell indicated that his heart and even his gifts were more in the academic arena than in editorial work. The Wheaton arrangement, he said, would be his life calling—teaching but two duplicate courses each semester and being on campus but four days a week on a generous salary with supplementary benefits. The arrangement, I told him, sounded too good to be true.

"My tension is twofold," he indicated. "I cannot do the writing I would like to do and must either make peace that it will not be possible . . . or place myself in a position where the opportunity will be available. The second problem is physical, having to do with Washington air pollution." On April 9, 1967, he reported that he would conclude his *Christianity Today* relationship in August to join the Wheaton faculty in September. "I can only hope," he wrote, "that the research and writing possibilities will materialize. . . . I do not see that your editorship makes that possible except as you conceive of your writings in the magazine as a fulfillment of that desire. . . . These have been three good years."

In Wheaton Lindsell bought a new home and settled into teaching. Six months later on February 1, 1968, came word: "Am getting on the research road—hopefully." Less than a week later came the call to *Christianity Today*'s editorship.

On February 20 he wrote me: "If I accept the editorship I'll go to Uppsala so that I am briefed and thus able to deal a telling blow to a movement that seems to presage the end of the age." The next week came a hurried visit to greet the staff. On March 9 Bell sent word that Lindsell had accepted the editorship the previous evening and that President Armerding of Wheaton would make a public announcement. Lindsell attended the Key Bridge III dialogue on March 10 and I congratulated him. Wheaton, he said, had given him a permanent leave of absence.

I told Lindsell that paid circulation was 158,688, near the all-time high, and that some 25 college and university libraries now offered *Christianity Today* in microfilm. I indicated with real regret that the April 12 issue would announce Jim Boice's resignation to become minister of Philadelphia's prestigious Tenth Presbyterian Church. Bob Cleath gave notice soon thereafter that he was leaving in the Fall to teach at California Polytechnic College. It grieved me to sense a kind of vocational uneasiness among staff. One by one, in the months ahead, the giants of what Dick Ostling called "the Camelot years" left and were replaced by others with less experience. Roland Kuniholm, circulation manager, gave notice that he would leave on September 1.

In a letter dated March 20 Lindsell asked: "Is there any agreement between you and the Board as to what they will do for you and you will do in return? I suppose all of this will be clearly spelled out to the mutual satisfaction of you and of the Board."

My dealings with Ockenga and Bell about the specifics of an editor-at-large relationship, I replied, were unsatisfactory. As formulated by Ockenga in late October, the executive committee proposed a $10,875 grant across eighteen months, and an additional $7,250 annual reimbursement as editor-at-large. It was indefinite, however, about tenure, and included no insurance benefits, contrary to initial assurances that full staff benefits were in view. Wilbur Benedict, the publisher, thought the proposal inept and I was inclined to decline it, because it called for twelve major essays a year—something that could only embarrass a successor-editor with too much copy from a single source and in addition would preempt the time and direction of my research.

The Board had voted in September, 1967, that the magazine should at some propitious time carry a mutually acceptable announcement of my leaving. As soon as Aiken Taylor's appointment as editor became imminent, the Board felt that this announcement should appear promptly in the January 5 issue. Nelson Bell hurriedly drafted a Board statement to which I objected because it gave the fallacious impression that I had initiated a departure, so I suggested tolerable ambiguities. Ockenga phoned me on December 14 and as Board chairman ordered me to run the original. I refused to run misleading copy and, for the first time, hung up the phone on him. Wilbur Benedict worked out a satisfactory revision. When Taylor's proposed editorship did not eventuate, Ockenga urged me to postpone the January 5 statement since it would fuel speculation about a possible successor. But it was too late; proofs had already gone to sixty religion editors for end of December news release. The announcement said merely that I was considering a research grant and editor-at-large relationship whose details were still pending.

I wished Lindsell better associations and experiences than mine with the executive committee. I assured him I would hold my tongue to provide opportunity for injustices to be undone—unless, of course, the writing of memoirs would take priority. In that case my conviction was and is that "pure religion can never be hurt by the truth."

Bell had virtually withdrawn from the Washington office for medical reasons. But during an office visit on February 28 he reverted to Ockenga's July 18 termination letter and volunteered: "Harold was mistaken and ought not to have sent it. He misread the minutes. He admits that now." Such admission never came to me. When a Dallas Seminary student fifteen years later wrote a doctoral dissertation on the history of *Christianity Today,* Ockenga insisted that I had resigned although he could produce no confirmatory resignation letter.

In my spring Editor's report to the Board, I told Lindsell, I would confirm to the Board the editor-at-large commitment. The executive committee stipulated and Lindsell concurred that I would produce a signed monthly page, with the additional possibility of occasional essays or interviews. The first copy was to reach Lindsell in mid-March, 1969; my name would not be listed as editor-at-large until the first issue in which the monthly page appeared. The research grant, I noted, running as it did through August 1970, offered "the possibility of staying in Europe for two years if that seems desirable. . . . I'll know better, after a year or more abroad, whether we'll settle down in Europe permanently (and try to forget American 'evangelicalism') or pursue an academic alternative somewhere in the U.S.A."

On April 1 Lindsell wrote that the *Christianity Today* Board had voted: "Dr. Lindsell will have complete authority and final word having to do with everything that appears in the magazine. This applies to all articles submitted by Dr. Henry. . . . Dr. Henry, as Editor-at-large, will not occupy any space in the office. . . . No one will officially represent the magazine at conferences, consultations, etc. except at the express request of Dr. Lindsell." Lindsell added: "If we need to consult we can do this by mail or telephone. . . . As far as your material is concerned—which will be submitted six months after you leave—I feel it would be unwise and premature for me to make any final commitments as to its use. . . ."

I replied on April 3 that Lindsell could count on me "not to presume to represent the magazine officially at conferences and consultations" and that any news releases after July 5 would identify me primarily as theologian and author, and minimize the relationship to *Christianity Today.* I noted that Ockenga, chairman of the Board and of the executive committee, had indicated that a signed monthly page (such as Nelson Bell's fortnightly page) "would raise the least problems" and that "this was acceptable to you. I shall now assume that everything is up in the air." When the monthly page finally got underway in *Christianity Today* as earlier projected, I decided for obvious reasons to caption it "Footnotes."

Meanwhile the March 29 issue of the magazine carried a box notice, over my signature, announcing that the Board had named Lindsell as editor effective in September, 1968.

I prepared a final Editor's report for the May 16 Board meeting, a brief summary of our editorial philosophy for the first twelve years. But the meeting did not eventuate and the report was buried in the files. I indicated, however, that I would cover the magazine's needs during the summer months before Lindsell's arrival in the Fall, and that I would not make advance decisions intruding on his area of determination.

On June 10 I gave the commencement address at Wheaton College and was given a gracious citation on the thirtieth anniversary of my graduation and was awarded an honorary Doctor of Letters degree. For my final summer at *Christianity Today* I invited J. D. Douglas, then editor in London of *The Christian and Christianity Today,* and the British theologian H. Dermot McDonald, and the Methodist evangelist Lon Woodrum, each to come for a month as editorial aides. A California Baptist minister and experienced news writer, Ed Plowman, came to handle news coverage from June through August. The July 5 issue led off with a spirited panel discussion at the American Baptist Convention in which I participated with Harvey Cox and George Young on "Technology, Modern Man, and the Gospel."

The Board had stipulated, I reminded Lindsell, that the July 5, 1968, issue would be my last, and hence the last to carry my name on the masthead. The September 27 issue would be the first to reflect his name as editor, but the Board wanted me nonetheless to remain through the Summer because of staff shortages and vacations. Lindsell contacted Nelson Bell and arranged to be listed promptly as Editor-elect in the absence of my name. Lindsell's name appeared as editor in the September 27, 1968, issue and remained so until he departed in 1978, when it was inscribed permanently as Editor-Emeritus and Bell's as Executive Editor (1956–63), while my name was obliterated from the masthead. In those years the magazine moved more radically to the right and I was depicted to Board members as being on the left; earlier written assurances that my contributions would be used were scrapped. While Lindsell served, paid circulation at one point fell below 100,000 and the magazine was in deepening financial jeopardy. Before he left for "writing, lecturing, and preaching," circulation had recovered to 155,000 paid as the magazine veered from its original stance as a professional thought journal to a largely lay-oriented publication.

As my severance from the magazine progressed, contacts with evangelical establishment figures waned. But academic institutions, by contrast, urged me to come their way. Among them was Trinity Evangelical Divinity School where Dean Kenneth Kantzer offered the department chairmanship in systematic theology. Ronald Nash projected faculty possibilities for me at Western Kentucky University and President J. Lester Harnish asked that after my research abroad I give Eastern Baptist Theological Seminary "the courtesy of first consideration."

Even during the last days of my editorship I tried to close ranks between independent and ecumenically identified evangelicals, and between evangelicals per se and radically independent fundamentalists. Carl McIntire invited me to address the Seventh World Congress of the International Council of Christian Churches on August 19 on "anything that you may wish to say to us all." I expressed hope of attending, but needed to wait for schedule clearance. On July 30 I indicated acceptance and gave my topic as "Demythologizing the Evangelicals." I was going to Cape May, I told my colleagues, "because we've said we'd go anywhere, anytime, for the peace of believers." On August 7 McIntire wrote again. He had not previously indicated, he said, that the original invitation went to Eugene Carson Blake, Billy Graham and me (possibly in the expectation that all of us would decline). "My original invitations to Dr. Blake, Billy Graham and yourself were not accepted," he wrote, "and when I did not hear from you a second time our program was finalized." I used my prepared remarks, without explicit reference to McIntire and his movement, in the last issue of the magazine that I supervised (Sept. 13, 1968). "Jesus chose disciples who would run with faith," I wrote, "not patriarchs who had to be carried. And they ran with joy, not with mace, or tear gas, or vituperation. I have to remind myself of this constantly; I do not speak in pharisaical self-righteousness. Every six months or so I have told colleagues at *Christianity Today* that it is time to 'ring the bells' again, to schedule a major editorial on the joy of being a Christian, the delight and dignity of walking with God."

The *Christianity Today* staff arranged a farewell dinner on August 16 at Key Bridge/Marriott. Although hosted by the Board, only those

Board members on salaried staff attended. Telegrams came from former staffers. Ockenga wrote that he had been involved in so many extra meetings for the magazine that he could not take the time. He expressed profuse appreciation: "It is impossible for me to adequately express my own appreciation of the tremendous task you have undertaken and effectively fulfilled as editor of *Christianity Today.* As the first editor, you initiated the magazine, directed its content and supervised its growth to enormous proportions. You are the one man in America who has been able to do this job and achieve it effectively. In a certain sense I receive some satisfaction out of this because I was the one who originally projected your name for the editorship." From within the Board came a treasured letter from Paul Rees: "I really feel perplexed and depressed over the way your magnificent term of service is coming to an end."

Frank Gaebelein, who had a month earlier written me a gracious personal letter, was asked to make dinner remarks. He read a 2,000-word "Portrait of an Editor"—a stylistic gem in which he spoke of our first acquaintance 34 years earlier during my journalistic apprenticeship on Long Island, of two years of transcontinental commuting during *Christianity Today* beginnings, of office presence at seven in the morning, migraine or no migraine, of single-minded devotion to editorial concerns. "Dr. Henry may not be the most patient of men," he said, "but working with him can be exciting as well as demanding." To my gratification he spoke at some length also of Helga's investment in the work: "a scholar . . . a teacher and writer" who "has loyally shared the cost of her husband's achievement." Our son Paul and daughter Carol were present, and noted that the reference to Helga's labors was the one point at which I coped with tears.

John Lawing, whom I had brought to the magazine as art editor, presented a framed cartoon showing all staff members at their posts and included their signatures. The staff presented me with one share of Communications Satellite common stock, a firm that later dissolved into Comsat and is now worth less than they paid for it. But their good will followed me as I left for Cambridge, and has followed me to the present through almost twenty years.

16

Cambridge

The observant visitor to Cambridge may on occasion sense the diverse interests that characterize Town and Gown, the gulf that separates ordinary townspeople from the academic élite. But only those who actually live in academe fully perceive the differences that underlie the two-tier social system. The university is indeed a world apart, and in some respects a world above, the secular city.

More than seven centuries ago Cambridge teachers attracted students. Modeled after Merton college, Oxford, the first Cambridge college, Peterhouse, came into being in 1281. Then appeared Clare college, founded in 1326 and refounded twelve years later by Lady Elizabeth Clare; I would come to know it rather as Charles F. D. Moule's lodgings where on Tuesday nights a small circle of us met with the distinguished New Testament scholar to assess post-apostolic apocryphal books. The university today recognizes not only nineteen colleges for men, the most recent being Churchill college (1960) with an emphasis on science and engineering, but also two colleges for women—Girton and Newnham.

King's Parade presents a magnificent panorama. The elegant chapel of King's college dominates the scene and remains one of Britain's best examples of perpendicular architecture. The college itself was at its founding in 1441 an edifice grander than any of its predecessors, and remained so for a century until the founding of St. John's college and then Trinity college. Established by Henry VIII in 1546, Trinity now ranks as the largest of all the Cambridge colleges. Among its illustrious scholars were Newton and Bacon, Macauley, Tennyson and Thackeray, Archbishop Trench and Henry Sidgwick.

Oblivious to tourists identifying among many sights the various colleges, Fitzwilliam Museum, the Round Church or St. Mary's, students roam or bicycle throughout the city in flapping academic gowns. Inevitably visitors discover "the backs," the lawns, gardens and meadows (some with grazing cattle) behind the five colleges ranged along the river Cam where skilled boatmen punt up-and-downstream. Never are the backs more beautiful than during their early spring show of crocuses and daffodils. Actually much of Cambridge is a labyrinth of brilliant-hued roses, asters, larkspur, lupines, poppies and snapdragons framed here and there by tall-stemmed hibiscus and hollyhocks.

But to the disciplined resident scholar Cambridge's well-bred lawns and peaceful gardens, its orderly paths and quiet walks reflect more than beauty; they suggest a higher world's impingement upon the senses: the university emerges as a cerebral megalopolis where the fortunes of truth and virtue are decided. The superior importance of learning over mere class attendance (to which dons can be highly indifferent), weekly sessions with tutors who assign scores of books and preparation of exhaustive and exhausting papers, access to brilliant faculty minds and writers of national and international repute, are but some facets of British heritage. In short, Cambridge is a call to an orderly life of reason motivated by the conviction that no person can be fully integrated without both maturity of mind and self-giving dedication to the service of society. That is not to say, of course, that all students miraculously lose their adolescence. Their occasional rampages, though not extreme, are well known to townspeople.

During the 1966 World Congress on Evangelism I tried to enlist Billy Graham for a special outreach to the student generation in England, one that would mean certain additions to his crusades approach. I suggested that Graham perhaps supplement his next major London crusade with an academically oriented witness simultaneously held in Royal Albert Hall. There, with the Christian Union taking a prominent supportive role, British evangelical professors might present papers or engage in panel discussions geared specially to the university mind. Albert Hall morning and afternoon meetings, with perhaps 1,200 participants, might even attract BBC television or radio interest. Graham's climactic nightly meetings would meanwhile go forward in the larger mass meeting arenas.

The Berlin Congress had noted that among the twenty million university students enrolled around the globe at that time, one could find almost all the world's future leaders in politics, science, religion, mass media, entertainment and the arts. Lord Thompson remarked not much later in *The Times* of London that in his lifetime alone the university population of the United States had grown from three to ten million while that of Britain had grown from 20,000 to 200,000. Since England was geographically much smaller than the United States, it could lend itself rather well, I felt, to some correlated effort of both a cognitive and spiritual kind.

The evangelical community in England included such respected scholars as Dr. J. N. D. Anderson, director of the Institute of Advanced Legal Studies at University of London, Dr. F. F. Bruce, professor of New Testament at Manchester University, Professor Donald Mackay of the department of communication at University of Keele, Dr. Donald Wiseman of the School of Oriental Studies at University of London, Professor R. L. F. Boyd, physicist and astronomer and director of the Mullard Space Science Laboratory at University College of London, Dr. David Booth of the psychology department at Sussex University, Dr. William J. Martin, senior lecturer in Semitic Languages at University of Liverpool, Derek Kidner, warden of Tyndale House, Cambridge, James Packer, warden of Latimer House, Oxford, and a growing company of younger scholars already beginning to make their mark, among them Alan Millard and Kenneth Kitchen.

My projected university outreach aroused only passing interest and, in any case, subsequent events at *Christianity Today* eclipsed it entirely. Graham wrote from his Melbourne crusade asking on March 22, 1969, if I would give time and thought to a second World Congress on evangelism, three times larger than Berlin, perhaps in Amsterdam in the Fall of 1971. About the same time he queried Stan Mooneyham inquiring about his willingness to be involved in a possible World Congress in 1972. From Melbourne Graham reported "open hostility and opposition, at times very violent, particularly among anarchist elements at the colleges and universities." I replied that I would gladly serve on a program committee, but not as its chairman or secretary. Mooneyham indicated his willingness to be involved, although not as coordinator, and only if such a congress were not an end in itself but part of a "total strategy." I heard nothing further.

I came to Cambridge in the Fall of '68 preoccupied with two intellectual fronts, one, the problem of religious knowledge, and the other, the doctrine of God. My initial projection was a volume on epistemology and another on ontology; half the academic year I would concentrate on the one, and remaining time on the other.

I was convinced—and this was, in fact, my first thesis about religious knowledge—that if we humans say anything authentic about God, we can do so only on the basis of divine self-revelation; all other God-talk is conjectural. I was no less persuaded that if God the living

Sovereign reveals himself, then he bears authority supremely over man and the world. Hence emerged the title, *God, Revelation and Authority.*

My first task was the orderly presentation of what we must say about God in consequence of his self-disclosure. In stating each successive thesis the challenge was to say neither too little nor too much, thus carrying the reader forward with a sense of intellectual excitement. At first I formulated only twelve theses, but the list divided and expanded to fifteen which, as it developed, provided the outline for the second, third and fourth volumes of what would finally become six in all.

Devoted to introductory concerns, volume one marked a sharp break with neoorthodox and existential theologies that internalized revelation and rejected appeal to objective considerations. Discussion of the religious a priori, in the closing chapters of that first volume, had been completed earlier during summers at Indiana University and then at Fuller. But chapters on the clash of cultural perspectives were readied, at least in preliminary form, on the edge of an unexpected invitation to give several public lectures in Cambridge.

Unexpected, I say, for such indeed it was. One Saturday night early in October a knock on our door admitted a tall, dignified stranger bearing a basketful of luscious grapes. The bearer was a leading Cambridge opthalmologist, Dr. Henry L. Backhouse, a lay leader of Queen Edith Chapel (Brethren) who later retired to Jerusalem, Israel, to devote his life in a professional tentmaker ministry to Israelis. Like Caleb's emissaries in the Old Testament, Dr. Backhouse said, he had "spied out the land" and found it propitious; he was inviting me at the behest of a community committee of clergy and professional men to give a sponsored series of public lectures in Sidgwick Hall. The lectures were publicly announced at a reception and dinner attended by more than fifty leaders—clergy, business and professional men and college personnel—in the Cambridge University Center. The initial lecture on "The Crisis in Evangelism: Is It Too Late for the Church?" we had agreed, would feature also a panel involving Dr. Simon Barrington-Ward, dean of Magdalene College; the Rev. Mark Ruston, vicar of the historic Round Church and chairman of the Cambridge television relay for the 1967 Graham Crusade; and Dr. Backhouse. Subsequent lectures were to be on theological-philosophical-apologetic issues of my own choosing. The lecture on "The Clash of Cultural Perspectives" I later expanded in *God, Revelation and Authority;* much of the other lecture material found its way into various chapters as well. The series, well-attended, drew not only clergy, professional men and literate laypersons, but also American chaplains from the U.S. air base at Alconbury.

The university had without any fee graciously given me access to any and all divinity school classes, faculty library privileges and open participation in the Cambridge Theological Society and in monthly meetings of the D Club. I attended Professor Charles Moule's lectures as well as those by Professor Donald M. MacKinnon, the Scottish philosopher who later gave the prestigious Gifford Lectures. I heard many of Professor Peter Baelz's lectures on metaphysics, several of Professor D. E. Nineham's Bultmannian-tilted excursions, but just one of Don Cupitt's ventures into post-Kantian agnosticism was quite enough. MacKinnon and Baelz were contributing to the "ontological revival" underway in the aftermath of logical positivism's decline, a turn of events that Norman Pittenger was trying, without much success, to exploit for process theology.

Moule and Baelz read lectures with professorial civility, Baelz being somewhat more open to occasional cross-questioning. MacKinnon was an untamed lion, a peripatetic venturing lionesque gyrations to mark a turn in the argument, or glaring at the classroom walls, ceiling or floor while he wrestled some important point. He had no use for existentialism and even less for logical positivism, which Cambridge had spawned; he insisted on the historical factuality of Christian redemptive acts and on the mental significance of divine revelation, although he did not much elaborate the latter. Now and then he set aside a lecture period to answer students' inquiries, and sometimes found in them a greater profundity than his inquisitors ever intended. MacKinnon's reputation for absent-mindedness was not wholly undeserved. One story about him, perhaps apocryphal, was that on his way to the classroom he one day left a pair of trousers at the tailor's for pressing only to discover later that beneath his academic gown he was garbed for teaching in nothing but underclothes.

In mid-winter we entertained Professor Moule for an enjoyable dinner and an evening of theological discussion. He came by bicycle (I would not have been more surprised had the eminent exegete arrived by rickshaw); for the murky return to his bachelor digs at Clare college I stashed his cycle in the trunk and insisted that he risk the ride back in my Cortina. During after-dinner tabletalk we discussed the resurrection of Jesus. He emphasized that, as he saw it, Jesus' resurrection from the dead remains a necessary presupposition both of the writing of the New Testament Gospels and of the formation of the Christian church. He declared himself ready, moreover, to affirm that the tomb was empty and that Jesus' resurrection was a bodily event. But Moule's view of Scripture and of the nature of Christ's atonement fell somewhat short of evangelical orthodoxy, and his statements of final redemption veered at times toward implicit universalism.

I recall attending Moule's monthly New Testament faculty discussion, which invited outsiders considered a treasured privilege. At one point when expounding God's mercy and wrath, Moule stressed that love is God's core attribute; all God's acts, he emphasized, display his love. I ventured to ask if he could conceive any act so horrendous, the crucifixion of Jesus by his foes, for example, or Hitler's extermination of six million Jews, that it would prompt a divine response other than love. When Moule was momentarily taken aback, Professor MacKinnon diverted the dialogue by discoursing on the complexities of human events and of the nature of the deity.

We also entertained Professor and Mrs. MacKinnon for a lively Sunday after-church dinner. I had bought two ducks the previous day which when Helga roasted them to a delectable brown became virtually meatless skeletons; I have never seen two ducks emerge from an oven with less excuse for existence. Until we learned some of the finer points of English shopping, cooking and eating, we simply made the best of such experiences and appreciated all the more our guests' gracious sufferance of well-intentioned culinary efforts. Professor MacKinnon entered into the situation with philosophical wit; his sense of humor was a gift of grace. He himself hosted the Monthly D Club where graduate students presented and defended papers; occasionally some Catholic heretic or Protestant theological deviant addressed the group. But MacKinnon himself presented the opening paper on "The Attributes of God." Meetings with him in or outside the classroom were never dull, and his psychological insights were at times as profound as his philosophical comments. At Christmas, Professor Baelz of Jesus College invited us to share their family holiday dinner, so that Christmas away from home and loved ones seemed less bleak.

Our apartment at One Latham Road a few miles from the inner city was located just beyond the Botanical Gardens. The apartment, easily accessible either on foot or for a six-pence fare by the Trumpington Road bus, we had rented in advance through the university. The London owners had renovated the old two-story red brick manor house into four apartments. One of these usually quartered Americans, who tended to sell to each succeeding occupant—and gladly—electricity converters, the so-called automatic washing machine and other British marvels. Our furnished quarters on the second floor consisted of a combination living-dining room, bedroom, kitchen and bathroom. An obtrusive gas heater was ensconced in the ancient and hollowed out fireplace. It supplemented the "central heating" (electrically heated bricks in metal cabinets) available for residential use only at night to preserve daytime energy for business and industry. The old velvet davenport with expiring springs, an equally antiquated stuffed chair, a small dining table and four chairs were hardly conducive to extensive entertaining, although student groups were not averse to sitting on window sills or on the floor. The kitchen stove was a spiritual challenge, especially the so-called grill.

A thirty-foot custom-made hurdle of extension cord wound from the bedroom with its converter box to sundry appliances around the apartment. Water was heated by a special gas unit. We bantered daily over who of us would first enter and exit the 50-degree bathroom, where one had to high-step into the deep tub and then struggle to climb out. I wondered whether that tub precipitated Helga's enrollment in Cambridge for swimming classes.

For all that, the apartment lent itself even in severe weather to study and typing. I spent many hours in Tyndale House library with its outstanding collection of evangelical books, as well as at the University library with its two million volumes and in King's college reading room with its specialized theology and philosophy collection.

Speaking engagements I limited mainly to weekends or to breakpoints in the academic schedule. A commitment to a small Churchill college service interdicted a later invitation to preach that same Sunday at Trinity college with full choir. Besides speaking to 300 members of the Cambridge Christian Union I addressed two meetings of the equally large Oxford Christian Union; later on I also spoke to the Christian Union at University of Liverpool and at University of Cardiff, Wales. In February, 1969, I addressed an Evangelical Alliance ministers' conference at Swanwick, Derbyshire; in May, I spoke in a Belfast church and addressed the Evangelical Fellowship of Ireland; in late June, I was conference preacher along with Dr. Barry White of Oxford University for the United Kingdom U.S. Air Force spiritual life conference at Swanwick.

I preached in many Cambridge area churches, including The Round Church and St. Paul's (Anglican), Zion Baptist, Roseford Chapel and Queen Edith's Chapel (Brethren). Additionally there were invitations to the U.S. air base chapels at Mildenhall and Alconbury, where I conducted a chaplain's retreat and became friends with the Base Chief Chaplain Bob Quigg and his wife Jean, who were fellow antique-scavengers.

Two major engagements took me outside Britain first to Singapore, and later to India and Ceylon. A month into the university schedule and the morning after the Cambridge reception announcing Sidgwick Hall lectures, I left on Friday, November 1, to address university students at the All-Asia Congress on Evangelism in Singapore. Helga meanwhile gladly sat in for me at university lectures (she never blanched at some of the peculiarities unique to that all male environment). In the Spring of 1969 a cable from Paul Rees indicated that Richard Halverson was unavailable for a pastors' conference May 19 to 30 in India and Ceylon. "Can you help?" he asked. The university term was over by then. I flew to Madras and, after sharing in the conference at Huebli, continued to Colombo and Kandy for meetings there.

Hardly a day passed, unless icy winds from Russia's Ural mountains swept over the Meadows, that we did not get out for a leisurely walk. At the nearby Botanical Gardens one could walk, read or simply meditate and reflect in a controlled environment that tolerated only the quacking of ducks and song of birds; radios, bicycles, guitars, indeed all mechanical or human noisemakers were off-limits.

Our apartment was several miles from the nearest branch post office and from King's Parade with its stately edifices on one side and, on the other, shops of all kinds. Buying ordinary supplies like carbon sheets and paper clips and typewriter ribbons could involve week-long delays due to stock shortages. Teahouses or pubs were often the best stops for tea or a hurried kidney pie or "mixed grill." Behind St. Mary's Church was the open market—dating from the 1500s—where we routinely bought fruits and vegetables in season. The nearby city's only self-service "supermart" offered cheeses galore. Delectable whole grain bread (some baked in open hearth ovens) was available at small home bakeries; supplies were quickly exhausted. Woolworths sold eggs and cottage cheese (not to mention toffees, Helga's weakness) and biscuits (cookies, we would say) that went together with tea like love and marriage. Somewhat baffling were the butcheries; one bought an indicated "joint" of beef rather than specific cuts. For pork we went to the pork shop, for fish to the fishmonger.

Saturday mornings we scouted used furniture stores (Cambridge had a constant turnover of useful items) and on occasion found magazine racks, piano benches and other mahogany or walnut pieces whose horsehair or velvet covers betrayed their Victorian vintage. For these Helga stitched needlepoint covers so that with some grace we could entertain (and seat) friends and students. Our home became a rendezvous for Sunday afternoon theological dialogue, and on certain evenings also for other guests.

On January 3, 1969, I addressed the Tyndale Society for Biblical Studies in London on "The Reality and Identity of God," a critique of process theology expanded for *Christianity Today* (March 14 and 28, 1969). On later visits to London I spoke at Spurgeon's College, and met with John Stott of All Souls, Langham Place, to discuss British ecclesiastical tensions. In Cambridge we welcomed visits by the gifted journalist Dr. J. D. Douglas and Dr. James Houston, lecturer in geography at Hereford College, Oxford, who shared his vision of Regent College in Vancouver. American chaplains came to discuss special concerns, as well as academicians like the Kidners, Millards and Shoesmiths, public relations specialist Michael Young and his wife Pauline who used their historic thatch-roofed home in Foxton for village ministries, American ex-patriots including the John Krommingas, Richard Longeneckers, Arthur Rupprechts and Jerry Horners.

We mailed parcels weekly to the States, items older than 1900 being exempt from customs charges. Browsing through an old rural barn marked "Antiques" I saw a dirty set of old dinner dishes of a Venetian geometric pattern in deep blue on white. The underside bore the symbol M, which I thought might perchance be the Minton hallmark. Yet the set was earthenware rather than porcelain and the entire lot, moreover, was priced at but $40. I returned next day with Helga and verified that it was indeed very old Minton. Because the post office conceded that they were irreplaceable, three pieces broken in shipment covered the entire shipping charges. The Minton factory confirmed that in the 1700s and early 1800s its products were of this sort.

Our most treasured Cambridge memento, however, is an eight-foot grandfather clock bought in nearby Cottingham. Of Welsh origin, with painted moon face, calendrical dial and heavy iron weights, the beautiful handcrafted mahogany timepiece is dated about 1791, the time of John Wesley's death and of Parliament's passage of Wilberforce's motion for abolition of the slave trade. It was shipped air freight for $165, and arrived at Dulles Airport in a huge casket-like box.

Information from the States was scanty, but ex-patriot friends shared timely news of evangelical developments. Not until March, 1969, did I learn that Evangelical Theological Society had elected me president at its December meeting, for a year when unfortunately I would be mostly in Britain. *Christianity Today*'s paid circulation, I learned, was slipping and advertising was down. News editor Dick Ostling announced in February that he would go on March 31 to *Time* magazine as religion reporter. My monthly page of "Footnotes" began appearing on March 14, 1969; updating Americans on England's theological climate, it familiarized readers with names like Harry Blamires whom most American evangelicals did not discover for themselves until a decade later. Harold Lindsell enlisted J. D. Douglas as Washington editorial assistant. Lindsell's occasional notes to me voiced increasing apprehension over spiritual conditions in America: "The trends in the U.S. seem to point away from adherence to Christianity more and more," he wrote. "The religious situation is deteriorating rapidly. . . . You'll find a different mood in America upon your return. The drift is pronounced, the problems are manifold."

In the States we had prepaid a new '69 Ford Cortina for Cambridge delivery in early October and for ultimate export to America. British labor problems delayed its delivery until mid-January, however, and then it malfunctioned for several months. We nonetheless scheduled two major Cortina trips while abroad, one in early June at the end of the university year, and the other at the end of July at the termination of our Cambridge residency.

The former, a trip to the English Lake District and then to Wales and the west coast of Scotland, fostered an important breakthrough in my final volumes on the doctrine of God. Whereas the outline for the earlier material on religious knowledge (revelation, inspiration, canon, interpretation) unfolded quite naturally, that relating to the doctrine of God in some ways seemed stubbornly elusive. As a concession to lay readers, I had already decided to canopy the volumes on revelation and religious knowledge with the rubric, "The God Who Speaks and Shows." From that, it was not a great leap to develop the doctrine of God under the heading, "The God Who Stands, Stoops and Stays," to stress divine self-existence, creation and redemption, governance and providence and last things. That leap did not occur to me, however, until Helga and I found unhurried and relaxed respite in the Lake District, where broad contours fell in place as we enjoyed nature's beauties and reflected on God's majesty and mercy. That trip took us to Coventry and Stoke-on-Trent and on to Liverpool, where I spoke to both the Graduates Fellowship and the Christian Union and lodged several days with the Semitic scholar William Martin and his wife Anne. We then drove to Broughton-on-Furness, staying with an appreciative clergyman reader of my early volumes. From there we continued to Wales.

What became clearer was the comprehensive framework within which, by way of preface, I felt my total literary effort should be set. Ancient Greek thinkers debated the alternatives of ultimate being or becoming; for the Middle Ages the overarching concern was the problem of guilt and redemption. The recent modern world considered human alienation and reconciliation the preemptive issues. The contemporary dilemma, it seemed to me, had deepened into a crisis over the very meaning of meaning and the intelligibility and utility of words. Two competing and conflicting power-centers in the late twentieth century were offering human beings a decisive opportunity for new selfhood—namely, the mass media with their stress on a new social image through physical enhancement and material aggrandizement, and the message of Christ the Mediator who bestows forgiveness of sins, spiritual and moral renewal and a reinstatement of human dignity. In short, the modern crisis of truth and word became the framework theme within which *God, Revelation and Authority* would present its claims.

The first publisher's welcome for my projected series was by Floyd Thatcher of Word Books who sent an advance contract assuring publication of what, in the early stages, loomed as two or perhaps three volumes. When I indicated that the series would likely be more extensive, Word Books was undisturbed; from the outset it was confident of a successful first edition. What neither Word nor I foresaw was that within a decade more than 60,000 copies of the individual volumes would be in print, as well as publication underway of Korean and Mandarin translations of the entire series.

Helga, too, found much that was personally rewarding in Cambridge. She registered for adult education classes in oil painting, swimming, Scottish cookery and music appreciation, the latter taught by the now internationally famous musician Christopher Hogwood. She visited museums and historic sites, made brass rubbings, lost herself in used book stalls and began gathering materials for her own Cameroun literary project. She spoke to women's groups at churches, military bases and in private homes. We attended chamber music programs and, most memorable of all, the King's college chapel Christmas readings and carols.

Signing up with the National Health Service and being fingerprinted were requirements that accompanied registering with the police as long-term residents. We found excellent whatever medical services we needed. Helga's alarming thrombosis-like confinement brought daily bedside visits and on-target diagnosis and treatment by a fine Christian medic that the Mayo staff later fully approved and carried forward for complete recovery. Dental visits had dramatic features. One lay down as on a stretcher, while huge lights beamed from above and the dentist did his thing as if in a surgical theatre.

Plans for the year beyond Cambridge were still uncertain, though I was not anxious. Invitations came for lectures during 1970 at Azusa-Pacific College, Earlham School of Religion, Houghton College, Messiah College and others, and to address a Southern Baptist evangelism conference in Nashville. Soon after my arrival in Cambridge President J. Lester Harnish of Eastern Baptist Theological Seminary had requested that, whenever I returned to teaching, I consider Eastern first. Gracious letters came almost monthly from Dean Kenneth Kantzer holding open the door in theology at Trinity Evangelical Divinity School and for Helga at Trinity College. In New England there was merger-talk between Conwell School of Religion in Philadelphia with Gordon College to create Gordon-Conwell Theological Seminary with Harold Ockenga as likely president. Ockenga urged consultation "before you make a decision" about a post for me in the divinity school and for Helga at Gordon College. Ockenga's conversations about a Gordon-Conwell presidency reflected the same ambivalence he had experienced concerning Fuller, except that now Park Street Church was about to call a successor.

Lindsell reported that *Christianity Today* had added to its staff Russell Chandler, religion editor of the *Washington Evening Star,* and that in September he would be adding Don Tinder, a church historian. I respected Chandler's gifts, but wished that *Christianity Today* would channel evangelicals into, not out of, the secular media.

Although the publisher, Wilbur Benedict, had earlier assured me that some 4,000 volumes available to the editorial staff could remain there until my return from Cambridge, unexpected word from the new editor instructed me to remove all my remaining books from the magazine offices. The request for prompt removal reached us just before Easter, 5,000 miles across the Atlantic, when our Arlington home was already occupied by the first secretary of the Japanese ambassador to the United States.

A surprise phone call came simultaneously from Cleo Shook, U.S. AID chief of mission for Southeast Asia, who was in London returning from a United Nations conference in Paris and during the weekend stopover wanted to visit us in Cambridge. We attended The Round Church, where I was speaking, and then settled into a leisurely afternoon. Cleo volunteered to take back to Washington a Pan Am carry-on bag containing much of the initial volume of *God, Revelation and Authority* in its earliest draft. Moreover, he also offered to facilitate removal of my books from *Christianity Today.* With the help of our son Paul, then a Congressional aide in Washington and who also had been informed about removing the books, Cleo trucked a good half of some eighty boxes to his home in Falls Church, Virginia, for basement storage. The rest were trucked at weekend by James Cudney, then U.S. AID program coordinator for Asia, to Eastern Baptist Theological Seminary in Philadelphia, where an office was being readied for my September arrival.

The commitment to Eastern, unknown to Lindsell, had been made only weeks before. Although teaching invitations followed me to England, I had determined to spend a full academic year abroad. A further letter from Lester Harnish invited me to full-time or part-time association with Eastern, and a choice of commuting from Virginia or residing in a seminary faculty apartment. The Eastern option somewhat troubled me; outside academic sources were not fully enthusiastic either about the student body or a number of the faculty. Yet the Eastern correspondence reached me just when our realty agent indicated that our Arlington renter would if at all possible like to remain at least another year. I accepted Eastern as visiting professor for a year and opted to live near the campus. Helga's brother, with a doctorate in theology as well as secular university studies in philosophy, was professor of theology and philosophy of religion there. A neoorthodox theologian had moved on to Villanova, a critical Old Testament scholar to Baylor.

In final months and weeks in Cambridge I made the most of extensive reading and research opportunities. We stayed through July and set aside the month of August for the Continent, where a ten-day teaching-preaching stint in eastern Europe would climax our sabbatical year.

The road from Cambridge to the Continent involved more than simply a geographical transition; it provided time for both reflection and evaluation no less than for anticipation. Thankful as I was for its intellectually stretching experience, I had become increasingly aware that Cambridge offered no cohesive "Cambridge theology"; in fact, England as a whole had few professional theologians. Although Cambridge had been its originating center, logical positivism had run its course and was now clearly on the defensive; no Cambridge philosopher now spoke of it except in a context of criticism. The emerging mood was post-Kantian and post-Ritschlian; the conviction was widening that some significant affirmations can indeed be made about the transcendent, although just what and why was a matter of much disagreement. Process philosophy was only of marginal interest, however; it was taught mainly out of respect for Whitehead as a thinker. Metaphysically affirmative views seemed therefore to be struggling for transcendent anchorage. While both philosophers and biblical scholars spoke of divine revelation they did so in terms of generalities or of personal-inferential considerations more than as a clearly formulated cognitive reality. There was no insistence on propositional revelation. Professors readily invoked the Bible in expounding their views, but they regarded the principle of an authoritative Scripture as passé. One had the sense that the reach toward metaphysical reality was "waiting for Godot"—perhaps for another prestigious German philosopher who would again channel all hesitant predications into some comprehensive speculative synthesis.

Cambridge was in fact a galaxy of different luminaries that spanned the distance from a radical Bultmannian view, reflected at times by Nineham, to the moderate evangelical view held by Moule. All professors in the theological school spoke of the "biblical witness" but then channeled it into divergent expositions. On the other hand Cambridge showed little of the Continental enthusiasm for dialectical and existential approaches to the transcendent that detached divine revelation from reason and history. MacKinnon spoke of Bultmann as sometimes "carrying out ingenious translations of clauses of the creed into the characteristic idioms of Martin Heidegger" (*Borderlands of Theology,* p. 52). And his references to Barth were often less than complimentary. If Christianity was to be intellectually significant, he averred, theological assertions must involve the same general standards of reason to which all valid thought is subject.

There was more Cambridge consensus on the resurrection of Jesus Christ than on some other credal affirmations. Yet G. W. H. Lampe spoke only of a "spiritual" resurrection to which he then struggled to give some external and objective basis. Both MacKinnon and Moule insisted on a bodily resurrection; the tomb was empty, Moule noted. Moreover, Moule and MacKinnon connected discussion of the transcendent with the life and work of Jesus of Nazareth; Christology was for them a decisive route to ontology.

While theological students at Cambridge reached for a wide view of the contemporary scene, they were by and large more evangelically rooted than their professors. Many were specially interested in biblical studies; in this respect nearby Tyndale House was already exerting a noticeable influence. Aware that the evangelical option gained growing literary support through Inter-Varsity's publication of works by biblical theists, many Tyndale resident scholars and other evangelical students aspired to write constructive dissertations at the frontiers of theological debate. After a period in which orthodox scholarship had seemed poised largely on the fringe of contemporary issues, and lacking in philosophical-theological impact, its competence and range became increasingly evident in the areas of ancient Near Eastern languages and related biblical studies.

The university nonetheless remained a world apart from the secular city; the churches, by contrast, were mandated to be present there as light and salt. During our year in Cambridge we had, in a sense, commuted between the two worlds. If we gained indelible impressions of the academic arena, so too we gleaned inescapable convictions about the secular sphere with and against which the English churches struggled.

Church-going even as merely a respectable custom had come to an end in England; except for some well-attended evangelical congregations most churches were conspicuously empty. Unitarians considered the church archaic and moved outside, where some of them espoused speculative theism or metaphysical idealism. On the whole, however, theism no longer seemed a significant term for identifying the stance of nonevangelical intellectuals. More and more the cognitive divide was between orthodox Christians and those with obscure commitments or with a growing immigrant population loyal to nonbiblical religions.

Since empty churches were not the best context in which to witness to an alienated world, house churches emerged in many places as the best remaining avenue for evangelical testimony. Yet the church's crisis had in some respects also become the crisis of the home. Church families were not immune to secular inroads, and the generation gap was severing an ambivalent youth-generation from its ambiguous parent-generation. The material-physical culture was sucking dry the soul of multitudes, and shaped a cavernous vacuum in the lives of the masses. It tugged at life in the churches and in evangelical homes as well, and beguiled some whose heritage had been Christian but who were shaken by the tightening grip of secularism in education, the workplace and on the mass media.

Periodic moves toward church merger nurtured the feeling that doctrinal differences are unimportant. Enthusiasm for ecumenism was much more evident among the religious hierarchy than among the laity. The unchurched often questioned the church's material wealth and investment in deteriorating buildings. Whereas ecumenical concern focused on the communication gap between church-and-world, secular society saw it rather as a credibility gap, and asked whether the contemporary church was really shaped by the teaching of Jesus. The question presupposed greater public respect for Jesus Christ as the Founder of the Christian religion than for the institutional church.

Evangelical congregations of whatever denomination were in some respects the exception to this ecclesiastical disinterest, although they were a minority. Even they were not without problems, however. While evangelicals had much more in common in terms of doctrine and practice than ecumenical pluralists, they nonetheless were divided into three groups. Some 2,000 Anglican congregations were determined, as spokesman John Stott put it, to reinforce the confessional stance of their church, confident that the future of Christianity in England depended upon Anglican fortunes. Then there were some 200 independent churches aligned with the Westminster Fellowship led by Martyn Lloyd-Jones, the gifted pastor of Westminster Chapel and champion of congregations without ties to an ambiguous ecumenical movement. Caught between these as a third group was the British Evangelical Alliance, whose 500 churches were vulnerable to pressure from the other two, and hindered therefore from making a significant cultural impact that would enlist evangelical orthodoxy across the board. Stott insisted that to publicize the differences would not serve the evangelical cause, since the leaders, though different in ecclesiastical convictions, respected each other and trusted one another's motives. But only when Billy Graham ventured to England for mass crusades did the three forces seem to mount a common effort; even in this context there were reservations of support. As we moved next toward the totalitarian atheism of eastern Europe, where to stand up and be counted as an evangelical believer cost much more than in Britain, one could not but reflect on the luxury and handicap of evangelical disunity.

An eastern European evangelism conference for pastors and workers in Soviet-sphere countries toward which we were now driving had been the vision of TEAM-European missionary Tom Cosmades ever since the 1966 Berlin World Congress. Yugoslavia was the only communist-bloc nation that had allowed participants—only two at that—to attend the Berlin conclave. Once the 1966 Berlin Congress ended, a carload of us passed through Checkpoint Charlie into the eastern sector and at a prayer meeting attended by East Zone Christian workers shared what had transpired in West Berlin. News of the global gathering then trickled albeit more slowly to other eastern European leaders.

Cosmades therefore projected an interdenominational eastern European pastors' conference to be held for ten days in mid-August, 1969, at the Baptist Bible Seminary in Novi Sad, Yugoslavia. To safeguard the event and protect its participants it was necessary to avoid advance publicity, a precaution that inevitably and understandably ruled out any invitation to Billy Graham. Cosmades's committee decided to invite Dr. Stephen Olford of Calvary Baptist Church, New York City, and me, to assume virtually all the teaching and preaching duties. Helga and I would drive from Cambridge to Novi Sad; Stephen would fly from New York to Belgrade.

At the end of our delightful ten months in Cambridge we drove late in July to Harwich and boarded the ferry for Hook of Holland, where that night we visited in The Hague with the Van Capellevans. Next we were off to Amsterdam for two nights, then to Cologne and nearby relatives from where we drove along the Rhine to Wiesbaden. The scenic German cities, familiar language, savory meals in picturesque villages were a relaxing tonic, as were stops in larger centers like Augsburg, Salzburg and Vienna. We entered eastern Europe at Bratislava, Czechoslovakia. The contrast from what we had left behind was enormous. Next day we proceeded to Hungary where border police and customs officials took several hours to examine our car and check passports. Unlike shabby Bratislava, Budapest was a beautiful, highly cultured metropolis and its people helpful and friendly. On Revolution Street we visited a Christian professional man who recalled how when the communist takeover made Bibles a rare commodity, he kept a

Bible in his waiting room and periodically replaced it so visitors could remove a treasured page for personal use and pass it on to others.

On Thursday, August 7, we entered Yugoslavia, and six hours later reached Novi Sad and the Seminary that would soon host a remarkable evangelical event. I joined the committee for the drive to Belgrade to welcome Stephen Olford.

Participants came from Poland, Romania, Hungary and Czechoslovakia—countries that had refused to issue visas to the Berlin/1966 congress. Russia, East Germany, Bulgaria and Albania refused visas to both Berlin and Novi Sad. Several leaders eager to come went on holiday to other eastern European countries from where they then secured permission to visit Yugoslavia. Far exceeding committee expectations, 130 eastern European pastors and workers came to Novi Sad; in addition, there were observers from five west European countries, including seminarians who helped with arrangements. Yugoslav authorities cooperated fully.

Many participants had suffered imprisonment and all manner of persecution; others were pressured to cooperate with communist policy as the price of annual preaching license renewal. A few had been permitted to come to Novi Sad only on condition that they make pro-communist speeches, which they did at lunch to knowing listeners. Many attendees wept with joy as they met friends after ten or more years of separation. Still others were overjoyed to meet for the first time other believers and workers who lived within miles of them. A score of first-time local decisions for Christ were made in Sunday services at outlying villages where Stephen Olford and I preached the Sunday before the conference began.

Translation of the Novi Sad messages into eight languages would pose a major problem. The largest linguistically compatible group occupied front seats in the chapel, where Dr. Josip Horak translated Stephen Olford's messages and Dr. Bronco Levric translated mine. Both had been to the Berlin Congress, Horak being active in the Baptist World Alliance, and Levric a medical doctor and promoter of evangelical literature in Yugoslavia. Other language groups were seated with translators to the rear left and right of the chapel, in the gallery, out of sight in either wing of the platform, and still others listened in basement rooms. We each spoke twice daily, Olford on practical facets of ministry whereas I spoke on theological and doctrinal concerns. By special request of participants Helga spoke one day for two hours on women's work in American churches and answered questions.

Since attendance far exceeded lodgings and meal expectations, Helga pitched in with Lila Cosmades and Carolyn Naujoks wherever help was needed, mending and ironing clothes worn by pastors and workers in travel, selecting, buying and transporting produce from the market and assisting kitchen and cleaning crews. She daily stirred huge cauldrons of soup and stew and helped wash or dry dishes and pots and pans and set tables for 130 people. Language barriers faded as the multinational ladies became a harmonious work force.

So self-evidently poor were conference participants that I removed my tie and wristwatch before undertaking any lectures, and Helga and others removed what little jewelry they wore. None of the attendees wore coordinated let alone matching clothes; they were oblivious to threadbare, drab attire. Each person, on return home, was taken privately to a room to select what he or she wanted of the clothing, kitchen utensils (many delegates had no cutlery whatever), dishes and other items that Cosmades had brought from believers in West Germany. I added to the clothes rack a heavy old suit worn in inclement Cambridge weather. One worker found it a perfect fit; recognizing me by its size as the previous wearer, he gave me a huge bear-hug. In tears he explained that this was the first time in twenty-two years that he had possessed a second suit, and a matching one at that. To my further embarrassment he added that never had so eminent a mantle fallen upon him. When I discarded into a trash can an old hat too disreputable to take back home an elderly man retrieved it at once.

These devout Christian workers in Marxist lands reminded me of Paul's observation to the Corinthians, "having nothing, and yet possessing everything" (2 Cor. 6:10, RSV). Their joyful discovery that in eastern European countries hitherto unknown workers were bearing faithful witness to Christ created and cemented new bonds. Early morning and late night private and group prayer meetings and eagerness to plunge more deeply into the Bible and its implications for ministry lent a sacred aura to the days. New friendships were formed amid appreciation of one another's special problems. All sang hymns in their own language and found in this multilingual and multinational gathering a foretaste of the regenerate church united by and in its Risen Lord.

The smallest language group numbered but three persons, one the translator. A husband and wife and the wife's sister had come incognito from a hostile eastern European country, traveling first on holidays to another country, and there gaining entry visas to Yugoslavia. The husband, a brilliant student who had learned English, had aspired to the Christian ministry. But communist authorities disallowed his continuance in university studies unless he pursued an engineering vocation "useful to the state." Police sought numerous times to arrest him and his wife for religious meetings in their home, where they invited students for musical evenings to study Bach, for example. The husband and wife were both believers in Christ, but not the sister. It was these three who in Novi Sad huddled in the tiny church nursery at the rear of the sanctuary. During every meeting the engineer carefully translated the messages for his wife and the unsaved sister.

One morning Stephen Olford and I were asked to tell the story of our conversion. It was a moving experience for everyone; some visitors were converted, and many participants rededicated their lives. On the final day another testimony and dedication hour was marked by an unexpectedly dramatic development. The engineer's sister, a talented organist, walked down the center aisle of the auditorium and moved directly to the organ. On her own initiative she triumphantly played parts of Handel's *Messiah,* climaxing the presentation with "I know that my Redeemer liveth." Since she knew none of the languages spoken by other participants, music became her vehicle of testimony that she, too, had become a believer in Christ.

Midway through the Novi Sad sessions Dr. Horak indicated that the regional communist police had invited him to bring Olford and me to a luncheon conference. Horak had had many confrontations with communist authorities; although now retired and devoting full time to Christian activities, during a lifetime's service in an industrial plant he was, because of his Christian convictions, excluded from a managerial post and worked under party bosses far less knowledgeable than he. For Olford and me the experience marked our first meeting with any but "closet communists," and we were unsure what lay behind the invitation to a candid conversation.

For an hour with Horak we drove into the mountains to a retreat camp concealed by trees and offering a commanding view of distant hills and valleys. An attractive cabin, one of several, had been readied for our relaxation before lunch. Suddenly Dr. Horak called us to meet our arriving hosts. We gathered around an outdoor table for sumptuous steaks prepared on an outdoor fireplace; nearby in a covered well a fresh spring kept watermelons constantly cool. Horak served as translator; I asked him to inquire if I might offer grace (adding that at worst our hosts would simply ignore an American's odd request). When the men consented, I thanked God for the beauties of his creation, for his provision of food, and for the gift of Christ our Savior.

I remarked to our host that Yugoslavia had for many Americans become an increasingly favored tourist resort. Americans, I added, are by and large interested in the fortunes of fellow Christians worldwide; they moreover welcome signs of religious tolerance in Yugoslavia. Immediately one of the communists replied: "Protestants have more freedom in Yugoslavia than they have in Spain or Italy!" I was surprised how well-informed he was about restrictions on Protestant activity in certain Catholic countries. But I decided to take another tack, namely, the difference between religious tolerance and religious freedom. "Tolerance, as you know," I said, "suspends liberty on the will of the state, so that it can at any time be modified or removed; religious freedom, on the other hand, makes the state responsible for preserving and promoting it." He smiled, as if surprised that I knew the philosophical distinctions. Thereupon we had a candid and hospitable conversation. Our hosts wished us all a successful conference and wanted all participants to enjoy their visit. Since the Yugoslavian communist police had access to the passports of all visitors and knew from which countries they came, it was clear that they wanted to be perceived as cooperative and friendly.

The conference closed on August 20 with a moving communion service. Bronco Levric, who had translated most of my twenty messages, was more exhausted than other interpreters. But he declared himself invigorated by an experience that had stretched him to see the importance of a Christian world-life view, and deepened his desire to go from medicine into a full-time literature ministry.

Early next morning we drove off to Zagreb to spend the night en route to Austria with a retired layman, Mr. Vukovic. A widower, he was deeply moved by the Novi Sad sessions. Since neither of us spoke the other's language, we communicated mainly by gestures. On arrival he welcomed us with two basins of water and some towels and insisted on washing our feet, then furnished us with slippers while he shined our shoes. He then seated us in the garden for a rest. When he called us to the meal he had prepared, we gulped with every swallow, suspecting that the delicacies lavished upon us were far beyond his own lifestyle or what he could properly afford. He did not eat with us, much as we importuned, but insisted on serving us. He slipped a towel into his belt and pointed to the Bible, as if to remind us that Jesus considered the servant role greatest of all.

Then we all drove to prayer meeting at First Baptist Church, where Dr. Horak translated my message. We returned for the night to Mr. Vukovic's home. Every hour before we fell asleep of exhaustion we heard our host slip outside to make sure our Cortina was not vandalized. At dawn Mr. Vukovic was outside washing down the car. He had readied early breakfast of Turkish coffee, tea, sausages and boiled eggs, and had packed enough food for several days. I do not know how far removed in heaven I shall be from Christ's glorious throne, but I expect that, after the martyrs, Vukovic will be numbered among the self-giving saints of God.

Our drive from Zagreb to Amsterdam, where we would board flights for London and the United States, took us through Salzburg and then on to the Czech border. I was scheduled to speak in Prague on Sunday afternoon at a cooperative evangelical Sunday service. But the previous Saturday was the anniversary of the Czech Revolution. Curt border guards waved us away with the announcement, "*Keine Ausländer!* (no foreigners!)." I left some American dollars with the police to phone Prague with information about my nonentry.

The gospel's far future in eastern European countries clearly rested not with tourists but with residents like the courageous leaders to whom we had ministered in Novi Sad. As we drove westward along the Danube to Regensburg and finally Nürnberg, Germany, our conversation alternated between memories of the recent eastern European experiences and those of the past year at Cambridge. We carried on to Würzburg and Mainz, and then took the Rhine River road, tarrying a few days and nights along the way for rest and relaxation. The final days of August we spent in Amsterdam, firming flight reservations, divesting ourselves of the Cortina for trans-atlantic shipment and buying two oil paintings. We flew out on Monday, September 1, 1969, to London/Gatwick, to pick up a 10 P.M. special charter flight to Philadelphia.

The London-Philadelphia charter did not leave as scheduled, however. We whiled away one weary hour after another until at last we were airborne at 3 A.M. About forty-five minutes beyond Shannon airport the plane lost an engine; we were fortunate indeed to limp back to Ireland. No replacement aircraft was available. We were all given accommodations in nearby Limerick, there to await further developments. Two days later TWA took some passengers to New York; others like ourselves were given tickets on Aer Lingus to Chicago with a connecting TWA flight to Philadelphia. We arrived in the City of Brotherly Love on Wednesday night, September 3, the night before my first class at Eastern. On hand to greet us was Dean Walter B. Davis. Unable to get information about the overdue charter, he had for two days met every flight arriving from London.

17

Undulations of Evangelical Witness

Next morning, after a courtesy call on President Harnish, I picked up registration data and taught the first class that put an editorial career behind me.

Eastern Baptist Tuesday-through-Friday classes accommodated off-campus students serving as pastors or assistants in Christian education or youth work. Such practical demands were heavy, and many students were interested mainly in classes that promoted their immediate ministries. Some were restive because so-called practical courses, especially preaching and Christian education, were more theoretical than experientially useful; they turned to courses in counseling. More and more were also aspiring to a doctorate of ministries degree that seemed increasingly an "in" thing to have.

For all that, a core of cognitively concerned students ventured into seminars with restricted enrollments. During the first term I taught contemporary theological trends and current theological literature; during the second term I introduced a seminar on the doctrine of the afterlife, a theme that was attracting interest even on secular campuses. My classes were more than filled; Thorwald Bender had energetically promoted their promise of serious theological study.

Our unfurnished third-floor faculty apartment at 6355 Lancaster Avenue greeted us on arrival with twin beds and a dresser. The ample premises were just below the top-floor apartment of Dr. Walter Davis, the devout Scotsman who taught evangelism and missions. Furnishing the empty apartment, a few blocks from campus, became an evening and weekend project. We plied suburban homes being vacated by Florida-bound retirees for everything from furniture and rugs to pots and pans. By mid-October the apartment looked as if we had been long-term occupants.

My return to seminary teaching came in the year of Richard Nixon's inauguration as thirty-seventh president and of Dwight Eisenhower's death, of Sirhan Sirhan's conviction for assassinating Senator Robert Kennedy and of Senator Edward Kennedy's misadventure at Chappaquidick that cost the life of Mary Jo Kopechne, of James Earl Ray's sentencing for the assassination of Martin Luther King, of the moon landing of American astronauts who then walked its powdery surface and of demonstrations by hundreds of thousands of Americans against the war in Vietnam that precipitated a gradual withdrawal of some 75,000 troops.

In this context the U.S. Congress on Evangelism was held in Minneapolis from September 8–13, 1969, the week following my initial classes. Halfway through the Congress came a phone call from B.G.E.A. treasurer George Wilson abruptly asking when I planned to arrive. "Arrive where and for what?" I asked. I had in fact no intimation that I was expected or even that the Congress was underway. Wilson explained that the program listed me to give a final morning summary and appraisal. But travel from Philadelphia after already scheduled classes would overlap most remaining Congress sessions; it would be unfair to assess a gathering that one had not attended. Later Canadian leaders invited me to address their national Congress on Evangelism in Ottawa at the end of August, 1970, on the theology of evangelism.

Eastern had asked me to deliver on October 23, 1969, the fall convocation address, not a technical theological discourse but an inspirational message with broad focus on the contemporary cultural crisis. In view of the deepening twilight of Western civilization I affirmed that "the barbarians are coming," noting the barbarian deployment of technology for evil ends, the barbarian reliance on violence and revolution rather than reason and persuasion, and the trendy modern religious accommodations of the pagan man. I then warned that the barbarians do not have the future to themselves, for "the Lord Jesus Christ is coming," the Lord of truth, the King of kings, the Man of righteousness. But I refused to leave matters there, as did much evangelical emphasis only on personal salvation and the Lord's return. "The barbarians are coming; the Lord Jesus Christ is coming; *but Christians are here now:* do they know whether they are coming or going?"

I devoted the last half of my address to the need for evangelical initiative and recovery of an apostolic stride. The message was striated with the importance of evangelical doctrine—the priority of the supernatural, man's creation in God's image, sin and the need of individual redemption, the lordship of Christ and his final universal judgment, the relevance of God's commandments to national life and culture, the role of the transracial and transnational church and the need for Christian engagement both in evangelism and in social and political affairs. Then came the emphasis on scriptural revelation: "The late twentieth century is bone-weary of the indefinite and inconclusive and indecisive; what it needs is a sure Word of God. . . . The Word of God is given, incarnate and incomparable, inscripturate and indelible. That God has revealed himself intelligibly, that Jesus of Nazareth is the incarnate Logos of God, that the Scriptures are the Word of God written, that the Holy Spirit uses truth as the means of human persuasion and conviction, that not even the twentieth century can cancel God's truth. . . . these emphases our generation needs desperately to hear."

The convocation concluded with a public signing of Eastern's doctrinal statement. I had not realized that my academic installation would be the occasion of the installation also of an Old Testament professor and of a New Testament professor whose doctrinal views were in question.

During the 1965–66 academic year Helga had commuted by train from Washington to Philadelphia as Visiting Professor of Christian Education. Her courses were so well received that the president of another seminary a thousand miles away called me and asked if I'd encourage his invitation that she commute there by air. She was elected as Eastern's first woman trustee in 1968, serving with people like John W. Bradbury of the *Watchman-Examiner,* C. Gordon Brownville, Harold Fickett, Lloyd Frederick, Harry Jenkins, Chester Jump, Frank Middleswart, J. Lee Westrate, President Harnish and former president Gilbert Guffin. But she resigned her trusteeship when I returned from Cambridge to teach at Eastern.

Eastern was founded in 1925 to prepare evangelical pastors for ministry in the Northern Baptist Convention. From the outset it incorporated certain tensions. On the one hand it opposed fundamentalist separatism, while on the other it promoted a conservative, biblically based ministry within a Convention in which liberalism was making disconcerting inroads. The Rev. Charles T. Ball was first president. Gordon Palmer, one of the seminary's early presidents, and prominent early trustees like Ralph Mayberry and David Miller, stood on the right both theologically and socio-politically in matters that the Federal Council of Churches usually championed on the left. But when the faculty repudiated the Conservative Baptist movement in the '40s, Palmer went along. The desire to avoid "excessive fundamentalism" and "extreme liberalism" had about it a certain ambiguity: persons on both sides could exploit the "middle ground" for positions that somewhat moderated the original doctrinal stance. Some faculty who when hired held conservative views, or who were perceived as standing on "the conservative side of the middle," exploited the Seminary's openness and modified their initial commitments.

Yet the "moderates" were not self-evidently correct when they later contended that Eastern's founders took middle ground between fundamentalism and modernism. A Philadelphia pastor actively involved in the beginning, Dr. A. C. Baldwin, wrote that "beyond doubt" the establishment of Eastern represented "the dissatisfaction of Eastern [East Coast] fundamentalists with our [Baptist] seminaries and their courses." In the book titled *What God Hath Wrought* edited by Gilbert Guffin, who was Eastern president from 1950–61, Norman Maring, Eastern alumnus and later faculty church historian, grants that "the surmise of Dr. Baldwin that Eastern was the offspring of the 'fundamentalists' was correct" (*ibid.,* Philadelphia, Judson Press, 1960, p. 16). Most early trustees had associated with Fundamentalist conferences, and nearly all early faculty members participated in pre-Convention programs that stressed loyalty to Scripture. The notion that Eastern's founders were concerned only to protect "the core of the biblical witness"—however one might choose to define that—and were disinterested in the question of the inerrancy or errancy of Scripture, and therefore open to negative higher criticism—gains no credence from the school's early history.

Only later, and gradually, did there emerge within Eastern an emphasis that biblical authority and inspiration are doctrines compatible with scriptural errancy and that affirmation of an inerrant Bible is uncritical and rests on a spurious doctrine of inspiration. Yet professors who rejected inerrancy were in numerous cases students of earlier Eastern professors who had already broken with an infallible Bible, yet who in the main correlated a critical view of Scripture with evangelical conclusions. Newly appointed faculty lacked a clear sense of what evangelical commitment implied for their view of Scripture, even as some already entrenched teachers were unsure. For a time some claimed to be fundamentalists without subscribing to the fundamentalist formulas; they maintained an evangelical life of faith but considered the view of an inerrant Scripture a barrier to biblical scholarship, to which in any case they contributed little. The doctrinal results gradually became evident in a caricaturing of the "fundies" by some later faculty members, a rejection of propositional revelation, the emphasis that an evangelical may question Jesus' virgin birth, the debunking of Satan as myth and the rejection of external supports for the resurrection of Christ. Finally the Seminary's offerings tilted more to social ethics and psychology than to theology and doctrine.

Eastern's commitment to evangelical orthodoxy was reaffirmed when Lester Harnish became president from 1968–1973. Harnish followed Thomas B. McDormand, a Canadian who was president from 1961–1967; many board members considered him theologically somewhat flexible, although the faculty welcomed him as a "British evangelical" mediating type. By contrast, Harnish was a Wheaton graduate who had taken theological studies at Eastern. He was loyal both to conservative theology and to the Northern Baptist Convention although opposed to its invading modernism. As a successful pastor he had been associated with the National Association of Evangelicals, took a leading role in Billy Graham crusades and served as president of the American Baptist Convention.

At the time Harnish became president most of Eastern's trustees wanted firmer theological affirmation. A number of faculty had defected from a wholly reliable Scripture. Students complained that the Old Testament was taught as a history of traditions that clouded any clear line between imagination and history; that objective factors were subordinated to personal faith in teaching Gospel accounts of the resurrection; that one professor taught an implicit universalism; and that the faculty as a group reflected little theological cohesion. Under Harnish's predecessor an Old Testament professor who ridiculed conservative views of the Bible transferred to another school. Trustees looked to Harnish to probe a neoorthodox teacher added without careful theological examination from the Southern Baptist seminary in Ruschlikon, Switzerland. Although conservative in christology, he held not only critical views of Scripture but also an openness to universal salvation in express contradiction of Eastern's doctrinal statement; after moving out of systematic theology into historical theology he too left Eastern's faculty.

Further questions were raised by Eastern's influential pastor-friends concerning the views taught by Professor Thomas McDaniel in Old Testament and Professor Glenn Koch in New Testament. Harnish met several times with McDaniel, who considered Harnish theologically too uninformed to decide the question of doctrinal acceptability. The combination of eager support for McDaniel by a prominent trustee who had been McDaniel's pastor and long-time advisor, hurried interviewing for a faculty appointment, the "old school tie" to alumni who had been McDaniel's classmates and faculty sympathies for a colleague were too strong to be overcome. Koch's critical views first became known through pastors attending his classes. Some trustees considered a faculty member's personal interest in students and admirable prayer life to be more important than doctrinal commitments; they emphasized that Koch and McDaniel were pious and gracious believers and accordingly championed their cause. Others could not cope with theological subtleties.

I was unaware of these tensions when I was asked to give the installation address followed by our shared signing of Eastern's doctrinal statement. Harnish had invited me to the theological faculty as a reaffirmation of Eastern's reason for being. Many of the faculty, eager for salary increases and a sabbatical program they considered overdue, were critical because the president needed to divide administrative time between the Seminary and Eastern Baptist College, as it was then known. Others criticized the president's effort to preserve a fuller evangelical emphasis as theologically retrogressive and as doctrinally unrepresentative of their stance.

The controversy over what Eastern meant by "evangelical" in time came to engulf faculty, trustees, pastors, students and the school's supporters. Baptist ministerial students were turning to other seminaries—Trinity, for example, had 500 applicants for the Fall and in view of its enrollment limit of 350 could accept only 98—while Eastern's meager growth was mainly due to non-Baptists who attended as a matter of convenience. When President Harnish encouraged faculty membership in Evangelical Theological Society, the faculty instead asked that a forum be arranged with the president and vice presidents to discuss the school's evangelical commitments. At the annual board meeting in May, 1971, the Faculty-Trustee Committee asked for a dialogue on "Eastern's evangelicalism" at the semiannual meeting on December 7, 1971, and requested board chairman Frank Middleswart to name a planning committee.

Dr. Middleswart wrote me on May 25 asking me to chair an Ad Hoc Committee for a December Trustee-Faculty Dialogue with Professors Norman Maring and Douglas Miller to represent the faculty and former Seminary president Guffin and Dr. Lloyd Frederick representing the trustees; Harnish and Middleswart would be *ex officio* members. The Ad Hoc Committee was to outline a procedure which, if the Executive Committee approved on October 25, would allow six weeks for preparation of the December 7 presentations on which both board members and faculty members would then comment.

I accepted the chairmanship and, since summer vacations were already underway, asked committee members to be ready early in September to indicate how Eastern might best give content to the term "evangelical": whether by an appeal to Scripture, church tradition,

Eastern's doctrinal basis, evangelical agencies like N.A.E. or E.T.S., promotional-funding requirements or some alternative.

Eastern's doctrinal basis did not expressly commit the Seminary either to the inerrancy or the errancy of Scripture. It read: "We believe that the Bible, composed of the Old and New Testaments, is inspired of God, and is of supreme and final authority in faith and life." Some trustees saw in this statement an implicit commitment to inerrancy, others to errancy. My comment to the committee was that the statement "does not explicitly affirm inerrancy" but that it would seem difficult to exegete the statement to mean that the writers intended scriptural errancy.

The weeks ahead brought from Dean Maring an unsolicited 2,000-word paper championing the doctrinal basis but deploring an interpretation that restricts its meaning of "evangelical" to "a particular view." Affirming biblical inerrancy, he emphasized, would in the view of some faculty violate Christian scholarly integrity. The other faculty committeeman, Dr. Miller, former Conservative Baptist pastor who in his initial faculty interview espoused inerrancy, held that the Seminary's doctrinal basis should be definitive. He disavowed the fundamentalist questioning of the salvation of all who deny inerrancy, yet affirmed scriptural inerrancy as the Bible itself interprets the doctrine. Hence Maring rejected inerrancy whereas Miller accepted it but offered no tangibly defined view.

From the two trustee committeemen came one-page letters. Dr. Guffin, who had become dean of religion at Samford University in Birmingham, suggested surveying the meaning of "evangelical" as understood in the New Testament, early Church history, Reformation, modern missionary era, Baptist doctrinal confessions, contemporary theology and finally in the purpose and role of Eastern. Dr. Frederick wrote that "as a busy pastor" of Central Baptist Church of Riverton-Palmyra, New Jersey, he would leave the theological and philosophical implications of Eastern's image to "able faculty members," but endorsed Maring's suggestion that Eastern "continue to minister within the broader tradition of Evangelicalism and not move to the right and thus make her stance more exclusive and confining."

I shared correspondence with the entire committee and suggested that the faculty committeemen meet initially on September 3. At that time Maring and Miller said that President Harnish had not indicated to them that our committee was to formulate a basis for future dialogue. They proposed that the entire Ad Hoc Committee meet on October 25 with President Harnish and board chairman Middleswart for an intermediate conference.

Meanwhile Maring wrote on September 11: "I hope we will not

become bogged down" on inerrancy "which I consider an abstraction." He had already readied (unrequested) a further paper should faculty or trustees consider inerrancy important, but he warned against polarization on "pseudo-issues." I circulated to the committee the 5,000-word paper by Maring, who indicated that he would be unavailable for meetings before October 30 because he was on sabbatical. "Our question," he held, "is not whether Eastern is an evangelical seminary, but what we mean by the adjective 'evangelical.' " Its main historical reference, Maring insisted, is to evangelistic concern and Christian piety; it is defined without reference to any view of Scripture. Eastern's alliances, he concluded, should be with all who affirm "Jesus Christ as Lord and Savior" and declare themselves to be evangelical.

Miller affirmed that the Bible implicitly teaches inerrancy. Disavowal of its inerrancy, he noted, strips the interpreter of any objective criterion for discriminating from error what he supposes to be truth. God's purpose, Miller explained, is expressed in the Bible not restrictively only in some of its parts (e.g. its redemptive message), but in the whole; Scripture in its totality is not merely trustworthy but true.

In dialogue with faculty members I identified myself with Miller's emphasis. If a school publicly affirms the authority and inspiration of the Scriptures, but disavows their inerrancy, I noted, a professor in Old Testament may dismiss the creation account as largely mythological, a professor in church history may insist that despite the Gospel accounts one need not consider the virgin birth of Jesus to be a necessary doctrine, a New Testament professor may depict Jesus' resurrection as a matter of faith not to be cognitively argued and a theologian may ridicule the very idea of revelatory divine truths or propositions. Each such professor, I added, may personally believe a great deal of what the Bible elsewhere teaches, and his isolated reservations may seem to him quite restrained. But a student sitting in all these classes will soon decide that scriptural authority and inspiration are compatible with rejection of all manner of Bible content, will boggle at the high theological pretensions of his teachers and will consider the tenet of biblical reliability too bewildering and confusing to comprehend.

A memorandum from President Harnish dated October 5 and read to the regular October 11 faculty meeting stipulated further: "This effort should not fall into the pit" of "again chewing over . . . biblical inerrancy. For evangelicals this is a matter of semantics. Let's agree that the Bible is a true, trustworthy, inspired expression of God's character and purposes, which we as a faculty accept and teach as our highest authority without reservation." Harnish intended this as a caution against refocusing the Seminary's doctrinal basis, but Maring welcomed it as a declaration of the irrelevance of inerrancy. The memorandum dissolved, Maring averred, "the real need for a director-faculty dialogue on the subject of our evangelicalism." Harnish reiterated his hope that the joint committee would, well in advance of the December 7 meeting, distribute to all faculty and board members a paper serving as a basis for dialogue.

When the joint committee reconvened on October 25 to prepare its document, I noted the recently stipulated directive that we not preoccupy ourselves with inerrancy, but distributed to the commitee a personal statement about the weaknesses and consequences of this approach. The session proceeded on the understanding that Eastern's doctrinal basis would be the starting point but that the errancy/inerrancy issue would not be a major item. The committee voted that the doctrinal basis be presupposed as the permanently valid statement of Eastern's theological position and then formulated for December 7 dialogue a sixfold preparatory statement. It began: "The Eastern Baptist Theological Seminary through its doctrinal affirmation is dynamically committed to the evangelical theological stance." The complete statement was distributed early in November to all faculty and trustees.

Dr. Walter Davis promptly expressed disappointment that the statement included no commitment to the inerrancy of the Scriptures. He asked whether any proposal had come to the committee to assess whether the Seminary actually operates in harmony with its doctrinal statement. "Certain of our students are declaring, on the basis of teaching received by them in Seminary classes, that we are not a conservative seminary, and that liberal doctrines are being promulgated," he wrote. "I do not see much point in making public statements about our conservative stance when we are obviously not convincing certain of our own students on this point."

I indicated to Dr. Davis that I would share at the next faculty meeting results of a poll taken in my *Recent Trends in Theology* class on the effect of Eastern courses on student beliefs about biblical authority, inspiration and reliability. Of twenty-eight students, mostly seniors, five students indicated that Seminary studies had weakened a higher view of the Bible held when entering; twenty-three conceded that they were already predisposed at entrance toward errancy of the Bible, but noted that Eastern had reinforced doubts about full scriptural reliability. One in four students indicated uncertainty about the meaning of revelation, the scope of the canon or the Bible's inspiration or authority.

Word of this poll had already reached and perturbed some faculty members. The acting dean informed me that they regarded my sampling as an affront and considered the testing device imperfect and untrustworthy; the faculty, moreover, would likely take me to task at its December 13 meeting. Any faculty distress, I commented, should concentrate not on the nature of the sampling technique but on the compromised outlook of senior seminarians about to be graduated for ministry in the churches. The matter never came up in faculty meeting.

In the Spring of 1972 the news was out that Lester Harnish was leaving as president. The trustees named as interim president for the 1972–73 academic year Dr. Henry Osgood, a Baptist pastor. During Osgood's stint McDaniel came up for faculty tenure. Not a single faculty member dissented [I abstained since I did not myself have tenure, and in any case had no firsthand information about what he taught]. Board chairman Frank Middleswart cast the only negative trustee vote. Attending the meeting was Daniel Weiss, the president-elect. A Wheaton alumnus and Gordon College vice president, he was perceived as a staunch evangelical who would reinforce Eastern's orthodoxy. Weiss, who served from 1973–81, counseled with McDaniel and on one occasion disciplined him; after that, McDaniel more readily presented alternatives to his own stance. But overall no conservative theological trend eventuated. When Stephen Olford complained that students sent by Calvary Baptist Church of New York to Eastern were disappointed and restive over their ministerial studies he was told that my position was Eastern's. Meanwhile Maring, back in the deanship after his sabbatical, worked unilaterally for greater diversity of theological emphasis.

In October, 1973, I confidentially told Weiss that I planned to leave at the end of the 1973–74 academic year. Weiss later pushed Ronald Sider for chairman of the theology department. Social concerns were Sider's preoccupation. When students protested the compression of virtually all theology into social ethics, Sider received part-time status. But Eastern was by now fully caught up in ecumenical patterns. Orlando Costas came in missions, advocating a qualified liberation theology; when Costas moved to Andover-Newton he was replaced by Latin American theologian Samuel Escobar who likewise channeled theology into a demand for radically altered socio-political structures. Eastern professors aligned themselves increasingly with the ecumenical thrust of American Baptist leadership at Valley Forge, including pro-Sandinista support in Nicaragua.

Weiss had to forego the presidency because of personal problems, later resolved. The election of Robert A. Seiple to the presidency in 1983 brought a devout but theologically untrained evangelical layman gifted in financial development. A proven fundraiser, Seiple had been vice president for development at Brown University.

Eastern's course was not decided in the long run by a handful of special-problem faculty. Its "middle ground" avoidance of extremes enabled those left of center to oppose the right and to espouse critical views. Lack of theologically literate trustees, gradual acceptance of the pluralistic denominational context it originally challenged, professing conservatives whose critical views emerged only after they were hired or received tenure and the translation of personal friendships into board support, all played a role. The offering of a doctor of ministries degree, attractive to aspiring pastors from all denominations, helped shift student interest from cognitive to practical subjects. Eastern's student body reflected not the original vision of providing evangelical pastors to serve in the American Baptist context, but a convenient degree program for pastors and laymen of divergent affiliations.

My own interest in social ethics involved me in the public debate over abortion. I took part in a seminar with Dr. C. Everett Koop, then surgeon-in-chief at Children's Hospital of Philadelphia, sponsored on November 7, 1970, by the Christian Medical Society in Tenth Presbyterian Church of Philadelphia. Later U.S. Surgeon General, Koop was already a famed pediatric surgeon; some prominent civic leaders owed their survival to his remedial surgery on birth defects. Many in the medical profession charged to preserve and protect life, I noted, were lending themselves instead to destruction of normal fetal life by abortion. Among the clergy, many of whom supported liberalizing abortion laws to permit abortion-on-demand, I added, the situation was "no less astonishing." In effect, they "accommodate a revival of infanticide, whereas ancient Christianity . . . revived the insensitive conscience of pagan parents who disposed of unwanted baby girls on public garbage heaps, and compassionately sought to lead the weak and unwanted to meaningful spiritual life in Christ. . . . Are modern exponents of abortion-on-request," I asked, "less barbaric than their pagan Roman counterparts because they approve a more sophisticated discarding of infant life with the medical trash? . . . The argument that abortion is an ideal method of birth control is spurious," I said; for "there are methods of birth control that avoid formation of the zygote. And the argument that the fetus becomes human only when the doctor spanks the baby's bottom at delivery is naïve. The clergy ought not to advocate nor the medics to accommodate the clamor for abortion-on-demand. . . . Let the clergy clarify the obscure line between right and wrong and the medics give themselves to the preservation and protection of life."

These were my convictions long before Francis Schaeffer made anti-abortion a cause célèbre, yet indirectly criticized me as lacking objective moral standards on the abortion issue, and before his more intemperate son Franky misrepresented me as being pro-abortion. To be sure, I indicated that the Church ought not to dictate "the laws of the secular community," but ought rather by precept and example "to exhibit the ethical principles of revealed religion." I noted that "the law recognizes the legitimacy of abortion when pregnancies are induced by rape or incest, or when the abortion is therapeutic," and added that "for Christian ethics a decision regarding termination of a seriously defective fetus is not easy." The churches cannot with integrity, I emphasized, demand the sparing of fetal life even under such extreme circumstances without a compassionate response, one that provides moral alternatives and financial and other help that makes meaningful life possible for those whose personal survival is haunted and shattered by such misfortune. When in 1984 misleading criticism prompted leaders of Inter-Varsity Christian Fellowship to withdraw from publication D. Gareth-Jones's *Brave New People,* I raised my voice for a well-reasoned rather than merely rhetorical response to the issues in debate. I wrote a blurb for Eerdmans's publication of a revised edition, as I had for the Inter-Varsity edition, persuaded that hammer-head negation cannot hope in intelligent circles to carry its positions even when they happen to be right, which they sometimes but not always are.

The Jerusalem Conference on Biblical Prophecy held June 15–18, 1971, was a brainchild of Gaylord Briley, Pennsylvania clergyman whose Madison Avenue flair depicted it as the equivalent of "a ringside seat at the Second Coming." It was well into the planning stage when I first heard of it. Dr. W. A. Criswell and Dr. Harold Ockenga were co-chairmen of a "call committee" that included numerous leading churchmen. The master plan called for a three-day prophetic conference in Jerusalem's massive convention hall, preceded and followed by related Holy Land tours arranged and escorted by evangelical evangelists and pastors.

As envisaged by Briley the conference was subsidiary to a larger projection of many planeloads of Holy Land pilgrims led by leading churchmen. Television and radio figures, he anticipated, might each fill an entire plane with friends and supporters. What Briley had not anticipated was that popular evangelists who enlisted large numbers for Holy Land flights would also expect to be major conference speakers. How then to salvage a significant program on prophetic themes was the problem when Robert Walker of *Christian Life* magazine and Briley asked me in 1970 if I would suggest speakers to lend credibility to a world prophecy conference and transcend the allocation of platform opportunities on the basis of churchmen bringing the largest tour groups. I was told that program involvement was hinted to many but no commitments had been made. I had too little time, I said, to make optional suggestions for a potluck program that might be routinely manipulated. I was willing to outline a comprehensive plan, and if it were approved (with acceptable countersuggestions) would try to enlist speakers, leaving Walker and Briley free to reject the whole if they wished. They asked me to go ahead.

Attended by 1,400 evangelical Christians from many lands, but mostly from the United States, the prophecy conference was the largest Christian gathering in the Holy Land since the state of Israel was founded in 1948. *Newsweek* (June 28, 1971) gave it lead religion coverage; *Washington Post* gave it three columns; and *The New York Times* handled it favorably.

Success of the conference and related tours in a time of great political uncertainty were remarkable. To be sure, not all my projections succeeded. To speak on the judgment of the nations I approached Lebanon's elder statesman Charles Malik, former chairman of the U.N. General Assembly and a devout Christian. Malik declined in a warm personal letter; he wished "political realities would permit it." But in the opening session David Ben-Gurion, Israel's first prime minister, welcomed participants; at 85, he was invited not in a political role but as a Hebrew patriarch in the land of the prophets. Explosive world political realities were evident not only in the Holy Land but elsewhere as well. En route to the Near East I had scheduled Poland for a ministry sponsored by evangelical Christians, but Warsaw authorities refused a visa on the ground that "it is forbidden for a foreigner to teach youth or adults."

Key messages in Jerusalem were by W. A. Criswell, A. Skevington Wood, Merrill C. Tenney, Oswald C. J. Hoffman, G. Douglas Young, Arnold Olsen, John Stott, Harold Ockenga, James M. Houston, Tom Skinner and Sam Wolgemuth. I was to speak on "Jesus Christ and the Last Days," but Doug Young became so preoccupied with "Contemporary Israel in Prophetic Focus" that he used up his time frame and mine; moreover, he unexpectedly introduced a surprise speaker, Professor Zvi Werblowsky of Hebrew University of Jerusalem. To keep the conference on track I simply forewent my remarks, since all major messages would appear in a post-conference volume. Two stimulating panels reflected sincere eschatological disagreement—one, on the rebuilding of the Hebrew temple, involved Edmund P. Clowney and Charles Feinberg, and another, on the future of Israel, featured Herman N. Ridderbos, John Walvoord and Zvi Werblowsky. One entire afternoon was devoted to scores of simultaneous panels in subsidiary convention hall rooms which gave well-known evangelists and pastors opportunity for presentation and discussion of special prophetic interests.

Among the most moving and memorable aspects of the conference were its opening and its closing. During opening ceremonies the Israeli symphony orchestra performed while Jerome Hines of the Metropolitan Opera Company sang. After Hines sang, an orchestra member came up in tears and identified himself as a fellow-believer. The final conference event was an outdoor communion service conducted by Richard Halverson.

Later in 1971 we drove to Florida for the marriage on August 25 of daughter Carol to William Bates in First Presbyterian Church of Pensacola. Bill was serving on the music faculty of University of West Florida. They had met at Indiana University, where Bill was a leader of the Baptist Student Union. Both were graduate students in the School of Music and now within a year or two of completing doctorates, he in organ, Carol in musicology. In 1972 both successfully took the doctoral exams. Meanwhile, in Grand Rapids, son Paul had added TV newscasting to his busy schedule at Calvin College, and Karen taught piano students besides shepherding the youngsters.

Although prohibitive plane fares even to Israel meant that few evangelical Asians attended the Jerusalem congress, their increasing vitality was evident at their home bases. Ecumenical diminution of the universal truth-content of revealed religion and emphasis instead on confession of Christ that clouded scriptural authority, openness to universal salvation and debatable Marxist-tilted socio-political proposals had motivated evangelical organization of the Asia-South Pacific Congress on Evangelism in Singapore in 1968. To the dismay of the ecumenical East Asia Christian Conference, evangelical Asian leaders were in the aftermath of the South Pacific Congress forging new alliances and planning their own theological institutions. The Asia Evangelical Theological Society was formed with branches in Japan, Korea and other nations. The ecumenical tendency to recognize the validity of nonchristian religions and to neglect evangelistic priorities spurred evangelicals to propose accredited institutes and seminaries to halt ecumenical inroads in the absence of evangelical educational alternatives. An immediate goal was to strengthen Union Biblical Seminary in India to widen its serviceability to Indonesia and the Middle East. The establishment of an evangelical seminary in Singapore was discussed, and also the upgrading of existing institutions in Japan, Korea and Taiwan.

At its 1968 Bangkok general assembly, the East Asia Christian Conference projected a consultation to encourage evangelicals to regard doctrinal differences as mutually enriching rather than as a basis of division. Set for July, 1970, the resultant consultation brought together ecumenical and evangelical spokesmen for a series of background papers, section workshops and preliminary discussions on church unity and mission. D. T. Niles, the announced chairman of the E.A.C.C. Committee for Life, Message and Unity, had requested Bishop Chandu Ray, former rector of the Anglican Cathedral in Karachi, to organize the conference. Then directing the Singapore coordinating office for evangelical evangelism in Asia, Bishop Ray invited me as an observer.

Although the consultation proceeded in good spirit, it did little to allay evangelical anxieties. Ecumenists tended to view evangelical theology as a Western distortion rooted in Greek rationalism, while European Barthianism was presented by its embracers as authentic biblical revelation. Ecumenical spokesmen presented divine judgment as always the underside of divine grace; universal salvation seemed an inescapable implication and the indispensability of evangelism therefore eroded.

For all that, Chandu Ray's own research indicated that 40 percent of Asian Christians had come to Christ as Savior through Bible-reading, and 30 percent through personal witness by believers. Pulpit preaching and evangelistic campaigns were thus but secondary methods of conversion. Correspondence courses advertised in newspapers were productive of enrollees in India and Ceylon. The importance of training lay Christians loomed with new force.

The mass media, moreover, were gaining ever widening significance among literate Asians and evangelicals needed new awareness of their potential. Two years later from July 16 to August 4, 1972, Helga and I were at Hong Kong Baptist College for a three-week Asian Christian Communications conference. From eleven countries it drew graduate students already active in Christian radio, television and print media, including some missionary veterans who after thirty to forty years of service in China had fled for their lives. The staff included Dr. Timothy Yu, then head of the communications department at Hong Kong Baptist College and founder of Rock House Press; later he established the communications department at the new University of Hong Kong in the New Territories.

Asians needed the reminder that the key to the future of Christianity in Asia rests not with non-Asians but with Asians. Asia's debt to Christianity needed to be told—how it had improved literacy, elevated women, sustained human worth, established schools and hospitals and social work—and most of all shared the good news of the living Redeemer who grants forgiveness and incomparable new life. Even where there was resistance to Christianity Asian Muslims and Buddhists were more receptive to fellow Asian Christians than to Westerners. The importance of reaching university youth, tomorrow's leaders, underscored the need for cognitively competent media craftsmen.

Asia had been increasingly caught in a pincers movement. Its big cities welcomed technocratic scientism, but with it came a tendency to consider God as irrelevant and to explain man by a naturalistic computer-analogy that Chinese communism could exploit in promoting a Marxist version of "the new man." To combat this secular tide Asian political leaders reasserted and reinforced their ancient spiritual traditions and cultural heritage, which meant a preferred status for nonbiblical religions and an ill-founded disposition to view biblical theism as a foreign import. Christians needed to develop skills in writing, photography, art and mass media techniques in order to clarify the transcendent in terms of the Judeo-Christian heritage whose historical roots were in fact Asian yet which was international in its significance.

While I shared in the media meetings, Helga addressed Christian education workshops, Christian women's clubs, women's retreats, seminary groups and a special luncheon of Christian educators. In Kowloon Baptist Church I shared speaking honors with Dr. Bob Smith of Bethel College for the annual Keswick week July 23–30, and spoke also at St. Andrews (Anglican). After Hong Kong we spent a week in Bangkok and a week in Singapore, where I preached before flying to the States for the annual September-December stint at Eastern.

Return meant a deluge of domestic speaking and lecture invitations. I addressed the Ohio Baptist Convention. I turned down a teaching invitation from Hawaii, in order to prepare for a Butler University centennial address in February, 1970, and for the Willson Lectures at Earlham Graduate School of Religion in the Spring. The Butler opportunity was gratifying since the student body invited three speakers: Loren Eiseley on "The Future of Science" and Eric Severeid on "The Future of Politics" while "The Future of Religion" fell to me. Despite perhaps the Winter's worst blizzard about 300 persons attended. Religion is so multiform, I emphasized, that it seems indefinable by contemporary scholars, whereas the nature of revealed religion is, in fact, clear and has an assured future that other religions lack. George Cornell's nationally syndicated Associated Press column featured my Butler address. At Earlham I emphasized that the insistence of some scholars that no event in the past is admissible unless analogues for it exist in the present is as arbitrary as the notion that all events in nature and history are causally uniform. Theology and philosophy lectures took me also to Houghton College, Judson Baptist and Eastern Baptist College, University of Oklahoma, Geneva College, Messiah College, Moody Bible Institute and for the Ryan Lectures to Asbury Theological Seminary. In addition, I took part in Cincinnati at the American Baptist Convention in a panel with Harvey Cox on the theology of revolution.

Meanwhile Trinity Evangelical Divinity School renewed its invitation to come in September, 1970, or September, 1971, and there were other options. The Eastern commitment required me to teach there for the September-December semester, but allowed me to give January-March to research and writing and to teach at Trinity for the April-June term, which I did.

Helga was soon extensively involved in lectures on Christian education in Philadelphia area churches and for recreation enrolled in an oil painting class. The January, 1970, *Christian Herald* featured her with other prominent evangelical women known for individual career contributions to the Christian cause. She, as well as I, was glad that our Arlington home would be available by Christmas, 1970. For the first time in several years the entire family could once again be together. Paul and his family drove from Grand Rapids where he had begun teaching political science at Calvin College and Carol flew in from Houghton College where she was teaching music.

Interwoven with teaching at Eastern and Trinity, conferences and seminars at home and abroad and various writing involvements, were my Board-stipulated relationships to *Christianity Today* as editor-at-large. Deterioration in these relationships was not long in coming and reflected changes both in the editorial staff and in Board personnel and policy. By December, 1970, paid subscriptions were down 30,000 from their peak and fund-raising was disappointing. Not only was my coverage in staff group insurance to be curtailed, but my editor-at-large reimbursement was to be reduced to $100 a month for "Footnotes" and even that contribution would be subject to annual Board renewal.

The death on November 27, 1971, of multimillionaire J. Howard Pew sent a shiver of uncertainty through the ranks at *Christianity Today.* Pew had nurtured the Sun Oil Company, founded by his father, from a small firm to one of the nation's top fifty businesses. He initiated an employee stock purchase plan in 1926 and during the Depression refused to lay off workers. One of his last acts was to help solidify the Gordon-Conwell merger in South Hamilton, Massachusetts. He was adverse to providing endowments; institutions are more spiritual, he told me once, if they are kept on their knees before the Lord and answerable to their constituencies. He thought *Christianity Today* should not acquire its own headquarters but rent serviceable premises. His will divided a massive fortune estimated at $400 million between the J. Howard Pew Freedom Trust, Grove City College and the Christian Freedom Foundation. Glenmede Trust Company, the executor, was to continue previous donations and grants "as long as circumstances indicate and justify."

By the Spring of 1971 *Christianity Today*'s paid circulation had sagged below 100,000, although a drive for lay subscribers later in the year brought partial recovery to 130,000. My name was increasingly bandied about as contributing to the magazine's misfortunes. All my magazine contributions were now considered probationary. The Board voted on January 11, 1972, to review my relationship as editor-at-large after one year. During that year some Board members were encouraged to think that I was moderating my evangelical commitments and becoming liberal.

I had in fact been enlisted by Baker Book House to project and edit a major *Dictionary of Christian Ethics* scheduled for publication in 1973. I engaged 263 evangelicals worldwide to handle topics ranging from abortion and apartheid to terrorism and wealth. In the preface I noted that "Reinhold Niebuhr rightly complained that evangelists tend to overvalue conversion as having a millenium-producing potential" but I declared also that Niebuhr's "one-sided expectation of social justice mainly from public structures was no less a serious miscalculation."

My supposed rupture with evangelicals was held to be verified by Larry Dean Sharp's thesis completed at Vanderbilt University in June, 1972, titled *Carl Henry: Neo-Evangelical Theologian.* Sharp discerned that the recent evangelical breakthrough in America depended upon a tenuous coalition between evangelical theologians and evangelists; the peak had been reached and passed, he held, because this coalition was now faltering.

Christianity Today notified me that since I was no longer "a permanent employee for full or part time" I should promptly remove boxes marked "Dr. Henry's Files" (actually magazine-related correspondence and background materials of historical value). Harold Lindsell sent a page proof of the masthead of the October 13, 1972 issue with the note: "I know you will be interested in the changes herein noted." It listed me as one of twelve editors-at-large. "Heading the list," Lindsell said in his Editor's Note, "is Dr. Carl F. H. Henry, former editor of *Christianity Today,* first editor-at-large, and author of the 'Footnotes column.' " In 1978, just before Dr. Kenneth Kantzer became editor, Lindsell struck my name from the masthead completely. My name remained unlisted until April 19, 1985, when it mysteriously re-emerged, unknown to me, below that of Billy Graham as founder.

Through the addition of many new lay readers the magazine in 1972 recovered to about 150,000 paid subscribers. Of these, only 36 percent were full-time pastors; more than 57 percent were laymen. Only 42 percent said they bought books on theology; some 68 percent did not regularly read editorials. In three short years the once predominantly clergy readership had been inverted in favor of lay readers;

even so, one in eight declared the magazine "hard to understand" and there was a large turnover of new subscribers.

Christianity Today maneuvered to recover its dwindling readership among reflective scholars, clergy and students. After Nelson Bell's death in 1973, the magazine launched a major visiting lectureship program in his name under which it would subsidize salaries of evangelical scholars to teach on major nonevangelical seminary campuses. The steering committee, chaired by Lindsell, by then editor-publisher, included five other persons most of whom had never taught either on a secular campus or in an ecumenical seminary. The effort, which was to provide $25,000 plus transportation for invited evangelical scholars, died for lack of funding and for lack of campus interest.

The Institute for Advanced Christian Studies (IFACS) was first projected in September, 1966, at a Christian higher education consultation at Indiana University. By funding research and writing, IFACS aimed to enunciate the Christian world-view in order to contain the secular tide that engulfs contemporary culture. At the outset it had five directors, and like all directors since, all served without remuneration. Dr. John W. Snyder, vice president and dean for undergraduate development at Indiana University, was the first president; while still editor of *Christianity Today* my role was that of vice president; Gordon J. Van Wylen, dean of the College of Engineering at University of Michigan was secretary. The other directors were Martin Buerger, professor of crystallography at Massachusetts Institute of Technology, and Orville S. Walters, director of Student Health Services at University of Illinois. Charles Hatfield, of the department of mathematics in the University of Missouri at Rolla, was executive secretary. Actively participating was Dr. Ruth Eckert of the University of Minnesota who on her own had for some years promoted somewhat similar interests.

The Institute hoped to locate in a lively academic area. Several target cities within easy access of major university complexes offered possibilities for a research center where mature scholars might be subsidized for a year to complete major works in their disciplines. But funds lagged for such a venture.

In 1971 the Lilly Endowment offered IFACS a $75,000 matching grant to solidify its program of research grants for competent evangelical scholars. That October I chaired a major two-day Chicago conclave of IFACS scholars and supporters on the theme, "The Search for Reality in Modern Life." Participants attended from Canada and the United States. Evangelical conferees who brought papers or served as consultants came from Ivy League schools including Harvard and Yale and Big Ten and other universities. Key addresses were published by Inter-Varsity Press under the title, *Christianity and the Counter Culture: A Search for Reality.*

By that time IFACS president John Snyder, following an interim as president of Westmont College, had become executive vice chancellor at the University of California-Santa Barbara; I had been reelected IFACS vice president, and was lecturer-at-large at Eastern; Orville Walters was secretary-treasurer. Other directors were V. Elving Anderson, professor of genetics at University of Minnesota, and Professors Buerger, Hatfield and Van Wylen. All of us probed available properties and funding prospects to meet the yearend deadline for the matching grant. Helga and I wrote hundreds of letters inviting a bit of extra tithe-money for the cause. By the end of 1971 we had raised $45,500 of the needed $75,000 and in a final offer the Lilly Foundation generously extended its deadline to March 31, 1972. The grant was finally totally matched only through a last-minute $10,000 assist from the educational arm of the Billy Graham Evangelistic Foundation.

In 1972 Charles Hatfield chaired an invitational scholars conference on "The Scientist and Ethical Decision" at the University of Michigan with papers and discussion by a dozen participating university scholars. Then president of the IFACS directors, I was asked to give the closing luncheon address on "The New Image of Man." Hatfield was vice president; C. Everett Koop, professor of pediatric surgery at University of Pennsylvania and editor of the *Journal of Pediatric Surgery* became a new director. IFACS's directive leadership consequently represented the fields of theology, history, psychiatry, pediatric surgery, genetics, crystallography, mathematics and engineering, and hoped to enlist still other directors from the humanities and from the sciences. United Press released nationally a news feature on my hopes for IFACS; *Washington Evening Star* in turn gave it a five-column headline on February 5, 1972. On August 5, 1972, United Press carried a second nationwide feature on IFACS. That same day the *Palm Beach Post-Times* gave it a six-column headline, and in its September 8 issue the Washington *Star-News* gave it a five-column headline.

But IFACS had begun implementing its mission even before receiving the 1971 Lilly matching grant. In its first four years it had assisted ten Christian scholars doing research on subjects related to evangelical faith. It had also gathered representatives of ten evangelical colleges to form an alliance that became a major factor in the emergence of the Christian College Consortium.

In 1972 IFACS directors approved two significant applications. A $10,000 grant was awarded Dr. Stephen V. Monsma, professor of political science at Calvin College, for a project that led in 1974 to publication of his book, *The Unraveling of America.* The other grant, of $14,000, went to Dr. Robert W. Lyon of Asbury Theological Seminary to complete a still-awaited work on the historical consciousness and concern of the Synoptic writers to underscore Christianity as a historically founded faith.

IFACS coordinated its semiannual Board meetings with panel discussions in major evangelical churches that gave visibility to its program. In Philadelphia several hundred persons, including many students, turned out in 1972 in blizzard conditions to hear a panel on "Christianity and Scientific Concerns." The following February a panel at Fourth Presbyterian Church of Bethesda, Maryland, discussed "Christianity and the Modern Mind." In the Fall of 1973 the Third Baptist Church of St. Louis hosted a panel on "Jesus Christ and the Modern World." In the Fall of 1974 a panel on "American Conscience in the Post-Watergate Era" convened in First Covenant Church of Minneapolis. The panel at Park Street Church, Boston, in early 1975, concerned "Suffering as a Human Problem."

Directors made a $1,500 grant in 1974 to its first Latin American recipient, Professor J. Andrew Kirk of Buenos Aires, to assist completion of his appraisal of the theology of revolution. That Fall IFACS elected Dr. Orville Walters as its third president. Dr. Ronald Nash, head of philosophy and religion at Western Kentucky University, became a director, as did Dr. John Scanzoni, then professor of sociology at Indiana University. A grant of $10,000 went to Dr. Samuel H. Moffett, church historian and veteran missionary in Korea, to shape a multivolume work on the history of Christianity in Asia.

When Dr. Walters died in February, 1975, Dr. Charles Hatfield succeeded him as IFACS president. That Spring Dr. Ruth Eckert (wife of Dr. John Hess McComb), recently retired Regents professor of higher education at the University of Minnesota, became the organization's first woman director, and Dr. John Snyder, by then executive vice president and provost of Kent State University, began a second four-year term as director. That year in July IFACS was one of nine academic groups that sponsored a conference of 150 scholars on "Human Engineering and the Future of Man."

Scholars applying for and receiving grants in 1976 included Dr. Nicholas Wolterstorff and Dr. Ronald Sider. Wolterstorff, professor of philosophy at Calvin College, received $9,000 to complete a work on the Christian philosophy of art, published in 1980 under the title, *Art in Action, Towards a Christian Aesthetic.* Sider, dean of Messiah College and later professor of theology at Eastern Baptist Theological Seminary, received $13,000 for a projected work—still uncompleted—on current historical methodology and the resurrection of Jesus.

IFACS bylaws precluded reelection of a director without at least a year's interim. To fill vacancies left by Professors Buerger and Hatfield, Dr. Arthur F. Holmes, chairman of the philosophy department at Wheaton College, was elected a director for the first time.

June, 1977, marked the Institute's tenth year. By that time it had awarded more than $80,000 to scholars proposing projects that relate the Christian faith to modern thought and life. Grant recipients through the years came, among other places, from Calvin, Greenville, Hagazian (Lebanon), Messiah and Wheaton Colleges, from Bethel Theological Seminary, University of Guelph, University of Illinois, Westminster Theological Seminary, Colorado State University and Indiana University. A survey by Ruth Eckert McComb showed that IFACS had funded 24 of 57 applications with grants ranging from $5,000 to $22,000, the median being $6,000. (The easiest refusal was a request for a one-year grant of $71,102.) IFACS assistance had wholly or partly funded ten volumes (completed or in process) and numerous significant articles. The Institute had also funded seven conferences and partially sponsored two others and had conducted panel discussions in many parts of the nation.

In all Lilly Endowment made four generous grants totaling $235,000; $188,110 was committed for scholar support, $36,045 for launching the Christian college consortium; and $26,454 for major conferences. Through the years a consistent supporter of the work has been Ken Olsen of Digital.

Overlapping this period was growing interest in what became known as Key '73, a movement first explored in a 1967 *Christianity Today* editorial that called for a united national evangelistic thrust. Despite America's far larger church attendance than in Europe, half of the U.S. population remained nonetheless outside the churches and synagogues; on any given Sunday only half the church members attended any service. Early in 1967 I had suggested that *Christianity Today* colleague Gene Kucharsky rough draft an editorial—along the lines of "somehow let's get together"—to prod evangelicals to simultaneous cooperation in a national outreach. Since mainly clergy and church leaders comprised our 180,000 paid subscribers, we foresaw their enlistment for clearly defined evangelistic objectives in their home communities. When the editorial appeared, it stimulated more response than any editorial in the magazine's entire history. More than 100 denominations subsequently committed themselves to the effort. *The New York Times* glimpsed implementation in terms of "the biggest evangelistic campaign ever undertaken ecumenically in the United States." An organizing committee named Dr. Theodore A. Raedeke of the Lutheran Church (Missouri Synod) executive director.

My eventual detachment from *Christianity Today* left the magazine more or less on its own to champion the effort which it had called into being. I nonetheless shared in related conferences at Eastern Baptist Seminary and elsewhere, and contributed supportive essays to *Eternity* and other publications. *Christianity Today* gave news coverage and some editorial bolstering. But it lacked the needed leadership, personal inspiration and coordinating direction for effective launching.

Key '73 achieved certain commendable goals; it was hindered, however, by the refusal of independent fundamentalist churches to cooperate in a witness to Jesus Christ that involved also ecumenically affiliated churches. A further deterrent came through ecumenically aligned spokesmen who under bureaucratic pressures sought to make social justice rather than personal evangelism the forefront thrust. American Jewish spokesmen assailed Key '73 as "anti-Semitic" because of its Christian intention to confront every American with the claims of the gospel of Christ. Any effort that embraced evangelization of Jewry was interpreted as a covert attempt to erase Jewish culture and identity; some Jews even likened a comprehensive Key '73 thrust to Auschwitz and Buchenwald. Secular religion editors generously publicized such frenzied assessments. After condemnatory statements had done their damage Rabbi Mark Tannenbaum acknowledged that Key '73 was not anti-Semitic after all.

Some churches—both fundamentalist and liberal—considered Key '73 a failure; its achievements were nonetheless worthwhile. In many communities Key '73 motivated Christians simultaneously if not cooperatively to creative ways of bearing a common witness. It roused interest in what other churches in other cities were doing. In these respects Key '73 paved the way for the American Festival of Evangelism, held in Kansas City in 1981; some spokesmen emphasize that the latter would not have eventuated without it. Had *Christianity Today* maintained personal liaison with key pastors and devoted a staff member full-time to related contacts and correspondence, as it had done for the 1966 Berlin Congress, the results might have been different. The venture could in fact have been channeled by way of followup into an annual event in which local churches focused on both the continuing evangelistic task and on glaring social injustices to be christianly confronted. In a panel of the Society for the Scientific Study of Religion that met in Washington, D.C., in October, 1974, I assessed the effort's potential and problems.

Early in Spring, 1973, we had returned to Israel for a World Bible Conference before I addressed the twenty-fifth Pasadena Rose Bowl Easter Sunrise Service. We continued to Australia and New Zealand for a three-week lecture tour in Sydney, Canberra, Adelaide, Melbourne, Perth, Christchurch and Auckland. American lectures that year included the Free Methodist Medical Fellowship, Ball State and Valparaiso universities, Pacific Union, Olivet Nazarene and Sioux Falls colleges, and the baccalaureate message at Houghton College which conferred the honorary doctor of humanities. Most important of my lectures was probably at Wright State University, on the tenth anniversary of the Schempp decision whereby on June 17, 1963, the Supreme Court struck down Bible reading and recitation of the Lord's prayer in public schools. I followed former Supreme Court Justice Tom Clark, who wrote the Schempp decision, in a major address. Since we happened to be on the same flight, he invited me to sit with him so we could chat. Although he attended National Presbyterian Church, he deplored "religionists" who saw church-state issues mainly in a negative light. He criticized Billy Graham, who when the Schempp decision was released was in Canada and—without having opportunity to read it, Clark contended—was quoted by the media as calling it "a victory for atheism." In my address I agreed neither with Graham nor with Clark on the decision's implications, but gave a long Footnotes series to it in *Christianity Today.*

During the summer of 1973 I spent five weeks in eight countries of Latin America, giving lectures sponsored by the Latin American Theological Fraternity. Evangelical Protestants there were being tug-of-warred by the charismatic movement on one hand, and on the other by social concerns already tinged by the emerging liberation theology. Protestant vitality had largely passed to Pentecostals who emphasized a working class lay witness more than professionally oriented clerical religion. But the emphasis on miraculous gifts, that stressed tongues-speaking and promoted a contemporary recovery of all apostolic powers, made it vulnerable. Other evangelicals felt that a vigorous challenge must be posed to the haunting poverty and social injustices in lands predominantly Roman Catholic but in which Protestant missionaries had also labored for a century. Evangelicals rejected the theology of revolution, which relied on violence for social change; most were hesitant to accept violence even as a last resort. They were reluctant, moreover, to champion a Marxist hermeneutic that read the Scriptures through the lens of socio-economic class struggle. But Orlando Costas, who joined the staff of Latin America Mission from a politically active ministry in the United States, promoted a bifocal approach to the Bible that seemed to elevate socio-economic interpretation to co-primacy with the normativity of Scripture. My mention of this in a Religious News Service report carried by many newspapers provoked Latin America Seminary faculty to adopt and publicize a self-serving resolution that did not clearly focus the issues. I ignored it, however, since the Mission had had a long and commendable record of evangelical social involvement on the edge of a virile evangelistic witness.

In country after country the proliferation of meetings led to an arduous and demanding lecture program. Even before I left home commitments made in my behalf by local committees had grown to more than sixty lectures in forty-five days, often to sometimes quite remote points. On my last day in Buenos Aires I spoke three times in different parts of the city and after evening dialogue with members of the New Testament Society I finally in a chilling rainstorm reached my lodgings in a taxi that lost its way.

The next day I arrived in Sao Paulo, Brazil, with a deep chest cold and laryngitis that required bed rest on penicillin. The one church service that I had to forego was the only engagement I have ever missed for health reasons. My former student Russell Shedd stood in for me but because he insisted on delivering my sermon, I had to preach it to him privately.

A few days later in Recife, where I addressed a joint meeting of university students, I learned from a Southern Presbyterian missionary, who had heard the news on a ham radio set, that Nelson Bell had died on August 2 at the age of 79. The cable sent by *Christianity Today,* asking for comments, was either missent or misdelivered; what I immediately volunteered by airmail from Recife apparently arrived too late to be used. The previous year, in June, 1972, Bell had become moderator of the Presbyterian Church in the U.S., with a membership of almost a million persons mainly in the South. His election came less than a year after he had repudiated the *Presbyterian Journal,* of which he had long been a director and associate editor. The move came, in part, because that magazine's board urged the conservative formation of a new denomination together with compatible church groups. Bell thought it unwise for conservatives to divide over the proposed future merger of the northern and southern churches; rather they should exert their influence from within the merged body. In the years after I left *Christianity Today* I seldom if ever heard from Bell. But in the months before his death, when he was in Washington for a periodic visit to the magazine, he phoned me late one afternoon and asked if Helga and I would that very evening be his dinner guests. It was too late to rearrange our plans; a social engagement would not in any event have been the best context in which to discuss long-standing concerns.

Other lectures were given in 1973 for the Theological Students Fellowship at Southwestern Baptist Theological Seminary, including chapel. Faculty on Southern Baptist campuses were increasingly questioning the complete reliability of the Bible. I was among those asked to contribute to the Spring, 1974, issue of *Review and Expositor* that Dr. Wayne Ward, a devout evangelical at Southern Baptist Theological Seminary had set aside on "Biblical Inspiration and Interpretation." Contrary to a growing tendency to say that all theology is manmade or that Baptists have no normative theology, Bernard Ramm stressed that the possibility of authentic theology lies in a conceptual element in divine revelation. My essay on Scripture interpretation ("Are We Doomed to Hermeneutical Nihilism?") later appeared in the fourth volume of *God, Revelation and Authority. Review and Expositor* carried a response by Morris Ashcroft, to which I in turn replied. The closing essays featured Eric Rust on the Bible and science; Harold Lindsell was respondent, and Rust brought a final rejoiner. It was later that year, or early in 1974, that Lindsell mentioned in our home that a book by him on biblical inerrancy was underway. It would be a bombshell, he said, showing ecumenical seminaries' confusion in the matter, and portending the same dilemma for mediating evangelical schools. Zondervan in time published *The Battle for the Bible.*

Late in November, 1973, some fifty evangelical leaders met in Chicago to discuss the need for unhesitating social involvement. Ronald Sider and a number of younger evangelicals staged the Thanksgiving holiday event to address Christian lifestyle concerns and to warn against misplaced national trust in economic and military power. While selective invitation and a prearranged agenda made room for diversity, it virtually assured an outcome serviceable to the merging social activist mood and critical of the evangelical establishment. For all that, it seemed better to attend and to strive for a balanced position than to simply accommodate a one-sided outcome.

While Christian indifference was blamed for many world problems, participants agreed that "radical reformation of the political structure must await God's doing" and they ruled out revolutionary violence as the preferred means of changing social structures. Left in midair, however, was the nature of ideal political reformation. The final draft of the Chicago Statement, labeled "a declaration of evangelical social concern," called for a bold attack on "maldistribution of the nation's wealth and services" but remained silent about Marxism's inability to produce wealth. Many participants were less than happy with some of the wording, but for different reasons: some felt it did not go far enough, others that in some respects it overstated or misstated a sound evangelical view. In any case, the Chicago Statement became the manifesto of Evangelicals for Social Action, which Sider for over a decade with only qualified success tried to propel into a significant social force.

In the April 26, 1974, issue of *Christianity Today* I contributed the lead essay, "Revolt on Evangelical Frontiers," a critically constructive appraisal of Richard Quebedeaux's book, *The Young Evangelicals.* Instead of giving editorial support, the magazine ran a pejorative letter from Jim Wallis of *Post-American* ascribing to me "a rather paranoid and unbalanced view of socialism" and affirming that I was uncritically devoted to "the present American economic and political system." My response to the editor was never acknowledged. Neither the National Association of Evangelicals nor *Christianity Today* nor the Graham crusades mounted any kind of a major thrust for national righteousness and social change. When Moral Majority emerged, it did so as something less than a specifically evangelical movement and skirted many concerns voiced by the Chicago Statement.

The Lausanne/1974 International Congress on World Evangelization was projected by Billy Graham in December, 1971, at White Sulphur Springs, West Virginia, during a meeting with 16 international champions of evangelism. Leighton Ford proposed a tenative program and Bishop Jack Dain of Australia served as chairman of the central steering committee. Graham was named honorary chairman and Ford, program committee chairman. I was asked to present the opening paper to one of the 50 panel groups and to chair the subsection on "evangelism and personal and social ethics." Lausanne gathered 2700 participants from more than 105 nations, and its plenary proceedings were translated into six languages. Stan Mooneyham of World Vision arranged and coordinated many of the dramatic and graphic visual features.

In *The Battle for World Evangelism* (Tyndale House, 1978) Arthur Johnston writes that Lausanne/1974 carried forward the Berlin/1966 emphasis on personal evangelism but focused more fully on the church as a cross-cultural community, and stressed the gospel's this-worldly utilitarian values more than man's destiny in eternity. It meshed evangelism into the current ecumenical controversies over the visible church as its authorizing instrument and appropriated the concept of mission and "holistic witness" that held together proclamation and service.

John Stott emphasized that social action is as integral to fulfilling the Great Commission as is evangelism; evangelism in the popular sense does not of itself fulfill the intention of the Great Commission. Stott and other plenary speakers insistently rejected violence as a catalyst of social change. The insistent demand by Third World speakers that the Church be in the forefront of socio-economic change left unsure, however, whether the prospect of present political liberation is an integral facet of the gospel. Nor did they clarify how the life and example of Jesus actually rather than symbolically undergirds such a view. Discordant notes were struck. Veteran champion of church growth, Donald McGavran, stressed the primacy of evangelism in terms of personal regeneration, whereas champions of "radical discipleship" like Samuel Escobar and René Padilla underscored repentance from social sins and the need to call for a changed socio-political order.

Differences at Lausanne/1974 that remained open-ended in the main sessions came into sharper focus in the subsection on Christian social concern where discussion built on my assigned paper on "Christian Personal and Social Ethics in Relation to Racism, Poverty, War and Other Problems" (cf. *Let the Earth Hear His Voice,* J. D. Douglas, ed., Worldwide Publications, 1975). Participants from more than twenty countries crowded out the sessions, many wishing that plenary illumination had been given to disputed issues.

Lausanne had many moving aspects and mirrored the evident evangelical momentum in many parts of the world, much of which I had already observed in my travels. Platform presentations seemed more panoramic than integrative of doctrinal, evangelistic and cultural concerns. Sponsors increasingly looked to a concluding Covenant to supply climactic cohesion. I was quietly asked if I would serve on an editorial redaction committee but felt too unfamiliar with Congress goals to serve.

Despite the contrary thrust of some plenary papers, the congress Covenant affirmed that "in the church's mission of sacrificial service, evangelism is primary." John Stott nonetheless interpreted the Covenant as championing an equal partnership of social action and evangelism (*The Lausanne Covenant,* pp. 30 f.). Lausanne doubtless linked evangelism and social concern more tightly than did Berlin. But Arthur Johnston concludes that the theology of Lausanne needs clarification and buttressing in numerous respects. Consequently the gathering postponed rather than resolved the conflicts and ambiguities in contemporary evangelicalism over the Church's socio-political involvement; ten years after Lausanne American evangelicals were still trying to resolve evangelism/social action issues. Moreover, the Covenant reflected a bias toward the visible institutional Church as the center of God's world purpose more than the spiritual body of regenerate believers. Its statement on Scripture (as without error "in all that it affirms"), moreover, was susceptible to conflicting interpretations. In the Lausanne emphases ecumenically oriented Protestants found an openness to enlarging cooperation that could very well weaken independent forces whose input had helped make Lausanne possible.

Five years after Key '73, and in the aftermath of the 1974 Lausanne conference, over 100 American church leaders decided in March, 1978, that Americans needed another major congress on evangelism. Despite the fact that the growing churches were conservative theologically, four out of five American congregations were not growing; evangelical leaders estimated, moreover, the number of unchurched Americans at 156 million. Dr. Thomas Zimmerman, member of the Lausanne continuation committee, was elected chairman of the projected American Festival on Evangelism. Paul Benjamin, head of the National Church Growth Research Center which was a byproduct of Key '73, was named executive director. The U.S. Congress on Evangelism twelve years earlier had been an invitation-only affair; the July 27–30, 1981, Festival in Kansas City did not restrict attendance. And it differed from Key '73 in being a national meeting.

Benjamin asked me to lead one of the 200 workshops on evangelism on a topic of my preference. With his consent I devoted my section to evangelism and public affairs, since the gospel's social impact seemed to be ignored or sidelined, rather than faced with precision. My section on "evangelism in public affairs" (as the program revised the topic) met in a hotel room a block away from the convention hall and drew about 50 persons. Out of the 200 workshops, three were devoted to the theology of evangelism. The Festival illuminated the alliance of theology and evangelism less than did Berlin/1966 and the alliance of evangelism and social action less than did Lausanne/1974. Since evangelism per se was the banner, the effort attracted not only evangelical Catholics but also partisans of traditional papal Catholicism. The participating 150 Protestant denominations and organizations ranged from high church Episcopalians and other mainline bodies to charismatics and establishment conservatives, and did little to clarify the identity of evangelicalism. Billy Graham flew in for the closing service attended by 11,000 persons. Speaking on "God Calls Us to Obedience," he asked each participant to win ten persons to Christ during the year ahead and to take an active role in establishing a new congregation in the next two years. The three-day Festival, which cost over $1 million, was attended cumulatively by 14,000 persons. It succeeded only partially in its announced aim of impacting on 225,000 congregations, although attendees were familiarized with the programs of 36 "parable churches" which for ten years had shown an annual growth of 10 percent in membership. The Festival provided notebooks or tapes containing workshop papers and granted permission to reproduce these for local church purposes; overprinting left the National Church Growth Research Center with a substantial debt in which other participants were reluctant to share. To what extent the Festival resulted in the planting of thousands of new churches is problematical. Many observers considered the expectation of 100,000 new churches in America by 1999 more millenially than realistically optimistic.

18

At Large with World Vision

The decision to become lecturer-at-large for World Vision International in a global ministry beginning in March, 1974, was announced in November, 1973, after six terms of teaching at Eastern. The appointment left me free as I wished to teach or lecture on any campus and to complete my writing. I was expected without added compensation to teach up to three months annually on foreign campuses.

The invitation had been extended for several years by World Vision president Stan Mooneyham, with whom I had worked closely during the 1966 Berlin Congress. Before that Mooneyham held a leadership role with National Association of Evangelicals and was editor of *United Evangelical Action.* He had organized numerous international conferences, was dean of the Graham crusades' School of Evangelism, and had been offered directorship of the international offices and vice presidency of one facet of B.G.E.A. International. Instead he opted for the presidency of World Vision beginning July 1, 1969, and under his direction it became the largest private voluntary relief organization in the world.

Mooneyham spoke frequently of the need of theological reinforcement on foreign fields. Evangelical schools that brought to America promising young scholars from Asia and Africa were unwittingly abetting the "brain drain" in other lands, since instead of returning home many of the brightest young people remained in the West. Foreign churches were thus routinely deprived of some of their ablest future leaders. Mooneyham saw the need of transporting evangelical scholars abroad for short-term lectures and courses benefiting students in their own cultural contexts.

The years in America after my return from Cambridge in September, 1969, gave me reason to question the depth and stability of the stateside evangelical resurgence. Still, the possibility remained, I felt, for a remarkable evangelical coalescence of theological learning, evangelism and social justice, one that could register decisively on American culture. After the initial year at Eastern, my involvements seemed as many-legged as a centipede: I spent a term annually teaching at Eastern, a term at Trinity in Illinois and the rest of my time in research and writing, interrupted by occasional lectures here and there that carried my convictions to classrooms and clergy. For Baker's *Dictionary of Christian Ethics,* which appeared in 1973, I had enlisted 263 world contributors from every continent, although it was apparent from numerous essays that important evangelical gains remained to be made in this sphere. Above all else I was concentrating energies on the massive work, *God, Revelation and Authority.* The main deterrent was lack of competent and sustained secretarial help, a liability that plagued me year after year.

When I turned 60 on January 22, 1973, Stan Mooneyham reiterated World Vision's offer of a world classroom while assuring time also for research and completion of my theological writing. International invitations multiplied after the religion editor of United Press International called me "probably the most noted evangelical theologian in the United States." World Vision's projected lectures abroad would accommodate teaching on American campuses also and preserve time to complete my volumes; moreover, I would be exempt from promotional-funding involvements. World Vision would make known my availability; I would be free to determine which engagements to accept, to apportion time as I preferred between writing and speaking. My lecture ministry was for students and teachers, rather than the more general pastors' conferences, although I would preach when and where I wished. World Vision would cover travel costs abroad and pay a modest stipend, but without retirement benefits or full-time secretarial help. In 1978, when I turned 65, World Vision carried me forward as a consultant on reduced reimbursement, but with essentially the same opportunities. Ted Engstrom, as president of the domestic arm of World Vision, was enthusiastically supportive of such a relationship.

World Vision was born at midcentury after Bob Pierce's compassionate visits to China and Korea. For twenty-five years before my official association as lecturer-at-large I had periodically served the effort in pastors' conferences with Pierce and others in many parts of the world. My first related team ministry in Asia came during my early Fuller years. After that I shared across the years in other pastors' conferences, sometimes several times in the same country, in Burma, Hong Kong, India, Malaysia, the Philippines, Singapore, Sri Lanka, Thailand and in Colombia and Latin America. On the edge of such ministries came frequent invitations to address seminary or university students. Already in 1952 Winona Lake School of Theology's "flying seminar" to Europe and the Middle East involved me in lectures in Greece and Switzerland, and later that school engaged me for a term of teaching in the Japan School of Theology summer session at Karuizawa. In early *Christianity Today* years the term spent at New College shaped lecture opportunities in Scotland. My 1963 sabbatical meant lectures on the Iberian Peninsula, in several African countries, then in Lebanon and in Italy and finally in England.

Billy Graham's invitation to address clergy on the edge of his European ministry provided a platform in numerous German and Swiss cities. The bid to come as visiting lecturer for the Latin American Evangelical Theological Fraternity involved addresses in ten countries. The 1969–70 Cambridge sabbatical provided numerous lecture opportunities in England and some in Wales. The 1970 Eastern European conference on evangelism opened other doors. When the Asian Center for Theological Studies and Mission was opened in Seoul I declined an invitation to serve as dean, in part because of the severe Korean winters, but came as the first visiting lecturer from abroad. By 1975 I had already taught, lectured or preached in more than thirty-five countries; some of my writing had been or was being translated into Italian, Japanese, Korean, Mandarin and Portuguese.

These teaching forays were not without some emotional as well as physical strain. The three-week Karuizawa stint was specially memorable. When I arrived in Tokyo by air nobody met me. Hour after hour I sat with my luggage while the loudspeaker periodically blared out: "Will the party meeting Dr. Henry from Washington please go to the waiting room?" Several hours had passed when Dr. Clyde Taylor, director of public affairs for the N.A.E.'s Washington office, unexpectedly came along; he was returning from India to the States with an overnight stop in Tokyo, and heard the announcement. Clyde had the Y.M.C.A. phone number and we repaired there for the night. My driver, it developed, had been given the wrong arrival date and met the previous day's flight. My first night in Karuizawa I was kept awake by the taunting of cuckoo birds; when I finally did get to sleep an earthquake from an active volcano in nearby Mount Asama soon jarred me awake.

The first World Vision lecture trip took us to Asia in 1974 for three months from mid-April to mid-July. I had determined that, whenever abroad for six weeks or more, Helga would go along at my expense. She served additionally in teaching or lecturing in Christian education, drilling students in English composition, speaking to women's groups and encouraging and counseling missionary wives and children. We hopscotched twelve airlines on a course that stretched from the States to Seoul, Taipei, Hong Kong, Bangkok, Singapore, Sri Lanka, India, Iran, Turkey and Greece, with a brief respite in Zürich and Salzburg before the Lausanne Congress on World Evangelization. Along the way my lectures and sermons had been translated into Farsi, Greek, Korean, Mandarin, Tamil and Turkish. While I was at Lausanne, Helga flew to Scotland for ten days; for the New York and Washington trip homeward our flights converged in London.

In Seoul, I taught two and a half weeks at the Asian Center for Graduate Theological Studies (later named ACTS), spoke at Asia's two largest seminaries (Presbyterian Theological Seminary and Seoul Theological Seminary) and at the Campus Crusade Center which was readying for Explo '74. I preached at four Sunday services (beginning at 6:30 A.M.) in the world's largest Presbyterian church, Yung Nak, which thirty years earlier had been founded by twenty-five beleagured refugees from communist North Korea. We paid a visit to the DMZ driving in a caravan led by the Sixth Army base commandant, Colonel King Coffman, whose car bore the emblem "Wise Men Still Seek Him," and who had been on the staff of Gen. William K. Harrison who signed the U.N. peace treaty with North Korea.

In Taipei I addressed meetings at China Evangelical Seminary and also spoke at Christ College, where the "little woman" Gladys Aylward lies buried. In both Hong Kong and Bangkok I addressed Evangelical Missions Fellowship gatherings. In Singapore I taught for five weeks at Evangelism International, where John Haggai had gathered forty-one students from ten countries for a program aimed at effective communication and practical ministry as much as at cognitive orientation. In Singapore, where Christianity had enlisted many professional leaders, businessmen and university students, I addressed over two hundred university graduates and faculty invited by Inter-Varsity leaders.

Scheduled next in Sri Lanka, I addressed four gatherings in Colombo and Kandy. We visited tea, coconut and rubber plantations, and also the gem factories for which Ceylon was already famous in earlier centuries. From there we flew to Bombay. The Indian driver's furious speed from the airport to our lodgings bounced my luggage off the top of his taxi. We regained our composure at the Church Missionary Society compound among mahogany trees planted by David Livingston, and were glad my lecture notes had survived intact.

Arriving in Iran in 110° weather, I addressed a large evening reception by the evangelical community (Persians, Armenians, Germans, French, Christian Jews and Americans). It was arranged by J. Christy Wilson and his wife, Betty, everywhere held in esteem.

Next came our first and only visit to Turkey. Religious liberty restrictions diluted our stopover mainly to a time of respite. We visited Istanbul's famed Topkapi Museum, the Blue Mosque, Roman aqueducts, the bazaar and other spectacular sights. By ferry we traveled to Heybeli Island in the Sea of Marmora to spend a few days with the parents of Tom Cosmades, European-based TEAM missionary. After a ferry trip by way of the Bosphorus to the Black Sea, where we saw Russian military vessels nearby, we returned for my one preaching engagement in Turkey, a small gathering of courageous believers who met in the security of the Swedish consulate.

From Istanbul we flew to Athens, where my mid-week message was translated into modern Greek. With an overnight stop in Switzerland, we then flew to charming Salzburg to recoup energies before I was to present a sectional paper at the Lausanne Congress.

I was aware that the influx of Western scientism, materialism and permissive lifestyles into the great urban centers of Asia was of ever-increasing concern to the inherited religions of the Orient. Lectures to Asian students provided an opportunity to test in the fiery furnace of broad academic relevance the challenge of *God, Revelation and Authority* to encroaching naturalism with its besetting inability to identify fixed truth and values. My own perspective, moreover, contrary to the tenets of Buddhism, Confucianism and Hinduism, was that of biblical theism which affirmed intelligible supernatural revelation. Whether the masses lived under the shadow of communist naturalism or of Free World humanism, these themes had international relevance.

Returning to the States I lectured at Albion College, Western Kentucky University and Mid-America Baptist Seminary, and shared in meetings of the American Theological Society, Society for the Scientific Study of Religion and Canadian Evangelical Theological Society. From September to mid-December, I worked in a lecture at University of Delaware after teaching at Trinity Evangelical Divinity School, where students from leading secular universities outnumbered those from evangelical colleges.

My 1975 itinerary took me abroad for almost ten weeks and 27,000 air miles of travel on eleven different lines flying westward around the globe for a lecture ministry in ten countries. This marked Helga's and my fourth consecutive Summer in Asia. We flew from Washington to Los Angeles to Auckland, New Zealand, where on arrival on April 17 I addressed the Evangelical Union at Auckland University. From there I hurried to the Bible College of New Zealand for a lecture.

Following the next day's address to the Christchurch Theological Society, I participated in a panel at the Asian Theological Association before continuing to Sydney, Australia.

My first Sydney engagement was the sermon for the annual university service in St. Andrew's Cathedral. The Anglican archbishop (The Most Rev. Marcus Loane), bishops, university chancellors and faculty, and the lieutenant-governor of New South Wales all had specific roles in the centuries-old traditional service. As we filed out of the service in colorful academic regalia, ushers who on entry had taken our academic caps in orderly sequence now returned them for donning outside. But there was a mixup; the dignified lieutenant-governor (the Hon. L. W. Street) got my mortarboard and I got his ceremonial busby-like headgear. We made an unobtrusive exchange, but I fear he saw less humor in the transfer than did I.

On Tuesday night, April 22, I gave the annual lecture at Baptist College of New South Wales. Wednesday I lectured twice and dialogued on evangelism and social concern at a conference of Anglican clergy of the Sydney diocese where Bishop Jack Dain presided. Our meeting was in cold and clammy church parlors, where I was more concerned with sheer survival than with a constructive response from clerics advantaged by woolen underwear. Before leaving Sydney I spoke also in Moore Theological College, an Anglican seminary known to me from college days through Principal T. C. Hammond's book *Perfect Freedom.*

At Melbourne I lectured Saturday afternoon and evening at the annual Toorak Convention of the Anglican Evangelical Fellowship of Victoria, and preached the following day, the day of Saigon's surrender, in city churches. By Tuesday we had flown to Adelaide, a city which when viewed from hilltops looks on a clear night like a 150-square-mile triplex opal. I lectured also in Australia Bible Institute at Victor Harbor.

On May 1 we continued to Perth, West Australia, where I gave the annual lecture sponsored by the Association of Evangelical Students and presided over by Professor D. Gareth-Jones at the University of Perth. We lodged with Principal and Mrs. Noel Vose of the Baptist Theological College of New South Wales, where the following day I addressed a Saturday theological conference. A subsequent buffet sponsored by the Evangelical Alliance gathered eighty leaders from university, religious and civil life and brought to a close our first three weeks away from home. In eighteen days in Australasia I had kept thirty-five different speaking engagements and lecture commitments, including a thirty-minute interview on national radio.

Tuesday we flew to Indonesia, where steaming 95° weather replaced

Perth's 45° reading, for what was to be simply an overnight rest stop in Jakarta. But an Indonesian serving with the World Bank unexpectedly met us at the airport. An orchid bouquet at Christian guest house lodgings carried an invitation to gather with nationals that night to discuss Campus Crusade work. Since we had reservations on an early morning flight, we asked the house boy to wake us at 5 A.M. He wakened us, indeed, but at 4, asking whether it was 4 or 5 that we wished to be called!

Hong Kong was our next stop. There, on crowded Nathan Road, we happened unexpectedly into Bob Pierce who had barely made it out of Saigon and was en route to Bangladesh with relief supplies. My two days of three-hour lecture and discussion periods—including Mandarin translation for those who spoke no English—drew capacity attendance. On Friday, May 9, I addressed another of a series of Asian Theological Association sessions that had begun in New Zealand and would include additional regional meetings also in Seoul, Colombo and Bombay.

Next day we flew to Seoul. Beginning May 12, I taught a three-week lecture course at Asian Center for Theological Studies and Mission (ACTS), which in its second year was growing vigorously. I also gave four public lectures and spoke to 400 students at Seoul Theological Seminary. During this Korean stint, I met happily and unexpectedly at the home of Sam and Eileen Moffett with Wheaton classmate Ken Taylor, who was in Seoul arranging a Living Bible translation. Stan Mooneyham was also present; he had come to Korea for a pastors' conference and reception by church and government leaders. Once again I spoke to all four services of the Yung Nak church and a week later preached to 1,500 persons in the so-called "millionaires' church."

At Christian Women's Club a scheduled speaker failed to materialize and Helga addressed 150 persons on short notice. A fun night was the celebration on May 30 of her Whang Nap (sixtieth birthday). She was first honored at a surprise birthday dinner, presented with a custom-made silk chongiri gown, then applauded by friends in traditional Korean dress who, one by one, solemnly knelt before her, bowing from head to floor as a mark of special respect to this newly aged, presumably retired, lady. To remind me of my friends in Korea I was presented, before we left Seoul, with a Buddhist scholar's desk, twelve inches high, requiring that one work at it while seated cross-legged on the floor.

We flew next to Colombo, Sri Lanka, stopping en route in Thailand. On Sunday, June 8, I preached in Bangkok churches, and had four major meetings in two days. Many missionaries were in transit from

Vietnam and had to renegotiate a Christian vocational calling now that Saigon had fallen under communist control.

On June 9 we flew to Colombo, where the following day I lectured and dialogued at a meeting of the Evangelical Alliance of Sri Lanka, and later addressed the Asian Theological Association. Six meetings in three days included a three-day conference for 150 Christian workers arranged by Celestine Fernando of the Bible Society. With little opportunity for rest I sometimes felt like the elephants we had seen in Sri Lanka lugging heavy logs. As we left Colombo we waved farewell to men in sarongs, women in saris and children often in nothing. We hoped that we had reinforced the evangelical witness.

On Thursday, June 12, we arrived in Bombay and lodged with the family of Scottish missionary Charles Wigglesworth. There I addressed another Asian Theological Society meeting attended by a goodly number of university-age Indian Christians.

We left Bombay airport, etched on my memory as one of the world's worst, on Friday night, and we arrived in Teheran at midnight. The next day we flew on to Shiraz, where I preached in St. Simon's Church, and on Monday addressed the Shiraz Christian Workers, a group encouraged by the Rev. Ron Axtell and by Glenn Deckert, active in university teaching as a tentmaking ministry. Petrol was thirty cents a gallon and shared taxi fares began at six cents. A most rewarding memory was the trip to ancient Persepolis that brought to life the times of Cyrus the Great. From Shiraz we flew to Isfahan where, on Wednesday night, I was to speak at a special service arranged by Bishop H. B. Dehqani-Tafti, convert from Islam and long head of the Anglican Church in Iran. In the later Khomeini revolution that overthrew the Shah, the bishop's son was murdered, the church properties were confiscated and the Bishop himself sought refuge in Britain. Although we had confirmed plane tickets, we were unaware that the flight to Isfahan was routinely oversold. When the Shiraz departure was announced, knowledgeable Iranians broke ranks like a street mob; foreigners and most women never made it aboard. Nor did the airline keep its promise to inform those who would be meeting our plane. I arrived a day late in time to address the student body of the Episcopal academy, having left a disappointed congregation the previous night without word of any kind.

In Teheran itself, missionary Keith Jones had arranged my schedule. I preached Friday (the Muslim "sabbath") in the Persian Church, lectured and then dialogued with the Teheran Evangelical Fellowship, and preached on Sunday, June 22, in a Southern Baptist church. There was little outward indication of serious national unrest. American Embassy environs were placid; a half-mile away we bought an ornate sheik's tea kettle hand hammered of tin, zinc and copper. Yet Iranian society was clearly a struggle between ancient and modern, provincial and cosmopolitan, Western and Middle Eastern ideologies. The main traffic circles and crosswalks of Teheran brought together at stoplights high coutured Iranians and Europeans, turbaned Bedouins, blue-jeaned longhaireds, veiled Muslim women, sheep and goats; one wondered how long such a mix would endure. The Marxist analysis of history did not fit Iran, so that revolution, should it come, was more likely to take the course of Islamic politicization. Some university students sensed such possibilities and hoped to escape the country for studies in America.

Early Monday morning we left Teheran on Air France for Paris and New York, reaching home late Tuesday night, June 24.

In the States I then participated in several conferences, including one on human engineering, and in symposiums, including one on academic freedom and commitment. Religious Heritage of America conferred on me its twenty-fifth anniversary award for contributions to education. Articles of mine appeared in *Commonweal, Christianity Today, Christian Herald* and *World Vision.* I curtailed domestic lecture opportunities, however, because I was committed once again for teaching at Trinity Seminary in the Spring of 1976.

Overarching these activities was progress in the writing of *God, Revelation and Authority.* Floyd Thatcher of Word Books had enthusiastically invited two volumes or more, if necessary; it was now clear that the work would run four volumes at least, one introductory, two on epistemology and the last on the doctrine of God. Providentially the appearance of each volume overlapped important contemporary developments in theological and philosophical arenas which I could assess. New views, projected mainly by speculative German scholars, were being carried to Asia and Africa by American and European ecumenists fascinated by theological novelties. It was not that German theologians had nothing to offer. Often they emphasized nuances in the Christian heritage that evangelicals had unfortunately neglected or missed. But they often did so in a theological context that distorted or defamed evangelical theism as an inadequate world-life view. They tended to reorient the Christian outlook in terms of some one-sided emphasis, at the same time blaming evangelicals for the intellectual gulf between the church and the world.

My lectures abroad and at home created a cresting anticipatory interest in *God, Revelation and Authority.* Copy for the initial volume, devoted to introductory concerns, was already at Word Books being prepared for publication, and material for volume two would now follow in a matter of months.

In August Helga and I celebrated our thirty-fifth wedding anniversary. Paul, still teaching at Calvin College, had now been elected as Kent County Republican Committee chairman, a post once held by Gerald Ford. Three active children, Kara, 7, Jordan, 5, and Megan, 1, now occupied Karen who additionally continued her teaching. In Florida, Carol and Bill Bates meanwhile maintained serious research and writing alongside university teaching and concertizing.

At the very beginning of 1976 the first two volumes of *God, Revelation and Authority* appeared simultaneously and set the pattern for the later coordinate publication of volumes three and four in 1978, and of five at the end of 1982 and six at the beginning of 1983. Asian interest in translations was already evident that Summer. Helga and I met at Chicago O'Hare airport and flew to Tokyo and Seoul to begin another multinational schedule in countries where copies of *God, Revelation and Authority* had already arrived by sea mail.

On our arrival in Seoul, President Albert Gammage, Jr., and his wife, Nettie, drove us 100 miles for a week of lectures at the Baptist Seminary in Daejon, where I later addressed Methodist seminarians, Southern Presbyterian university students, the Christian Academy, missionary leaders and church groups. Returning to Seoul, I gave a lecture series at ACTS, where I had been "founding lecturer" three years earlier, and where the eight graduate students had grown to twenty-five. Sessions were now being held in the complex that Bob Pierce had originally acquired as World Vision's Korean headquarters. I also addressed chapel services in the Presbyterian and O.M.S. seminaries.

Next stop was Hong Kong for lectures at China Graduate School of Theology where Dr. Philip Teng translated into Cantonese. I also addressed the Asia Theological Association, where the program theme, in contrast to motifs popular in ebullent Christian America, was persecution and suffering as integral to Christian commitment. Already under subtle pressures was Hong Kong Baptist College, founded as a Southern Baptist effort; few suspected that less than a decade later only 30 percent of the faculty would be professing Christians, the school would rely on government funding and many student leaders would be open to Marxism.

Asian urban centers were more and more vulnerable to Western secular naturalism and to communist atheism, options that called urgently for illumination and assessment by the Christian world-life alternative. Emphasis on the rational significance of Christianity became the larger framework into which much of my activity channeled. The subtle outside cognitive pressures upon Asian countries were evident to Dr. James Taylor, great grandson of J. Hudson Taylor, who had invited me to conclude my Asian ministry of forty-five days—with 38 addresses in all—on the campus of China Evangelical Seminary in Taipei, which was thriving under his presidency. Christian Literature Society of Korea had already planned to translate and publish the initial volume of *God, Revelation and Authority,* and now a Mandarin translation was being discussed both in Hong Kong and in Taipei.

Back in the States I taught another term at Trinity Seminary, which now listed me as visiting professor. Confusion and conflict seemed to be settling over evangelical ranks in the States. *Newsweek*'s October 25, 1976, issue heralded "The Year of the Evangelical," a verdict on American religious vitalities that George Gallup, Jr., had encouraged. For all the secondary warning notes in *Newsweek*'s essay, one spokesman after another for the evangelical establishment jubilantly heralded evangelicalism's religious triumph. *Newsweek* had not, however, spoken of "the *decade*" and far less of "the *century*" of the evangelical.

In the series of 1975 "Footnotes" in *Christianity Today* I surveyed reactionary and counterreactionary trends that signaled trouble ahead for the evangelical thrust in America. The movement was riding the crest of a wave; its forward momentum would carry it to still uncharted levels of impact and influence. But the future should not be taken for granted. "The growing impasse between evangelical groups, each of which deliberately and perhaps stubbornly advances its own approach and emphasis," I wrote, "creates misunderstanding and sacrifices gains that might accrue to the whole evangelical front by solidifying agreements. . . . New centers of evangelical power and conviction will almost inevitably come into being in the next decade; what is unsure is whether their input into the total evangelical context will be disruptive or constructive."

Evangelical editors apprehensive over the prospect of squandered opportunities busied their pens. *Sojourners* carried a major interview on "Evangelical Identity," and *Eternity* on "The House Divided." Under the title of *Evangelicals in Search of Identity* Word Books in 1976 reprinted ten successive essays of mine that had appeared as monthly "Footnotes." Although the tiny volume was selected in *Eternity*'s list of "choice books of the year," it was disconcerting to establishment evangelicals who regarded any questioning of evangelical triumphalism as a matter of religious disloyalty. Yet one needed only to move outside the evangelical "in group" and, for that matter, to take note of the conflicts and ambiguities within evangelicalism itself, to sense that all was not well.

Northwestern University in Evanston meanwhile invited me to give three lectures on "The Essence of Christianity." In New York I took part in an American Theological Society panel on "how to do theology"; elsewhere I shared in a conference on Religion and the Presidency, and spoke at a U.S. Army chaplains' retreat. In addition, I contributed articles invited by *Interpretation* and *Theology Today.* Each context was one in which historic evangelical Christianity was being rivaled by formative competing views. I managed to complete by yearend an essay on "Christological Neglect by a Mission-Minded Church" for the Festschrift titled *Scripture, Tradition and Interpretation* to honor the seventy-fifth birthday on October 7, 1977, of my early Fuller colleague, Everett F. Harrison, and an essay also on "The Undoing of the Modern Mind" for the volume *Evangelical Roots,* edited by Kenneth Kantzer and published in 1978 as a memorial tribute to Wilbur M. Smith, another Fuller founding colleague. Smith, who had died in 1976 at the age of 81, had spent his final teaching years at Trinity. The other early Fuller colleague, Harold Lindsell, was in 1976 approaching the end of his eight years' editorship of *Christianity Today,* and announced impending retirement in 1977.

Lindsell was not dislodged by cabal as I was, nor was he necessarily pressured into resigning. But paid subscriptions had fallen to 90,000 and disconcerting deficits accumulated. Harold Myra, who had made an impressive financial success of *Campus Life* magazine, was enlisted by the Board as publisher to bolster circulation and the magazine's financial base. He reduced editorial staff and promoted circulation by appealing for lay readers. Gift offers of the *Living Bible,* made available far under market price, restored part of the lost circulation, lifting it from 90,000 to 120,000. The Pew Foundation made a $100,000 gift, although it indicated this would be its last.

Graham was active in the search for a new editor. He decided on Kenneth Kantzer, dean of Trinity Evangelical Divinity School, who before that had been head of the division of Bible and apologetics at Wheaton College. Graham wrote for my counsel just before the announcement was made. I applauded Kantzer as a marked improvement—a scholarly theologian, evangelically firm yet irenic, and an esteemed friend. I noted, however, that at 60 Kantzer could hardly establish himself before retirement would loom and search for a successor again confront the magazine.

Myra from the outset wanted to be and increasingly became a dominant editorial force. The magazine's improving financial condition, he felt, merited a voice in respect to editorial content and format. But, stressing that Graham had assured him of editorial freedom, Kantzer hoped to restore some of the magazine's earlier theological and editorial guidelines. Kantzer's effort to restore my name to the masthead as the founding editor was unsuccessful.

The Board soon named Myra both publisher and president. With Myra's encouragement the Board voted on January, 1977—five days after President Carter's inaugural address—to move the magazine from its twenty-year Washington location a block from the White House, to Carol Stream, Illinois, a suburb of Wheaton. Board chairman Ockenga told *Newsweek* that the moral pollution and deleterious influence of the District of Columbia ran counter to the magazine's concern for Christian ethics and lifestyle. Others, however, considered the move to this heartland of evangelical independency and political conservatism as consolidation into the "evangelical Vatican," so named because of the area's conglomerate of evangelical enterprises like National Association of Evangelicals, Tyndale House, Youth for Christ International, Scripture Press, *Christian Life* and others. The magazine would, of course, be accessible to Wheaton College, where construction was soon to begin on the $15.5 million Billy Graham Center. The Graham Association and the Pew trust established grants of $150,000 to assist construction of the magazine's headquarters building. Of the editorial staff only Lindsell, who was soon to be succeeded, agreed to make the move.

The relocation announcement came as a complete surprise to me. "The decision to relocate," I told *Newsweek,* "seems to reverse the ideal of evangelical penetration of secular society that motivated the founders of *Christianity Today.*" The *Washington Post* on February 6, 1977, in its lead editorial titled "Exodus," commented that if Washington is the "moral mess" that Harold Ockenga thinks is the case, there was "every reason . . . to stick around and try to change our ways. After all, perhaps the most famous evangelical Christian in the country has just moved into the White House, with a view to doing something along those lines. And what makes Mr. Ockenga think that small-town America is relatively sin-free, anyway? We'd put Peyton Place up against Washington any old day in the moral pollution sweepstakes. . . ." *Newsweek*'s religion page subsequently depicted the move in terms of "Capital Flight."

Months before announcement of Lindsell's impending retirement and of the magazine's relocation, I was being drawn increasingly into full-scale interviews by secular and religious journals. For thirty-five years I had interviewed others; now it was the other way around. The occasion for these interviews was at first twofold: the appearance at the beginning of 1976 of *God, Revelation and Authority* with its emphasis on the cognitive importance of the Christian revelation for all aspects of the modern culture-crisis, and the growing concern about evangelical identity. The identity debate focused in part on the widening use of the evangelical label by Catholics, Anglicans, charismatics, neoevangelicals and so-called conservative evangelicals alongside establishment evangelicals. Moreover, many fundamentalists differentiated themselves from evangelicals. To worsen the confusion, President Jimmy Carter was placarded as a "born-again evangelical" while some theologically modern denominational spokesmen insisted that Southern Baptists were not evangelicals. But confusion was precipitated also through the dismissal as "false evangelicals" of all who do not affirm biblical inerrancy, even if they subscribed to all the early credal commitments. The position was championed by Schaeffer at a convention of the National Association of Evangelicals and by Lindsell in his *The Battle for the Bible* (1976). Had Schaeffer and Lindsell spoken of "inconsistent" rather than of "false" evangelicals they might have served the cause more positively. As it was, scholars like F. F. Bruce, G. C. Berkouwer and a score of others who stood firmly within the creeds of Christendom and who had in fact served *Christianity Today* from its beginnings in one role or another, and shared in its rejection of modernist, dialectical and existential theology, were now unfortunately categorized as false evangelicals, even though most considered the Bible reliable and criticized not the Book but its critics. A further byproduct of such overstatement was that mediating schools, Fuller among them, could look better than they deserved.

I concurred that the ecumenical seminaries chaotically disagreed over the nature of biblical authority and that a creeping compromise of biblical reliability was underway even in many professedly evangelical colleges and seminaries. But I feared that extremist statements disadvantageously formulated evangelical concerns in a way that could unwittingly harm essentially evangelical institutions and personalities no less than mediating agencies. *Christianity Today* was from the outset committed to biblical inerrancy as a matter of doctrinal consistency, but it nonetheless enlisted as allies all scholars who fought well on implicit biblical grounds for the great articles of faith, rather than excluding some from the evangelical camp. National media attention would now focus on a controversy that would make evangelicals look like oddities at the very moment when they were poised to reap significant public gains.

When the Council for Biblical Inerrancy was formed in the fall of 1977, one of its first burdens was to escape commitment to embarrassingly excessive formulations of its positions. Its next major and continuing problem, having consolidated its membership and leadership in independent evangelical seminaries and colleges, was how to involve conservative scholars on major university campuses and in ecumenically oriented seminaries in an enterprise that had been launched on too narrow a base. Instead the organization moved toward solving this impasse by enlisting prominent laymen.

Lindsell's *Battle* conceded that I supported inerrancy, but then added that I did not consider it important, contrary to my published stance. My *God, Revelation and Authority* incorporated an affirmation of inerrancy, but not as the very first thing to be said about the Bible. Secular as well as religious publications interested in the cultural relevance of the Christian message now sought interviews to gain evangelical perspectives on science, culture and the contemporary moral crisis. (Many of these are included in the volume, *Conversations with Carl Henry: Christianity for Today,* published early in 1986 by The Edwin Mellen Company). When *Time* magazine devoted its religion page (Feb. 14, 1977) to "Theology for the Tent Meeting" the invitations for domestic teaching and lectures multiplied, as did requests from abroad under World Vision commitments. *Time* had put its finger on the pulse of the contemporary debate, and recognized the significance of the claim that reason is on the side of evangelical theism, and that modernism, neoorthodoxy and existentialism are mired in subjectivity. From distant religious centers and missionary libraries on all continents came requests for *God, Revelation and Authority;* the volumes are now available in hundreds of learning centers around the world. A Christian layperson sent publication copies of the two volumes to 100 leaders of thought and many offered appreciative comments, among them Charles Malik, Fulton J. Sheen and D. Elton Trueblood. Television and radio interviews came in the aftermath of the *Time* article.

Only six months after publication, *God, Revelation and Authority* went into a second printing; the volumes were featured as an Evangelical Book Club selection and tied for first place in *Eternity*'s annual survey of best books. As book reviews appeared the mounting interest surprised even the publishers. In *Eternity* Bernard Ramm welcomed "the broadest, the most learned, the most incisive comprehensive work on revelation in our current evangelical tradition." In *Christianity Today* Ronald Nash, head of the philosophy and religion departments at Western Kentucky University, declared it "a publishing event of the first magnitude." In the *New Review of Books and Religion* Robert A. Traina declared it "a significant milestone in evangelical thought." Kenneth Briggs, religion news editor of *The New York Times,* considered the volumes "the most important work of evangelical theology in recent times" and added that they may "help the evangelical churches make a sounder transition from the periphery to the mainstream of American religious life." William Willoughby, religion editor of the *Washington Star,* called it "the most definitive work on biblical theology in this century."

The tributes came from across religious lines. Martin Marty, writing in *Context,* said that "here at least, and at last, is an attempt to set evangelicalism on a theological course." In *Christian Century* Richard Caemmerer wrote: "This is a tremendously assiduous effort and will become the encyclopedia . . . for the exposition of biblical authority in the conservative movement." In the *Time* essay religion editor Richard C. Ostling remarked that the publication established its author as "the leading theologian of the nation's growing evangelical flank." A personally signed note from President Jimmy Carter voiced appreciation and his desire to read the work.

Lindsell wrote me on February 14, 1977, saying that on May 1 he would begin his "terminal leave" at *Christianity Today;* he thought it "most inappropriate for former editors of a magazine to have their long shadows hanging over the magazine. . . . To give the new editor full freedom to proceed," he wrote, "I have decided that the Footnotes column will come to an end with the September issue. That means that my successor who we hope will come in September, will not be caught with either the first or the second editor as an overhang." My final essay, "On Saying Good-bye," appeared in the September 9, 1977, issue and on October 21 my name vanished from the masthead.

My writing continued nonetheless at an energy-exhausting pace. And under the World Vision umbrella I spent six weeks in 1977 giving lectures in Europe—in England, in Germany (including chaplains' retreats in Heidelberg, Nürnberg, Frankfurt and Ramstein, and preaching also in military chapels), in France, and finally three weeks in Yugoslavia on the theological faculty of Matija Vlacic Illrik in Zagreb, where I lectured on "The Christian View of History," that contrasted the biblical view with Marxist and other approaches. In midsummer I taught at Regent College, Vancouver, where faculty colleagues included R. Hooykaas and Donald Mackay.

But for Helga, 1977 was a critically decisive year for her health, career, our home and in fact life itself. Occasionally she had experienced intense and inexplicable facial pain. By the time we reached Salzburg en route to Lausanne her suffering was almost unbearable. We were singing a congregational hymn in a German church service when she suddenly dropped the hymnal and sank into the pew.

Helga little suspected what was involved and at stake. Remissions of several days or weeks were a welcome respite but only such. When we returned to Virginia her malady was diagnosed as dread *tic douloureux* and the usual drugs were prescribed. The neurologist gave little hope for cure and intimated eventual permanent impairment of certain brain functions. He counseled her to give up all public speaking and teaching, since attacks were unpredictable.

After several years of drug therapy had accomplished little, I wrote the National Institutes of Health for information about their research and recommendations. N.I.H. responded that Dr. Peter J. Jannetta of Presbyterian University Hospital in Pittsburgh was performing highly successful but still experimental surgical procedures. I wrote him but heard nothing. I therefore arranged for Helga to go to Mayo Clinic. The neurologist there merely changed her medication and hesitated recommending a surgical procedure that Mayo was not yet ready to approve.

Meanwhile Dr. John Huffman, Jr., minister of First Presbyterian Church, Pittsburgh, whom I had known as a lad when his father was president of Winona Lake School of Theology, replied to my inquiry about Dr. Jannetta. A member of his congregation, Dr. Donald Reigel, had spent a year assisting Dr. Jannetta, Huffman reported. Head of the department of neurological surgery in the School of Medicine at University of Pittsburgh, Jannetta was becoming so remarkably successful and sought after for trigeminal neuralgia surgery that he was deluged by patients even from abroad. Dr. Reigel interceded in our behalf and over Labor Day weekend we drove to Pittsburgh.

Traditional procedures had been to sever the offending trigeminal nerve which permanently paralyzed the face, or to inject alcohol which treatment required repetition every six months and in any case guaranteed no sure relief from pain. Such remedies sought to cope with consequences, not causes of the affliction. Dr. Jannetta's surgery was predicated on a conviction that *tic douloureux* resulted from pressure of an artery to the brain on all or part of the trigeminal nerve. Very summarily stated indeed, the microscopic surgery involved, after a cranial incision behind the ear, separation of nerve and artery at their point of impact. Here Dr. Jannetta inserted a small cushion of flesh as permanent barrier to further friction. The incision was then sutured. After the almost four-hour surgery, Helga was in the recovery room for an additional four hours and in intensive care for a full day. After but one day in her own room she was wandering about, encouraging fellow-sufferers next in line for the same surgery, thanking not only the medics, but God her heavenly Caretaker. Two weeks after arrival in Pittsburgh, Helga was back home in Virginia.

In all our travels as well as personal problems we had the prayer support of our neighborhood Bible study group, which had met fortnightly since Key '73, and still met in our home whenever feasible. We had the support also of our "youngsters" who gathered with us at Christmas. This year was a time of relaxed thanksgiving. Helga's recovery was complete. Paul was enjoying a mini-sabbatical and completing a book; Carol had completed her Ph.D. dissertation (650 pages in 3 volumes) in musicology and her husband Bill Bates had finished his D.Mus. (organ) document of 450 pages.

January, 1978, marked Harper & Row's publication of the sixth volume in the Contemporary Evangelical Thought series. Titled *Horizons of Science,* it enlisted twelve prominent evangelical scholars in illumining modern scientific frontiers in evangelical perspective. At the same time it brought to view the debate between evangelical scholars over whether science can legitimately claim to convey objective truth or is limited to describing "what works," and even then, always subject to revision. The only other volume I had hoped to include in this symposium series was one on Christian social ethics, but some of the scholars I considered most competent were precommitted and therefore unavailable.

On April 7, 1978, Kenneth Kantzer became editor of *Christianity Today.* We had long been friends, and I applauded the choice, although I feared it would cost the evangelical movement (as in the case of Ed Carnell) the theological books Kantzer aspired to finish. In view of changes and pressures at *Christianity Today* I was unsure how effectively it could be recaptured for theological dialogue with nonevangelicals. I nonetheless gladly contributed essays as requested and helped Kantzer as much as I could. We served together on the board and editorial committee of IFACS.

My three-month annual trips to foreign learning centers were now a fixed pattern. In the Spring of 1978 I lectured or taught concentrated courses on campuses that trained selected Christian students from 35 Asian and African countries: in Manila at Asian Theological Seminary, where I gave the commencement address on March 31, five days after giving the Easter sunrise message to 8,000 persons in the beautiful Folk Arts Theatre; China Graduate School of Theology in Kowloon and Lutheran Seminary in the New Territories; China Evangelical Seminary in Taipei and the Presbyterian Theological College in Tainan (where I met with the faculty for a dialogue on Scripture), Asian Center for Theological Studies and Mission and also Seoul Theological Seminary in Korea; and in Singapore, Discipleship Training Center and the Haggai Institute for Advanced Leadership Training.

All along the way we were welcomed by former students, many now twenty- to thirty-year missionary veterans. Say what one may critical of para-church efforts, almost everywhere we found evidences of a remarkable evangelical energy that would have been absent had it not been for Wycliffe Translators, Far East Broadcasting Corporation, Inter-Varsity, Campus Crusade, Young Life, Child Evangelism, Christian academies and day schools, Laubach and other literacy programs, Christian publishing ministries and bookstores, not to mention World Vision and much else. To observe World Vision's twenty-fifth anniversary in Korea, over 39,000 "alumni"—including many orphans for which the movement had found sponsors and homes, and some now prominent in Seoul's business and professional community—held a banquet at which attendees presented WV with a substantial cash gift to further its work. By then, Korea was but one of thirty-four countries in which World Vision was already ministering, and the orphan and child care ministries now but one of many programs.

In June we returned to the States where, the following month, I taught at Gordon-Conwell summer school. Among enrollees were Pearl Hamilton and Ann Horsford of the Bible Study Fellowship movement, who had driven from California to make the classes part of their summer vacation. Volumes 3 and 4 of *God, Revelation and Authority* had come off the press in mid-May; we had celebrated publication of volume 1 in Korean while in that country and learned that in Taiwan the Mandarin translation was progressing well.

In Grand Rapids Paul's political interests had encouraged his race for the Michigan state legislature and subsequent election by 74 percent of the vote. We applauded the effort. There were multiplying advantages to Christian vocation in the governmental arena, not least of them that one could address community and national issues in a context of public moral concern with high visibility, while at the same time working actively for better alternatives. With their Indiana University doctorates completed, Carol and Bill (Bates) moved to teaching appointments at the University of South Carolina in Columbia, Bill as head of the division of organ and church music, and Carol as adjunct in the music department.

1979 brought opportunity to preach several times in Westminster Chapel, London, where R. T. Kendall had succeeded Martyn Lloyd-Jones. It also accommodated a media conference in London and two weeks of research in Cambridge that revived warm memories of 1968–69 residency there. Three weeks in India under my World Vision commitment involved the All-India Conference on Social Action in Madras, where I was the only invited foreign lecturer. I addressed also Christian faculty members at Madras University. In Bangalore I lectured under auspices of the Evangelical Fellowship of India Committee on Relief and then went to Yeotmal for a series of lectures at Union Biblical Seminary. My ministry concluded with preaching in Bombay. The taxi-driver driving me to the largest Anglican church in Bombay lost his way, and I arrived just in time to don a robe in the processional already moving into the church. My query about preaching time elicited the rector's suggestion of "10 minutes." The contrast with London's Westminster Chapel was remarkable. There I was told that the congregation would expect a 45 to 50-minute sermon, and that if the morning prayer ran less than 15 minutes many in the congregation would wonder if I really knew how to pray.

Before the 1979 trip abroad I gave the Staley Lectures at the University of Virginia during a blizzard that cancelled all other activities on campus; preached the Easter sunrise sermon at the cemetery in Fredericksburg where Mary Washington is buried; held religious life meetings at Milliken University; shared in the Notre Dame colloquy on "Loss and Recovery of the Sacred"; taught in the C. S. Lewis Institute adjoining the University of Maryland; spoke in Houston at the National Conference on Church Renewal; and conducted theological renewal meetings at the First Baptist Church of Conway, Arkansas.

But the highlight of 1979 was publication of volumes 3 and 4 of *God, Revelation and Authority,* which was being read increasingly by nonevangelical students. I was elected vice president of American Theological Society and continued active in IFACS which was projecting a college textbook series on Christian world-life themes. Northwestern College (Reformed Church in America) conferred an honorary doctorate.

Paul and Karen and family came for Thanksgiving and Carol and Bill Bates for Christmas. Paul was completing his first term in the Michigan legislature. Carol was at work on a post-doctoral project involving research in France and Britain, and in Italy where she had uncovered a long missing seventeenth century volume of harpsichord music.

New Year's Day had hardly passed when on January 3, 1980, we flew again to Seoul for my fifth teaching stint at the Asian Center for Theological Studies and Mission. During the visit Word of Life Press committed itself to translation and publication of the remaining volumes of *God, Revelation and Authority.*

From Korea we flew to Japan for a lecture and preaching ministry sponsored in Tokyo, Ariga, Osaka and Kobe by the Japan Evangelical Theological Society and the Japan Protestant Council. As its tenth anniversary project JETS had translated and published, unknown to me, my book, *A Plea for Evangelical Demonstration.*

We returned home by way of Pasadena where I taught at Fuller's three-week intersession; it was the first such involvement in twenty years at the school I helped found. When one of the professors who held permissive views of biblical inspiration installed sound equipment to record my every comment "because of the historical importance of my remarks," I promptly evicted the mechanical eavesdropper. In days that followed, many students voluntarily indicated that mine was the first course in their Fuller experience where the importance of a completely reliable Scripture was presented. We were glad that many evangelical emphases survived, yet we noted the considerable theological diversity among faculty. The policy of accepting a colleague's differences from the norm, one professor observed, was the price each teacher paid for the unchallenged acceptance of his own departures; few faculty dreamed, however, that the end result would be so far-reaching.

The American Theological Society elected me as president at its 1980 spring meeting. Teaching during that year carried me to Columbia Bible College Graduate School and lectures to various campuses east and west, including a Theological Vacation Conference for Lutherans in Colorado along with Paul Holmer and Krister Stendahl, and to Bluefield College to address the Virginia Baptist Pastors Conference.

In August I returned to Seoul to share in the '80 World Evangelization Crusade attended cumulatively by 7½ million persons on four nights. Probably no larger meeting to date has occurred in Christian history. American evangelists emphasized the need for the new birth, whereas Asian evangelists emphasized the need of dedicated and sacrificial service by believers. I had the privilege of addressing 12,000 high school and college students in an overflow meeting.

Upon my return Helga and I celebrated our fortieth wedding anniversary with gratitude for health, happiness and ongoing ministries. Our children were established in gratifying careers as dedicated believers. Paul was now in his second term in the Michigan legislature. Carol was both teaching and completing a post-graduate research project. Her husband Bill had given organ concerts in King's college chapel, Cambridge, in Notre Dame Cathedral, Paris, and in various German cities. Helga continued to address women's retreats, bore the main load of carrying forward the neighborhood Bible study, handled as much personal correspondence as possible, helped with literary work as I labored to complete the fifth and sixth volumes of *God, Revelation and Authority* for publication in 1983, was reviving her missions research on a segment of her parents' years in Cameroon—all these over and above her activities as homemaker.

In November came Helga's second and my third trip to Asia in a single year, this time for a lecture-preaching-teaching mission in Hawaii, the Philippines, Taiwan and Japan. During Staley Lectures in Honolulu I also addressed students at the University of Hawaii where a religion professor had invited me to teach two large classes. To the frustration of Muslim and lapsed Christian students I vigorously defended the doctrine of the Trinity against attacks recently made upon it in the classroom. We ended up in a large, packed-out classroom where during an hour-long free-for-all four professors behaving like Thrasymachus in Plato's *Republic* hurled questions without waiting for replies, until even students agreed that rational discussion presupposes some semblance of order.

We observed Thanksgiving in Manila at the Asian Theological Seminary and Christmas in Taiwan. After lectures at the China Evangelical Seminary in Taipei we proceeded to Hsilo for lectures at the Conservative Baptist college there and then spent the Christmas holidays with its president, Jim Cummings, former Fuller student. Jim's oldest son meanwhile flew to Hong Kong as one of Taiwan's participants in the All-Asia basketball finals. We sent along for eventual transfer to mainland China two copies of the Mandarin version of volume 1 of *God, Revelation and Authority,* just off the press. Less than two years later we would learn about a Chinese philosophy student who, after reading it, sought out an English teacher from Australia to make a personal commitment to Christ.

1981 dawned for us in Osaka, Japan, where under the leadership of Dr. Stephen Hatori I gave a series of expository messages to inaugurate an annual New Year's observance by Christians. We then flew back home, having spent six weeks in three countries.

In the States both secular and religious publications welcomed interviews on the spiritual temperature of the nations and of the evangelical movement in America. Some evangelists were badgering audiences with dire statistics of cultural doom and almost in the same breath exuberantly publicizing their own personal world-changing impact. Christian colleges and seminaries told of burgeoning enrollments, yet by far the larger number of students were on secular campuses and were still outside the reach of the Christian view and its vitalities. Both George Cornell in his nationally syndicated AP religion column and *Christianity Today* welcomed feature interviews. In three states there were television opportunities. In the Spring I gave the retiring presidential address to the American Theological Society on revelation and culture. At the American Festival of Evangelism in Kansas City I presided over and addressed a seminary on evangelicals and public concerns. Then I criss-crossed Canada on an eight-city lecture tour sponsored by the Canadian Fellowship of Evangelicals on "Theology for the '80's." Student lecture series took me to Western Conservative Baptist Seminary, Western Evangelical Seminary, Gordon-Conwell Theological Seminary, George Fox College and Newberry College. In addition I addressed leaders of the Christian College Coalition, Protestant inter-service chaplains at Bolling Air Force base, Kinney anniversary Christian Life meetings in Cincinnati, National Association of Evangelicals regional meetings in California and Virginia, Washington Congressional Wives at Fellowship House and a Washington Presbyterian dialogue on Scripture.

Besides serving on the IFACS board and editorial committee I was elected to the boards of the Ethics and Public Policy Center and of Prison Fellowship, as well as functioning on the advisory boards of the Christian College Coalition, Institute for Religion and Democracy and other agencies.

After fifteen years of continuing effort, early 1982 rewarded me with completion of the final manuscripts for *God, Revelation and Authority;* volume 5 appeared in November of that year, and Word scheduled volume 6 for publication in February, 1983.

In May World Vision duties carried us to Taiwan for lectures once again at China Evangelical Seminary coincidentally with the appearance in Mandarin of volume 2 of *God, Revelation and Authority.* As on previous visits, I spoke at The International Church in Taipei. I returned home to read proofs and to prepare for upcoming speaking commitments in the States.

In June I was invited along with other religious and civil leaders to a White House luncheon with President Reagan and Vice President Bush after a conference on voluntarism in meeting community needs.

By the end of August I was aloft again, this time to Africa, with an intermediary stop in London to preach at Westminster Chapel. Then, at the invitation of the Accrediting Council for Theological Education in Africa, I gave ACTEA's initial series of annual lectures, addressing joint gatherings of seminarians arranged in five countries by Dr. Paul Bowers: Liberia, Nigeria, Cameroun, Zaire and Kenya.

Soon after the month-long mission, I flew to Portland for the annual lecture series at Western Conservative Baptist Seminary. The year 1982 had carried me to eleven states for addresses and lectures of one kind or another, as well as on separate lecture trips to Asia and to Africa.

Christmas holidays brought Paul and Karen and their three children from Michigan, where Paul had now been elected state senator, and Carol and Bill Bates from South Carolina with seventeen-month-old Stephen. A prestigious Paris publisher planned to issue Carol's modern edition of LaGuerre's seventeenth and eighteenth century harpsichord works.

With the calendar turn to January, 1983, when I reached seventy, I was increasingly reminded that all the years of our lives are a divine gift. In that month my friend and near neighbor, and former colleague, Frank E. Gaebelein, reached the end of his earthly course. Within a few years Francis Schaeffer, Harold Ockenga, Merrill Tenney and Gordon Clark would all slip away. In May, 1983, Helga and I were again on a World Vision lecture trip aboard KAL flight 007 from New York to Seoul, the flight which Russian missiles later that year demolished in midcourse. In any case, I recalled that God had given me thirty-five years more of life and service than at one time, in my teens, I thought I would ever have.

The year had opened with publication of the sixth and last volume of *God, Revelation and Authority.* Word Books timed the publication date to coincide with the fortieth anniversary banquet of National Religious Broadcasters, which I addressed in Washington, D.C., and where to my complete surprise Jarrell McCracken and Floyd Thatcher presented me with a leather-bound set of the entire six-volume project. They also announced that a volume on my theological contribution was to be published later in 1983 in the *Makers of the Modern Theological Mind* series which had been largely preempted by nonevangelical theologians.

Staley Lectures carried me to Erskine College and to Wheaton College; other lectures included Calvin College, Denver Conservative Baptist Seminary, the Gaebelein memorial lectures in Denver and a week's survey of the life and epistles of Paul at Bible Study Fellowship in San Antonio. The three-week Denver course on the Christian world-life view and the mind of modernity was responsible indirectly, and quite unexpectedly so, for my return for three semesters to full-time teaching, and on a secular rather than evangelical campus, from September, 1983, through December, 1984.

Before that turn of things, however, we were headed to Asia on the aforementioned KAL 007. Our Korean stop had two prongs: the growing and expanding campus of the Asian Center for Theological Studies and Mission, where I gave a lecture and chapel address, and Seoul Theological Seminary in Bucheon. At the conclusion of the Bucheon lectures the Seminary in cooperation with ACTS and Word of Life Press hosted a reception that gathered scores of evangelical lay leaders and clergy to dedicate and celebrate the publication in Korean of the third volume of *God, Revelation and Authority,* translated by New Testament scholar Jonathan Lee, the Seminary's president-elect.

In Taiwan, our next stop, I lectured also from volume 3, newly translated into Mandarin by Paul Kang and published by China Evangelical Seminary Press. While in Taipei I spoke also in both Christ College chapel and The International Church and had numerous contacts with the expatriot community.

Next came Hong Kong, that perpetually fascinating city of waterways and junks, concrete jungle apartments, intriguing shopping centers and street markets, all of this increasingly under the shadow of the 1997 expiry of Britain's lease and approaching domination by mainland China. Both at China Graduate School of Theology and at Alliance Bible Seminary on Cheung Chau Island I was asked to assess and confront this prospect in evangelical context.

From Hong Kong we jetfoiled to the tiny Portuguese colony of

Macao, where at the newly formed Bible institute I addressed the first class of thirteen students. Eight were from mainland China. Before leaving Macao we tarried at the gravesite of Robert Morrison, father of Protestant missions in China, and saw, still towering above earthquake-shattered cathedral ruins, the surviving cross that in 1825 inspired Morrison's fellow countryman and consul to Canton, Sir John Bowring, to write the hymn, "In the Cross of Christ I Glory."

The temporary return to full-time teaching as distinguished visiting professor of Christian Studies at Hillsdale College in Michigan, came about quite remarkably. When I was teaching in Denver, John Andrews, former Nixon speechwriter who was one of the first to resign in criticism of Watergate, and then director of Shavano Institute for National Leadership, attended one of the lectures. He encouraged the Hillsdale Center for Constructive Alternatives to invite me to lecture on the Bible and American values at a projected bicentennial conference. The lecture was well received. Faculty dean John Muller asked if I could be persuaded to teach some courses in religion. Hillsdale had been founded more than a century earlier as a Baptist college but during the modernist era its trustees had made a complete break with a specific religious heritage, and there was admittedly little student interest in religion courses. Although Hillsdale was one of the better independent liberal arts colleges and its president, George Roche, was known as a fearless foe of federal encroachment on education, its location two hours' drive from Detroit Metropolitan Airport in wintry Michigan and its student body of but 1,000 discouraged my serious consideration. But Hillsdale importuned, indicating a willingness to invite me at department head level as distinguished visiting professor, permitting me to determine what two courses I wanted to teach, and offering to fly me routinely between Virginia and Michigan. As Hillsdale continued to probe, I began to weigh the challenge of stepping into a nonevangelical college that takes educational concerns seriously and was open to setting biblical perspectives alongside the contemporary secular outlook.

I remained at Hillsdale for three semesters, although I was invited to continue. During that time three other Michigan campuses asked if I would duplicate the Hillsdale experience. During my stint a somewhat beleaguered vanguard of evangelical professors was drawn together, a growing interest was reinforced in the Christian Studies major projected by Dr. Tom Burke, the small Inter-Varsity and Campus Crusade chapters were encouraged to do some things cooperatively, campus links to local clergy and lay leaders were tightened, interest was solidified in an annual Christian Studies seminar sponsored by the Center for Constructive Alternatives and an annual prayer breakfast shaped for faculty, clergy and businessmen. I had the joy of leading to Christ a member of the faculty and also a student who had entered college as a vocal atheist and declared himself a humanist when he enrolled in my introductory religion course but later privately expressed his desire to become a Christian.

The family once again gathered at Christmas—four grandchildren and their parents—with Paul, serving in the Michigan senate, wondering whether he should encourage approaches that he run for ex-president Gerald Ford's former seat in Congress. Carol had added piano teaching at Columbia Bible College to her adjunct teaching responsibilities at the University of South Carolina.

Vital Speeches in its first January, 1984, issue, printed in its totality my address on "The Crisis of Modern Learning," giving it national exposure. In May I addressed the annual banquet of the Evangelical Press Association on "God's Press Corps in the Cultural Cross-Fire" and Multnomah Press distributed complimentary copies of my new volume, *The Christian Mindset in a Secular Society.* The volume, my twenty-eighth, contained various lectures and addresses previously unavailable in book form. That same month Gordon-Conwell conferred an honorary doctor of divinity degree specially commending the completion of *God, Revelation and Authority,* which had won the Evangelical Christian Publishers Association gold medallion award in the theology and doctrine category.

The years 1984 and 1985 were the first in a decade in which I did not lecture outside North America. For one thing, Korean and Mandarin publication of volume 4 of *God, Revelation and Authority*—an extensive volume on biblical inspiration, inerrancy and interpretation—was not scheduled until 1986. For another, the worsening ambiguity of American evangelicalism seemed to me to justify a concentration of effort at home. The *Washington Times* carried a full-page Easter question-and-answer interview in its religion section. Television opportunities included participation in the Christmas Sunday NBC *Today* program with David Brinkley. Numerous publishers had expressed interest in an autobiography, but Floyd Thatcher of Word Books sent a contract and urged completion by yearend 1985 for publication in 1986.

In 1984 I taught or lectured at Emmanuel School of Theology, International School of Theology, Hope College, Huntington College, Spring Arbor College, Taylor University and Westminster of California. In addition I addressed the Shavano Institute for National Leadership and served on a panel with Dr. Frank Stanger at the 200th anniversary of American Methodism. I was requested to serve on the resolutions committee of the tumultuous Southern Baptist Convention in Kansas City at which conservatives elected Dr. Charles Stanley over candidates promoted by the convention staff and nonconservative churchmen. I continued an active role as board member of Ethics and Public Policy Center, Institute for Advanced Christian Studies, Prison Fellowship and Institute for Religion and Democracy, of which I was named vice president. In addition, I served on the advisory board of the Christian College Coalition, *The Modern Age* and numerous other enterprises. Helga and I team-taught, as before, at the National Church Growth Center's writers' conference.

Alongside these activities there were book reviews and articles and addresses to prepare, and a dispiriting amount of correspondence. Out of the whole I carved a bit of time (Ted Engstrom once said that "God gives us enough time to do everything he wants us to do") to supervise the several hundred azaleas, many of them raised from cuttings, that blanket our back yard and in the spring turn our Arlington property into a splash of color that only the fall foliage can rival.

In the Fall of 1984 Paul ran for Congress from Michigan's Fifth District and won in a 63 percent sweep of the ballot box that outpaced the Reagan landslide by several points. Although his family decided to remain in Grand Rapids, where Karen and their three children have cherished associations and involvements, he lodged with us until after the inauguration, and after that met with us periodically for early breakfast or a late snack. Bill Bates, Carol's husband, had composed Reformation Day anthems, and Carol had completed for publication in Paris a major contribution to contemporary musicology. Both families were with us for Christmas.

The year 1984 also finally sealed the fortunes of *Christianity Today* as an essentially popular news and feature magazine with theological overtones of broad evangelical dimension. Already in 1981, when the magazine held its twenty-fourth anniversary luncheon in Kansas City on the edge of the American Festival of Evangelism, Harold Myra solicited names for a prospective successor to Kantzer, whose editorship had begun four years earlier. Kantzer had indicated that he would like to serve as editor until he was 65 and that he would resign on August 31, 1982, six months after reaching 65, in order to return to teaching. Although Myra had taken over control of the magazine before Lindsell's departure and was really editing as well as publishing it when Kantzer arrived, Kantzer insisted upon filling the role of editor and on being perceived as the responsible spokesman for editorial content. In the spring of 1982 the Board named as editor-elect Dr. Gilbert Beers, an alumnus of Wheaton College and member of its board of trustees, who had served many years with David C. Cook

Company. Beers was consciously an evangelical and a graduate of Northern Baptist Theological Seminary; he was, however, neither an avowed theologian nor technically an editor. Myra's leadership was geared to increasing magazine appeal to a wider, largely lay leadership. Trustees hailed the magazine's financial success but recognized its increasing loss of theological virility. As early as August, 1980, Dr. David Baker, a long-time Board member and son-in-law of J. Howard Pew, resigned in protest because "*Christianity Today* is no longer the magazine it was founded to become"; it has become "more of a Christian family magazine than another *Christian Century* dedicated to the defense and propagation of historic Christianity. Most of the older members of the Board will fully understand this comparison."

The year 1985 opened with several opportunities of special challenge. For several years the Harvard Divinity Students Fellowship had probed possibilities of a lecture; finally, on Maundy Thursday afternoon, I spoke on "Did Jesus Really Rise from the Dead?" a lecture which the divinity faculty joined in sponsoring and which filled the divinity school chapel. The following morning I addressed pastors of the New England Fellowship of Evangelicals on "The Importance of the Resurrection for the Present Day." The Harvard experience led, in turn, to an invitation from the Christian Study Center in New Haven to give three lectures in the Yale Divinity School common room with Professors Hans Frei, Richard Hays and Paul Holmer responding. I addressed the Connecticut convention of the Evangelistic Association of New England on American evangelical prospects. Much of the year was given to correlating and first-drafting materials, many of them still boxed from the *Christianity Today* years, for this autobiography. Once done, the whole needed final editing to excise certain historical and other details of interest only to certain groups of readers. For that reason a copy of the original unabridged and unedited manuscript is secured at Trinity Evangelical Divinity School, to which I have donated my personal library of some 10,000 volumes. When I spoke on October 11, 1985, at the dedication of the library's new extension I learned that a special unit is designated the Carl F. H. Henry Research Center, a microform room with such collections as Migne, STC-I and STC-II that offers immediate access to some 60,000 volumes not on the library shelves.

Other activities included addresses to the president's council at Gordon-Conwell Theological Seminary, lectures to evangelical students at Southeastern Baptist and Southern Baptist seminaries bearing on the debate over biblical authority, a centennial lecture at Moody Bible Institute, preaching at Moody Memorial Church and a satellite radio interview on WMBI carried by ninety-five stations. Commencement addresses at Point Loma College in San Diego and at DeKalb Academy in Atlanta, in San Antonio on the Gospel of John to sixty Bible Study Fellowship teaching directors, a course on current hermeneutical theories at Northwest Baptist Theological College in Vancouver, British Columbia, were additional commitments. Added also were conferences with Christianity Today Institute on church-and-state issues and on the mission of the church in the world.

In many ways 1986 loomed no less auspicious. For the spring term Calvin Theological Seminary in Grand Rapids enlisted me as distinguished visiting professor of systematic theology, and Westminster Theological Seminary as well as Calvin to give commencement addresses in May. From June 30 to July 10 was reserved for the Lutheran Institute for Ecumenical Research in Strasbourg, France, as participant in a top-level dialogue on revolution theology. August 4 to September 6 was scheduled for perhaps a last visit to Asia, coordinated with Korean and Mandarin publication of volume 4 of *God, Revelation and Authority,* with lectures first in Singapore, then in Hong Kong and next in Taipei and Seoul. Beyond that, in mid-September, was an invitation by University of Missouri Law School to lecture on the Judeo-Christian heritage and human rights in a series with Secretary of Education William Bennett and Dr. Max Stackhouse of Andover Newton Theological Seminary.

Trinity Evangelical Divinity School invited me to come annually as visiting lecturer in systematic theology beginning the Spring of 1987. If God should spare me for the effort, I would still like to complete a one-volume work on the Christian revelation of world-life ultimates.

During the period from its early pastors' conferences in the 1940s to the present time, World Vision has been an incomparable partner in extending the compassionate outreach of Christians in ten Western nations to less fortunate millions upon millions in eighty non-Western countries. Decades before Live-Aid and other secular programs, and even many denominational programs, awakened to the need, World Vision had pointed the way. Within that framework I tried as best I could to participate specially in the theological training of Third World candidates for national and transcultural service. World Vision added, in the fullest sense, an "at large" dimension to my ministry, and to its credit maintained with integrity every commitment it had made to me. I shall be ever grateful.

19

The Evangelical Prospect in America

I have two main convictions about the near-term future of American Christianity. One is that American evangelicals presently face their biggest opportunity since the Protestant Reformation, if not since the apostolic age. The other is that Americans are forfeiting that opportunity stage by stage, despite the fact that evangelical outcomes in the twentieth century depend upon decisions currently in the making. The saddest side of this forfeiture is that many evangelical leaders bask promotionally in the movement's towering success instead of pointing it to repentance, rededication, reformation and renewal. Worse yet, even some so-called renewal movements have promotive and exploitative facets.

The evangelical recovery during the past half century has been nothing less than phenomenal. For perspective on that resurgence one need only remember the recent past and note some turning points decisive for evangelical fortunes. When one recalls the secure modernist takeover of evangelical colleges and seminaries, the Federal Council (later the National Council) of Churches' dominance of the ecclesiastical scene and then the gradual collapse of liberal ecumenism in the wake of the stunning reemergence of evangelical Christianity, it is no wonder that some persons speak today with almost millennial anticipation of a cresting conservative revival.

Fifty years ago the uncontested voice of American Protestantism was the *Christian Century,* a skillful advocate of ecumenical pluralism and of the theological and socio-political left. Not only were the evangelical clergy beleaguered and outmaneuvered, but the very term evangelical was in ecclesiastical disrepute. When modernism swept over the churches in the 1920s and 1930s, seven in ten Americans were church members; some four in ten attended quite regularly and the Bible was the nation's most popular book (even if not faithfully read). By the early 1940s, when I earned my doctorate in theology, only 41 percent said they had read the Bible in a year.

Then a series of remarkable developments posed an accelerating challenge to the religious scene: formation of the National Association of Evangelicals in 1942, founding of Fuller Theological Seminary in 1947, national headlines for Billy Graham's evangelistic crusades beginning in 1949, founding of *Christianity Today* magazine in 1956. These enterprises informally linked some of evangelicalism's ablest leaders for an overall witness contributory to evangelical ecumenism, evangelism, theology, apologetics and social ethics. Vigorous new student groups—movements like Youth for Christ, Navigators, Campus Crusade and Young Life—emerged to supplement the outreach of Inter-Varsity Christian Fellowship. Into evangelical colleges and seminaries they funneled a floodtide of eager ministerial and missionary candidates, and young scholars pursuing doctorates in biblically related fields. By the mid-1970s American evangelicals were riding the crest of religious influence.

This escalating conservative church growth and evident evangelical vitality in a time of religious confusion finally prompted *Newsweek*'s cover story on October 25, 1976, proclaiming "The Year of the Evangelical." *Newsweek* affirmed that "the religious phenomenon of the '70s" is "the emergence of evangelical Christianity into a position of respect and power." A Gallup survey indicated that half of all Protestants and a third of all Americans—in summary, nearly fifty million American adults—claimed to be "born again." In a seven-page photographic essay titled "Born Again" *Newsweek* noted that both Jimmy Carter and Gerald Ford professed to be evangelical believers. *Newsweek* added that, while found in every Protestant denomination in every part of the nation, evangelicals "are particularly strong among Southern Baptists." The northern evangelical establishment, said *Newsweek,* was represented by the National Association of Evangelicals, National Religious Broadcasters, Billy Graham Evangelistic Association and *Christianity Today* ("the unofficial voice of established evangelical opinion"). Many evangelical spokesmen promptly declared that a sweeping national religious revival was underway.

Yet none of the major contributory evangelical movements fully achieved its original goal. While N.A.E. coordinated independent evangelicals and Pentecostals, comparatively few clergy and lay leaders from ecumenically aligned churches found its orientation stimulating. Although Fuller brought to many evangelical seminaries a new sense of academic excellence, it foundered for lack of administrative leadership, moderated its initial biblical commitments and became infatuated with numbers. While Graham crusades won a host of converts and provoked several mainline denominations to recognize anew the importance of evangelism, they did not fulfill expectations that evangelism could reverse a progressively secularizing culture nor did they restore evangelism to priority in most local churches. *Christianity Today,* once considered an indispensable theological guide by clergy and reflective laymen, tilted to a mass market philosophy and thereafter competed less with nonevangelical journals than with evangelical magazines. While the burgeoning evangelical colleges emphasized a theistic world-life view alternative to secular humanism, they sponsored no program to confront the secular mindset on its own terrain, and evangelists instead established rival universities whose result was more protective than penetrative.

During the past twenty-five years American evangelicals have in fact several times failed to walk through open doors that might spectacularly have set their cause ahead with important consequences for the nation's religious fortunes. In each case the movement's leaders retreated from a significant possibility for deeper penetration of the socio-cultural arena.

One was in 1960, when they lost the opportunity to launch a major Christian university in a great metropolitan area, in this case in the New York-New Jersey vicinity giving students striking access to vocational and professional careers. Today even churches in New York City struggle for effective memberships and financial consultants counsel evangelical telecasters to avoid Manhattan as "a graveyard for evangelism."

Another was in 1968, when directors repositioned *Christianity Today,* I believe, on a general editorial course that led in 1977 to a lay-oriented policy and to the magazine's removal from Washington to suburban Wheaton, Illinois.

Another was in the 1970s when important openings arose for evangelical realignment on an enlarged N.A.E. base. Carl McIntire's American Council of Christian Churches had withered, and some fundamentalists were already reaching for constructive alternatives. Meanwhile Reformed, Wesleyan, Pentecostal and other subgroups of N.A.E. met independently to address their own theological concerns. Although doubts existed that a super-N.A.E. offered a hopeful alternative—particularly if Southern Baptists were to be drawn into larger evangelical liaison—yet only a minority, mainly a vocal Christian Reformed vanguard, looked affirmatively toward the National Council of Churches. In the early 1970s Graham was still the one charismatic personality who might have rallied evangelicals for a long, hard look at their need of more comprehensive unity and at the neglected issue of evangelical ecclesiology. Graham was the one figure who could have rallied larger response among Southern Baptists. But interest on Graham's part in a new and larger non-NCC movement would have seriously complicated relationships of his crusades to ecumenically oriented churches, since he exacted their endorsement as the price of city-wide meetings.

Key '73 had only limited success in offsetting evangelical independency. On the one hand, ecumenically affiliated denominations were more interested in social protest than in personal evangelism; on the other hand, fundamentalist churches were reluctant to cooperate with evangelicals in ecumenically identified churches.

The next and perhaps final opportunity to probe a larger movement enlisting more evangelicals from NCC-affiliated churches and perhaps also more Southern Baptists, came with *Newsweek*'s 1976 proclamation of the evangelical high tide. But precisely at that time N.A.E. was preoccupied with a building program in Wheaton and confined its sights to existing membership perimeters. The growing prominence of the electronic evangelists soon elevated National Religious Broadcasters over N.A.E. in the public eye as a mirror of evangelical vitalities. The Graham Center subsequently sponsored conferences on the future of evangelicalism, but the inerrancy debate complicated the discussion from the outset. When Francis Schaeffer sketched a vast laymen's movement predicated on inerrancy, a former Southern Baptist Convention president replied that such special focus would put off many Southern Baptists. The next Graham Center conference on evangelical futures featured Martin Marty as speaker.

The evangelical movement was now coping with theological imprecision in some of its own schools. It had emerged from obscurity to dramatic resurgence through a remarkable coalition of evangelical evangelism symbolized by Graham and of evangelical theology symbolized by *Christianity Today,* which had rallied an international, multidenominational corps of scholars articulating conservative theology. But the sudden refocusing of all issues on the criterion of biblical inerrancy—precisely at the peak of the movement's public impact—exposed the evangelical cause as itself deeply split over the issue of religious authority. Even evangelical colleges and seminaries, the supposed guardians of evangelical orthodoxy, were depicted by evangelical spokesmen as seriously compromised.

In its 1976 overview *Newsweek* noted certain troublesome conflict areas inside evangelicalism: over biblical infallibility, over involvement in public affairs, over radical young social activists, over whether spiritual obedience yields health, happiness and material abundance or requires a sacrificial lifestyle and perhaps suffering. Speaking of such divisions, *Newsweek* concluded that "1976 may yet turn out to be the year that the evangelicals won the White House but lost cohesiveness as a distinct force in American religion and culture." *Newsweek* noted, moreover, the growing determination of certain Southern Baptist spokesmen to distinguish their denomination from the evangelical movement. Despite its evangelistic vitality and new visibility, some wondered whether the evangelical "movement" was held together by computerized mailings and pungent media comment of a few vocal leaders more than by a carefully knit philosophy of evangelical engagement.

Mainstream evangelicalism assumed, as did neoorthodoxy and liberalism, that fundamentalist independency was terminally ill. While fundamentalists had many strong local churches, active Sunday schools and Christian day schools, they had withdrawn from cooperative evangelism and from public involvement. The formation of Moral Majority in 1979 swiftly changed that scenario.

The evangelical establishment had looked largely to evangelism as the primary and indispensable social solvent, and it avoided political debate over controversial public issues. It largely commended right-wing Republican commitments but formulated no program of civic engagement. Public activism became the prerogative of left-tilting young evangelicals like Jim Wallis and Ronald Sider, the former promoting disarmament and hostility to nuclear missiles, and the latter advancing the notion that rich Christians and capitalists were somehow specially responsible for world poverty.

In this context fundamentalists dramatically reentered the public arena. Founded in 1979 with Jerry Falwell as president, Moral Majority signaled a deliberate incursion of conservative Christian activism into political debate and public policy advocacy. Mainline churches and synagogues had already set an ecclesiastical precedent for a high intensity blitz during anti-Vietnam war protests and in the civil rights movement of the 1960s and 1970s. Moral Majority now took a stand wherever public policy seemed to collide with other Christian values. Faced by an articulate rival activism, the ecumenical mainline quickly deplored such conservative involvement as promotive of an ecclesiastical political takeover, an attempt to legislate Christian theocratic controls on a pluralistic nation. Although some early Moral Majority pronouncements invited such criticism that the movement aimed to establish (or reestablish) a Christian government in America, Falwell soon announced that the thrust of Moral Majority was ethical rather than theological, and that it spoke for many Mormons and conservative Jews no less than for Christians.

Assessments that this conservative involvement in public affairs was simply a strategic offsetting by the right of what ecumenically aligned leaders were promoting on the left obscured its deeper significance. Such hasty judgment overlooked the fact that in earlier generations evangelical orthodoxy was deeply involved in socio-political concerns. Fundamentalist withdrawal from cultural and public affairs in the generations after 1920 contrasted sharply with the nineteenth century impact of Shaftesbury, Hutchison and others during the evangelical revival in England and the evangelical protest against slavery in America. The fundamentalist privatization of piety and withdrawal from public concerns had stirred my *Uneasy Conscience.* Falwell now made clear that the far-right would speak up on national issues that Graham, *Christianity Today* and the National Association of Evangelicals had largely skirted.

An evangelical leadership vacuum contributed indirectly to the reemergence of a bold fundamentalist presence at frontiers of social criticism. To preserve harmony within its rather diverse constituency, N.A.E. avoided controversial socio-political commitments, and its Wheaton headquarters moreover exerted no leadership role in the deepening national moral crisis. Bill Bright's Campus Crusade, Oral Roberts's mass meetings and other efforts by new charismatic figures including Pat Robertson of "The 700 Club" and Jim Bakker of PTL network viewed the success of global Christianity as hinging specially on their evangelistic energies and depicted their enterprises as world-changing. They confronted national moral decline mainly by underscoring the need for personal spiritual commitment and religious renewal, although Robertson more than others voiced the need of a Christian thrust in government. *Christianity Today* had lost a nonevangelical reader audience and gave only sporadic attention to public concerns and the clash over rival values reflected in legislative proposals. Billy Graham had amiable ties to the Nixon White House and during one crusade in Tennessee he and Nixon traded tributes. But after Watergate Graham resolved to avoid White House entanglement (and largely did so during the regime of his "born again" fellow Southern Baptist Jimmy Carter), only to renew ties during the Reagan era.

Given visibility by his weekly national telecast, Falwell became an instant media resource, all the more since public relations aides offered the networks his prompt sound-blips on any controversial moral issue. Yet the evangelical movement now lacked a leader whose personal authority and charisma could gather all evangelicals together for a common effort transcending cooperative evangelism, which was increasingly recognized as unable by itself to entrench social justice. Looking back over his tenure as editor of *Christianity Today,* Kenneth Kantzer singled out the shift toward political and social engagement as the most striking change in American evangelicalism during the years 1977–1982.

What then shall we say concerning the evangelical situation at present?

1. My assessment is that the evangelical phenomenon in the United States is broadening but not significantly deepening. It lacks cohesion. No intellectually articulate spokesman has both acknowledged authority and universal acceptance to speak for the entire enterprise. Television personalities like Pat Robertson, Jerry Falwell, Jim Bakker, Robert Schuller and Oral Roberts have become its household names, and Billy Graham gets a significant national press when he goes to Soviet-bloc nations. The secular media are more interested in Falwell's pungent one-liners than in what mainline evangelical college presidents or editors have to say.

2. The term evangelical during the past fifteen years has become ambiguous through deliberate distortion by critics and needless confusion invited by some of the movement's own leaders. Nonevangelicals are somewhat unsure of the term's connotation except for emphasis on the "new birth," the divinity of Jesus Christ and the importance of the Bible. Many evangelicals now measure growth mainly in terms of numbers; distinctions of doctrine and practice are subordinated in a broad welcome for charismatic, Catholic, traditional and other varieties of evangelicals. Theological differences are minimized by evangelical publishers and publications reaching for mass circulation, by evangelists luring capacity audiences and even by evangelism festivals seeking the largest possible involvement. Church growth seminars have even embraced "miracle-growth" churches that claim to raise the dead and to reproduce all other apostolic gifts. Numerical bigness has become an infectious epidemic.

At the same time nonevangelicals who for secondary reasons link themselves to the evangelical resurgence further cloud questions of confessional orthodoxy. Ecumenical pluralists welcome evangelicals with leftist political commitments, and liberal seminaries extend visibility for conservative scholars who embrace biblical criticism and accommodate liberation theology. Among Southern Baptists nonevangelical spokesmen project a choice between evangelism and biblical inerrancy as rival priorities (as if the Great Commission were self-authenticating). While N.A.E. gives platform prominence to radical denunciations of "false evangelicals" subscribing to biblical errancy, some of the organization's own spokesmen disavow inerrancy. Fundamentalists dwell on differences and frequently depict evangelicals as neoevangelicals. Falwell boasted in *The Fundamentalist Phenomenon* that fundamentalists had hijacked the evangelical jumbo-jet, while at the same time he urged mutual cooperation. Jack Van Impe and several others meanwhile sought to transcend the lingering fundamentalist-evangelical rivalries.

3. Although somewhat restrained, secular modernity is tightening its hostility to supernaturalism. Secular thought considers Christian theism a cultural oddity. Like Soviet communism, Anglo-Saxon humanism, process philosophy and contemporary theology all promote a one-layer theory of reality. By contrast, even ancient pagan intellectuals conceded the reality of the supernatural, and insisted that human meaning and worth cannot long survive its eclipse. History has reserved for renegade humanity in our century an eager embrace of what ancient, medieval and early modern sages fled like a dread disease—the illusion that the human species is the sole crown of the cosmos, generator of the good, touchstone of truth, fashioner of the future and designer of destiny.

While evangelicals seek to penetrate the culture, the culture simultaneously makes disconcerting inroads into evangelical life. This is specially evident in the widening notion that divorce and remarriage are simply matters of free moral choice. The church's credibility is compromised by an evaporation of discipline even when congregational values are deeply breached. A disturbing number of church members cling to the idols of money and material things, sex and status, that bewitch the Western world.

The evangelical impact on society has not altered the basic humanist stance of the campus, the media or the political arena. Criticism of media permissiveness has provoked countermovements that malign evangelicals as hostile to freedom, given to censorship and addicted to book-burning. Some mainline publishing houses are waiting for the evangelical epiphenomenon to pass away.

Yet the worldly quest for self-fulfillment leads instead to self-frustration and to a questioning of the value of personal survival. In the aftermath of ethical relativism those who seal their souls against the supernatural soon doubt the existence of wisdom, goodness and happiness. Only a diminishing list of social conventions preserves from chaos the daily life of many moral vagabonds. Not a few social critics warn that only our fascination with scientific technology and our preoccupation with media entertainment obscures an encroaching "dark ages." Some think we should dress even now for a wake for Western culture, one for which Solzhenitsyn has crafted an appropriate funeral oration.

4. The strength of evangelical theism lies in its offer of religious realities that human unregeneracy desperately needs and cannot otherwise provide. In a time of spiritual rootlessness Christianity proclaims God the self-revealed heavenly Redeemer. In a time of intellectual skepticism, it adduces fixed truths about God's holy purpose for man and the world. In a time of ethical permissiveness, it offers moral absolutes and specific divine imperatives. In a time of frightful fear of the future, it presents a sure and final hope. In a time when daily life has turned bitter and sour for multitudes of humans, it offers a life-transforming dynamic.

Amazing short-sightedness refocused the evangelical dialogue—just when the world-press publicly conceded "the year of the evangelical"—on epistemological differences that depicted evangelicals as openly at odds with each other. An opportunity existed of rallying the whole evangelical enterprise to socio-cultural engagement in which even a crippled soldier might somehow serve the cause of faith. Instead, exulting in their evident public gains, evangelicals indulged in the luxury of internal conflict and channeled theological energies into the controversy over biblical inerrancy. The secular media gleefully mirrored the controversy over evangelical sheep and goats, wheat and tares, that ranged school against school, faculty against faculty, pastor against pastor.

The point is not that Scripture's comprehensive reliability is an unimportant second-order issue. Those who think that without a trustworthy Bible they can preserve the priority of the Great Commission or even an orthodox doctrine of Jesus Christ, cannot see the sun beyond the rain. Yet there was a better way than to warn the world against fraudulent evangelicals, a tactic that could only stimulate the counterformation of an evangelical anti-defamation league.

The Bible is the authoritative book about creation life, redemption life and resurrection life. The very truth and Word of God are accessible to our nation in more English versions than most people have heard of, and in several thousand other languages if English will not do. Almost all versions offer light enough to banish the night, to turn the soul toward God, to light the lamp of faith, to lead the worst sinner to salvation.

Even liberal thinkers now warn modern biblical scholars that their critical partitioning of the Bible has led to irreconcilable disagreements, and that the time is long overdue to hear the biblical canon in its comprehensive unity. To be sure, liberals are not about to return to a fully authoritative, specially inspired, inerrant canon, nor are they outlawing documentary and historical criticism. They place new emphasis, however, on letting the Bible speak for itself, letting it make its own claims, utter its own denunciations, until we all ask, "Is it I, Lord?" The liberals have shrewdly left it to evangelicals to confound the world by emphasis on false evangelicals and untrustworthy evangelical scholars and schools.

The Council for Biblical Inerrancy became a rallying cry among independent evangelicals and institutions that champion flawless autographs. It has moved beyond its initial polemical phase to scholarly conferences on scriptural reliability and interpretation, and to publication at least of some quality books addressing frontier issues. But it now belatedly faces the difficult task of enlisting kindred spirits from many denominations who ought to have been carefully recruited and involved before independents hurriedly sounded their call to arms. It may be that prominent lay leaders for whom scriptural inerrancy is a firm presupposition rather than a battle cry, and who came to the Christ of the Bible not through family tradition but rather out of spiritual rootlessness and intellectual skepticism and moral relativism, can lend the movement a necessary broader identity. The fact that an ecumenically oriented Lutheran bishop has recently said that all faculty posts in denominational seminaries should be reserved for non-inerrantists holding critical views of the Bible, may be the provocative turn that makes the issue a mainline *cause célèbre.* The proposal would entrench as official policy what many denominational schools now already routinely practice.

While scriptural authority must be part of any authentic evangelical renewal, evangelicals will affirm it to their own reproof apart from the cry, "Let my heart be broken" and filled with the truth and grace of God. Christian integrity is nullified if spokesmen for scriptural inerrancy combine it with perverse misjudgment and distortion of others' views.

5. The evangelical movement looks stronger than in fact it is. Evangelicalism presumptively acts as if it were the permanently appointed preserver of "the faith once-for-all delivered" and specially entrusted with ecclesial keys to the Kingdom. But no earthly movement holds the Lion of the Tribe of Judah by the tail. We may need for a season to be encaged in the Lion's den until we recover an apostolic awe of the Risen Christ, the invincible Head of a dependent body sustained by his supernatural power. Apart from life in and by the Spirit we are all pseudo-evangelicals.

Evangelicals appear stronger than we really are because deep and besetting problems plague other religious communities. Multitudes of American Roman Catholics oppose the Pope on cardinal doctrines such as birth control and priestly celibacy and abortion. Jews are also openly divided on fundamental issues. Protestant ecumenism is in dire trouble; conservative churches have sidelined many former mainline churches during a decade of evangelical growth.

Americans overall are committed to belief in God, to the importance of the family, to the work-ethic and to love of country. Social scientists fully expect that between now and the end of the century the prevalent form of religion will not differ much from its present conservative contours. There remains among much of the populace a Christian subconsciousness of sorts, one increasingly repressed by self-interest.

For all that, church membership is frequently inflated; some Southern Baptist observers put the miscalculation at 5 percent to 10 percent. Those who move or join other churches often do not notify congregations they have left, and pastors with a self-interest in imprecise statistics are reluctant to "trim the fat." Although 72 percent of Protestants are church members, more than 60 percent of them do not attend worship in a typical week. In some cities, rapidly growing Asian churches, most notably Korean, have outpaced American churches. Evangelicals seem not to halt their routines long enough to consider that, although 95 percent of Americans believe in God, only 66 percent identify the deity as the personal God of biblical revelation. Only 15 percent read the Bible daily. Only seven in ten believe in life after death. Mormon churches, which emphasize traditional values but champion unorthodox doctrines, have grown in twenty-five years from 1,500,000 in 1960 to 5,600,000. In the aftermath of Asian and African immigration more and more Muslim mosques and Buddhist temples arise alongside churches and synagogues. America's more than 400,000 local churches align into hundreds of denominations, so that not only foreign converts but Asian immigrants as well are sometimes confused as to whether the Christian God is Baptist, Methodist, Pentecostal, Presbyterian or independent.

6. Global statistics on religion underscore the continuing urgency of evangelism. Despite programs to "win the lost in our lifetime" stretching from the Student Volunteer Movement through the Graham Crusades, there are proportionately fewer Christians (32.4 percent) in the world today than there were in 1980 (32.8 percent) or in 1970 (33.7 percent) or in 1900 (34.4 percent). This scenario is the more disturbing in view of the fact that the unevangelized population has reportedly fallen from 48.7 percent at the beginning of our century to 27.9 percent at present—although in actuality a wholly unevangelized world is born every generation. Missiologists estimate that of the world's 2.8 billion non-Christians, most being adherents of other religions, some 2.4 billion fall outside the reach of the usual Christian activities of evangelism.

In the period from 1900 to 1985 the face of the Christian movement has altered considerably. In the West, the number of Christians in Latin America has more than doubled (largely through Pentecostal evangelism); in North America the number has advanced only slightly. Europe, heartland of medieval Christianity and then of the Protestant Reformation, has seen its Christian community reduced almost to half of what it was. In England, France, Germany and Scotland both church membership and attendance are pitifully low. In the U.S.S.R.—once sturdily Eastern Orthodox—the percentage of Christians has dropped from 18.6 percent in 1900 to 7.2 percent at present. The most dramatic Christian gains have occurred in Africa and in South Asia. In Africa the percentage of believers has leaped from 1.7 percent in 1900 to 13.4 percent in 1985, and in South Asia from 3.1 percent to 10.1 percent. On a global basis, in fact, 1,000 new churches come into existence weekly; of these, six new churches are formed every day in Korea.

In overall world context Christianity has nonetheless during the past half century lost some ground, as have Jews and Buddhists. Spectacular growth is registered by Muslims. Yet almost every appraisal of resurgent Islam notes the Muslim religion's militant character, and that it has yet to experience the scientific revolution and to multiply amid religious freedom in a pluralistic society. Islamic reliance on the sword for an extension of Koranic influence may shape the future of the Near East, in the light of both Persian Gulf and Israeli restrictions on Christian missionary activity, more than many observers now suspect.

The percentage of nonreligious persons in the world has far outpaced the growth of any of the world's religions, rising from .2 percent in 1900 to 15 percent in 1970 and 16.9 percent in 1985. Whereas in 1900 avowed atheists numbered one-tenth of one percent of the world population, they number 4.4 percent in 1985. These include hard-core communists, post-Auschwitz Jews and Anglo-Saxon and European naturalists. In China less than 1 percent of the intellectuals are members of the Communist Party, and the Bible can now be brought into the country as a textbook.

American evangelicalism's continuing vitality as a global missionary base is noteworthy. The new pilgrims to America are Hispanics and Oriental refugees. They may help shape America by way of religious transition or of Christian renewal in unforeseen ways. A key test of evangelical vitality will be concern for religious liberty. If this is narrowed simply to protection of legitimate evangelical interests in a pluralistic society, and fails to speak up also for the religious freedom of nonevangelicals and even of non-Christians, we will forfeit a powerful witness. In contrast to intolerant national religions and totalitarian atheism, evangelicals should actively commend and emphasize religious voluntarism. The best context in which to present the Christian gospel is "Choose you this day whom you will serve" (Josh. 24:15). A religion that can make headway only by legal prescription is not worth having.

Yet American evangelicals may also be missing an historically unprecedented home missions opportunity for effective witness to devotees of non-Christian religions. The influx of Asian immigrants has brought to the United States hundreds of thousands of refugees for many of whom an Oriental faith has been little more than a cultural tradition. Among these immigrants there are present also thousands who while abroad became eager Christian converts. To challenge, train and support Christian workers in a powerful evangelistic witness borne to Asians in their own tongue by fellow Asians holds unparalleled possibilities. No convert better knows that superiority and singularity of Christ than one who experientially knows what Buddhism, Confucianism, Hinduism and other isms fail to offer.

Hard-core ecumenism will doubtless increasingly affirm truth in all religions, and disavow the New Testament claim that Jesus is the only Savior. It will not deny that Jesus is "a way" of redemption and that Christians witness that he is Savior and Lord. But today not only a secular humanist or a defector from Christian circles will disavow the singular uniqueness of Jesus Christ, but even a denominational theologian in a confessional college sacrificially supported by mission-minded believers. So, for example, in "A New Future for Jews, Christians and Muslims" (in *Dialogue,* Spring, 1984, pp. 124 f.), Norman A. Beck, chairman of the theology department of Texas Lutheran College, urges Christians to give up claims of "religious exclusivism" and "one-wayism."

7. Debate over political philosophy narrows for many evangelicals to discussion of the propriety of a Christian government. Even those who applaud the idea are much confused over what this implies. Some mean only that we should revive a Christian consensus, which they assumed to have prevailed during the American Revolution and in the subsequent drafting of our charter political documents. Others think that Christians should routinely be preferred as candidates for public office, although nobody wants an evangelical Constantine. Yet spiritual devoutness need not imply political expertise and, in any event, the Constitution disallows a religious test for office. The real question is whether Christians—devoted by definition to biblical principles and to the implantation of scriptural values in society—are to observe the constitutionally stipulated political rules of a pluralistic society.

Christians have biblical reason for seeking a predominantly regenerate society. But do they—as a body of believers within corporate society—have reason also to legislate all scriptural principles upon public institutions including government and schools? Even if they should become the majority, would it be wise to do so? The seventeenth century Puritans of Massachusetts Bay constituted a self-declared Christian society which sought to base all community values on the Bible, restricted political office to Christians and conditioned the right to vote on spiritual qualifications.

Many Christians hold that a contemporary Christian government, one founded on theocratic principles, would be more harmful than helpful. When a supposedly Christian government's policy or program fails (for whatever reason), the Church is inevitably blamed. Will not Christians be disillusioned and in fact discredited if by political means they seek to achieve goals that the Church should ideally advance by preaching and evangelism?

The organizational entrenchment of both liberal and conservative political views now makes it likely that the conflict over values in public policy will shape up increasingly and perhaps permanently as a clash between diverse religious bodies. Long-established denominations with officially subsidized staff resources can promote their views more routinely than can independent agencies relying on solicited contributions. The Roman Catholic Conference of Bishops, Protestant ecumenism and Moral Majority are not the only politically aggressive agencies affirming religious values; Jews and Mormons are also politically influential, and humanists remarkably so.

Although evangelical spokesmen have recently promoted specific political objectives, they have not impressively succeeded in altering the dominant culture or even in securing passage of preferred legislation. Evangelical evangelists are photographed with President Reagan, but Roman Catholics are rewarded with an ambassador to the Vatican and with strategic cabinet posts. Despite all the media tumult over Moral Majority and the high public visibility of its leader, its extensive solicitation of funds during a six-year political crusade—claiming to speak for six million households—has not achieved passage of a single major piece of legislation cherished by the conservative right.

Protestant political engagement overall has been weak because of its lack of a comprehensive philosophy. Two generations ago American Christians expected from education alone more than an accelerating modernist utopianism could deliver. During the past generation, many evangelicals expected from evangelism more than evangelism alone can deliver. Now many fundamentalists seem to expect from political engagement more than it can deliver.

The evangelical churches view the issues of abortion and school prayer as compelling ethical and religious concerns. Their opposition was provoked by the government's policy of funding abortions and of excluding prayer from public schools, actions which the churches regarded as intrusions into the realm of religious values.

Current flashpoints include the issues of equal access to school facilities, religious displays and observances on public property, and the long-standing debate over diplomatic relations with the papacy. Equal access legislation presently allows voluntary student groups, secular or religious, to meet in public high schools before or after class hours.

Public religious observances have become increasingly controversial. Particular religious referents are a much-debated aspect of government celebrations. Some critics would end Christmas observance as a government holiday; others would even replace the abbreviations B.C. and A.D. by B.C.E. (before the common era) and A.C.E. (after the common era). Church-state separation, they hold, requires an exclusion of all religious symbols from public life. Some support public observance of Christmas on the ground that it has become a secular folk-festival devoid of religious significance. Others insist that the First Amendment was not intended to deprive public holidays of any and all acknowledgment of their traditional religious nature.

The school prayer issue is exceedingly difficult. The rightful and traditional place which religion has had in education is not simply in marginal worship but as part of cognitive classroom content. A prefatory prayer followed by a dismissal of theistic considerations from the classroom could reinforce the impression that such concerns are only emotionally and volitionally significant. Officially stipulated prayers have been declared unconstitutional. A successive panorama of doctrinally conflicting prayers would be more confusing than no prayer at all. A moment of silence would be more compatible with humanist awe in the presence of the universe than with the Judeo-Christian emphasis that divine-human communication is verbal.

Religion will continue in the near future to be a conditioning factor in the lives of most Americans. It will not be constricted to private life, but will be a shaping force in public policy. Many values at stake in the current political debate are values nurtured by the nation's Judeo-Christian religious heritage. This anchorage of moral values in transcendent religious realities is no mere contemporary emphasis; it is mirrored by the affirmation of the Declaration of Independence of "inalienable rights" conferred by the Creator of all mankind and in the Establishment and Free Exercise clauses of the Constitution that assure religious freedom.

In the pluralistic context of American life a "civil religion" of sorts has always emerged to impact on the public outlook in terms of a popular consensus. Some critics view civil religion only as a bastard byproduct that is best eradicated. But civil religion is an ineradicable phenomenon, and is best improved rather than merely deplored.

There is no hard evidence that evangelicals constitute a monolithic political bloc, or that evangelical collegians and seminarians do. The political right includes Moral Majority (not strictly an evangelical effort), Pat Robertson's Christian Broadcasting Network, establishment conservatives in the N.A.E. and N.R.B., Christian Voice and smaller groups as well as many individuals not in these groupings. The CBN constituency favors a presidential bid by Robertson (whose father was a distinguished U.S. Senator from Virginia), who seeks increasingly to be perceived not as an evangelist but as a television personality. Jerry Falwell of Moral Majority reportedly has personally endorsed Vice President Bush and Gary Jarmin of Christian Voice has reportedly endorsed Congressman Jack Kemp. The Christian right's political agenda opposes abortion-on-demand and public school teaching of secular humanism and evolutionary scientism, while it advocates school prayer and teaching of "scientific creationism."

The evangelical return to politics poses no threat to democratic civility. To be sure, there are occasional abortion-clinic bombers and pamphleteering defamers of any who disagree even in part with intemperate crusaders, but every movement must contend with a radical and extremist fringe. There is no real basis for classifying evangelical political involvement with Islamic fundamentalism or Soga Gakkai Buddhism, Rhoshtriya Swayam Hinduism or Edah Haredit Judaism as do liberals who swiftly brand all nonpluralistic movements as intolerant. All political action involves judgments, ideals, values and goals; the notion that these are uncivil and intolerant if they proceed from the right rather than from the left is sheer bigotry. It is incredible that ecumenical pluralists should have been roused to fury over the fundamentalist effort to impose Christian legislation upon pluralistic America, while they said little about atheistic communism's arbitrary restrictions on Christians and Jews in Eastern Europe, and about Islamic leaders who, if they could, would impose Allah's *sharia* upon the whole world. Commentators who link American fundamentalism with Islamic fundamentalism reflect an uncritical bias. The media elite's identification of evangelical political action as religio-political fanaticism, and a seedbed of political intolerance, is more imaginary than real.

A national survey of college and seminary students shows that less than half of evangelical seminarians and less than a fourth of evangelical collegians on major religious campuses approve Moral Majority's goals. The movement's early ambiguous emphasis on a "Christian America" as the aim of political action doubtless somewhat colored this judgment. Only one in eight seminarians would support a Constitutional amendment to make Christianity the official religion of the United States. Yet there was no commendation of a pagan America, or of the hedonistic lifestyle of the '60s, or of the secular humanist incursion into education, politics and the media. Evangelical college and seminary students are politically more conservative than other students, and more conservative still than the American population as a whole. The notion that *Sojourners* magazine reflects evangelical student opinion is not well founded.

From recent surveys J. D. Hunter concludes that "the coming generation of American Evangelicals fits well within the boundaries of political civility." The representation of Protestant conservatives as extremists he ascribes in part to the fact that commentators on the New Christian Right "tend to share a bias against theologically conservative Protestants" ("Political Civility and American Evangelicals," in *Journal for the Scientific Study of Religion,* Vol. 23, No. 4, December, 1984, pp. 375 f.).

The disturbing fact is that no bold, creative counterproposal and counterassault exist to invade the educational, media and political arenas with a comprehensive alternative. No evangelical college, organization or publication presently charts that course. Contemporary evangelicalism lacks coordination of its theological, evangelistic and socio-cultural concerns. There is no broad evangelical vision, no commitment to dynamisms and goals sufficiently inclusive to contain and reverse the temper of the times.

What is now and then offered as a courageous evangelical initiative reduces to an individual projection with entrepreneurial overtones linked to a funding appeal to support a particular program which, however commendable, cannot hope to constitute, simply on its own, more than a pilot project or isolated effort. Individual fundamentalists have during the past five or ten years discovered poverty in the Third World and some have announced new programs of compassion without the on-site capabilities of established agencies; some have yet to discover poverty at home. Some rush for the media limelight to promote new proposals as if they were pioneer efforts, and speak as if mere public announcement guarantees the desired end-result much as miracle-medicines work in television commercials. Often these proposals combine sound commitments with highly debatable correlatives. Sometimes many years pass before prematurely publicized projections become reality, if they eventually do. Sometimes leaders with prophetic self-assurance will counsel evangelicals publicly to invest in South

African Krugerands. Some spokesmen speak uncritically of Israel, which is indubitably of high importance for U.S. military policy in the Middle East and also has biblical significance, as if that nation can do no wrong; they are less critical than Yahweh is of Israel's spiritual rebellion. The evangelical movement's hard-won prominence and momentary security can be opportunistically exploited in view of constituency appeal and in quest of potential funding.

Some proposals have much merit—for example, that well-to-do congregations consider adopting poverty-ridden congregations to get them on their feet; that adoption agencies be formed to assist abortion-minded unwed mothers; that regional clothes-and-pantry closets aid families in emergency need; that congregations organize to find work for their unemployed. Yet statistics will attest how limited is the impact of such voluntary effort in coping on its present basis with the problem as a whole. To be sure, even limited success is to be highly commended, and emphasis on voluntarism is preferable to cosmetic bureaucracy that taxes citizens for programs which benefit administrators more than the needy. But a comprehensively coordinated effort could become sociologically significant.

Present patterns should provoke the evangelical community to sustained discussion of immediate and long-term goals. Are the movement's ultimate objectives clearly defined and deeply shared? How do present objectives anticipate and contribute to future goals? Do evangelicals really know what they want in the political arena, or even what they have a right to expect? Some observers say that at the 1988 Republican convention evangelicals may control some 20 percent of the delegates and may significantly influence platform commitments and candidate selection. On their own say-so, Presidents Reagan, Carter and Ford all were evangelicals; Nixon privately claimed also to be one, at least in earlier years. Do evangelicals ultimately want congressmen and congresswomen proportionate to the evangelical population? Is there any guarantee that national leadership reflective of religious blocs would improve either national or evangelical fortunes? And what then happens to church-state separation?

Constituency confidence in mainline denominations waned notably as a consequence of ecumenical politicization. Are evangelical churches less vulnerable to such disaffection simply because their politicization would be on the right rather than on the left?

Evangelicals need in any case to set an agenda of public priorities. If despite doctrinal disagreement over ecclesiology and eschatology they can cooperate on evangelism as an inescapable mandate, they should be able likewise to shape an orderly list of public goals and approved means to serve as salt, light and leaven in American society. To be sure, some individual leaders have spoken out in fearless protest, and have sponsored such cultural para-efforts as Christian day schools, religious colleges, evangelical media and so on. These have value in a day when the secular mainstream is highly erosive of Christian values, and nobody should understate their contribution. Apart from the rivalry that characterizes some of these enterprises and that fragments their evangelical impact, they largely enable the secular mainstream to go its own way and pose little challenge to it; moreover, they seldom achieve in their special spheres of operation the excellence that commends Christianity at its historic best. The evangelical witness is worthy of a coordinated effort.

8. The evangelical movement is woefully confused on free enterprise issues. While it staunchly opposes communism as an ideology of totalitarian atheism and statist restriction on human rights, especially religious freedom, it is ambivalent about Marxist economic analysis. Neither evangelical colleges nor seminaries prepare logic-wary young people for clear distinctions. Few seem aware that socialism is demonstrably a miserable failure in country after country where it has been tried, while Third World capitalistic countries like Korea and Taiwan have experienced economic revival.

Poverty is an ever-present phenomenon of human history. Only the emergence of capitalism in recent modern times offered the lower class an opportunity to rise to middle class status through personal industry. Socialism has no means of creating wealth.

Christian theism approves private property and ethically acquired wealth. The Bible regards individual possessions as a divine entrustment and commends compassionate response to fellow-believers' and to others' survival needs.

Yet some evangelicals, writing as if capitalism were intrinsically unjust, promote forced redistribution of wealth as a divine necessity. One's possession of more than others have, even if hard-won by creative labor, is considered a mark of injustice.

In this context Christian giving loses status as voluntary compassion and instead becomes a legal due. Evangelicals in fact increasingly cloud the distinction between justice and charity and compassion. Compassion comes to be seen as a distribution of economic benefits to the poor through a state monopoly of social services. To be sure, private charity is not a substitute for social justice, and when voluntarism fails there is ample reason for government to intervene. But the notion that charity is a right and that the state ideally advances human welfare by implementing economic equality virtually nullifies the distinction between justice and charity. If charity is a legal obligation a just government must necessarily implement it by taxation and voluntary compassion will inevitably wither.

9. No less disconcerting is a reconstruction of educational philosophy

toward which some evangelical colleges are moving through a growing preoccupation with praxis. One can applaud evangelical emphasis on social involvement, all the more after fundamentalism's lamentable withdrawal from the public arena a generation ago. Salvation Army, World Vision and other humanitarian agencies have commendably assisted impoverished millions. Evangelical college graduates responded laudably to Peace Corps opportunities. College students manifest a growing career interest in social ministries aiding the poor and underprivileged. Nor ought we to fault their interest in a marriage of perspective-courses to applied learning that will enhance career opportunities.

Yet, in distinction from a vocational school, an evangelical liberal arts college has cognitive studies as its proper priority. The excitement of evangelical learning properly centers in the clash of ideas from which spring conflicting views of life.

Increasingly, however, activist social scientists and philosophers debunk as Greek rather than biblical any primary student focus on ideas rather than on social involvement. The unjustifiable contrast between "concrete" Hebrew thought and "abstract" Greek thought is extended into a contrast between action-centered and idea-centered learning. The fact that Christianity requires that truth be "done" and not only "known" is made a rationale for shifting student concentration to public engagement. On some campuses students protest that so many community involvements are now required that they cannot do justice to liberal arts studies for which they enrolled.

Champions of the emerging philosophy contend that book learning has for many students lost its excitement, and that practical involvement can restore flair to the curriculum. Educators eager for large enrollments are ready to accommodate community-service courses, all the more since it constitutes good public relations. But should liberal arts students be charged tuition for engaging in social work? Should they be coerced by the curriculum to engage in social welfare activities for classroom credit?

Some evangelical proponents of the activist philosophy do not stop there. The aim of education, they stress, is active promotion of the kingdom of God in society and, accordingly, they urge an activation of the whole educational enterprise. Trustees and faculty should aggressively condemn nuclear missiles, capitalism, South Africa and much else. Students should directly engage in radical social protest and public confrontation in a demand for swift social change—all this is an essential aspect of their academic studies. A false view of God's image in man, they say, currently obscures "creativity" as the crucial aspect of the *imago.* The traditional emphasis on man's rational and ethical capacities, they complain, is really "Hellenistic."

It remains to be seen whether any student will make the grade if he or she opts to actively protest against these very activist notions, declaring them motivated more by partisan political preferences than by academic authenticity, and resting in fact upon a highly debatable philosophy of education and tendential theology of the *imago Dei.* Only the reading of good books and wrestling of influential ideas will dispute the intellectual novelties which in every generation some proponents eagerly sponsor in the often defamed name of progress and creativity.

The sobering fact is that only 85,000 of the 12 million college and university students in the United States are enrolled in the 70 member-schools of the Christian College Coalition, and some of these very campuses already face worsening problems of attrition. What task force bears greater responsibility than evangelical faculties and students for illumining to secular scholars the cognitive power of the Christian option and the debilitating weaknesses of contemporary alternatives? And will not Christian students seem like Hogan's Army in the midst of millions of university students in an all-out activism aiming by unargued alternatives to change the world?

The evangelical movement can hardly be theologically revitalized if students are detoured from thought to action; if evangelical pastors yearn for doctor of ministry degrees that concentrate on method more than truth; and if laymen remain like some of their clergy too pragmatically preoccupied and too intellectually lazy to grapple cognitive concerns. In the present naturalistic cultural milieu the humanist world-view disparages the Christian revelation as a rational monstrosity. If evangelicals try to live like theists while they think about nature and history and about man much as secular pagans do, they are condemned to survive as intellectual schizophrenics. Nor will the religious colleges defy the culture if their presidents are chosen for public relations skills and trustees for financial ability, while academic committees approve for faculty posts candidates whose convictions they only loosely probe or whom they hesitate to exclude because of peer pressures. The most competent campus professors sometimes have studied only on some prestigious secular campus where evangelical concerns are privatized. Some evangelical campuses initially accommodate diversity as a mark of maturity, until finally no central core of scholars is any longer earnestly devoted to evangelical world-life commitments. Understandably, such colleges have no program or strategy for altering the mindset of the secular universities.

* * *

Fifty years ago I had, as a young Christian, grand visions of the world impact of evangelical Christianity; today, as a timeworn believer,

I still dream at times of the movement's profound potential. Admittedly, it is difficult, especially in the latter years, to distinguish dreams from hallucinations.

I remain profoundly convinced that evangelicals are now facing their biggest opportunity since the Reformation, and yet are forfeiting it; unless soon enlarged, the present opening, at least in the United States, may not long remain. Some may say that larger evangelical expectations are in any case visionary and beyond the bounds of sober analysis. Given the movement's present disarray, some say, any implementation of larger possibilities would require an evangelical pope or a massive religious bureaucracy. There is too little organizational commitment to selfless engagement, and too little burden for massive national cooperation, too little spiritual desire for epoxy to mend the broken parts. Several high-visibility evangelicals, gifted and creative leaders, have told me that American evangelicals have already run past their opportunity without recognizing it, and that what can now be rescued may not be worth the effort.

Perhaps it is foolhardy then to speak of an opportunity that remains. My hesitant proposals in any event include no costly national congress (far less international) that would corral all evangelicals into a spectacular "hoopla" that once again yields verbal agreement and then leaves local implementation to an already overburdened national committee. Such an effort could only be "the last hurrah" of an evangelical movement gone introvert.

The coming decade of decision will be marked either by evangelical penetration of the world, or by the world's penetration of the evangelical movement and an inner circle's reactionary withdrawal into some modern Dead Sea Caves. This ferment is already underway. The Year of the Evangelical was not annually self-renewing. Some already lost opportunities are irretrievable. The theological instability of some educational institutions and approaching retrenchment of evangelical colleges, the unending proliferation of evangelical independency, the decline of formative cultural impact, are eventualities which evangelicals must now accept in the absence of any comprehensively compelling alternative.

Yet I have wondered whether evangelicals might not during these next few years still cooperatively marshall their available resources of prayer and projection in order to initiate in 1990 a national impact to climax the twentieth century in its final decade with a massive outpouring of spiritual and moral energy. Such an effort would encompass Christ's mandate to preach the gospel and to illumine the moral criteria by which God will judge our nation. It would address the evident hunger of many Americans for a personal faith, and simultaneously advance an alternative to secular humanism's cultural domination. A comprehensive program of renewal, evangelism and social engagement would enlist independent evangelicals and fundamentalists, including evangelicals active in ecumenically aligned churches.

Suppose the 35 million adult evangelicals were to engage in sustained personal prayer and corporate prayer in connection with Sunday services or midweek meetings or neighborhood Bible study sessions. Might this not spark a revival of ailing weekly prayer meetings, rekindle the duty of personal evangelism, nurture concern for public righteousness? Could not one of our great Bible institutes—perhaps Moody Bible Institute—volunteer a full-time director of a national prayer vigil, provide office and secretarial help and a WATS line to further such an effort?

Suppose the Billy Graham Center provided leadership to integrate a nationwide decade of evangelism meshing television and radio activity, citywide crusades, regional outreach and local teams of witnessing believers from different congregations.

Suppose evangelical scholars seriously wrestling Christian world-life concerns—both on secular campuses and in evangelical colleges—met in Labor Day weekend conference to identify the intellectual arena's currently ruling tenets and to discuss available means and resources for christianly addressing these premises in cassettes, journals, books and media presentations, and in three-day gatherings of professors and student leaders. Suppose the Christian College Coalition, Institute for Advanced Christian Studies and Inter-Varsity Press at its University of Wisconsin-Madison base, perhaps with Campus Crusade headquarters in Arrowhead Springs aiding West coast engagement, became frameworks for coordination of a major academic thrust. Suppose for each of the 12 million college and university students without a Bible, American Bible Society were to provide a special student edition with the supportive help of Zondervan and Thomas Nelson and Tyndale Press and other Bible publishing houses, and of Gideons? Suppose Christian librarians drew up a list of the 100 most important books for college students seeking light on the Christian view of God and the world and its implications. Suppose knowledgeable faculty members were enlisted to give a related lecture each month on every major campus in America.

Suppose National Religious Broadcasters were to sponsor provocative media presentations including interviews, panel discussions, debates, feature coverage and other programs through CNN satellite television and the Christian Family radio network. Suppose that International Media Service were to establish links to key evangelicals in the secular media—religion editors, newscasters, reporters, columnists and editorial writers—enlisting suggestions and help in focusing on the decade of decision. Suppose the Evangelical Press Association maintained weekly contact with the dynamic frontiers of the developing national program and channeled appropriate news releases and interpretative features to smaller daily and weekly papers across the nation, and suggested local photo and feature story opportunities.

Could not *Christianity Today, Moody Monthly, Christian Herald, Eternity* and other publications call evangelicals to their knees in community commitment until the world asks itself whether evangelical renewal is indeed underway?

Suppose evangelicals in conference and discussion forged an annual agenda of national and local social and political concerns, so that instead of dividing on secondaries evangelicals would advance their commonalities. Suppose the N.A.E. public affairs office and Christian Legal Society and Prison Fellowship Ministries' Justice Fellowship were to correlate evangelical engagement on religious liberty, abortion, pornography, crime and other social concerns, annually concentrating on certain priorities to challenge and roll back the permissive humanist tide. Suppose a weekend conference of evangelical leaders in government were to convene at The Cedars in Arlington to discuss how best to promote national righteousness at the executive, judicial and legislative levels, including evaluation of desirable political goals, platform commitments and policies, and feasible options in view of existing differences over priorities. Suppose evangelical office-holders were to counsel political action groups on the subtleties of legislative procedure and political compromise, distinguishing the realistically possible from the ideally preferable. Suppose that on the local level evangelical concern for social righteousness emerged so that in every city and hamlet true believers would stand shoulder to shoulder to protest the single most glaring infraction and to sponsor a community alternative.

Suppose that, in view of unemployment problems, evangelicals were to identify two local work projects that would best cater to unmet community needs of the majority and of the largest minority, and explore the possibility of advancing such projects with the assistance of voluntary agencies such as churches and service clubs and merchants associations and, as a final resort, government also. Suppose that the Salvation Army, World Vision and World Relief Commission could map a strategy, in cooperation with churches and rescue missions, to reach and restore the needy to self-supportive survival with the Army working in cooperation with inner-city missions, and World Vision and World Relief Commission with immigrant families from Asia and Latin America. Suppose that evangelical college and university students and unemployed local teenagers were to donate a week of vacation time to repainting and repairing homes in impoverished slum areas, with materials furnished by building supply stores that would ultimately benefit from greater respect for property preservation.

Suppose 35 million evangelicals in the United States were encouraged to write a tax-deductible check for $10 to The Decade of Decision, providing funds to launch the effort in 1990. Suppose 12 evangelically oriented corporations or foundations and 12 of the largest inner-city churches were to underwrite the salary, office space, WATS line and secretary for one or more of the major coordinators (of prayer, evangelism, academe, media, public affairs, immigration, unemployment and so on) for the three planning years 1987–1990. Suppose a national letter solicitation invited every evangelical's participation through his local church or a national coordinating office. Suppose a computer network were to correlate the effort which—for the first time since the Protestant Reformation—would bring to the Christian cause all the national energies and dynamisms of which Christianity is worthy.

The profoundest element, to be sure, must always be the free, unpredictable and quite unmanageable presence and power of the Holy Spirit, who comes when hungry hearts ache for him. Apart from his dynamic we are trying to repair broken ecclesiastical furniture with kindergarten putty.

Is it possible that from among 35 million believers enough evangelical men and women of vision will rise to chart a nationwide thrust that reaches for America's heart—its mind, its will, its affections? Or is it already too late? Have evangelicals given up on the cultural importance of Christ's cause? Do they really think the spiritual future of America is critically important for the future of the world? Or has decision-time already passed us by?

* * *

For hours I had been waiting in the airport lounge for a long-delayed flight when suddenly I dozed off. I shrugged myself awake once or twice, but soon was drowsing again.

Suddenly a young man seated nearby addressed me. He seemed about twenty years of age. "You haven't been a Christian all your life," he said.

His words startled me, for I had no reason to think we had met before. And how did he know that I was a Christian? Or was he perhaps asking a question rather than stating a fact?

"If you had it to do over," he continued, "would you spend your life doing what you're doing?"

I suspected now that he was not a stranger, which made the situation all the more perplexing. Nonetheless I replied: "I could have made it in the media—the secular press, surely; radio very possibly; television maybe. Yet I had to do what God called me to do, and not run for the limelight."

"Are you *sure* God called you to do what you have done—all that theological reading and research, all those books, all those lectures, all that travel?"

It was somewhat impertinent, I thought. But just as I was about to ask, "Who in the world are you, anyway?" I decided instead first to meet the question.

"More lucrative options, more comfortable ones too, were available," I remarked. "But I really lived and worked out of a sense of imperative—divine imperative. I don't claim infallibility for what I've done. But I've tried in good conscience to be a responsible servant. There have been gratifying rewards but also some disappointments. Some doors opened unexpectedly, some closed just as unexpectedly."

"Do you ever feel that other Christians, some of them anyway. . . ." He paused, and I thought I had missed his point. But then he continued in a soft, subdued voice that expected a reciprocal whisper: "Do you ever feel they played you false or maybe even betrayed you?"

I was indignant. But to react emotionally to such probing, I felt, might be read as concealing my true feelings and convictions, and a refusal to reply might give a wrong impression. "God will have to sort out our motivations and deeds and fortunes . . . yours too!" I remarked.

Then I made an astonishing discovery. My interrogator, I noticed, looked very much like my own son—and, for that matter, in some ways looked remotely like me when I was twenty. But almost at once he posed another question. "Tell me," he said, "what you really think about your life. . . . What do you treasure most?"

"You stated before," I responded, "that I haven't always been a Christian. The big turn came," I added, "when I was twenty, and received Jesus Christ as personal Savior and Lord of my life. Into the darkness of my young life he put bright stars that still shine and sparkle. After that encounter I walked the world with God as my Friend. He prodded me to go to college, to choose my career and my mate and still leads me day after day."

"Your greatest treasure?" he asked.

"Family aside," I said, "I'd begin with Scripture . . . the most read book of my life. And communion with God . . . waiting before God. I have done less waiting than working, and my works would have been better had I waited more. But I have enjoyed God's incomparable companionship. I have been blessed with wonderful friends—none more fantastic than Helga, your mother—and have spent long and happy hours with them. But my deepest memories are those spent waiting before God, often praying for others, and not least of all for you and your sister, sometimes waiting before him in tears, sometimes in joy, sometimes wrestling alternatives, sometimes just worshiping him in adoration. Heaven will be an unending feast for the soul that basks in his presence. And it will be brighter because some will be there whom I brought to Jesus, and others whom I encouraged to become pastors and missionaries and teachers, or to invest their God-entrusted gifts in other constructive careers. The tides of history that seem to us so all-important and all-consuming in this lifetime will fade overnight into a vast panorama in which Christ and not modern celebrities will hold center-stage. It is Christ alone who will give unending meaning to a future that will become and remain ever present."

Suddenly, while making these remarks, I awoke, confused. My son, I knew, was no longer twenty, but more than twice that, and I myself already in my early seventies. I had been dreaming. I had spanned a long lifetime in a short reverie about my anticipated final flight to the Father's house. On that trip there would be no carry-on baggage other than God-given moral and spiritual assets, and with Christ as the pilot I would travel first-class. I could be thankful for a sound mind, for eyes that welcomed trifocal lenses as the world began to fade, and that my time-worn body still slept comfortably at least in one position while it awaited a resurrection replacement without need for quinidine sulphate, Wigraine or extra-strength Bufferin. Suddenly I remembered Vance Havner's prayer, "Lord, get me safely home before dark."

Index of Names